H. (Hermann) Loew

Monographs of the Diptera of North America Part 4

Prepared for the Smithsonian Institution

H. (Hermann) Loew

Monographs of the Diptera of North America Part 4
Prepared for the Smithsonian Institution

ISBN/EAN: 9783742818799

Manufactured in Europe, USA, Canada, Australia, Japa

Cover: Foto ©Thomas Meinert / pixelio.de

Manufactured and distributed by brebook publishing software
(www.brebook.com)

H. (Hermann) Loew

Monographs of the Diptera of North America Part 4

SMITHSONIAN

MISCELLANEOUS COLLECTIONS.

VOL. VIII.

"EVERY MAN IS A VALUABLE MEMBER OF SOCIETY WHO BY HIS OBSERVATIONS, RESEARCHES,
AND EXPERIMENTS PROCURES KNOWLEDGE FOR MEN."—SMITHSON.

WASHINGTON:
PUBLISHED BY THE SMITHSONIAN INSTITUTION.
1869.

CONTENTS.

ADVERTISEMENT.

The present series, entitled "Smithsonian Miscellaneous Collections," is intended to embrace all the publications issued directly by the Smithsonian Institution in octavo form; those in quarto constituting the "Smithsonian Contributions to Knowledge." The quarto series includes memoirs embracing the records of extended original investigations and researches resulting in what are believed to be new truths, and constituting positive additions to the sum of human knowledge. The octavo series is designed to contain reports on the present state of our knowledge of particular branches of science : instructions for collecting and digesting facts and materials for research : lists and synopses of species of the organic and inorganic world : museum catalogues : reports of explorations : aids to bibliographical investigations, etc., generally prepared at the express request of the Institution, and at its expense.

The position of a work in one or the other of the two series will sometimes depend upon whether the required illustrations can be presented more conveniently in the quarto or the octavo form.

In the Smithsonian Contributions to Knowledge, as well as in the present series, each article is separately paged and indexed, and the actual date of its publication is that given on its special title-page, and not that of the volume in which it is placed. In many cases, works have been published, and largely distributed, years before their combination into volumes.

While due care is taken on the part of the Smithsonian Institution to insure a proper standard of excellence in its publications, it will be readily understood that it cannot hold itself responsible for the facts and conclusions of the authors, as it is impossible in most cases to verify their statements.

JOSEPH HENRY,
Secretary S. I.

(vii)

SMITHSONIAN MISCELLANEOUS COLLECTIONS.
219

MONOGRAPHS

OF THE

D I P T E R A

OF

NORTH AMERICA.

PART IV.

PREPARED FOR THE SMITHSONIAN INSTITUTION

BY

R. OSTEN SACKEN.

WASHINGTON:
SMITHSONIAN INSTITUTION.
JANUARY, 1878.

ADVERTISEMENT.

The present publication is the fourth part of a work on the Diptera of North America. It has been prepared at the request of the Smithsonian Institution by Baron R. Osten Sacken, and is based almost exclusively on his own collections.

Parts I and II of the series were written by Dr. H. Loew, of Meseritz, Prussia, principally from the examination of specimens furnished by Baron Osten Sacken. Part III, also by Dr. Loew, is in an advanced state of preparation. The work is published in successive monographs of families and genera, when sufficient material is on hand for illustrating particular groups, without reference to systematic sequence.

JOSEPH HENRY,
Secretary S. I.

SMITHSONIAN INSTITUTION,
WASHINGTON, December, 1868.

PHILADELPHIA:
COLLINS, PRINTER.

PREFACE.

Διὸ δεῖ μὴ δυσχεραίνειν παιδικῶς τὴν περὶ τῶν ἀτιμοτέρων ζῴων ἐπίσκεψιν. Ἐν πᾶσι γὰρ τοῖς φυσικοῖς ἔνεστί τι θαυμαστόν· καὶ καθάπερ Ἡράκλειτος λέγεται πρὸς τοὺς ξένους εἰπεῖν τοὺς βουλομένους ἐντυχεῖν αὐτῷ, οἳ ἐπειδὴ προσιόντες εἶδον αὐτὸν θερόμενον πρὸς τῷ ἰπνῷ ἔστησαν (ἐκέλευε γὰρ αὐτοὺς εἰσιέναι θαρροῦντας· εἶναι γὰρ καὶ ἐνταῦθα θεούς), οὕτω καὶ πρὸς τὴν ζήτησιν περὶ ἑκάστου τῶν ζῴων προσιέναι δεῖ μὴ δυσωπούμενον ὡς ἐν ἅπασιν ὄντος τινὸς φυσικοῦ καὶ καλοῦ.

(Wherefore we ought not childishly to neglect the study even of the most despised animals, for in all natural objects there lies something marvellous. And as it is related of Heraclitus that certain strangers who came to visit him, when they found him warming himself at the kitchen-fire, stopped short—he bade them enter without fear, for there also were the gods; so we ought to enter without false shame in the examination of all living beings, for in all of them resides something of nature and beauty.)

ARISTOTELES, de partibus animalium, I, 5.

The present volume contains the first part of a monograph of the North American *Tipulidæ*, that is, the *Tipulidæ brevipalpi*, the *Cylindrotomina*, and *Ptychopterina*. The *Tipulidæ longipalpi* are reserved for another volume.

The ground covered in this monograph is the same as that of my former essay: *New genera and species of the North American Tipulidæ with short palpi, with an attempt at a new classification of the tribe* (in the *Proceedings of the Academy of Natural Sciences of Philadelphia*, 1859), that is, it embraces all the known North American species,[1] at the exclusion of those from the West

---

[1] The described species belong to the Atlantic States of the Union; only two Californian species have been added.

(iii)

Indies and Mexico. But if, instead of the sixty pages which the above-mentioned essay contains, the present volume fills nearly three hundred and sixty, this is owing partly to the increase of materials at my disposal, partly to the much greater development which I have given to the paragraphs concerning the classification. When, in 1859, I adopted an entirely new distribution of the *Tipulidæ*, I considered it as only provisional, because it was based exclusively on North American species. Since then, however, it has proved available in a more general application, and has been introduced by Dr. Schiner in the European fauna. I have therefore deemed it necessary to explain my views on that distribution with more accuracy, and have treated the classification with almost as much detail as if I was writing, not a faunistic, but a general monograph of the family. I only regret that my opportunities for studying the European fauna have been so limited. As to the *Tipulidæ* from the other parts of the world, besides Europe and North America, they are hardly known at all. The little I have seen of them in the principal museums of London, Paris, Berlin, and Turin, has been made use of by me.

My principal collecting grounds have been the environs of Washington, D. C., and of New York. I have made occasional excursions to different parts of the States of New York and Pennsylvania and in New England; moreover, I have received contributions from my friends in New England, and not unimportant collections from the northwestern region of this continent, sent by the lamented Robert Kennicott. Thus, as far at least as the more common species are concerned, the Middle and Northern States may be said to be tolerably well represented in this volume; less so, the region west of the Alleghanies and the British Possessions. The country south of Washington is almost unexplored.

I owe a debt of deep gratitude to my friend Mr. Samuel Powel, in Newport, R. I., who devoted a great deal of valuable time to the preparation of magnified photographs of the wings, intended to be represented on the plates I and II to this volume. These photographs were transferred to steel by the process of Baron Egloffstein. The plates thus obtained present a degree of fidelity to nature hardly attainable by the ordinary processes. The plates III and IV, drawn by my own unskilful hand, are reproduced from my earlier essay; only the arrangement of the figures on them has been changed.

The measurements are given in decimal fractions of an inch (as in the former volumes of these monographs).

I am under manifold obligations to my friends Director Loew, of Guben, Prussia, and Dr. Schiner, of Vienna, for their assistance in my work.

R. OSTEN SACKEN.

New York, April, 1865.

TABLE OF CONTENTS.

APPENDIX I.

DIPTERA

OF

NORTH AMERICA.

I.

ON THE NORTH AMERICAN TIPULIDÆ.

(Part First.)

INTRODUCTION.

1. *Characters of the family.*

THE *Tipulidæ* belong in the number of those large families of *Diptera*, the limits of which are equally well defined on all sides. In the *Dolichopodidæ* and *Asilidæ* we have instances of families of the same kind, and the words of Mr. Loew about the latter "that not a single dipteron has yet been found, the position of which as belonging or not belonging to this family is questionable"—these words may, with almost equal propriety, be applied to the *Tipulidæ*.

The presence of a transverse V-shaped suture across the mesonotum, would alone be sufficient to distinguish the *Tipulidæ* from the neighboring families. The completeness of the venation and the structure of the ovipositor of the female are of equally general application. Through the whole family, and all the modifications in the other organs notwithstanding, the venation is arranged according to the same plan, the characteristic features of which are, the great length of the two basal cells, the development of the auxiliary vein, and the presence, in the majority of cases, of a discal cell. The veins, in their last subdivisions along the margin of the wing, are from ten to twelve in number (if *Clado-*

lipes and *Toxorrhina* (Tab. I, f. 6) have only nine veins, the obliteration of a vein is in both cases evident). The *Culicidæ* and *Psychodidæ* come next to the *Tipulidæ* with regard to the completeness of the venation; but they have no discal cell; among all the other *Diptera nemocera*, this cell occurs only in *Rhyphus*.

The size and structure of the ovipositor, with its two pairs of long, horny, pointed valves, is common, with very rare exceptions, to all the *Tipulidæ* (the ovipositor of the other *Diptera nemocera* generally consists of two hardly projecting inconspicuous valvules). The only genera exceptional in this respect are *Cryptolabis* and *Bittacomorpha*; their ovipositors do not show any horny appendages.[1]

These three leading characters of the *Tipulidæ*—thoracic suture, venation, and the structure of the ovipositor—sufficiently isolate this family among the other *Diptera nemocera*; but we render the contrast still more striking, if we direct our attention to the different parts of the organization of the *Tipulidæ*, and compare them with the corresponding parts in other families. Thus the eyes here are rounded or oval, and never excised on the inside (reniform or 'lunate), like those of most *Culicidæ*, *Chironomidæ*, *Psychodidæ*, *Simulidæ*, and some *Mycetophilidæ*. The ocelli are, with rare exceptions (*Trichocera* and perhaps *Pedicia*), wanting, or, at least, imperceptible; and this character the *Tipulidæ* share with the *Culicidæ*, *Chironomidæ*, *Psychodidæ*, *Simulidæ*, and a part of the *Cecidomyidæ*. The joints of the antennal flagellum are, with rare exceptions, well marked in their divisions, the shape of the whole antenna being in most cases setaceous, that is, gradually attenuated towards the tip. The joints are never absolutely cylindrical, as in some *Cecidomyiæ* (*Asphondylia*, *Spaniocera*), or of the compressed disciform shape, so common among the *Mycetophilidæ*; only *Rhipidia* has them pedicelled (a character common among the *Cecidomyiæ*). The antennal joints are in most cases verticillate (a character very rare among the *Mycetophilidæ*); never bushy (a character of general occurrence among the males of the *Chironomidæ* and *Culicidæ*). With regard to the number of antennal joints, the *Tipulidæ* do not differ much from the other *Nemocera*; the

[1] I have neglected the opportunities I have had to examine the ovipositor of *Bittacomorpha* on fresh specimens; in dry ones, I perceive only a pair of short, coriaceous appendages.

great majority of them have 2 + 11, 2 + 12 or 2 + 14 joints; the great majority of the *Mycetophilidæ* have 2 + 14, the *Culicidæ* 2 + 12, the *Chironomidæ* from 2 + 10 to 2 + 13 (in the male sex; much less in the female); the *Cecidomyidæ* 2 + 12, or double this number, 2 + 24.

The feet of the *Tipulidæ* are comparatively much longer than those of the other families of *Diptera nemocera* (except perhaps the *Blepharoceridæ*); but the coxæ are never so long as in the *Mycetophilidæ*, the femora never dentate, as in *Ceratopogon;* the tibiæ, although often spurred at the tip, are never beset with spines, as in the majority of the *Mycetophilidæ.* The ungues have sometimes teeth on the under side, like those of some *Chironomidæ* and *Mycetophilidæ;* empodia are often distinct, but pulvilli, like those of *Bibio*, have not been observed.

In size, the majority of the *Tipulidæ* are considerably larger than the other *Diptera nemocera*, and the contrast in this respect is very striking.

Among the families usually placed in the vicinity of the *Tipulidæ*, the *Blepharoceridæ* alone may have a claim to a distant relationship with them. In the structure of the incomplete thoracic suture of *Blephorocera*, I perceive, if I am not mistaken, an approach to the *Ptychopterina;* but as my knowledge of the *Blepharoceridæ* is confined to a single species, I would not insist upon this relationship. The *Blepharoceridæ* have three ocelli and a peculiar venation; the inner horny parts of the mouth of *Blepharocera* are much more developed than those of the *Tipulidæ;* and the eyes are divided by a distinct cross-line into two portions, one with large, the other with small facets; a character which I have never observed among the *Tipulidæ.*

The connection between the *Psychodidæ* and the *Eriopterina* is of a very obscure kind, and unless farther developed by observation, cannot have any scientific value.

The position of the genus *Chionea* among the *Tipulidæ*, is determined chiefly by the structure of its ovipositor, the want of a thoracic suture notwithstanding. Moreover, the relationship of *Chionea* to *Trimicra* is evident.

The case of *Dixa*, likewise deprived of a thoracic suture, is more doubtful. This genus has been referred to the *Mycetophilidæ* by Meigen and Zetterstedt; to the *Tipulidæ* by Macquart and Westwood; Rondani connects it with *Trichocera*, and Halliday places it provisionally, together with *Orphnephila*, in an artificial group, *Heteroclita*. *Dixa* has no thoracic suture; the ovipositor of the female, according to Mr. Halliday, is different from that of the *Tipulidæ*, consisting of two short, broad, round lamels; the presence of only six longitudinal veins, the shortness of the auxiliary vein, the absence of both subcostal and marginal cross-veins, the peculiar course of the first longitudinal vein, the constant absence of the discal cell, etc., constitute a type of venation which separates *Dixa* from all the known *Tipulidæ* and shows some points of analogy with *Ptychoptera* only. The rather extraordinary larva of *Dixa* (described by Stæger) is one ground more for separating this genus from the *Tipulidæ*. Altogether, I incline to the opinion of Mr. Halliday in leaving *Dixa*, temporarily at least, in an isolated position.

2. On the larvæ of the Tipulidæ.

During the larva stage, the species of this family are as well marked among the Diptera, as in the perfect stage of their existence. At the same time, they exhibit a remarkable conformity in the more important parts of their organization, all the differences in the external conditions of their life notwithstanding. About a dozen more or less complete descriptions of such larvæ have been given by former authors,[1] and I have had occasion myself to examine several larvæ of *Limnobia*, *Tipula*, *Pachyrrhina*, and *Ctenophora*. The following account is based upon these data (some more details concerning all the known larvæ of this family will be given under the head of the respective genera):—

The principal character, distinguishing these larvæ from those

[1] Perris, *Ann. Soc. Entom. de Fr.* 1849, p. 331, Tab. VII, f. 4 (*Ula pilosa*); the same, l. c. 1847, p. 37, Tab. I, f. 3 (*Trichocera*); the same, l. c. 1849, p. 331, Tab. VII, f. 5 (*Limnophila dispar*); *Chionea* by Brauer (*Verh. Zool. Bot. Ver.* 1854); *Cylindrotoma* in Schellenberg, *Genres de Mouches Dipt.*, and in Zeller, *Isis*, 1842, p. 808; *Phalacrocera* in Degeer; *Ptychoptera* in Réaumur and Lyonnet; *Ctenophora* in Fischer, *Oryctogr. du Gouv. de Moscou*, Bouché, etc.; *Tipula* in Réaumur, Degeer, Bouché, etc. Besides the detailed descriptions, numerous short notices about single larvæ are scattered in the different authors. I cannot refrain from noticing here, that what Mr. Dugès describes as the larva of *Limnobia platyptera* Macq. (*Sitzungsber. der Wien. Acad.* Vol. XI, 1853) is a *Mycetophilideous* larva, probably *Bolitophila*.

of the neighboring families is, that as far as known they are metapneustic, that is, they have a single pair of spiracles at the anal end of the body. The genus *Trichocera*, anomalous in many respects, is the only one, provided Mr. Perris' statements are correct, which has two pairs of spiracles, a thoracic and an anal one. A second characteristic peculiarity of these larvæ is the structure of the mentum, which consists of a horny plate, pointed in front, and with several more or less deep indentations on both sides of this central point. I found this organ in all the larvæ which I have dissected; it is entirely different from the corresponding organ in the larvæ of the *Mycetophilidæ* (compare my description of these in the *Proc. Entom. Soc. Phil.* 1862, p. 151, Tab. I).

The head of the larva is comparatively large, imbedded nearly up to the mouth in the first thoracic segment; it consists of a horny shell, open on the under side and in front; the parts of the mouth are inserted in the latter opening. The comparatively large labrum, lapping over the mouth when it is in motion, has a rather complicated structure, partly horny, partly fleshy, varying in the different genera; often, for instance in *Tipula*, with bristles and microscopic hairs in front. The mandibles are horny, very strong (not flat, as in the *Mycetophilidæ*), generally bifid at the tip and often with several indentations on the inner side. The maxillæ are likewise large and stout; more or less fleshy on the inside, but strengthened on the outside by horny plates; they have a short palpus on the outside and the usual lobe, coriaceous, often provided with an entanglement of hairs and bristles, on the inside. The mentum, already alluded to above, is a horny lamel of variable structure; in *Tipula* and *Ctenophora* I have found it triangular in front, the sloping sides bearing several small indentations; in a larva of *Limnobia* this organ had five large teeth in front. Under the mentum, inside of the buccal cavity, I have perceived in the larvæ of *Tipula* and *Ctenophora* another smaller, rounded, horny lamel, with indentations on its anterior side. The plane of this second lamel is parallel to that of the first, and it may be seen moving up and down, when the mouth is in motion. The antennæ, placed on the sides of the mouth, consist of a rounded, fleshy basal piece, and a cylindrical, horny shaft, ending in one or several stout bristles.

The body of the larvæ is grub-like, of a uniform grayish, brownish, or whitish color. It consists of twelve segments (counting the anal segment among them). The nature of the outer integuments depends on the mode of life of the larva. The larvæ of *Ctenophora*, living in wood, have a soft, white, smooth skin, similar to that of the larvæ of longicorn beetles or of the *Asilidæ*, living in similar conditions. The larvæ of *Tipula*, living in the soil, or the larvæ of those species of *Ctenophora* which are found in wood so far decomposed as to be like soil or vegetable mould, have a much tougher skin, and are covered with a microscopic, appressed pubescence. This toughness, as well as some stiff bristles, scattered over the surface of the skin, is probably useful in burrowing. Thus the larva of *Trichocera*, digging in vegetable mould or in fungi, is covered, according to Perris, with microscopic erect bristles; the larva of *Ula*, living in fungi, has, according to the same author, still longer bristles. The larvæ living in water (as some *Limnobina*) are soft and slimy, of a dirty greenish color, and with a peculiar clothing of appressed microscopic hairs, not unlike those of the larvæ of *Stratiomyia*. The most anomalous of all the Tipulideous larvæ are those of the *Cylindrotomina*. That of the *Cylindrotoma distinctissima* lives upon the leaves of plants, as *Anemone*, *Viola*, *Stellaria*, almost like a caterpillar; it is green, with a crest along the back, consisting of a row of fleshy processes. The larva of *Cylindrotoma* (*Phalacrocera*) *replicata*, according to Degeer, lives in the water, on water-plants, and is distinguished by numerous filaments, which, although resembling spines, are flexible and hollow on the inside. Degeer took them for organs of respiration.

The organs of locomotion of the larvæ generally consist in transverse swellings on the under side of the body provided with exceedingly minute, stiff bristles. Sometimes these swellings run round the whole body; in such a case, their dorsal portion is less developed than the ventral. The anal end of the body is truncate, and the two spiracles are placed upon the truncature. The margins of the latter are for the most part provided with fleshy retractile processes of various size and shape, usually four, sometimes six or more. The truncature can be contracted at the will of the larva, and then the fleshy processes are shortened and the spiracles are inclosed in the cavity thus formed at the end of the body. The fleshy processes are sometimes, especially in the Tipulidæ, strengthened on the inner side by small horny plates; sometimes they are replaced by horny, pointed processes (I have found a larva of this kind, belonging to Tipula or Pachyrrhina). The larvæ of some Ctenophora (as C. strata, nigricornis, etc., belonging to the subgenus Xiphura Brullè), have no processes at all round the truncature. In the aquatic larvæ of Ptychoptera, a long tube at the end of the body, serves for breathing, for which purpose it is raised to the surface of the water.

On the under side of the last segment is the anal opening. Immediately in front of the anus, on the under side of the body, some larvæ, belonging probably to the genus Tipula, have a certain number of soft, digitiform, retractile processes, varying in size, shape, and number. (The usual shape is figured in Réaumur, IV, Tab. XIV, f. 10, where there are six large processes; but sometimes they are much smaller.) I do not know the use of these singular organs.

The pupæ of the Tipulidæ are extricate, like those of nearly all the Diptera orthorapha. The thorax usually bears two horn-like processes, varying in length and structure. They represent the thoracic spiracles. In Ptychoptera one of these processes acquires a great length, in order to allow the pupa to breathe under water. The abdominal segments of the pupæ are provided with transverse rows of hairs, bristles or spines, which enable the pupa to extricate itself from its place of concealment, preparatory to the escape of the perfect insect. These processes are usually more numerous and stronger in the genera Tipula, Ctenophora, etc., than among the brevipalpous Tipulidæ.

3. *Historical account of the classification of the Tipulidæ.*

The word *Tipula* was used by the Latin classics to designate some long-legged insect, running over the surface of the water, perhaps *Hydrometra.* I have not been able to ascertain when and where this word was first applied to the crane-flies;[1] but it

[1] The quotations from *Plautus, Varro* and *Festus* about *Tipula* or *Tippula,* are to be found in all Latin dictionaries. Aldrovandi, whose work, *De Animalibus Insectis,* appeared in 1602, reproduces these quotations (p. 709), and describes as Tipulæ two water insects; one of them is *Ranatra,* which is also figured; the other is apparently *Hydrometra.* Monfet (*Insect. Theatr.* 1 [?]34), under the name of *Tipula,* likewise means *Hydrometra* (p. 162); but in

was used in this sense some time before Linné introduced the
name in his zoological system. His two genera, *Culex* and
Tipula, embrace the whole of the present *Diptera nemocera*,
but, in his arrangement, they were not placed alongside of each
other. *Culex*, on account of its long proboscis, was put in the
same group with *Empis, Conops,* etc.

Fabricius, in his earlier works (*Syst. Entomol.* 1774), followed
Linné in adopting these two genera and locating them on account
of the structure of their proboscis.

Latreille, in 1802 (*Hist. Natur. des Crustacés et des Insectes,*
Vol. III), introduced the name *Tipulariæ* for the division which
he afterwards called *Diptera nemocera*, and which he distinguished on account of the structure of the antennæ. The genera
admitted by him at that time, besides *Culex* and *Tipula*, were
Ceroplatus, Bibio, Simulium, Scatopse.

While Fabricius tried to found his arrangement upon the
structure of the mouth, Latreille upon the structure of the
antennæ, the comparative length of the feet and also the structure
of the mouth, Meigen struck in the right direction by showing
the importance of the venation. This character enabled him to
establish at once a series of genera, which have been retained
since. He did it first in an essay (*Versuch einer neuen Gat-
tungseintheilung der europ. zweiflügl. Insecten,* in Illiger's
Magasin, etc., II, p. 259, 1803), and a year later in his first
independent work (*Klassification und Beschreibung der europ.
zweifl. Insecten,* 1804). Without introducing any family divisions, these works give a series of definitions of genera. The
following genera belonging to our family of *Tipulidæ* are mentioned in this way by Meigen : *Trichocera, Erioptera, Limonia,
Tipula, Nephrotoma, Ptychoptera, Ctenophora.* Except *Tipula,*
all of them were new.

The fourteenth volume of Latreille's *Hist. Natur. des Crustacés
et des Ins.,* containing the Diptera (the third volume, mentioned

another chapter (p. 70) he mentions the word *Tipula* among the Latin names
commonly applied to crane-flies. In 1722 Frisch (*Beschr. v. allerl. Ins. in
Deutschl.* part IV, p. 24), speaking of the crane-flies, says : " Flies which
are called *Tipulæ* by the naturalists who have written before me." Réaumur (about 1736) also calls them "tipules." Linné quotes Frisch and
probably borrows the name from him. It is not impossible that Aldrovandi's figure of *Ranatra* has been mistaken for a crane-fly (*Tipula*), by
one of the subsequ-

above, gave only the general classification), appeared a few months
after Meigen's work. Although acquainted with Meigen's labors,
Latreille does not adopt his new genera, except *Limonia*. The
subdivision of Latreille's *Tipulariæ* (afterwards called *Diptera*
nemocera) is rather confused, but the character derived from
the length of the last joint of the palpi, which became so important soon after, is introduced here. The genera with an
elongated last joint of the palpi are : *Tipula* (corresponding to
the present genus *Ctenophora*), *Tanyptera* (for *Ctenophora*
atrata Fabr.), and *Tychoptera* (containing species of the genus
Tipula and *Ptychoptera*). The genera with a short last joint
of the palpi are *Limonia*, *Molobrus* (*Sciara*), and *Oligotropha*
(*Cecidomyia*).

In Latreille's next work—*Genera crustaceorum et Insectorum*,
Vol. IV, 1809—a considerable progress is apparent. Here for
the first time, the family *Tipulidæ* in our sense is distinguished
as a separate tribe *Tipulariæ terricolæ*, co-ordinate to the
Tipulariæ aquaticæ (*Culex, Chironomus*), *fungicoræ* and
florales. The *Tipulariæ terricolæ*, characterized by the structure of their antennæ, the absence of ocelli and the length of
their feet, are divided into two groups, according to the length
of the last joint of the palpi. The group with an elongated joint
is composed of the genera *Ctenophora, Pedicia, Tipula, Nephro-*
toma, Ptychoptera; the group with a short joint, of *Limonia* and
Hexatoma (now *Anisomera*). *Limonia* which, in the sense of
the author, includes *Trichocera* and *Erioptera*, is further subdivided in four sections, based upon the structure of the antennæ
and the venation. Among the genera *Pedicia* and *Hexatoma*
are new.

The name *Diptera nemocera* has been proposed for the first
time by Latreille in 1817, in the *Nouveau Dictionnaire d'Histoire*
naturelle, in the articles *Diptères* and *Entomologie*.

Fabricius's principal work on Diptera, published in the mean
time—*Systema Antliatorum*, 1805—did not add anything of importance to the knowledge of the distribution of the *Tipulidæ*.

In Meigen's great work—*Systematische Beschreibung der*
bekannten Europäischen zweiflügligen Insecten—the first volume
of which, containing the *Tipulidæ*, appeared in 1818, the *Diptera*
nemocera were called *Tipulariæ* (*Mücken*), and subdivided in
the sections : *culiciformes* (now Culicidæ and Chironomidæ),

gallicolæ (now Cecidomyidæ), nortuæformes (Psychodidæ), rostratæ (Tipulidæ), fungicolæ (Mycetophilidæ), lugubri (genus Sciara), latipennes (Simulidæ), muscæformes (Bibionidæ and Rhyphidæ). The Tipulariæ rostratæ (oor Tipulidæ) were defined thus: " Eyes rounded, separated by the front above; no ocelli; head prolonged in a snout; palpi incurved; thorax with a curved transverse suture in the middle; abdomen with eight segments; tibiæ more or less spurred." The following genera were added to those adopted in the "Klassification," etc.: Rhipidia, Nematocera, Anisomera. The name Limonia (from λειμών, meadow), as objectionable on account of a foreign idea which might be connected with it, was changed in Limnobia. Hexatoma Latr., was changed in Nematocera, rather arbitrarily, the only reason for this change being that Meigen himself wanted to use the name Hexatoma for one of his genera. Limnobia was defined in the following manner:—

" Antennæ setaceous, 15-17 jointed; first joint cylindrical, the second cyathiform, the following elongated or globular.

Palpi incurred, cylindrical, four jointed; the joints of equal length.

No ocelli.

Wings (generally) incumbent in a parallel position to each other; veins glabrous."

The definition of Tipula differs only in the statement about the structure and the number of joints of the antennæ (thirteen); the prolonged last joint of the palpi and the divaricate wings.

In the sixth volume of the same work (1830) the genera Glochina, Rhamphidia, Symplecta, and Dolichopeza were added. The latter genus, however, had been originally proposed by Curtis (British Entomology, II, 62) in 1825.

In reviewing the first steps taken in the classification of the Tipulidæ, we cannot but notice the contrast between the talents of Latreille and Meigen. The correct definition of all the large subdivisions, as the separation of the Diptera nemocera, the recognition of the Tipulidæ as a family, and the subdivision of this family in longipalpi and brevipalpi are due to Latreille. But the adoption of all the leading genera is the work of Meigen.

Contemporaneously with Meigen's work, Wiedemann's Diptera Exotica (1821) and Aussereuropaeische Zweiflügelige Insecten

(1328–30) appeared. They did not introduce any change in the classification, but added two new genera to the system: *Polymera* and *Megistocera*.

Macquart, in both of his works (*Diptères du Nord de la France*, 1825, and *Hist. Nat. des Ins. Diptères*, Vol. I, 1834), retains Latreille's designations: *Diptera nemocera* and *Tipulariæ terricolæ*. To the latter family, in the last of the two works, he adds the genus *Dixa*, placed by Meigen among the *Tip. fungicolæ*. He also follows Latreille in subdividing the *Tip. terricola* in the *longipalpi* (genera: *Ptychoptera*, *Ctenophora*, *Tipula*, *Pachyrrhina*, *Nephrotoma*, *Pedicia*) and *brevipalpi* (*Orodicera*, *Rhipidia*, *Rhamphidia*, *Idioptera*, *Limnophila*, *Limnobia*, *Cylindrotoma*, *Symplecta*, *Erioptera*, *Polymera*, *Megistocera*, *Trichocera*, *Bolichopeza*, *Dixa*, *Anisomera*, *Chionea*). Among these genera *Orodicera*, *Idioptera*, *Pachyrrhina*, *Limnophila*, and *Cylindrotoma* were new. *Chionea* had been described, in 1816, by Dalman, and correctly referred to the *Tipulidæ*. The principal innovation of Macquart was the introduction of the genera *Pachyrrhina* and *Limnophila*, which broke up Meigen's large genera *Tipula* and *Limnobia*.

The most important publications on the Diptera in general, since Macquart's last quoted works, are Zetterstedt's, Walker's, and Rondani's. Zetterstedt (*Fauna Lapponica*, 1840, and *Diptera Scandinaviæ*, tenth volume, 1851) introduced several new genera, but did not improve the distribution of the family of *Tipulidæ*. The subdivision into *longipalpi* and *brevipalpi* was entirely abandoned by him, and the genera belonging to these two groups were arranged promiscuously. The genus *Chionea* forms a separate family for itself, between which and the *Tipulidæ* the *Mycetophilidæ* are inserted. Zetterstedt's new genera are *Psiloconopa*, *Dicranota*, *Tricyphona*, all of which had been originally adopted in his earlier work in 1840.

Walker (*Insecta Britannica, Diptera*, Vol. III, 1856) adopts, in the main, Meigen's distribution of the *Tipulidæ*. Macquart's genera *Limnophila* and *Pachyrrhina* are introduced as subgenera only. The genera *Geranomyia* and *Ula*, originally proposed by Mr. Haliday, in 1833 (*Entomol. Magaz.* Vol. I), are introduced here, and the genus *Amalopis* is suggested by the same author in a note (*Addenda*, p. xv), but not introduced in the body of the work.

Mr. Rondani, in his *Prodromus Dipterologiæ Italicæ*, Vol. I
(1856), proposed the following distribution :—¹

Fam. XXV. *Tipulidæ*.

I. Stirps *Limnobina*,

A. Eleven or twelve longitudinal veins reach the margin.

1. *Erioptera* (type: *E. obscura* M.; therefore syn. *Molophilus*).—2.
Chionalina, n. g. (type: *Erioptera tænionota* M.).—3. *Ilisomyia*,
n. g. (type: *I. subipunnis*, n. sp.).—4. *Ilisophila*, n. g. (type:
Erioptera lutea M.).—5. *Ormosia*, n. g. (type: *Erioptera nodulosa*
Macq., which, in my distribution, would be a *Rhypholophus*).—
6. *Spylopterra*, n. g. (type: *S. meridionalis*, n. sp.; also a *Rhypholophus*, according to Dr. Schiner).—7. *Limnea*, n. g. (type: *Erioptera florescens* Lin.).—8. *Symplecta*.—9. *Rhamphidia*.—10. *Cylindrotoma*.—11. *Taphrona*, n. g. (syn. *Goniomyia*).—12. *Ureomyia*,
n. g. (type: *O. aprona*, n. sp.).—13. *Ilisia*, n. g. (type: *Erioptera
maculata* M.).—14. *Elaeophila*, n. g. (type: *Ephelia marmorata*
Rgg.).—15. *Limnophila*.—16. *Bophrosia*, n. g. (syn. *Trieyphona*).
—17. *Trichocera*.—18. *Idioptera*.—19. *Ula*.

AA. Only ten longitudinal veins reach the posterior margin.

20. *Dolichopeza*.—21. *Anisomera*.—22. *Nematocera*.—23. *Dixa*.—24.
Pelusia, n. g. (type: *P. albifrons*, n. sp.).—25. *Glochina* (type:
G. arrica M.).—26. *Taphrophila*, n. g. (type: *Dicranomyia
inusta* M.).—27. *Limnomyia*, n. g. (type: *Limnobia tripunctata*
M.).—28. *Limnobia* (type: *L. chorea* M).—29. *Rhipidia*.

II. Stirps *Tipulina*.

1. *Ctenacra* (syn. *Dictenidia* Brullé).—2. *Siphona*.—3. *Ctenophora*.—
4. *Ctenacra*, n. g. (type: *Psychoptera pectinata* Macq.).—5.
Psychoptera.—6. *Pidiria*.—7. *Nephrotoma*.—8. *Alophroida*, n. g.
(type: *A. cinerea*, n. sp.).—9. *Pachyrrhina*.—10. *Tipula*.—11.
Pterelachisus.

Fam. XXVI. *Chionaidæ*.
Fam. XXVII. *Orphnephilidæ*.
Fam. XXVIII. *Bertidæ*.
Fam. XXIX. *Asthenidæ*.
Fam. XXX. *Rhyphidæ*.

It is unnecessary to enter into a detailed criticism of this

¹ I have seen Mr. Rondani's first volume only, containing the general
synopsis of all the families of Diptera, and it is from this volume that the
extract which I give is reproduced; I do not know whether the volume
containing the *Tipulidæ* has appeared at this date or not.

distribution, as its comparison with the one adopted in this volume can be easily effected.

As early as 1854 (*Stettiner Entomol. Z.* p. 203), I had suggested that the proper way to subdivide the genus *Limnobia* Meigen, would be, to base this subdivision on the number of the submarginal cells, instead of the posterior cells (as Macquart has done it). At the same time, I observed that a division established upon this character, would be very well supported by characters taken from the structure of the forceps of the male.

In 1859 (*Proc. Acad. Nat. Sciences Philad.* p 197) I carried out these suggestions, by applying them to the North American fauna. The distribution of the *Tipulidæ brevipalpi* into six groups, proposed by me, was based upon a combination of characters, taken from the number of submarginal cells, the number of antennal joints, the presence or absence of spurs at the tip of the tibia, and the position of the subcostal cross-vein. This distribution required the adoption of a considerable number of new genera.

In 1864, Dr. Schiner, in his work *Fauna Austriaca, Diptera*, adapted my distribution to the European fauna.

As the present volume contains the development of the same distribution, the necessary details about it will be given at the proper places below (compare also the § 5 of this Introduction).

In the same year, Mr. Lioy arranged the *Tipulidæ* (his family *Rostrattili*) into four subfamilies: *Paludicolini* (our Ptychopterina), *Lignicolini* (genus *Ctenophora*), *Terricolini* (our Tipulina), *Limnocolini* (embracing all our *Tipulidæ brevipalpi*). He proposed several genera, which I will mention in the list given below.

I conclude this review of the progress of the classification of the *Tipulidæ* with a list, in chronological order, of all the generic and subgeneric names, which have been proposed in this family, whether finally adopted or not. Further historical details about the *Tipulidæ* will be given under the heads of the different genera.

Tipula Linné, Animalia per Sueciam observ. 1736.
Trichocera Meigen, Illiger's Magaz. 1803 (Limnophilina).
Erioptera Meig. l. c. (Erioptorina).
Limonia Meig. l. c. (changed afterwards in *Limnobia*).
Nephrotoma Meig. l. c. (Tipulina).

Ptychoptera Meig. l. c. (Ptychopterina).
Ctenophora Mrig. l. c. (Ctenophorina).
Tanyptera Latreille, Hist. Natur. des Crust. et des Insectes, Vol. XIV, 1804 (syn. Ctenophora).
Tychoptera Latr. l. c. (syn. Tipula and Ptychoptera).
Pedicia Latr. Genera, etc. Vol. IV, 1809 (Amalopina).
Hexatoma Latr. l. c. (syn. Anisomera).
Chionea Dalman, Kon. Vetensk. Akad. Handl. 1816 (Erioptorina).
Limnobia Meig. System. Beschr. Vol. 1, 1818.
Nematocera Meig. l. c. (syn. Anisomera).
Anisomera Meig. l. c. (Anisomerina).
Rhipidia Meig. l. c. (Limnobina).
Gonomyia Megerle in Meigen, l. c. 1818 (now Goniomyia, Erioptarina).
Polymera Wiedemann, Dipt. Exot. 1821 (Amalopina ").
Megistocera Wied. l. c. (originally Metistocera).
Helobia (syn. Symplecta).   } St. Fargeau, Encyol. Méthod.
Megarhina (changed afterwards in Helias). } Insectes, 1825, Vol. X, p.
Helius (syn. Rhamphidia).   } 885 et Index.
Dolichopesa Curtis, Brit. Entomol. 62, 1825 (Tipulina).
Glochina Meig. System. Beschr. etc. 1830, Vol. VI (Limnobina).
Rhamphidia Meig. l. c. (Limnobina anomala).
Symplecta Meig. l. c. (Erioptorina).
Leptorhina Steph. Catal. Brit. Ins. 1829 (syn. Rhamphidia Meig.).
Dicranomyia Steph. l. c. (Limnobina).
Xiphura Brullé, Ann. Soc. Entom. de Fr. 1, p. 306, 1832 (Ctenophorina).
Dictenidia Brullé, l. c. II, p. 402, 1833 (Ctenophorina).
Molophilus Curtis, British Entomology, 444, 1833 (Erioptorina).
Geranomyia Halliday, Entomol. Magaz. Vol. 1, 1833 (Limnobina).
Ula Dalid. l. c. (Amalopina).
Limnophila Macquart, Hist. Nat. Dipt. 1834, Vol. I.
Pachyrrhina Macq. l. c. (Tipulina).
Ozodicera Macq. l. c. (Tipulina).
Idioptera Macq. l. c. (Limnophilina).
Cylindrotoma Macq. l. c. (Cylindrotomina).
Aporosa Macq. Webb et Berthelot, Hist. Nat. des Canaries, 1835 (syn. Geranomyia Hal.).
Limnobiorhynchus Westw. Ann. Soc. Entom. de Fr. IV, p. 683, 1835 (Limnobina and Rhamphidina).
Caloptera Guérin in Westw. l. c. (changed afterwards in Erasioptera, Anisomerina).
Anoplistes Westw. Zool. Journ. V, p. 444, Tab. XXII, f. 10-13, 1835 (Limnophilina).
Gymnoplistia Westw. (same as preceding; only name modified) Lond. and Edinb. Philos. Magaz. VI, p. 280, 1835.
Ptilogyna Westw. Zool. Journ. l. c. Tab. XXII, f. 14, 15; Lond. and Edinb. Phil. Mag. l. c. (Ctenophorina).

Oncoera Westw. Zool. Journ. I. e. (changed afterwards in *Ceraxodia*).
Ceroxodia Westw. Lond. and Edinb. Phil. Mag. I. c. (Limnophilina).
Hemioteima Westw. Zool. Journ. I. c. (Ctenophorina, syn. *Uzodicera* Macq.).
Bittacomorpha Westw. Lond. and Edinb. Phil. Magas. VI, p. 231, 1835 (Ptychopterina).
Poronocera Cortis, Brit. Entomol. 589, 1838 (Anisomerina).
Evanioptera Guérin, Voy. de la Coquille, Zoologie, Texte I, 2, p. 287, Tab. XX, f. 2. The text was published in 183., the plates, upon which the genus was called *Cs-aptera*, in 1830 (Anisomerina).
Leptotarsus Guérin, I. c. (Tipulina).
Ctenogyna Macq. Diptères Exotiques, Vol. I, p. 42, 1838 (Ctenophorina).
Bricoera Macq. I. c. (Anisomerina).
Psiloconopa Zetterstedt, Ins. Lapponica, 1840 (Erioptera).
Dicranota Zett. I. c. (Amalopina).
Tricyphona Zett. I. c. (Amalopina, syn. *Amalopis*).
Pterelachisus Rond. Guérin, Magas. de Zool. 1842, No. 106 (Tipulina).
Prionocera Loew, Stettiner Entom. Zeitung, 1844, p. 170 (Tipulina, syn. *Stygeropis*).
Styringomyia Loew, Dipterol. Beitr. I, p. 6, 1845 (Limnobina anomala).
Apsilesis Macq. I. c. 1er Supplemt. 1-40 (Tipulina).
Chailotrichia Rossi, Systemat. Vers. Oester. Zweifl. p. 12, 1848 (Erioperina).
Pterocoramus Walker, List of the Dipt. Brit. Mus. I, p. 78, 1848 (Anisomerina).

Trichoneura, Calobamon, Haploneura, Tanymera, Tanysphyra, Ataracta, Allarithmia : Loew, *Über d. Bernstein und die Bernstein fauna*, 1850. (These genera are named, but not described.)

Toxorrhina Loew, Linnæa Entomologica. V, p. 400, 1851 (Rhamphidina).
Macrochile Loew, I. c. p. 402 (Ptychopterina).
Chamallda, Elleomyia, Illeophila, Ormosia, Spylotera, Limnæa, Illsia (all Erioptera) ; Rondani, Prodr. Dipterol. Ital. I (1856).[1]
Taphrona (syn. *Geniomyia*), Rondani, I. c.
Orosmyia }
Palosia } Rondani, I. c. (location unknown to me).
Elaeophila Rondani, I. c. (syn. *Ephelia* Schin. ; Limnophilina).
Taphrophila, Limnomyza, Rondani, I. c. (Limnobina).
Bophrosia Rondani, I. c. (syn. *Trirgphous*).
Ceroctena Rondani, I. c. (syn. *Dictenidia* Bralld ; Ctenophora M.).
Ctenocaria Rondani, I. c. (Ptychopterina).

Alophroida Rondani, l. c. (Tipulina?).

Amalopis Haliday, Walker's Ins. Brit. Dipt. III, p. xv, 1856 (Amalopina).

Oligomera Doleschall, Naturk. Tijdschr. v. Nederl. Indie, Vol. XIV, p.
11, Tab. VII, f. 3, 1857 (Anisomerina).

Dicranoptycha.
Antocha.   } Limnobina
Elephantomyia.   } anomala.
Teucholabis.
Gnophomyia.
Cryptolabis.   } Eriopterina.   O. Sacken, Proc. Acad. Nat. Sc.
Cladura.   }   Phila. 1859.
Lasiomastix.
Epiphragma.   } Subgenera of
Dactylolabis.   } Limnophila.
Dicranophragma.
Arrhenica.   Anisomerina.
Protoplasa.   Ptychopterina.

Physecrania Bigot, Ann. Soc. Entom. de Fr. 1854, p. 122, Tab. III, f. 1
(Anisomerina).

Eristes Rondani, Atti Soc. Ital. Sc. Natur. Milano, II, p. 58, with fig. 1862
(location uncertain).

Rhypholophus Kolenati, Wiener Entom. Monatschr. IV, with fig. 1860
(Eriopterina).

Crunobia Kolenati, l. c. (Amalopina).

Trimicra O. Sacken, Proc. Acad. Nat. Sc. Phila. 1861, p. 290 (Eriopterina).

Penthoptera (Anisomerina).   }
Dasyptera (Eriopterina).   }
Trichosticha (Eriopterina).   } Schiner, Wiener Entom. Monatschr.
Epihelia (Limnophilina).   }   Vol. VII, 1863, and Dipt. Austriaca,
Pacilostola (Limnophilina).   }   Vol. II, 1864.
Elliptera (Limnobina anomala). }
Triogma (Cylindrotomina).   }

Phalacrocera (Cylindrotomina).

Holorusia Loew, Berl. Entomol. Zeitschr. Vol. VII, 1863 (Tipulina).

Stygeropis Loew, l. c. (Tipulina).

Platytoma Lioy, Atti Inst. Ven. 3d series, Vol. IX, X, 1864 (Eriopterina).

Macroptera Lioy, l. c. (Amalopina, syn. Ula).

Anomaloptera Lioy, l. c. (Tipulina).

Dicera Lioy, l. c. (Ctenophorina).

Plettosa (Limnobina, syn. Geranomyia). }
Ctedonia (Limnophilina).   } Philippi, Verh. Zool. Bot.
Polymeria (Limnophilina?).   }   Gesellsch. in Wien, 1865,
Idioneura (Eriopterina, syn. Symplecta).}   p. 593 sqq. (with figures).
Lechnocera (Eriopterina?).   }

Tanyderus Philippi, l. c. p. 760, Tab. XXIX, f. 57 (Ptychopterina).

Cladolipes Loew, Zeitschr. für Gesammte Naturw. 1865, p. 369 (Anisomerina).

Diacobola O. Sacken, Proc. Entomol. Soc. Phila. 1865 (Limnobina, syn. Trochobola).

Paratropesa (L. anomala). ⎫
Cloniophora (Limnophilina). ⎬ Schiner, Verh. Zool. Bot. Gesellsch. in Wien. 1866. •
Peripheroptera (Limnobina). ⎭

Thaumastoptera Mik, Verh. Z. B. G., etc., 1866 (Limnobina anomala).
Macrothorax Jen. Schr. d. Senkenb. Ges. (Tipulina).
Rhipnoptila Now. Verh. Zool. Bot. Ges. in Wien, 1867, p. 337 (Limnophilina). •

Trochobola (Limnobina). ⎫
Orimarga (Limnobina anomala). ⎪
Atarba (id.). ⎰ ⎪
Sigmatomera (Eriopterina). ⎪
Empeda (id.). ⎬ Genera and subgenera adopted in the present volume:
Mesocyphona. ⎫ ⎪
Acyphona. ⎬ Subgenera of Eriopterina. ⎪
Hoplolabis. ⎭ ⎪
Ulomorpha (Limnophilina?) ⎪
Plectromyia. ⎱ Anisopina. ⎪
Rhaphidolabis. ⎰ ⎭

4. Division of the TIPULIDÆ into LONGIPALPI and BREVIPALPI

Some Tipulidæ have the last joint of the palpi much longer than the three preceding taken together, whiplash-shaped, almost reaching the fore coxæ in the living insect. Others have this last joint hardly longer, or even shorter, than the two preceding taken together, cylindrical or subcylindrical and not whiplash-shaped. If we exclude the small and anomalous groups of the Ptychopterina and the Cylindrotomina, this division of the Tipulidæ in longipalpi and brevipalpi will, upon examination, prove natural enough, and supported by a considerable number of subsidiary characters. Among the brevipalpi the genus Pedicia is the only one which has the last joint of the palpi rather long (nearly once and a half the length of the three preceding joints taken together), and this induced Latreille, when he established this genus, to place it among the longipalpi. In all other respects, the position of Pedicia among the brevipalpi is not in the least doubtful.

Besides the structure of the palpi, the following are the characters which may be used as tests for determining the relationship of doubtful forms with either of the two divisions. Some of these characters, perhaps all, may not be of universal occurrence

2 May, 1868.

In the groups in which they prevail ; but their importance arises from their characterizing the great majority of the species :—

1. In the *T. longipalpi*, the auxillary vein ends in the first longitudinal vein, being incurred towards it ; beyond the humeral cross-vein there is no other cross-vein connecting the auxillary vein with the costa or with the first longitudinal vein. In the *T. brevipalpi* the auxillary vein, as a rule, ends in the costa, and is connected by a cross-vein with the first longitudinal vein.

2. The structure of the cells in the vicinity of the stigma is totally different in the two divisions. The first longitudinal vein in the *T. longipalpi* is usually incurred towards the second vein and attenuated in a peculiar manner before ending in it ; an oblique cross-vein connects the first vein, a short distance back of the tip, with the costa ; this cross-vein, together with the anterior branch of the second vein, form near the anterior margin a small, trapezoidal cell, very characteristic of the *T. longipalpi* (it is wanting, however, in *Dolichopeza* and some related species). In the *T. brevipalpi* the first longitudinal vein ends in the costa, and the cross-vein, at its tip or some distance before it, connects it with the second longitudinal vein ; no structure like the trapezoidal cell is apparent.

3. The structure of the discal cell and the direction of the veins surrounding it is different in the two divisions. In the *T. longipalpi*, the vein separating the two last posterior cells (the posterior laterealary vein of Mr. Loew ; compare *Monogr. of N. A. Diptera*, I, p. xxiv, fig. 3, v) issues very near the inner end of the discal cell, usually from the angle, between this cell and the great cross-vein ; this, in most cases, gives the cell a pentagonal shape, unless, as for instance in the genus *Pachyrrhina*, the vein has no contact at all with the cell, and has the appearance of the direct prolongation of the fourth longitudinal vein ; in such cases the discal cell is a parallelogram. In the *T. brevipalpi* the posterior interealary vein issues from the latter end of the discal cell, and its origin is quite distant from the great cross-vein, which is usually near the inner end of the discal cell. The *Amalopina* show some approach to the *T. longipalpi* in the position of the interealary vein and in the shape of the discal cell ; still the origin of the interealary vein in the *Amalopina* is usually rather distant from the great cross-vein. *Amalopis umnalis* O. S., is the only species which, in this

respect, is like the *T. longipalpi*; the intercalary vein of this species issues from the angle between the cross-vein and the discal cell, at the inner end of the latter.

4. In the *T. longipalpi* a distinct fold generally runs across the wing from the inner end of the stigma, over the discal cell, to the penultimate posterior cell; it is usually marked by a paler coloring of the membrane of the wing and by a discoloration of the wing-veins; it is more or less distinct in the different genera. In the *T. brevipalpi* this fold is not apparent, and a slight trace of it may sometimes be observed in the partial discoloration of the veins at the inner ends of the discal and of the penultimate posterior cells.

5. The *T. longipalpi* usually keep the wings divaricate in repose, while the *T. brevipalpi* fold them over the abdomen. *Pedicia*, which reminds us of the *longipalpi* by the length of the last joint of the palpi, also keeps the wings divaricate in repose.

6. The rostrum of the *T. longipalpi* is usually more prolonged and its upper part projects in the shape of a point (*nasus*), clothed with hair; a very marked character, seldom wanting among the *T. longipalpi*, and not observed among the *T. brevipalpi*.

7. The antennæ of the normal types of *T. longipalpi* are 13-jointed; those of the *T. brevipalpi* are from 14 to 16-jointed; exceptions are comparatively rare. The structure of the joints of the flagellum, common among the *T. longipalpi*, is different from that of the majority of the *T. brevipalpi*.

8. The male genitals of the *T. longipalpi* are of a more complicated structure and more voluminous than the simple forceps of the *T. brevipalpi*; still, in this respect, intermediate forms occur.

9. The size of the *T. longipalpi* is generally considerably larger; their feet and especially the tarsi, are longer.

The *Ptychopterina*, as I have said above, are an anomalous group, which does not well fit in either of the two principal divisions of the *Tipulidæ*. Their palpi are long; but this length depends on the elongation of all the joints and not of the last joint in particular; this applies especially to the genera *Protoplasa* O. S. and *Tanyderus* Philippi. The auxiliary vein in *Bittacomorpha* and *Ptychoptera* ends in the costa, and there is no cross-vein connecting it with the first longitudinal vein; in

Protoplasa and Tanyderus, this cross-vein exists, and its position is altogether as in the T. brevipalpi. The rest of the venation of the Ptychopterina is peculiar and distinguished by the absence of the sixth longitudinal vein; still this venation is more like that of some T. brevipalpi, than of any T. longipalpi; there is hardly any vestige of a fold across the wing. The general appearance and the coloring of the body and of the wings are much more like the T. brevipalpi; tho structure of the antennæ and the number of their joints also remind us of them. The elongated epistoma, however, in Bittacomorpha and Ptychoptera, shows something of the nasus peculiar to tho T. longipalpi; it is not apparent in Protoplasa. The Ptychopterina keep the wings divaricate in repose (I do not know whether this applies equally to Protoplasa).

In the Cylindrotomina, tho course of the auxillary and first longitudinal veins strongly remind us of the T. longipalpi; the T. brevipalpi with a single submarginal cell, as far as known, never have spurs at the tip of the tibiæ, whereas the Cylindrotomina partake of both of these characters at the same time; the T. brevipalpi with a single submarginal cell always have only four posterior cells, Cylindrotoma distinctissima and C. americana have a single submarginal cell and five posterior cells. At the same time, the number of the antennal joints of the Cylindrotomina (16), the position of the posterior intercalary vein and the structure of the palpi, are characters belonging to the T. brevipalpi. The Cylindrotomina, except in the above quoted instance, have four posterior cells, a character of common occurrence among the T. brevipalpi, and, as far as I know, not observed yet among the T. longipalpi. (Compare, for more detail, the chapter on the Cylindrotomina.)

Thus, if we adopt the division into T. longipalpi and T. brevipalpi, it will be necessary to form a third group which will be artificial and contain the intermediate and anomalous forms.[1]

[1] It was with this intention that I introduced in the first volume of the present series (Monographs, etc., Vol. I, p. 11) the group Ptychopterina, co-ordinate with the T. longipalpi and brevipalpi (following Mr. Loew's precedence, I then called them Tipulina and Limnobina). With the Cylindrotomina I was hardly acquainted at that time, as I had found on this continent only a single doubtful specimen. It may not be amiss to notice here, that the two last lines of the above quoted page contain a lapsus calami, which

But as the *Tipulidæ* are divided now into a larger number of natural groups or sections, the subdivision into *T. longipalpi* and *brevipalpi* has lost somewhat of its importance. These names are, nevertheless, very convenient terms for designating the two large groups of which the family is composed; and they are the more convenient in the present publication, as the two parts of which it is intended to consist will nearly coincide with these groups.

---

5. *Distribution of the* TIPULIDÆ BREVIPALPI *in sections.*

The bulk of the *T. brevipalpi* is represented in the genus *Limnobia* Meigen, which contains the most heterogeneous elements. Several attempts have been made to subdivide it into sections, or to break it up altogether; but strange enough, all these attempts were based upon secondary characters, whereas the number of submarginal cells was either entirely overlooked, or applied to the distinction of subordinate groups only. Thus, both Zetterstedt (*Dipt. Scand.* X, 1851) and Walker (*Ins. Brit.*, *Diptera*, III, 1856) use for their primary subdivision of *Limnobia*, the presence or absence of the discal cell; and next to this, the number of posterior cells. The consequence is, that one of Prof Zetterstedt's ultimate subdivisions contains the following species in the same order as they are given here: *L. didyma* M. (a *Dicranomyia*; section *Limnobina*; one submarginal cell); *L. pilipes* F. (*Trimicra*; section *Eriopterina*; two submarginal cells); *L. replicata* L. (*Phalacrocera*; section *Cylindrotomina*); *L. trisulcata* Schum. (*Triogma*; section *Cylindrotomina*); *L. tristis* Schum. (*Dicranomyia*; one submarginal cell); *L. fuscescens* Schum. (*Dicranoptycha*; section *Limnobina anomala*; one submarginal cell); *L. murina* Zett. and *hyalinata* Zett. (probably *Dicranomyia*; one submarginal cell); *L. pilicornis* Zett. (probably *Cloniomorpha*; section *Limnophilina*; two submarginal cells); *L. pilosa* Schum. (*Ula*; section *Amalopina*; two submarginal cells); *L. ciliaris* Schum. (*Erioptera*; two submarginal cells); *L. lugubris* Zett. (perhaps a *Psiloconopa*? section *Eriopterina*; two submarginal cells); *L. morio* F. (*Dicrano-*

requires correction; in the penultimate line, read *first* instead of *second*; in the last line read *auxiliary*, instead of *first longitudinal*.

myia; one submarginal cell); L. gracilis Zett. (probably Goniomyia; section Eriopterina; two submarginal cells). Among
fourteen species, six different sections of the Tipulidæ and at
least ten genera are represented!

Earlier than Zetterstedt and Walker, Macquart had divided
Limnobia Meig. in two genera: Limnobia, with four posterior
cells, and Limnophila, with five. If Mr. Zetterstedt did not
seem to attach any importance to the number of submarginal
cells, except as a specific distinction, Macquart is somewhat in
advance of this author; he uses this character, but without
recognizing yet its full importance. His genus Limnobia is subdivided into two groups, the first of which, with a single submarginal cell, answers to our genera Dicranomyia and Limnobia;
the second, with two submarginal cells, contains the species: L.
sylvatica M. (a Limnophila, with four posterior cells); L. platyptera Macq. (the same); L. diana Macq. (an Eriocera), etc.

The presence or absence of a discal cell is, in most cases, a
character of a very secondary value, often unreliable even for the
distinction of species. The presence of a fifth posterior cell is
not always indicative of a corresponding modification in the
other organs. Closely allied species, in the genera Eriocera
and Penthoptera for instance, have a different number of posterior
cells. The number of submarginal cells is a character of a much
higher value, and can be applied with advantage to the whole
group of Tipulidæ brevipalpi, and not to the genus Limnobia
Meigen, only. But, used alone, it does not overcome the principal difficulty, which consists in eliminating from the genus
Limnobia, in Meigen's sense, all the foreign elements which it
contains. In order to attain this end, we have to use several
other characters. In the Proc. Acad. Nat. Sciences of Philadelphia, 1850, I have proposed a distribution, based upon the
number of submarginal cells, the presence or absence of spurs at
the tip of the tibiæ, the presence or absence of empodia, the
structure of the ungues, the number of antennal joints, and the
position of the subcostal cross-vein. The scheme of this distribution, which is retained in the present volume, is the following:—[1]

[1] Instead of the names ending in formis, which I applied to the sections
in 1859 (Limnobiæformis, Eriopteræformis, etc.), I adopt here the more
convenient termination in inæ. The name of the sixth section, Policia-
formis, is changed in Amalopina.

1. A single submarginal cell.

Antennæ 14-jointed.	Antennæ 16-jointed.
Sect. I. **Limnobina.**	Sect. II. **Limnobina anomala.**

II. Two submarginal cells.

No spurs at the tip of the tibæ.	Tibiæ with spurs.
Sect. III. **Eriopterina.**	

Auxiliary cross-vein posterior to the origin of the second vein.	Auxiliary cross-vein anterior to the origin of the second vein.
Antennæ 16-jointed. Antennæ 6 or 10-jointed. Sect. VI. **Amalopina.**	
Sect. IV. **Limnophilina.** Sect. V. **Anisomerina.**	

Besides the leading characters, mentioned in the table, almost all the sections have some other characters peculiar to them, as may be seen in the following definitions :—

I. **Limnobina.** One submarginal cell ; four posterior cells. Normal number of antennal joints[1] *fourteen* (sometimes apparently 15). Eyes glabrous. Tibiæ without spurs at the tip ; ungues with more or less distinct teeth on the under side ; empodia indistinct or none.

II. **Limnobina anomala** (artificial group). One submarginal cell (none in *Tasorrhina*). Normal number of antennal joints *sixteen*.

III. **Eriopterina.** Two submarginal cells ; four posterior cells (five cells in *Cladura* only) ; discal cell sometimes closed, but very often open. Normal number of antennal joints *sixteen*. Eyes glabrous. Tibiæ without spurs at the tip ; empodia distinct ; ungues smooth on the under side.

IV. **Limnophilina.** Two submarginal cells ; usually five, seldom four posterior cells ; discal cell generally present ; subcostal cross-vein posterior to the origin of the second longitudinal vein, usually closely approximated to the tip of the auxiliary vein (considerably distant in *Trichocera* only). Eyes glabrous (pubescent in *Trichocera*). Normal number of antennal joints *sixteen*. Tibiæ with spurs at the tip ; empodia distinct ; ungues smooth.

V. **Anisomerina.** Two submarginal cells (only one in *Cladolipes*) ; three, four, or five posterior cells ; discal cell closed or open ; subcostal

---

[1] Each one of the sections has a number of antennal joints, which is the *normal* number of this section. If a genus or species belonging to it have a smaller number, it can usually be shown that this number is due to the coalescence of some joints. This is for instance the case with *Elephantomyia* and *Tasorrhina* (compare these genera). Occasionally a larger number of joints is met with, as in the genus *Nephrotoma*, among the *Tipulidæ longipalpi* ; or among some foreign genera of *Limnophilina* ; but these are exceptions.

cross-vein near the tip of the auxiliary vein, posterior to the origin of the second vein. Eyes glabrous. The normal number of the antennal joints is *six* in the male and not more than *ten* in the female. Tibiæ with spurs at the tip; empodia distinct; ungues generally smooth.

VI. **Amalopina.** Two submarginal cells; discal cell closed or open; subcostal cross-vein far removed from the tip of the auxiliary vein, anterior to the origin of the second longitudinal vein. Tibiæ with spurs at the tip; empodia distinct. Eyes pubescent; front usually with a more or less distinct gibbosity. Normal number of antennal joints *sixteen* (seldom 17), or *thirteen*.

The second of these groups is called artificial, because it is destined to receive all the genera with a single submarginal cell which, at the same time, have sixteen-jointed antennæ. All such genera are so very peculiar in their characters, that it is natural enough to isolate them from the first section; but with all that, most of these genera do not show any relationship to each other and their juxtaposition is therefore artificial. The connecting links between them may not have been yet discovered, or they may have been lost in the course of geological ages; nevertheless, the adoption of this artificial group will be found of great advantage in the system. If it should be proved that one of these genera is related to some genus of another section, it will have to be removed to that section. Thus, in the genus *Cladolipes* Loew, closely related to *Anisomera*, one of the branches of the second vein has disappeared, and hence the genus has only a single submarginal cell. Nevertheless, as the natural relationship of this genus is evident, we place it among the genera with two submarginal cells. The aim of all classification is to increase our knowledge of the structure of organic beings by illustrating their natural relationship. If the natural relationship of some organic form be obscure, we may, for the sake of convenience, locate it provisionally on account of some artificial character; but this provisional state has to cease, as soon as the true relationship is found out. In this sense, the location of several of the genera of the second group may be only provisional and connecting links between them and the other sections may yet be discovered.

The other sections, as far as known, have very well marked

limits, and there are but very few forms of transition from the one to the other.

The *Erioptcrina*, through the entire disappearance of the short anterior branch of the second vein in *Goniomyia*, may show a leaning towards the group of *Limnobina anomala;* on the other side, some genera of *Erioptcrina* may come very near those *Limnophilina* which, with only four posterior cells, combine exceedingly small, almost obsolete, spurs at the tip of the tibiæ. These connections are as yet very obscure, and we have to wait for further discoveries. Another question which may be naturally raised here is, whether *Cladura*, which alone among the *Erioptcrina* has five posterior cells, is not rather to be considered as a genus of *Limnophilina*, the tibial spurs of which have become obsolete. A more detailed study of the organization of *Cladura* will have to show on which side its relationship is the strongest. The *Anisomerina*, especially the genus *Eriocera*, are closely related to the *Limnophilina;* but the number of antennal joints establishes a distinct limit between the two sections. Intermediate forms are, as yet, unknown, although they may be in existence. *Trichocera*, the only genus among the *Limnophilina*, which has pubescent eyes and the subcostal cross-vein far remote from the tip of the auxiliary vein, shows, in this respect, a leaning towards the *Amalopina;* in other respects, however, its relationship to the *Limnophilina* is manifestly stronger.

The more characters peculiar to each one of the sections we accumulate, the stronger we render the basis upon which the classification is established and easier the solution we prepare for all future doubtful cases. In this respect, a great deal yet remains to be done. The progress of this study depends very much on the observation of fresh specimens, and these cannot always be had when wanted. Thus very good characters may be derived from the comparison of the size and structure of the different parts of the thorax and of the abdomen; especially of the segments of the latter preceding the forceps. But these parts are subject to shrinkage in drying, and in this state it is easy to take an erroneous view of them. It is for this reason that I have abstained from entering upon their detailed description. The structure of the other soft parts of the body, as the palpi, the

forceps, and in many cases the antennæ, has been noted down by
me, almost invariably from living or fresh specimens.

At the end of the Tipulidæ brevipalpi I place the two sections
which I consider as intermediate between them and the T. longipalpi (compare above, p. 19): the Cylindrotomina and Ptychopterina:—

Sect. VII. Cylindrotomina. One submarginal cell: first longitudinal
vein incurved at the tip towards the second, instead of ending in the
costa (exception: Phalacrocera replicata Lin., where the first vein takes
the usual course): four or five posterior cells; a discal cell; the auxiliary
vein is abruptly interrupted before the stigma, without ending either in
the costa, or in the first longitudinal vein. Eyes glabrous. Normal number of antennal joints sixteen. Tibiæ with spurs at the tip. Empodia
distinct. Structure of the forceps and the ovipositor peculiar and
characteristic.

Sect. VIII. Ptychopterina. Only a single longitudinal vein posterior
to the fifth vein; two submarginal cells. Labium largely developed; palpi
long. Tibiæ with spurs at the tip.

After having given an account of the distribution into sections,
I have to add a few words on the genera. I am opposed to a
too great multiplication of the genera, and I believe that as the
contrast between large and small groups exists in nature, it
should also be brought before the eye in the classification. In
the genus Erioptera, for instance, the relationship of the groups
which compose it is a much more striking feature than the
characters which separate these groups. If we set up the groups
as genera, with only three or four species in each, the difference
between the large group, now called Erioptera, and smaller
groups, such for instance as the genera Gnophomyia, Trimicra,
and all the genera of the group Limnobina anomala, this difference, so strongly marked in nature, would remain unexpressed in
the system. Subdivisions of the larger genera should of course
be carefully marked, but less strongly than the intervals between
the small genera, and in such cases a subgeneric subdivision may
be useful. This is the course which I have followed.

6. General remarks on the structure of the TIPULIDÆ BREVIPALPI.

In this paragraph I do not intend to undertake a general comparative description of the external structure of the Tip. brevi-

palpi. My purpose is, to give a review of those characters only, which have been used in the classification, and to furnish some explanations necessary for the better understanding of the present monograph.

The organs of the mouth of the *Tip. brevipalpi* afford comparatively few characters for the classification. The prolongation of the head in front, called the *rostrum* (compare *Monograph,* etc., Vol. I, p. xiii) is generally shorter here than in the *Tip. longipalpi;* it is considerably prolonged in the genera *Rhamphidia, Tororrhina,* and *Elephantomyia,* and then bears the palpi at its tip. The outer envelope of the rostrum has sometimes the shape of a short tube ripped open on the under side; often, however, it is hardly tubular at all, but has rather the appearance of a labrum, and is either short and stout, or long, narrow, and linear (*Geranomyia*). Whenever I wanted to designate this outer envelope of the rostrum separately, as an independent organ, I have called it *epistoma.* The *proboscis* consists chiefly of the under lip, with its suctorial flaps; it projects more or less beyond the epistoma; the flaps are usually somewhat pubescent, linear in the *Limnobina,* more-stout and fleshy in the *Limnophilina, Amalopina,* etc.; (in *Geranomyia* the under lip is very much prolonged and bilobed, the lobes being likewise long and linear). The palpi incurved backwards, when at rest, are four-jointed; a fifth joint, sometimes perceptible at their basis, probably represents a rudimental maxilla; Mr. Westwood (*Introd.* etc. II, p. 525), who makes this suggestion, adds, that the texture of this fifth joint is different from that of the other four. The last joint of the palpi is usually longer than the preceding, somewhat linear; but, except in some rare cases, as in *Pedicia,* it is never very long. Immediately under the part which I call the epistoma, is a linear, pointed organ, called the *tongue;* it is especially long in *Geranomyia.* Meigen (Vol. VI, p. 281), in dissecting the mouth of *Glochina,* also mentions a pair of horny, linear, pointed *maxillæ.* A comparative study of the parts of the mouth of the *Tipulidæ* is yet to be made.

The eyes are oblong or rounded, separated above by a front which is more or less broad in different genera, but not perceptibly broader in one sex than in the other. On the under side of the head, the eyes are usually more approximate, often almost contiguous. There is no striking difference in the size of the

facets of the upper and of the lower part of the eyes, nor a distinct dividing line between them.[1] The eyes are glabrous, except
in the *Amalopina* and in the genus *Trichocera*, where they are
pubescent. Ocelli are wanting, except in *Trichocera*, where
they are distinctly perceptible; *Pedicia* also shows some traces
of them.

The antennæ are composed of a cylindrical, elongated first
joint; a short, cyathiform or rounded second joint, and from 12 to
14 joints of the flagellum. The *Anisomerina* have an abnormal
number of joints (from 6 to 10); and in some foreign genera, the
number of the joints is larger (compare *Gynoplistia*, *Cerozodia*,
Clerkonia, etc.). The usual measure of the antennæ is, that when
bent backwards, they nearly reach the root of the wings; they
are much shorter than this in the genus *Amalopis*. The male
sex in the *Anisomerina*, especially in some American species of
Eriocera, has enormously prolonged filiform antennæ, sometimes
three or four times the length of the body. Some *Limnophilæ*,
also *Cylindrotoma*, have the antennæ of the male considerably
longer than those of the female and pubescent on their whole
length; usually, however, this difference in length between the
sexes is much less perceptible. The male has often, on the under
side of the three or four basal joints of the flagellum, a dense,
short pubescence, which is much less perceptible in the female;
in some cases this pubescence extends on both sides of the whole
antenna. It is worthy of notice that when the antennæ of the
male are long and pubescent, the first basal joint is very apt to
be shorter than usual; this is the case for instance with *Limnophila tenuipes*, *Cylindrotoma americana*, *Ula*, etc. Pectinate
antennæ occur only in *Rhipidia* among the native species, but
several foreign *Limnophilina* have them also.

The feet are long and slender, more or less pubescent; the
presence or absence of spurs at the tip of the tibiæ, of empodia,
and of teeth on the under side of the ungues constitute the basis
of the principal subdivisions of the *T. brevipalpi*, and will be
sufficiently noticed below. The spurs, whenever present, are two

[1] In the genus *Blepharocera* (fam. *Blepharoceridæ*, Monogr. Vol. I, p. 8)
the eyes are divided in two portions, the upper one with large, the lower
one with small facets; the upper portion is comparatively smaller in the
male than in the female; in life, these portions differ in their color; the
upper one, in *B. capitata* Lw., is reddish-green, the lower one purple.

in number on each tibia, and occur on all the three pairs of tibiæ; I have not observed a single case of spurs occurring on one or two pairs of tibiæ only.[1] The last tarsal joints show a sexual character, tho very general occurrence of which has, I believe, not been observed before: In tho male, the interval between tho last and the penultimate joint is excised on tho under side, which enables this joint to be bent under the preceding (a similar structure in a *Tipula* is figured by Westwood in Walker's *Ins. Brit. Dipt.* Tab. XXVIII, fig. 5 *d*). In such cases the last joint itself is modified in its structure, generally more elongated,[·] slender, somewhat curved, and beset with bristles on the under side. This structure prevails through nearly all the genera, although it is sometimes wanting in single species of a genus in which it otherwise prevails.

The prothorax (collare) varies in breadth and the remaining parts of the thorax in shape. These modifications, although mentioned in the descriptions, have not served to establish any important subdivisions. On the front part of the mesonotum there is often a pair of black dots, one on each side, immediately back of the humerus; sometimes they assume the appearance of small pits, with a brown or black, shining bottom. I do not know what they are; they may have some connection with the prothoracic spiracle, which is not far from them, immediately below. There is no vestige of them in some species and genera (for instance in *Pedicia* and *Amalopis*). In other cases, they are quite conspicuous, as in the group of *Limnophila*, represented by *L. lucipennis*. These latter species have, besides the pits, two closely approximated shining dots, black or brown, near the point of contact of the intermediate thoracic stripe with the collare.

The abdomen is nine-jointed; the eighth joint is often narrow; the ninth usually consists of an upper half segment and of the genitals. The external sexual apparatus of the male consists of a forceps, by means of which the end of the female abdomen is seized from below, a little before the ovipositor, in such a manner, that the latter organ is stretched out on tho upper part of the abdomen of the male. This done, the male with a second, inner, clutching apparatus seizes the orifice of the inner genital

---

[1] *Atarba* may, perhaps, form an exception; compare this genus.

organs of the female and adjusts thereon for copulation. The structure of this outer forceps offers many modifications and is for this reason very useful in the classification.

The usual structure of the outer forceps is, that it consists of two, generally subcylindrical basal pieces, to each of which two elongated, pointed, movable appendages are fastened (compare Tab. IV, f. 23, 24, 25, 29). The two pairs of these appendages are not of the same consistency, the outer one being generally horny, the inner one often of a less hard texture. The modifications, however, of this primitive type are numerous. Sometimes the two appendages on the same side are soldered together, so as to represent a kind of horny hook (Tab. III, fig. 6, 7; Tab. IV, fig. 11, 18). In the genus *Dicranomyia* the forceps is represented by a pair of movable fleshy lobes, with horny, beak-shaped projections on the inside (Tab. III, fig. 3, 5). Among the *Eriopterina* the structure of the forceps is often complicated and subject to considerable modifications (T. IV, f. 14, 15, 17-20). The outer forceps, as far as I have been able to observe, is put in motion by a kind of horny frame, fastened to its basis on the inside and communicating with the proper muscles; this frame expands and contracts by means of a hinge in its middle (compare Tab. IV, fig. 29, and 29 a, the forceps of *Erioecra spinosa* and the explanation, appended to the figure; I have observed a somewhat similar structure in *Dicranoptycha sobrina*). This inner frame is also connected with the inner clutching apparatus, the structure of which has not been used, however, for descriptive purposes. Among the *Limnobina*, a single, immovable, styliform organ is visible immediately below the forceps; I have called it the *style*; this organ is not perceptible in most of the other sections. It is replaced, however, by a slender, horny, often curved and pointed piece, which is entirely concealed when the forceps is closed, and projected when it is open; I have called it *aculeus*. Among the *Cylindrotomina*, the aculeus has the shape of a lamel, more or less trifid at the tip. (For more details on the structure of the forceps, compare the explanation of Plates III and IV.) A more detailed study of the structure of the male genitals and also of the shape of the abdominal segments immediately preceding the forceps, would undoubtedly afford very valuable characters for the discovery of links of relationship otherwise latent. But this study is difficult, because it can give positive results only when pursued upon fresh specimens.

The female ovipositor consists of two pairs of horny valves, usually attenuated and pointed at the tip. Their length and shape afford occasionally useful characters.

The most important and at the same time the most tangible of all the characters used for the classification of the *Tipulidæ* are afforded by the wings and their venation.[1] The shape of the wings, their breadth in comparison to their length, the shape of their anal angle, etc., deserve to be noted. Their membrane, when examined under a strong magnifying power, will always appear pubescent (the wing of *Antocha* appeared pubescent under a power of 150); nevertheless in describing a wing, we call it glabrous, when the pubescence is not discernible to the naked eye nor to a lens of low power, and however indefinite the limit between a pubescent and a glabrous wing, in our sense, may seem, the practical application of these terms is hardly ever doubtful. In the same way, the wing-veins are always pubescent; but we call them so only when the pubescence is long enough to be striking under an ordinary entomological lens; otherwise we consider them as glabrous.

The terminology of the venation used by me is, in the main, that of Mr. Loew, as explained in the first volume of these *Monographs* (pp. xv–xxiv). In some respects, however, it had to be modified, in order to be rendered applicable to the *Tipulidæ*. The principal difficulty lies in the name to be given to what I will call below the *great cross-vein* and to the portion of the fifth longitudinal vein, beyond this cross-vein. If the diagram below is compared to the three diagrams given on page xxiv of the first volume of the *Monographs*, it will be easily perceived that the portion of the fifth vein, lying beyond the cross-vein in the *Tipulidæ*, corresponds to the *posterior basal transverse vein* of the wing of *Ortalis* (*Monogr.* I, p. xxiv, fig. 1, q). The *great cross-vein* of the *Tipulidæ*, if traced back to the wing of *Ortalis*, would be found to form a part of the fifth longitudinal vein (i. e. fig. 1, ggg). The course of the fifth longitudinal vein of *Ortalis*, if traced out upon the wing of a Tipulid, would be found to run along the great

---

[1] The term *venation*, used by English authors, is certainly preferable to *neuration*, which has been used in the first volumes of these *Monographs*.

cross-vein, then along the discal cell, between the two intercalary
veins, to the posterior margin (see l. c. fig. 8, the wing of *Empis*,
which in this respect resembles that of the *Tipulidæ*, and compare it to the wing of *Ortalis* and to the diagram which I give
below). Thus, if we force upon the *Tipulidæ* the terminology
introduced originally for the families of Diptera with a less developed venation, we meet with inextricable difficulties. But
there is no more reason for doing this than for following the
opposite course, adopting a terminology for the *Tipulidæ* first
and forcing it afterwards upon the *Muscidæ*. It is perfectly
arbitrary at which end of the system of Diptera we begin to
trace out the homologies of the venation. This study of the
homologies has two distinct aims in view: the scientific aim of
showing that the ground-plan of the venation is the same in all
the families of the order; and the practical aim of adopting a
terminology for descriptive purposes. We cannot carry out a
terminology on solely theoretical grounds; we will have to vary
the details of it according to the peculiarities of structure occurring in different families, the main plan remaining the same. This
is done in all the departments of zoology, and I do not see why
the venation of the Diptera should be treated differently.

In accordance with these views, I call *fifth longitudinal vein*
the whole vein immediately following the second basal cell and
the last of the posterior cells; I call *great cross-vein* (in contra-
distinction from the *posterior cross-vein* of the *Muscidæ*) the
cross-vein connecting the fifth vein with the vein preceding it.
The *fourth vein*, I look upon as including the discal cell between
its two main branches.[1] The posterior of these branches is almost
always forked (the posterior branch of this fork corresponds to
Mr. Loew's *posterior intercalary* vein, *v*, in the wing of *Empis*,
Monogr. I, p. xxiv, fig. 8); and the cross-vein, connecting this
fork with the anterior branch, closes the discal cell; hence, when
the discal cell is open, through the disappearance of this cross-
vein it coalesces with the second posterior cell (as in Tab. 1, fig. 1),
or with the *third*, when there are five posterior cells (as in Tab.
II, fig. 17). Such is the case with the majority of the genera
which have the discal cell open, as *Orimarga, Empeda, Cryptolabis, Erioptera* (subgenera: *Erioptera* and *Molophilus*), *Plec-*

---

[1] In this I follow Dr. Schiner's views.

tromyia, Dicranota, and *Rhaphidolabis*. In those genera where
the discal cell is open in some species only, or in some specimens
of certain species, the same rule prevails; it coalesces with the
second posterior cell, when there are four such cells, and with the
third, when there are five (compare the genus *Dicranomyia*).
Cases, where the anterior branch of the fourth vein is forked and
the posterior not; in other words, where, with four posterior cells,
the discal cell coalesces with the *third* posterior cell (as in Tab.
I, fig. 15); such cases are rare, and occur more commonly only
in the section *Eriopterina* (compare the general remarks on
this section); outside of it, the genera *Thaumastoptera* and
Elliptera (Tab. I, fig. 10) only possess this character. In *Dicranomyia pubipennis* O. S., also, when the discal cell is open, it
coalesces with the third posterior cell; a singular exception
from among all the *Dicranomyiæ*. Outside of the *Tipulidæ
brevipalpi*, this structure may be observed in *Ptychoptera* (Tab.
II, fig. 19). The occurrence of five posterior cells, without any
fork on the posterior branch of the fourth vein, can take place
only when the anterior branch of this vein has a double fork.
This is the case with *Dolichopeza*; but I have not met with any
instance of this kind among the *Tipulidæ brevipalpi*, except in
the *Limnophilina*. It is worthy of notice, that in this section
where the discal cell is, as a rule, always closed, whenever an
abnormal specimen is met with, where this cell is open, the
branching of the fourth vein is very apt to appear like that of
Dolichopeza.

The fork of the anterior branch of the fourth vein is formed by
the insertion of the vein which Mr. Loew calls the *anterior intercalary vein* (u in *Monogr.* I, p. xxiv, fig. 3). It is the addition
of this vein which raises the number of posterior cells to five.

The small cross-vein usually forms the inner end of the first
posterior cell. In some rare cases the inner end of the submarginal cell is in immediate contact with the discal cell (as in
the wing of *Triogma*, Tab. I, fig. 7), and in such cases there is,
of course, no small cross-vein. This structure characterises the
genera *Triogma* and *Paratropeza* Schiner; it also occurs in most
specimens of the North American *Cylindrotoma nodicornis* and
adventitiously in the genus *Rhamphidia*.

I call *præfurca* (a term which has been used by Mr. Haliday
in Walker's *Ins. Brit. Dipt.* III, p. 304) the portion of the second
3   June, 1868.

vein between its origin and the emission of the third longitudinal
vein. The *petiole* of the first submarginal cell is the portion of
the second longitudinal vein between the tip of the profurca and
the inner end of that cell. In order to describe the relative
position of the tips of the veins and of cross-veins, I have used
the term *opposite*; two points are opposite each other when, projected on the longitudinal axis of the wing, they appear eqni-
distant from its basis. The following diagram explains the other
terms, which have been used by me :—

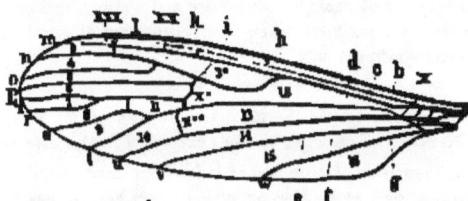

Diagram of a wing with two submarginal and five posterior cells
(Cladura indivisa).

Cells.

1. Costal.	6. Second submarginal.	14. Anal.
2. Subcostal.	6–10. First to fifth posterior.	15. Axillary.
5. Marginal.	11. Discal.	16. Spurious.
5°. Inner marginal.	12. First basal.	
4. First submarginal.[1]	13. Second basal.	

Veins.

b i. Auxiliary.	d g r i. Fourth longitudinal.
c m. First longitudinal.	q r. Fork of the anterior branch: the
4 a e. Second longitudinal.	posterior branch of this fork,
4 f. Profurca.	ending in r, is Mr. Loew's an-
4 n. Anterior branch of the second	terior intercalary vein.
L. vein.	a f. Fork of the posterior branch of
4 e. Posterior branch of the second	the fourth vein; the branch
L. vein.	of this fork, ending in f, is
f b. Petiole of the first submarginal	Mr. Loew's posterior inter-
cell.	calary vein.
f p. Third longitudinal.	e u. Fifth longitudinal.
	f v. Sixth longitudinal.
	g x. Seventh longitudinal.

[1] In my paper: Description of some new Genera and Species of North
American Limnobina, *Proc. Phil. Entom. Soc.* 1865, p. 225, I have called
this cell the *second marginal*; the proper term, however, in accordance with
the terminology originally adopted by Macquart, is *first submarginal*.

a. Humeral.
xv. Subcostal.
sm. Marginal.

Cross-veins.

s*. Small, or anterior cross-vein.
s**. Great cross-vein.

Other terms which have been used.

When the veins between the end of the præfurca (i) and the great cross-vein are more or less in a line, I designate them by the collective term *central cross-veins*.

Veins or cross-veins not found in the ordinary venation and therefore not separately named, have been called *supernumerary*, when they are of constant occurrence and distinguish a genus or a species; *adrentitious*, when their occurrence is accidental in abnormal specimens only.

7. *Comparison of the North American and of the European* TIPULIDÆ *of the eight sections described in this volume.*

The knowledge of both faunas is far from perfect, and in this country, as well as in Europe, almost every year brings with it the discovery of some of the more rare and more interesting forms. Only the general features of these faunas can therefore be compared with a certain degree of confidence, and our statements with regard to the details, the numerical proportions of the species, and the comparison of the smaller genera must, in a certain measure, be considered as only provisional.

What strikes us most, when we compare the number of European and North American species in the eight sections of the *Tipulidæ* described in the present volume, is the remarkable agreement, in this respect, between the two faunas. The comparison of the number of species occurring in Germany (according to Dr. Schiner's enumeration), with those of the Atlantic slope of this continent (as far as represented in my collection) stands thus:—

Large Groups.	N. Am.	Germ.	Small Groups.	N Am.	Germ
Limnobina . . .	35	31	Limnobina anomala	10	5
Eriopterina . . .	35	34	Anisomerina . . .	6	5
Limnophilina . .	34	85	Amalopina . . .	13	14
			Cylindrotomina . .	4	4
			Ptychopterina . .	3	5
Total . . .	104	100	Total . . .	36	33
	species	species		species	species

Sum total of the eight first sections of the *Tipulidæ* (that is, the *T. brevipalpi*, including the *Cylindrotomina* and *Ptychopterina*) for North America 140, for Germany 133 species. The number of species described in Zetterstedt's *Diptera Scandinaviæ*, embracing Sweden, Norway, Denmark, and Finland, is nearly equal to the total for Germany.

The total number of the species of *T. brevipalpi* in Europe, according to Schiner's *Catalogus Dipterorum Europæ*, is 240, but a proper synonymy would very considerably reduce this number.

The striking features of the above given table are : 1. That each of the three large groups is represented by nearly the same number of species in both countries; 2. That the number of species in each of the three large groups is nearly equal to the number of species of the other two large groups, and nearly equal to the number of species in the five small groups taken together; in other words, that both in North America and in Germany, the number of species in each of the large groups is about one-quarter of the whole number; 3. That the number of species of the small groups is somewhat larger in North America than in Germany. If we extend this comparison to the genera, we will find that the large genera are represented by nearly the same number of species in North America and in Germany (*Dicranomyia* 19 and 15, *Limnobia* 9 and 12, *Erioptera* 15 and 15, *Rhypholophus* 7 and 6, *Limnophila* 27 and 29).

Among the smaller genera, some are common to North America and to Europe (we need not confine ourselves to the German fauna here), and others peculiar, as far as known, to one of the two continents.

The N. A. genera peculiar to the American continent are :— *Elephantomyia* (1 sp.), *Toxorrhina* (2 sp.), *Teucholabis* (1 sp.), *Eriocera* (4 sp.), *Cladura* (2 sp.), *Atarba* (1 sp.), *Cryptolabis* (1 sp.), *Plectromyia* (1 sp.), *Rhaphidolabis* (2 sp.), *Rillacomorpha* (1 sp.), *Protoplasa* (1 sp). *Gnophomyia* (2 sp.) is represented in Europe by *Psiloconopa* (3 or more species).

The following genera have been found as yet only in Europe :— *Elliptera* (2 sp.), *Orimarga* (2 or 3 sp.), *Thaumastoptera* (1 sp.), and *Cladolipes* (1 sp).

Common to both continents are : *Geranomyia* (2 Eur., 3 N. Am. sp.); *Trochobola* (2 Eur., 1 N. Am. sp.); *Rhipidia* (2 Eur.,

3 N. Am. sp.); *Rhamphidia* (2 Eur., 1 N. Am. sp.); *Dicranoptycha* (2 Eur., 8 N. Am. sp.); *Antocha* (1 Eur., 1 N. Am. sp.); *Trimicra* (2 or 3? Eur., 1 N. Am. sp.); *Symplecta* (3 Eur., 1 N. Am. sp.); *Goniomyia* (5 or 6 Eur., 4 N. Am. sp.); *Empeda* (4 Eur., 1 N. Am. sp.); *Chionea* (2 Eur., 2 N. Am. sp.); *Epiphragma* (1 Eur., 2 N. Am. sp.); *Trichocera* (5 Eur., 4 or 5 N. Am. sp.); *Anisomera* (8 Eur., 1 N. Am. sp.); *Penthoptera* (2 Eur., 1 N. Am. sp.); *Amalopis* (about 8 or 9 Eur., 5 N. Am. sp.); *Dicranota* (about 5 Eur., 2 N. Am. sp.); *Pedicia* (1 Eur., 1 N. Am. sp.); *Ula* (2 Eur., 2 N. Am. sp.); *Cylindrotoma* (2 Eur., 2 N. Am. sp.); *Triogma* (1 Eur., 1 N. Am. sp.); *Phalacrocera* (1 Eur., 1 N. Am. sp.); *Ptychoptera* (5 Eur., 3 N. Am. sp.).

The comparison of the smaller genera again discloses a remarkable agreement in the number of species; the differences, where they occur, are in most cases in favor of the European fauna, and are probably due, in a great measure (for instance in the genus *Anisomera*), to the imperfect knowledge of the North American fauna.

I have shown the points of agreement between the two faunas. The statement of the differences requires much more caution, as the incomplete knowledge of the North American fauna is here to be especially taken into account. It is almost certain that some of the genera, enumerated above as peculiar to America, will never be found in Europe (for instance *Toxorrhina*, *Elephantomyia*, *Eriocera*); on the other hand, it is far from certain that the genera hitherto found in Europe only, may not yet be discovered on the American continent (as *Orimarga* and *Elliptera*). As for as my knowledge goes, the difference between the two faunas may be expressed in the following terms : *Whenever the North American fauna differs from the European in the occurrence of a peculiar generic form, or in a marked prevalence of another, this difference is due, either to an admixture of South American forms, or of forms peculiar to the amber fauna.*

If we look over the North American genera, not occurring in Europe, we find that, among those genera, *Toxorrhina* is a South American and West Indian form ; *Elephantomyia* occurs in amber ; *Eriocera* with short antennae are abundant in South America ; those with long antennae in the male sex have been found in amber. *Protoplasa* is represented by *Tanyderus* in

South America and by *Macrochile* in amber. *Teucholabis*, and some allied, and as yet undescribed forms, are well represented in South America and Mexico; *Gnophomyia* likewise.

Geranomyia is represented in Europe by two rare species; it is common in North America, and still more abundantly represented in South America. Those North American species of *Epiphragma* and *Rhipidia*, which are not represented by analogous forms in Europe, are South American forms.

Some species, characteristic of North America, as *Limnophila* (Lasiomastix) *macrocera* Say, *Limnophila tenuipes* Say, and some other species with long antennæ in the male sex, are represented quite abundantly by analogous forms in amber; one of them, *Limnophila longicornis* Loew, seems to be closely allied to *L. macrocera* Say.

It would be interesting to push the comparison of the two faunas still farther, and, by taking up the genera singly, to compare the North American and the European species, so as to arrive at some results as to analogies or differences in their structure, coloring, or size. From want of materials for such a task, my remarks will be very fragmentary.

In this family, as in most of the other families of Diptera, there is a certain number of species, which are apparently common to Europe and to North America. I say apparently, because with such species one is never sure whether the comparison of a larger number of specimens would not disclose a constant difference. And as every kind of difference, even if constant, does not necessarily constitute a specific character, cases of this kind are often doubtful, and their decision more or less arbitrary.

My opportunities for comparing specimens having been small, it is with such reservations that I have to introduce the list of identical or analogous species of both continents.

The following species, as far as ascertained, seem to be common to Europe and to North America: *Dicranomyia liberta* O. S., *D. longipennis* Schum. (syn. *D. imm篏ior* O. S.), *Rhipidia maculata* Meig., *Symplecta punctipennis* Meig., *Antocha opalizans* O. S.

The identity of the following species is less certain, their resemblance, however, very great: *Dicranomyia morio* Fab. and *morioides* O. S., *Trochobola annulata* Lin. and *T. argus* Say; *Ephelia* (an unnamed European species in my collection, perhaps

guttata Macq.) and *F. aprilina* O. S., *Idioptera pulchella* Melg.
and *I. fasciolata* O. S.; *Amalopis tipulina* Egger and *A. incon-
stans* O. S.; *Cylindrotoma distinctissima* M. and *C. americana*
O. S. Judging from the description of *Limnobia varinervis*
Zett., which is an *Amalopis*, it must be very like *A. hyperborea*
O. S.

Closely resembling, but certainly different species are *Pedicia
rivosa* L. and *P. albivitta* Walk., *Rhipidia uniseriata* Sebin.
and *R. fidelis* O. S., *Limnobia annulus* Lin. and *L. cinctipes*
Say, etc.

An undescribed European *Ula* is very like *U. elegans* O. S.
The European and North American species of *Trichocera* are
closely alike in appearance, but require comparison.

The comparison of the large genera gives occasion to the
following remarks :—

In the genera *Limnobia* and *Limnophila* the species with
handsomely pictured wings seem to be more abundant in Europe.
The species *Limnobia flavipes* Melg., *sylvicola* Schum., *nubeculosa* M., *nigropunctata* Schum., and similar ones, have no
corresponding representatives in North America. The same
remark applies to the subgenus *Poecilostola* Sehiner (Limnophila), represented by four species in Germany, and not discovered yet in North America.

In the genus *Erioptera* I am not aware of the occurrence in
Europe of the subgenera *Mesocyphona* O. S. and *Acyphona* O. S.;
however the European *Eriopterae* are very imperfectly classified.

If my limited knowledge prevents me from pushing very far
the comparison of the North American with the European fauna,
I have still less means for a comparison with the faunas of the
other parts of the world. Almost nothing is known about them;
the scanty facts in our possession will be mentioned, however, in
the respective sections and genera.

8. *On the species of North American* TIPULIDÆ BREVIPALPI (including the *Cylindrotomina* and *Ptychopterina*), *described in
former publications.*

Forty-four Tipulidæ coming within the scope of the present
volume have been enumerated in my *Catalogue of the Described
Diptera of North America*, Washington, 1858. Omitting two
collection-names of Mr. Harris, which had never been published

before, and five species from the West Indies and Mexico, thirty-seven species remain. These are :—

1. *Erioptera caliptera* Say, described below under the same name.

2. *Erioptera fascipennis* Zett. ; a *Rhypholophus*, closely allied to *R. nubilus*, but apparently distinct ; unknown to me ; its description is reproduced in the *Appendix* I.

3. *Pedicia albivitta* Walk. is described below under the same name.

4. *Limnobia argus* Say = *Trochobola argus* (comp. below).

5. *Limnobia badia* Walk. = *Dicranomyia badia* (comp. below).

6. *Limnobia biterminata* Walker (*Dipt. Saund.* V, p. 137), according to the author's description, has two submarginal and five posterior cells ; the first submarginal with a very short petiole ; the præfurca rectangular near its origin, etc. I know of no species to which this description can be applied ; it suggests *L. luteipennis*, but this species is three lines long, and not six, the antennæ are not tawny at the basis, the wings are not "grayish," but brownish ; the second marginal cell has not a short, but a long petiole ; the third vein does not form a very obtuse angle near its basis. Moreover there is a contradiction in Mr. Walker's description ; the diagnosis says "abdomen basi fulvum;" the description on the contrary has: "abdomen tawny at the tip." This description is reproduced at the end of this volume.

7. *Limnobia cana* Walk. I have seen the original of this species at the British Museum and took it for *Symplecta puncti-pennis*. I overlooked at that time Mr. Walker's statements about the differences between these two species (*List, etc.*, I, p. 49). Nevertheless these statements are not quite clear, and would not influence my opinion in the absence of the original specimen.

8. *Limnophila carbonaria* Macq. is a species unknown to me, the description of which is reproduced at the end of this volume.

9. *Limnobia cinctipes* Say is described below under the same name.

10. *Limnobia contermina* Walk. is probably a variety of *Pedicia albivitta* (compare this species).

11. *Limnobia fascipennis* Say = *Epiphragma fascipennis*.

12. *Rhamphidia flavipes* Macq. is described below under this
name.

13. *Limnobia gracilis* Wied. is either a *Limnophila* or an
Amalopis, distinguished by its large size (7 lines) and its abdomen being much longer than the wings. The description of this
species is reproduced in the Appendix to this volume.

14. *Limnobia humeralis* Say; a *Limnophila*. I would incline to the opinion of Wiedemann and consider this species
as synonymous with *L. tenuipes* Say. If in a copy of Wiedemann's
work at the Academy of Natural Sciences in Philadelphia I had
not found a marginal note, in Say's handwriting, positively denying this synonymy. Say describes only a female; the venation
is the same as that of *tenuipes*, and altogether the resemblance
of the two species must be very great. I reproduce the description of *L. humeralis* in the Appendix.

15. *Limnobia ignobilis* Walk. (*Dipt. Saund.*) has the venation
like Meigen, Tab. VI, fig. 5, that is, a single submarginal cell;
there is a stump of a vein near the origin of the præfurca. I
know of no such species. The description will be reproduced
in the Appendix to this volume.

16. *Limnobia macrocera* Say = *Limnophila macrocera* (comp.
below).

17. *Limnobia prominens* Walk. is very probably *Rhamphidia
flavipes* Macq.

18. *Limnobia ricœma* of Fabricius' *Fauna Grœnlandica* is
probably *Pedicia albivitta*, which is indeed very like the European
Pedicia ricœma.

19. *Limnobia rostrata* Say = *Geranomyia rostrata* (comp.
below).

20. *Limnobia simulans* Walk. = *Dicranomyia defuncta* O. S.
I have seen the original at the British Museum, an old and faded
specimen. Mr. Walker describes the species as "pale yellow,
legs yellow, tips of thighs, of the shanks and of the feet black;"
whereas, in reality, the body is blackish, the legs are dark brown,
almost black, with a white band before the tip, etc.

21. *Limnobia tenuipes* Say = *Limnophila tenuipes* (comp.
below).

22. *Limnobia turpis* Walk. (*Dipt. Saund.*). Venation like
Meig. Tab. V, fig. 5, that is, a single submarginal cell and five
posterior cells. All the known *Limnobiæ* with a single sub-

marginal cell have four posterior cells, and there is only one exception to this rule: *Cylindrotoma distinctissima* and its vicarious North American form—*C. Americana*; Meigen's figure represents the wing of the former. Therefore Mr. Walker's description must either refer to some species entirely unknown to me, or more probably, the statement about its wings being like Meigen, Tab. V, fig. 5, must be erroneous. Moreover, the name *L. turpis* cannot be retained, as Mr. Walker himself has described another *L. turpis* in the *Insecta Britannica, Diptera*, Vol. III, p. 300, in the same year 1856. The description is given in the Appendix to this volume.

23. *Limnobiorhynchus canadensis* Westw. = *Geranomyia canadensis* (comp. below).

24. *Anisomera longicornis* Walk. = *Eriocera longicornis* (comp. below).

25. *Chionea aspera* Walk. = *Chionea valga* Harris (comp. below).

26. *Chionea scita* Walk.; unknown to me; the description is reproduced in the Appendix.

27. *Chionea valga* Harris, described below under the same name.

28. *Trichocera bimacula* Walk.
29. *Trichocera gracilis* Walk.
30. *Trichocera brumalis* Fitch.
31. *Trichocera scutellata* Say.

The descriptions of these somewhat doubtful species are reproduced in the Appendix I; compare also the genus *Trichocera*.

32. *Trichocera maculipennis* Meig.; a European species said to occur in Greenland, according to Stæger.

33. *Trichocera regelationis* Lin.; also a European species, quoted by Otto Fabricius, as occurring in Greenland, which requires confirmation.

34. *Gymnoplistia annulata* Westw. I have seen the original specimen in Mr. Hope's collection at Oxford, and have never met with any other. Mr. Westwood's description is reproduced in Appendix I.

35. *Dittacomorpha clavipes* is described below under the same name.

36, 37. *Ptychoptera metallica* Walk. and *quadrifasciata* Say are unknown to me; their descriptions will be found in the Appendix.

Since the publication of my *Catalogue*, etc., a *Limnobia nigricola* Walk. has been described in the *Trans. Lond. Entom. Soc.*
V, N. S. pt. VII, p. 66. It is apparently my *Gnophomyia
luctuosa*.

The result of the foregoing examination is the following :—
Omitting the six species of the genus *Trichocera*, which requires
an entire revision, eleven species, among the thirty-two which have
been described, have not been identified ; of these six or seven,
because they have not been among the number of species which
I have had for examination : *Limnophila carbonaria* Macq. ;
Gynoplistia annulata Westw. ; *Rhypholophus fascipennis* Zett. ;
Limnobia gracilis Wied. ; *Ptychoptera quadrifasciata* Say and
metallica Walk. ; *Chionea scita* Walker may perhaps be added
to the number. The four remaining species (*L. humeralis* Say,
interminata, ignobilis, and *turpis* Walker) have not been identified on account of the insufficiency of the descriptions.

TABLE FOR DETERMINING THE GENERA.[1]

1 { Two longitudinal veins between the fifth vein and the posterior
    margin.   2
    Only one longitudinal vein between the fifth vein and the posterior
    margin: Tab. II. fig. 19 and 20 (Sect. VIII. Ptychopterina).   45

2 { Last joint of the palpi shorter or not much longer than the two pre-
    ceding joints taken together; the auxiliary vein usually ends
    in the costa, and is connected with the first longitudinal vein
    by a cross-vein.   3
    Last joint of the palpi very long, whiplash-shaped, much longer than
    the three preceding joints taken together; the auxiliary vein ends
    in the first longitudinal vein: no cross-vein between it and either
    of the two veins running alongside of it (Tipulidæ longipalpi).

3 { A single submarginal cell :[2] Tab. I, fig. 1–13.   4
    Two submarginal cells :[3] Tab. I, fig. 14–20, and Tab. II, fig. 1–18.   9

[1] This table contains all the known European and North American
genera of the eight first sections of the Tipulidæ; the table for the following sections (Tip. longipalpi) will be appended to the volume treating
of them. In using dichotomical tables it should always be remembered
that to construct them in such a way as to meet all cases, to include all
the anomalous structures, is impossible, and if it were possible, it would
be only through the use of anatomical characters, which would defeat the
object in view, the facility of determination. Thus, if, in order to accommo-
date Chionea, we had abstained from the use of any character connected
with the wings, we would perhaps have rendered the table more precise,
but certainly less useful. As it is, Chionea, although wingless, is placed
among the genera provided with two submarginal cells, where it belongs.
These imperfections of the dichotomical tables occur especially in those
portions of them which refer to the larger divisions; as soon as the genera
and species are reached, more precision can be expected, although even
there it can never be absolute.

[2] Toxorhina has none at all.

[3] Cladolipes has only a single submarginal cell, although it belongs to
this division.

Section I. Limnobina.

---

[1] In *Elephantomyia* the antennæ are 15-, in *Toxorrhina* 12 jointed; in
both cases through the evident coalescence of several joints at the basis
of the flagellum; but as both genera have a rostrum which is nearly as
long as the body, they will not easily be mistaken.

[2] The spurs being sometimes very small, the tibiæ have to be very
closely examined.

Section II. Limnobina anomala.

13 { Rostrum conspicuously prolonged, at least as long as the head, some-
times nearly as long as the whole body; no marginal cross-vein
(Subsection *Rhamphidina*).   14
Rostrum shorter than the head.   1d

14 { Wings without submarginal cell; Tab. I, fig. 6.
                                              Gen. VIII. Toxorrhina.
Wings with a submarginal cell.   15

15 { Rostrum not much longer than the head.   Gen. VI. Rhamphidia.
Rostrum not much shorter than the whole body.
                                              Gen. VII. Elephantomyia.

16 { Discal cell open.   17
Discal cell closed.   19

17 { Second basal cell considerably shorter than the first, the great cross-
vein being placed about the middle of the wing.   18
Second basal cell of about the same length with the first, the great
cross-vein being in its usual position; Tab. I, fig. 1.
                                              Gen. XI. Elliptera.

18 { The discal cell being open, is coalescent with the second posterior
cell; Tab. I, fig. 9.   Gen. X. Orimarga.
The discal cell being open, is coalescent with the third posterior cell.
                                              Gen. XV. Trachantrepra.

19 { No vestige of a marginal cross-vein; Tab. I, fig. 13.
                                              Gen. XIII. Ayaela.
Marginal cross-vein extant (although sometimes weakly marked).   20

20 { The first longitudinal vein ends in the costa nearly opposite the inner
end of the submarginal cell, or very little beyond it.   21
The first longitudinal vein ends in the costa very far beyond the inner
end of the submarginal cell, the distance being about equal to
the breadth of the wing; Tab. I, fig. 6.   Gen. IX. Dicranoptycha.

21 { Submarginal cell as long or but little longer than the first posterior
cell; Tab. I, fig. 12.   Gen. XIV. Trichocladus.
Submarginal cell much longer than the first posterior cell; Tab. I,
fig. 11.   Gen. XII. Antocha.

Section III. Erioptarina.

22 { No wings.   Gen. XIX. Chionea.
Wings present.   23

23 { Five posterior cells.   Gen. XXVI. Clalmbia.
Four posterior cells.   24

24 { The inner marginal cell has the shape of an almost equilateral triangle; Tab. II, fig. 11.   Gen. XXV. Cryptolabis.
The inner marginal cell has the usual elongated shape.   25

25 { Wings conspicuously hairy on the whole surface or along the
veins. 26
Wings not conspicuously hairy on the surface, veins glabrous, or
almost so. 27

26 { Wings conspicuously hairy on the whole surface.
Gen. XVI. Batrmolopha.
Wings conspicuously hairy along the veins and not in the cells.
Gen. XVII. Eriopters.

27 { The first submarginal cell is remarkably short, half as long as the
second or less; Tab. II, fig. 2, 4. 28
The first submarginal cell is much longer than half the length of the
second. 29

28 { Marginal cross-vein wanting. Gen. XXIII. Gonomyia.
Marginal cross-vein present. Gen. XXIV. Empeda.

29 { The distance between the subcostal cross-vein and the tip of the
auxiliary vein is more than twice the length of the great
cross-vein. 30
The distance between the subcostal cross-vein and the tip of the
auxiliary vein is moderate or small (usually not more than the
length of the great cross-vein). 31

30 { Seventh longitudinal vein straight; Tab. II, fig. 1.
Gen. XVIII. Trimicra.
Seventh longitudinal vein conspicuously bisinuated; Tab. I, fig. 20.
Gen. XX. Symplecta.

31 { Body uniformly black. Gen. XXI. Crupromyia.
Body black, scutellum and pleura marked with yellow.[1]
Gen. XXII. Philocompa.

Section IV. Limnophilina.

33 { Wings pubescent. Gen. XXIX. Ulomorpha.
Wings glabrous. 33

33 { Seventh longitudinal vein very short, abruptly inserted towards the
anal angle; Tab. II, fig. 13. Gen. XXX. Taicnocera.
The seventh longitudinal vein follows the ordinary course. 34

34 { A supernumerary cross-vein between the auxiliary vein and the
costa. Gen. XXVII. Epiphragma.
No supernumerary cross-vein between the auxiliary vein and the
costa. Gen. XXVIII. Limnophila.

Section V. Anisomerina.

35 { Three posterior cells. 36
Four or five posterior cells. 37

---

[1] I am not sufficiently acquainted with the European genus *Philocompa*
to distinguish it from *Gnophomyia* in a satisfactory manner; the distinction
given here is merely empirical. (Compare their descriptions below.)

35 { A single submarginal cell   Gen. XXXII. CLADURA.
{ Two submarginal cells; Tab. II, fig. 12.   Gen. XXXI. ARMOMERA.

37 { The stigma occupies nearly the whole space between the tip of the auxiliary vein and the marginal cross-vein; pubescence of the wing-veins hardly perceptible. .   Gen. XXXIII. EMPEDA.
{ The stigma occupies but a small portion of the space between the tip of the auxiliary vein and the marginal cross-vein; pubescence of the wing-veins distinct.   Gen. XXXIV. PENTHOPTERA.

Section VI. Amalopine.

35 { Antennæ 16- or 17-jointed.   39
{ Antennæ 13-jointed.   41

39 { Four posterior cells; wings pubescent.   Gen. XXXVII. ULA.
{ Five posterior cells; wings glabrous.   40

40 { The small cross-vein is nearly at right angles with the longitudinal axis of the wing; last joint of the palpi not longer than the two preceding joints taken together.   Gen. XXXV. AMALOPIA.
{ The small cross-vein is in a very oblique direction with regard to the longitudinal axis of the wing, and in one line with the great cross-vein; last joint of the palpi longer than the three preceding joints taken together.   Gen. XXXVI. PEDICIA.

41 { Two cross-veins between the first longitudinal vein and the anterior branch of the second vein; Tab. II, fig. 16.   Gen. XXXVIII. DICRANOTA.
{ Only one cross-vein between the first longitudinal vein and the anterior branch of the second vein.   42

42 { Four posterior cells; Tab. II, fig. 18.   Gen. XXXIX. PLECTROMYIA.
{ Five posterior cells; Tab. II, fig. 17.   Gen. XL. RHAPHIDOLABIS.

Section VII. Cylindrotomina.

43 { Head and intervals of the thoracic stripes with dense, deep punctures.   Gen. XLII. TRIOGMA.
{ Head smooth.   44

44 { Coloring of a Pachyrhina: yellow and black.   Gen. XLI. CYLINDROTOMA.
{ Coloring of a Tipula: brownish and grayish.   Gen. XLIII. PHALACROCERA.

Section VIII. Ptychopterina.

45 { First submarginal cell much shorter than the second.   Gen. XLVI. PROTOPLASA.
{ Second submarginal cell much shorter than the first.   46

46 { Three posterior cells; Tab. II, fig. 20.   Gen. XLV. BITTACOMORPHA.
{ Four posterior cells; Tab. II, fig. 19.   Gen. XLIV. PTYCHOPTERA.

SYSTEMATIC DISTRIBUTION OF THE TIPULIDÆ.[1]

I. TIPULIDÆ BREVIPALPI.

A. A single submarginal cell.

1. Antennæ 14-, sometimes apparently 15-jointed.

Section I. **LIMNOBINA**.

Gen. I. Dicranomyia.	Gen. IV. Limnobia.
Gen. II. Geranomyia.	Gen. V. Trochobola.
Gen. III. Rhipidia.	

Gen. *Peripheroptera* Schin. (S. Amer.).

2. Antennæ 16-jointed.

Section II. **LIMNOBINA ANOMALA**.

(Subsection *Rhamphidina*.)	Gen. X. Orimarga.
Gen. VI. Rhamphidia.	Gen. XI. Elliptera.
Gen. VII. Elephantomyia.	Gen. XII. Antocha.
Gen. VIII. Toxorrhina.	Gen. XIII. Atarba.
	Gen. XIV. Teucholabis.
Gen. IX. Dicranoptycha.	Gen. XV. Thaumastoptera.

Genera: *Styringomyia* Loew (in amber and copal) and *Paratropeza* Schin. (Mexico, S. America).

B. Two submarginal cells.

1. No spurs at the tip of the tibiæ.

Section III. **ERIOPTERINA**.

Gen. XVI. Rhypholophus.	Gen. XXII. Psilocomopa.
Gen. XVII. Erioptera.	Gen. XXIII. Goniomyia.
Gen. XVIII. Trimicra.	Gen. XXIV. Empeda.
Gen. XIX. Chionea.	Gen. XXV. Cryptolabis.
Gen. XX. Symplecta.	Gen. XXVI. Cladura.
Gen. XXI. Gnophomyia.	

Genera. *Sigmatomera* O. S. (Mexico) and (?) *Lachnocera* Phil. (Chile).

---

[1] Besides the European and North American genera, this table mentions the other genera hitherto described; they are printed in italics and not numbered. Most of them I have not examined, and have no opinion about their value. Those, the position of which in the section where they are placed, is doubtful, are marked with a query.

1 June, 1868.

2. Tibiæ with spurs at the tip.

 a. Subcostal cross-vein posterior to the origin of the second
 longitudinal vein.

  a. Normal number of the antennal joints sixteen.

Section IV. LIMNOPHILINA.

Gen. XXVII. Epiphragma.   Gen. XXIX. Ulomorpha.
Gen. XXVIII. Limnophila.   Gen. XXX. Trichocera.
Genera: Gynoplistia Westw. (Australia, America), Cloninphora
Rdln. (Australia), Cerazodia Westw. (Australia), Cledonia
Phil. (Chile), ? Polymoria Phil. (Chile).

  b. Normal number of antennal joints from six to ten.

Section V. ANISOMERINA.

Gen. XXXI. Anisomera.   Gen. XXXIII. Eriocera.
Gen. XXXII. Cladolipes.   Gen. XXXIV. Penthoptera.
Genera: Erantioptera Ost. (S. America), Pterocosmus Walk.
(Asia), Oligomera Doleseh. (Java), Physeorania Bigot
(Madagascar). N. B.—All these genera are closely allied to Erio-
cera, some of them probably synonymous with it.

  b. Subcostal cross-vein anterior to the origin of the second
 longitudinal vein.

Section VI. AMALOPINA.

Gen. XXXV. Amalopia.   Gen. XXXVIII. Dicranota.
Gen. XXXVI. Pedicia.   Gen. XXXIX. Plectromyia.
Gen. XXXVII. Ula.   Gen. XL. Rhaphidolabis.
  Genus ? Polymera.

II. TIPULIDÆ INCERTÆ SEDIS.

Section VII. CYLINDROTOMINA.

Gen. XLI. Cylindrotoma.   Gen. XLIII. Phalacrocera.
Gen. XLII. Triogma.

Section VIII. PTYCHOPTERINA.

Gen. XLIV. Ptychoptera.   Gen. XLVI. Protoplasa.
Gen. XLV. Bittacomorpha.
  Genus Tanyderus Phil. (Chile).

III. TIPULIDÆ LONGIPALPI.

•

Section I. LIMNOBINA.

One submarginal cell; four posterior cells. Normal number of antennal joints fourteen (sometimes apparently fifteen). Eyes glabrous. Tibia without spurs at the tip. Ungues with more or less distinct teeth on the under side. Empodia indistinct or none.

The group thus characterized is natural and compact. It comprises about one-fourth of the known brevipalpous *Tipulidæ* of the United States (35 species among 135), and it seems that in Europe nearly the same proportion obtains (in Austria 31 species among 127, according to Dr. Schiner's enumeration). The forms of this section, belonging to the temperate regions of Europe and America (and hardly anything is known about the species from warmer climates) afford but little structural diversity and their relationship is so great and evident that one is almost more tempted to unite them all in one genus than to subdivide them in several.

The *Limnobina*, together with the *Limnophilina*, constituted the bulk of the genus *Limnobia* in Meigen's sense. These two groups also very nearly correspond to the first subdivision of Meigen's genus by Macquart, in *Limnobia* Macq. and *Limnophila* Macq. Thus, we may look upon these two groups as the representative ones of the brevipalpous *Tipulidæ*. It was the great similitude of their outward appearance, more than anything else, which caused the species belonging to them to remain united together in the same genus from Meigen's time up to that of the latest publications, whereas genera like *Rhipidia*, *Rhamphidia*, *Erioptera*, *Antomera*, *Pedicia*, etc., were singled out and separated quite early, not on account of any real knowledge of the peculiarities of their organization, but merely on the ground of some one conspicuous character distinguishing them. And yet, the contrast of characters, presented by the *Limnobina* and the *Limnophilina* is very great and extends to almost every portion

of their organization. This contrast is expressed in the following two columns:—

Limnobina.	Limnophilina.
Epistoma longer than broad.	Epistoma generally transverse (broader than long).
Flaps of labium linear, narrow.	Flaps of labium broad and fleshy.
Antennæ 14-jointed.	Antennæ 16-jointed.
One submarginal cell.	Two submarginal cells.
Auxiliary vein often short, its tip being then anterior to the inner end of the submarginal cell.	Auxiliary vein generally long, its tip being almost always nearly opposite the inner end of the submarginal cell.
The great cross-vein is almost always at the inner end of the discal cell, or before it.	The great cross-vein is very often opposite the middle of the discal cell.
Four posterior cells.	Five (seldom four) posterior cells.
Tibiæ without spurs at the tip.	Tibiæ with spurs.
Ungues dentate on the under side.	Ungues smooth.
Empodia indistinct or none.	Empodia distinct.
A horny, elongated, immovable style on the under side of the forceps, in the male.	No horny, immovable style on the under side of the forceps.
Upper valves of the ovipositor often very short (especially in the genus *Dicranomyia*).	Upper valves of the ovipositor generally long.

The teeth on the under side of the ungues of the *Limnobina*
seem to be peculiar to this section. They must not be confounded
with the more or less square or sharp projection on the under side
at the very basis of the ungues, forming a part of the thickening
which always exists there. The tooth of the *Limnobina*, even
when single, is distinct from this thickening, and placed before it
(outside of the *Limnobina*, *Antocha* is the only genus which
seems to have something like this tooth). The style on the under
side of the male forceps is also peculiar to this group; I have
observed something analogous to it only among the *Tip. anomalæ*
(*Dicranoptycha*, *Antocha*).

The North American and European *Limnobina*, as far as
known, may be divided in two natural groups, one of which has,
in most cases, a short auxiliary vein, the marginal cross-vein
always at the very tip of the first longitudinal vein, and the male
forceps formed of two fleshy lobes (*Dicranomyia*, *Rhipidia*,
Geranomyia); the other group has, with rare exceptions, a long

auxillary vein, the marginal cross-vein is sometimes at the tip, but
more often at some distance from the tip of the first longitudinal
vein, and the male forceps consists of two horny hooks (*Limnobia,
Trochobola*). Little is known about the forms of *Limnobina*
peculiar to the tropical regions and foreign to Europe and North
America. The Berlin Museum possesses several species from
Mexico and Brazil, with a supernumerary cross-vein in the submarginal cell; the auxiliary cross-vein has its tip nearly opposite
the origin of the second longitudinal vein; the ungues have strong
and distinct teeth; the wings are spotted. These species will
form a distinct genus.[1] Another, still more aberrant form from
South America, is represented by several species in the same
museum. In Mr. Bellardi's collection, in Turin, I have seen a
species from the Philippine Islands, remarkable for its coloring;
it is black, with smoky wings; the thorax is orange red.

As far as I can judge from the description of the genus *Peripheroptera* Schiner (*Verh. Zool. Bot. Ges.* etc. 1866, p. 933, and *Reise
d. Novara*, etc. *Diptera*, p. 47), it is only a form of *Dicranomyia*;
the generic character will be found in the *Appendix* II.

Gen. I. DICRANOMYIA.

One submarginal cell; four posterior cells; discal cell present or absent;
marginal cross-vein at the tip of the first longitudinal vein; tip of the
auxiliary vein generally opposite or before the origin of the second longitudinal vein, seldom beyond it (wings of *Dicranomyia*, Tab. 1, fig. 1, 2, 3).
Antenna 14-jointed, joints subglobular, elliptical, or short subcylindrical.
Proboscis not longer than the head. Feet slender, tibiae without spurs at
the tip; empodia indistinct or none. The forceps of the male consists of
two movable, soft, fleshy, subreniform lobes and a horny style under them
(Tab. III, fig. 2, 3, 5).

Rostrum subcylindrical, projecting; epistoma longer than
broad, narrowed at the sides; the narrow, linear, pubescent
flaps of the under lip project more or less beyond it. In *D.
rostrifera*, rostrum and proboscis are nearly as long as the head;
usually, however, they are shorter; palpi short. Eyes large,
glabrous, front rather narrow. The antenna are comparatively
short, as they do not reach the root of the wings, when bent backwards; the joints of the flagellum are subglobular or elliptical;

[1] *Limnobia dira* Schiner (*Reise d. Novara, Diptera*, p. 46), from Brazil, is
apparently a species of this kind.

seldom short subcylindrical (as in *D. immodesta, gladiator*); with moderately long, often inconspicuous verticils (in the two species just named, the verticils are somewhat longer than usual). The collar is broad, well developed, triangular at a side-view; with a neck-like prolongation, carrying the head; thoracic suture well marked. The feet are slender, with a very inconspicuous, almost microscopic pubescence, and, as a general rule, of a uniform coloring. Most of the species have a distinct tooth on the under side of the ungues, near the basis, sometimes followed by a smaller one. In *D. defuncta*, these teeth are replaced by a few notches on the under side of the ungues. In some species, as in *D. haretica*, the teeth are very small and difficult to perceive.

The venation follows rather closely a certain uniform type, and but few of the characters taken from it can be used for the distinction of the species. The auxiliary vein generally ends in the costa nearly opposite the origin of the second longitudinal vein; in some species it is still shorter and ends before the origin of the second vein (*D. rostrifera, brevivena,* and *floridana*), and it is an exception when it reaches considerably beyond the origin of that vein (*D. defuncta, pubipennis, rara, globithorax*). The distance of the subcostal cross-vein from the tip of the auxiliary vein, which is variable, affords good specific characters. The first longitudinal vein ends in the costa near the posterior end of the stigma, nearly opposite the tip of the fifth longitudinal vein and more or less beyond the inner end of the submarginal cell; often at one-third, at the utmost about the middle of this cell; the marginal cross-vein is close at the tip of the first longitudinal vein; in most species, this cross-vein forms a nearly straight line with the tip of the first longitudinal vein; often, however, the upper half of this straight line recedes a little backwards and in such cases it appears as if the first longitudinal vein was incurved towards the second and ended in it, while the cross-vein in such a case seems to connect the first longitudinal vein with the costa. Such is the case with *D. pubipennis* (Tab. I, fig. 2) and *globithorax*; sometimes this character is not specific, but merely adventitious. The course of the second longitudinal vein varies in the relative length of the two portions of this vein, before and after emitting the third vein. The inner portion or the præfurca is remarkably short in those species which have a very short auxiliary vein (*D. rostrifera, brevivena, floridana*).

The submarginal cell is always a good deal longer than the first posterior cell; the relative proportion of their length is subject to slight variations. When the discal cell is open, which characterizes several species, it coalesces with the second posterior cell, in consequence of the absence of the cross-vein, connecting the two first veins emitted by it towards the margin of the wing. *D. pubipennis* (Tab. I, fig. 2) is the only exception I know of, to this rule; whenever in this species the discal cell happens to be open, it coalesces with the *third* posterior cell, because it is the cross-vein connecting the *two last* veins, emitted by the discal cell, which is wanting. As a rule, the discal cell is open in *D. immaculata, gladiator, rostrifera, floridana, longipennis, brevivena;* it is closed in *D. diversa, pudica, halterata, distans, stulta, haeretica, liberta, defuncta, rara, humidicola, morioides.* Among twenty specimens of *D. pubipennis* five had the discal cell open; of my two specimens of *D. globithorax* one has this cell open, the other closed. But even in the species which have the discal cell either open or closed as a rule, occasional exceptions occur; this character is therefore not an altogether reliable one, and can be established only upon the comparison of a number of specimens. The shape of the discal cell is more or less square; its inner end is either in a line with the small cross-vein, or somewhat arcuated and projecting on the inside beyond this cross-vein. The position of the great cross-vein is generally in a line with the inner end of the discal cell; sometimes a little anterior or posterior to this line; it varies in different specimens of the same species.

The male forceps consists of a pair of movable, fleshy lobes, oblong, often subreniform, each being armed on the inside with a short, curved horny appendage, somewhat resembling a beak (I call it *rostriform* appendage); it often bears upon its convex side one or two stiff bristles (see Tab. III, fig. 3 and *b, d*). To the upper side of each of the lobes, another horny appendage, long, slender, attenuated, curved, is closely applied (*falciform* appendage); its point of attachment is the basal piece below (fig. 6 and 3, *b*). The forceps of *D. humidicola* (fig. 2) and that of *D. liberta* (fig. 3), with their full, rounded lobes may be considered as typical. Often, these lobes are more slender, sinuated or excised on the inside, such are for instance, those of *D. defuncta* (fig. 1); or somewhat club-shaped towards the tip, as in *D. haeretica.* Below these lobes, at the end of the body, on the under side, is the *style* (fig. 1 and 5a, e, and fig. 3, a), a horny projection, characteristic of this group.

The European species *Dicr. autumnalis* and *D. stigmatica* (placed by Stæger in the genus *Glochina*) show a remarkable modification in the male forceps. In *D. stigmatica* the fleshy lobes are much larger than usual, and their skin is a delicate whitish membrane (compare the figures given by me in the *Stett. Entomol. Zeitschr.* 1854, Tab. I, fig. 5–7); their rostriform appendages are very large, branched, antler-like; below the lobes, there is a second, hairy, coriaceous forceps; below this, a pair of conical processes, clothed with long hair and pointing towards each other; the horny style is between them. *D. autumnalis* (l. c. fig. 6) has these conical processes largely developed; in other respects, its forceps has the ordinary structure.

The ovipositor of *Dicranomyia*, among those of the other sections of *Tipulidæ*, is remarkable for its smallness. The upper valves are short, narrow, arcuated, pointed; the lower ones are straight. The ovipositor of *D. haretica* is exceedingly small.

The coloring of the body in this genus is rather monotonous and dull; grayish, brownish or ochraceous; without the well-marked stripes, bands, and spots which adorn the body, the feet, and the wings of *Limnobia*. Among nineteen species of North American *Dicranomyiæ* only two, rather abnormal species in more than one respect, have spotted wings (*D. defuncta* and *D. rara*); a single species has them clouded (*D. humidicola*). In Europe, *Dicranomyiæ* with clouded wings seem to be more numerous. The European *D. ornata* has handsomely banded wings. However, I am not sufficiently acquainted with the European fauna to make any general statement about the numerical proportion between the species with immaculate and those with clouded wings.

The habits of the larvæ are probably aquatic, or subaquatic. I am not aware that any larva of this genus has been described, but I have observed near Washington, D. C., a larva, which I have every reason to suppose is that of *D. defuncta*. It lived upon the wood-work of a mill-dam, with a stream of water constantly passing over it. However, Mr. Winnertz reared *D. dumetorum* from decaying beech stumps (*Linnæa Entomol.* VIII, p. 281).

Dicranomyia probably occurs in all parts of the world,

although it may be principally at home in the more temperate latitudes. *D. vicariana* from Aukland and *D. morionella* from S. America, have been described by Dr. Schiner in the *Reise d. Novara, etc., Diptera*, p. 46. The *Limnobiæ funsipennis, chorica, ægrotans*, and *gracilis* from New Zealand, mentioned in Walker's *List of Dipl. Brit. Mus.*, are all *Dicranomyiæ*. The genus *Ataracta*, found in amber (Loew, *Bernst. u. Bernstein-fauna*) is apparently synonymous with *Dicranomyia*.

This genus is very closely allied to *Limnobia*, still the differences between them are numerous. They consist:—

1. In the structure of the body: The feet of *Dicranomyia* are generally more slender; the vagues have usually but one distinct tooth, whereas in *Limnobia* there are several; the male forceps in the two genera has a different structure. As to the latter point, however different the two forms may be, I look upon them as modifications of the same plan of structure, the whole difference consisting in the more or less development of the fleshy lobes. If we represent to ourselves the large fleshy lobes of *Dicranomyia* lessened, the rostriform horny appendage, being closely applied to the falciform appendage (marked *b* on the figures of Tab. III), will form the double horny hook of *Limnobia*. Intermediate forms really occur in some species; the forceps of *Trochobola*, for instance, is one of them. We have already noticed above the contrast in the coloring between the two genera; that of *Limnobia* being more intense and brilliant, with well-defined stripes, bands, and dots on the body, the wings and the feet.

2. In the mode of life: Most of the larvæ of *Dicranomyia* are probably aquatic or subaquatic, whereas those of *Limnobia* live in wood, fungi, etc.

3. In the venation: The auxiliary vein in *Dicranomyia* is in most cases shorter; it usually ends in the first longitudinal vein nearly opposite the origin of the second vein or before it. In exceptional cases only (in four North American species among nineteen), this vein is prolonged a considerable distance beyond the origin of the second longitudinal vein. Just the opposite is the case with *Limnobia*; the auxiliary vein is, almost without exception, prolonged considerably beyond the origin of the second vein. The only exception I know of is the European *L. macrostigma* Schum., the auxiliary vein of which is prolonged only a short distance beyond the origin of the second longitudinal vein.

The relative position of the subcostal cross-vein and of the tip
of the auxiliary vein is somewhat different in the majority of the
species of both genera. In both of them, the cross-vein is sometimes placed at the tip of the auxiliary vein; but whenever it is
removed from this tip, it is *always* situated between the first
longitudinal vein and the auxiliary in *Dicranomyia*; in *Limnobia*, on the contrary, it is *very often* situated between the
auxiliary vein and the costa; in which case, the auxiliary vein
ends in the first longitudinal vein, and not in the costa, as usual.
This latter structure, as far as I have observed, occurs only in
the genus *Limnobia*.

The relative position of the marginal cross-vein and of the tip
of the first longitudinal vein, gives occasion to a somewhat similar
observation. In *Dicranomyia* this cross-vein is *always* at the tip
of the first longitudinal vein (about the peculiar structure, sometimes occurring here, compare above, page 54). In *Limnobia*
the marginal cross-vein is *often* some distance back of this tip, so
as to cut the stigma in two, or even to be placed near its inner
end. This latter character, as far as my observation goes, may
be useful in doubtful cases, as it occurs principally in the less
typical *Limnobiæ*, some of which, as for instance *L. macrostigma*,
might be mistaken for *Dicranomyiæ*. The typical *Limnobiæ*
(*cinctipes*, *solitaria*, etc.) have the cross-vein close at the tip of
the first longitudinal vein, like *Dicranomyia*.

We may also notice here, that the discal cell is often open in
the genus *Dicranomyia*, whereas I know of no such case among
the *Limnobiæ*.

In my previous essay on the *Tipulidæ brevipalpi*, the genera
Rhipidia, *Geranomyia*, *Dicranomyia*, and *Limnobia* have been
united as subgenera of a single genus *Limnobia*. This was done on
the ground that *Rhipidia* and *Geranomyia* are much more closely
allied to *Dicranomyia* than the latter is to *Limnobia* (in the
narrower sense). If therefore we leave *Limnobia* and *Dicranomyia* united, we should not separate *Rhipidia* and *Geranomyia*
from them. If, on the contrary, we separate *Rhipidia* and *Geranomyia* from *Dicranomyia*, we should, *à fortiori*, separate *Dicranomyia* from *Limnobia*. This separation has been introduced
in the present publication.

The name *Dicranomyia* (from δίκρανον, fork, and μυῖα, fly) has
been first used in J. Stephens's *Catalogue of British Insects*, in

1829, for the species *D. lutea*, *inusta*, *modesta*, *dumetorum*, *didyma*, etc.   In Holiday's *Catalogue of Diptera occurring about Holywood, Devonshire* (*Entomol. Magaz.* I, 147) in 1833, the same generic name is introduced for the species *lutea*, *inusta*, *modesta*, *chorea*, and *oscillans* n. sp.   This generic name has not been used in the systematic works which have appeared since (Macquart, Walker, and Zetterstedt) until it was reinstated by me in the *Proc. Acad. Nat. Sci. Phila.* 1859, as a subgenus of *Limnobia.*

The genus *Glochina*, introduced by Meigen in his Vol. VI, p. 280, 1830, for *Glochina sericata* Meig., has not been sufficiently characterized by him, and has never obtained a definite meaning since.   The alleged distinguishing characters are the fourteen-jointed antennæ and five-jointed palpi; but it must be borne in mind, that Meigen called the antennæ of *Limnobia* from 15- to 17-jointed (compare above, page 10), and that, for this reason, fourteen-jointed antennæ, which we know now as belonging to the whole section of *Limnobina*, must have seemed unusual to him.   As to the palpi, the fifth basal joint is often visible, and not in *Glochina* only; as Mr. Westwood suggests (*Westw. Introd.* II, p. 525) it probably represents the maxilla.

Macquart (*Hist. Nat. des Dipt.* I, p. 179) rather oddly places *Glochina* among the *Tipulariæ florales* of Latreille, between *Rhyphus* and *Simulium*, on the ground that "*Glochina*, together with *Culex* and *Bolitophila*, are the only nemocerous diptera hitherto observed which are provided with maxillary setæ; they are, moreover, distinguished by five-jointed palpi, the third of which is incrassated, like the second in *Rhyphus.*"

* We find *Glochina* introduced with a query, in Halidny's *Catal. Dipt. Holyw.* for *D. leucocephala* M. (syn. *morio* Fab.) and *dumetorum*, as well as in the *Synopsis*, etc. at the end of Westwood's *Introduction*, etc. Vol. II, for the same species.

Staeger (Kröjer's *Naturh. Tidskr.* Vol. III, 1840) placed three species in it, *Gl. stigmatica*, *autumnalis*, and *frontalis*, which are *Dicranomyiæ*; at the same time, other *Dicranomyiæ*, as *modesta*, *dumetorum*, *chorea*, *didyma*, are left by him in the genus *Limnobia.*   Thus it does not appear upon what the claims of the genus, in this author's sense, are established.   Unless the peculiarities in the structure of the male genitals of *G. autumnalis* and *stigmatica*, already alluded to above (p. 56) prove of

sufficient importance to justify a generic separation of those few
species which possess them, the genus *Glochina* will have to be
abandoned. By all means *Glochina* cannot be maintained as a
name of the group now called *Dicranomyia*. This name, as
shown above, has been proposed a year earlier, and was, from
the beginning connected with a series of those very species which
constitute it now.

Table for the determination of the species.

1 { Wings remarkably narrow, lanceolate (Tab. I, fig. 1).
                             1 longipennis *Schum.*
    { Wings of the usual shape.   2

2 { Tip of the auxiliary vein nearly opposite, or before, or only a short
          distance beyond the origin of the second longitudinal vein.   8
    { Tip of the auxiliary vein a considerable distance beyond the origin
          of the second longitudinal vein.   16

3 { The whole antennae, or at least their basal joints, pale.   4
    { The whole antennae black or brown.   7

4 { Discal cell open.   5
    { Discal cell closed.   6

5 { Thorax with a single brown stripe in the middle. 2 immodesta *O. S.*
    { Thorax with three brown stripes.   3 gladiator *O. S.*

6 { Flagellum of the antennae and halteres infuscated. 4 diversa *O. S.*
    { Flagellum and halteres not infuscated.   5 pudica *O. S.*

7 { Discal cell (in normal specimens) open; tip of the auxiliary vein
          considerably anterior to the origin of the second vein; the pre-
          furca is about equal in length to the distance between the origin
          of the third vein and the small cross-vein, or even shorter.   8
    { Discal cell closed; tip of the auxiliary vein nearly opposite the origin
          of the second vein (or, when anterior or posterior, the distance
          small); prefurca distinctly longer than the distance between the
          origin of the third vein and the small cross-vein.   10

8 { Rostrum and proboscis nearly as long as the head. 6 rostrifera, n. sp.
    { Rostrum and proboscis much shorter than the head.   9

9 { Thorax ochraceous.   7 brevivena, n. sp.
    { Thorax brown.   8 floridana, n. sp.

10 { Thorax shining black, pleura with a silvery reflection.
                           15 morioides *O. S.*
    { Thorax brownish or grayish.   11

11 { Femora with a rather broad pale band at the tip. 14 badia *Walt.*
    { Femora without such a band.   12

12 { The distance between the tip of the auxiliary vein and the subcostal
          cross-vein is nearly as long as the stigma.   13
    { The distance between the tip of the auxiliary vein and the subcostal
          cross-vein is shorter than half the length of the stigma.   14

13	Halteres unusually long.	13 halterata, n. sp.
	Halteres of the ordinary length.	9 distans O. S.

14 The cross-vein separating the discal cell from the first basal cell is arcuated in such a manner, that the inner end of the discal cell is but little more distant from the basis of the wing than the inner end of the submarginal cell. 10 stulta O. S.

The cross-vein separating the discal cell from the first basal cell is not conspicuously arcuated and hence, the inner end of the discal cell is distinctly more distant from the basis of the wing than the inner end of the submarginal cell. 15

15	Thorax gray, with a brown stripe in the middle.	11 liberta O. S.
	Thorax brownish-yellow, with a brown stripe in the middle.	12 haeretica, n. sp.
16	Wings immaculate.	17
	Wings spotted with brown.	18
17	Stigma distinct.	16 pubipennis O. S.
	No vestige of a stigma.	17 globithorax, n. sp.
18	Wings brownish, three or four brown spots along the anterior margin.	18 vara, n. sp.
	Wings with brown dots in all the cells.	19 defuncta O. S.

Description of the species.

1. D. longipennis Schum. ♂ and ♀.—Ochracea, thorace rufescente, vittis tribus obscurioribus; pleuris vitta fusca; alis angustis, immaculatis, areola discoidali aperta; costa, venaque longitudinali prima pallide flavis; vena auxiliaris pone initium praefurcæ perparum extensa.

Ochraceous, thorax reddish above, with three darker stripes, pleura with a brown stripe; wings narrow, immaculate; discal cell open; the costa and the first longitudinal veins pale yellow; the auxiliary vein is extended very little beyond the origin of the praefurca (Tab. I, fig. 1). Long. corp. 0.25—0.3.

Syn. *Limnobia longipennis* Schum. Beit. etc. 104, 2.
    Dicranomyia immemor O. Sacken, Proc. Ac. Nat. Sc. Phil. 1861, p. 287.

Head brownish, rather elongated, rostrum brown, also somewhat prolonged; palpi and antennæ brownish; second joint of the latter stout; thorax reddish-yellow above, with three indistinct brownish stripes, the intermediate one with a faint yellow line in the middle. Pleuræ with a brown line, bordered with whitish, running from the humeri towards the basis of the halteres; the latter have a whitish stem and a brownish knob; abdomen brownish; feet pale yellow, tip of the tibiæ and tarsi infuscated; wings narrow, lanceolate, their basal, narrowed portion rather long, their color is subhyaline; anal angle small, hardly projecting; stigma elongated, pale; costa and first longitudinal veins pale yellow, the other veins brown; tip of the auxiliary vein very little beyond the origin of the prefurca; subcostal cross-vein immediately opposite this origin; tip of the first longitudinal vein a little anterior to the middle of the submarginal cell; the latter rather long, longer than the first posterior cell; the discal cell being open, the first and second posterior cells are of equal length; the third is one-half the length of the second; seventh longitudinal vein somewhat bisinuated.

Hab. Trenton Falls, N. Y., where I caught numerous specimens on a meadow.

In general habitus this species is different from the other *Dicranomyia;* its very narrow wings with their yellow costal and first longitudinal veins, forming a contrast with the brown color of the other veins, make it easily recognisable. The structure of its male forceps belongs to the same type with those of the other species of the group. I had at first described *D. longipennis* under the name of *D. immemor,* but recognized afterwards its identity with a species belonging to eastern Europe.

2. D. immoderata O. S.   ♂ and ♀.—Ochracea, thorace vitta fusca; antennis fuscis, basi pallidis; alis hyalinis, stigmate pallido, areola discoidali aperta; vena auxiliaris apex lutile prefurcæ plus minusve oppositus; venula subcostalis transversa ab auxiliaris apice stigmatis longitudine remota.

Ochraceous, thorax with a brown stripe; antennæ brown, pale at the base; wings hyaline, stigma pale; discal cell open; the tip of the auxiliary vein is nearly opposite the origin of the prefurca; the subcostal cross-vein is at a distance from the tip of the auxiliary vein, which is about equal to the length of the stigma. Long. corp. 0.25—0.3.

Syn. *Dicranomyia immoderata* O. Sacken, Proc. Ac. Nat. Sc. Phil. 1859, p. 211.

Rostrum pale, palpi infuscated; antennæ fuscous, pale at base; verticella rather long; front and vertex infuscated. Thorax ochraceous, paler on the pleuræ; a dark brown stripe, extending over the collare, in the middle; this stripe is abbreviated behind and does not reach the transverse suture; the lateral stripes are not perceptible; both ends of the scutellum and a stripe in the middle of the metathorax usually infuscated. Knob of the halteres dusky; feet pale tawny, coxæ and basis of the femora pale yellow; tips of the tarsi darker. Abdomen infuscated above; forceps pale. Wings nearly hyaline; stigma elliptical, pale; veins pale brownish; tip of the auxiliary vein nearly opposite or a little before the origin of the præfurca; the sub-costal cross-vein is separated from the tip of the auxiliary vein by a distance at least equal to the length of the stigma, if not longer; the cross-vein, forming the inner end of the discal cell, is straight; discal cell always open.

Hab. Washington; Trenton Falls; Maine.

When I first described this species I had twenty-five specimens for comparison. *D. immodesta* is not unlike the European *D. modesta*, the discal cell of which, however, is closed.

2. D. gladiator O. S. ♂ and ♀.—Ochracea, fuscis-nervis; thoracis vittis tribus fuscis; antennis fuscis, basi pallidis, alis hyalinis, stigmate infuscata; areolâ discoidali apertâ; venæ auxiliaris apex infra præ-furcæ plus minusve oppositus; venula subcostalis transversa ab auxili-aris apice stigmatis longitudine remota.

Brownish-ochraceous; thorax with three brown stripes; antennæ brown, pale at base; wings hyaline, stigma infuscated; discal cell open: the tip of the auxiliary vein is nearly opposite the origin of the præfurca; subcostal cross-vein removed from the tip of the auxiliary vein at a distance equal to the length of the stigma. Long. corp. 0.25—0.3.

Syn. *Dicranomyia gladiator* O. Sacken, Proc. Ac. Nat. Sc. Phil. 1859, p. 212.

Rostrum pale ochraceous, front brownish-gray, palpi infuscated, antennæ brown, pale at base. Thorax brownish ochraceous, with three distinct brown stripes; the intermediate one extends over the collare; the lateral ones extend beyond the suture; scutellum and metathorax brownish in the middle; mesosternum with two large, round brown spots between the fore and middle coxæ and several smaller, indistinct spots; halteres pale at base; knob brown; feet brown, coxæ and base of femora pale; tip of the latter brown. Abdomen brown, posterior margins of the seg-ments and the genitals paler; falciform appendages of the male forceps very large (Tab. III, fig. 4); they are very striking in the living insect, and when their points touch each other, they form a kind of arch or bridge over both lobes. (The name of the insect is derived from these sword-like appendages.) Wings nearly hyaline; stigma elliptical, more or less infuscated; venu-tion exactly like that of *D. immodesta.*

Hab. Washington; In June.

I found fourteen specimens of this species upon one occasion in Washington. If it was not for the difference in the structure of the male forceps, I would have taken this species for a darker variety of *D. immodesta.* The venation of both is exactly the same.

4. D. diversa O. S.   ♂ and ♀.—Ochracea, antennis fuscis, basi pallidis ; alis hyalinis, stigmate pallido ; areola discoidali clausa ; venula subcostalis transversa ab auxiliaris apice stigmatis longitudine remota ; venæ auxiliaris apex initio præfurcæ plus minusve oppositus.

Ochraceous, antennæ brown, pale at the base ; wings hyaline, stigma pale : discal cell closed ; subcostal cross-vein removed from the tip of the auxiliary vein at a distance equal to the length of the stigma ; the tip of the auxiliary vein is more or less opposite the origin of the præfurca. Long. corp. 0.2—0.25.

Syn. *Dicranomyia diversa* O. Sacken, Proc. Ac. Nat. Sc. Phila. 1859, p. 212.

The body is ochraceous ; the head above, the halteres and the abdomen are infuscated ; genitals ochraceous. Antennæ more or less infuscated, basal joints pale. The tip of the auxiliary vein is more or less opposite the origin of the præfurca ; the sub-costal cross-vein is at a considerable distance from the tip of the auxiliary vein, this distance being at least equal to the length of the stigma ; the discal cell is closed ; the stigma has a slight brownish tinge.

Hab. Washington, D. C.; Maryland ; In the spring

This species is much smaller than *D. immodesta,* and moreover is easily distinguished from it by its closed discal cell ; the verticils of its antennæ are much shorter.

I possess three specimens collected by Mr. R. Kennicott, near Fort Resolution, H. B. T. ; they are very like *D. diversa,* but have the thorax darker, the feet more brown above, and the halteres paler. They may belong to a different species.

5. D. pudica O. S.   ♂ and ♀.—Pallide ochracea tota ; oculis nigris, tarsorum apicibus fuscis ; alis pallide flavescentibus ; venis pallidis ; venæ auxiliaris apex initio præfurcæ parum anterior ; venula subcostalis transversa ab auxiliaris apice parum remota.

Altogether pale ochraceous ; eyes black : tip of the tarsi fuscous ; wings with a pale yellowish tinge : veins pale ; the tip of the auxiliary vein is a short distance anterior to the origin of the præfurca; the subcostal cross-vein is at a short distance from the tip of the auxiliary vein. Long. corp. 0.3—0.35.

Syn. *Dicranomyia pudica* O. Sacken, Proc.ᵈ Ac. Nat. Sc. Phil. 1859, p. 212.

There is not much to add to the diagnosis; the stigma is scarcely apparent; the auxiliary vein joins the costa a little before the origin of the præfurca; the cross-vein is not far from its tip (at a distance shorter than half the length of the stigma); the antennæ are yellow.

Hab. Illinois (Kennicott).

At the time when I prepared the original description of this species, I had two male and four female specimens before me.

6. D. restrifera, n. sp. ♂ and ♀.—Fusca, thoracis vittis obscuriori, rostro et proboscide elongatis, fuscis; antennis nigro-fuscis; venæ auxiliaris apex præfurcæ initio anterior; præfurcâ brevi; cellulâ discoidali apertâ.

Brown, the thorax with a darker stripe; rostrum and proboscis elongated, brown; antennæ brown; the tip of the auxiliary vein is anterior to the origin of the præfurca, the latter short; discal cell open. Long. corp. 0.2—0.25.

Head, including rostrum, palpi, and antennæ fuscous; rostrum and proboscis unusually prolonged, being almost as long as the head. Thorax fuscous, sericeous with yellowish above and with a dark brown stripe in the middle; sericeous with cinereous on the pleuræ; scutellum tawny, metathorax brown. Halteres with an infuscated knob, stem pale. Abdomen brown; genitals subferruginous. Feet dark tawny, coxæ pale. Wings hyaline; stigma short oval, pale; the tip of the auxiliary vein is anterior to the origin of the second longitudinal vein by about half the length of the stigma or more; the subcostal cross-vein is at about an equal distance from the tip of the auxiliary vein; the first longitudinal vein has the marginal cross-vein close by its tip; the præfurca is short, not much longer, if longer at all, than the distance between the origin of the third longitudinal vein and the small cross-vein; discal cell open.

Hab. New York; three male, one female specimen. The venation of this species is exactly like that of *L. brevivena.* I

5 July. 1868.

could not very well describe the color of the front which, in all
my specimens, is shrunken.

7. D. brevivena, n. sp. ♂ and ♀.—Ochracea vel fusco-ochracea;
rostro ochraceo; antennis nigro-fuscis, thorace vittis tribus fascis; venæ
auxiliaris apex præfurcæ initio anterior; præfurcâ brevi; cellula discoidali plerumque apertâ.

Ochraceous or brownish-ochraceous; rostrum ochraceous; antennæ brownish-black; thorax with three brown stripes; the tip of the auxiliary
vein is anterior to the origin of the præfurca; the latter short; the
discal cell in most specimens open. Long. corp. 0.2—0.23.

The coloring of the body is either of a light brownish-yellow,
or a more ochraceous yellow; head brownish, front infuscated in
the middle; rostrum yellow; antennæ dark brown. Thorax
ochraceous with three brown stripes, the intermediate one broad
and distinct, the lateral ones extending backwards beyond the
suture are slightly pruinose with grayish; collare brown above,
prolonged in a distinct neck; scutellum infuscated at both ends,
metathorax brownish, pruinose with grayish; pleuræ ochraceous,
more brownish posteriorly; stem of halteres pale at the basis,
knob infuscated. Abdomen brownish above, pale below; male
genitals ochraceous. Feet dark tawny; coxæ and base of the
femora pale; tarsi brown towards the tip. Wings almost hyaline, very slightly tinged; stigma pale. The tip of the auxiliary
vein is anterior to the origin of the præfurca by about half a
length of the stigma; the cross-vein is at about an equal distance
from the tip of the auxiliary vein; the first longitudinal vein has
the marginal cross-vein by its tip; the præfurca is short, in some
specimens shorter than the distance between the origin of the
third longitudinal vein and the small cross-vein; in other specimens, it is a little longer. The discal cell is usually open; one
of my specimens (among ten) has it closed.

Hab. New York; also in Washington, D. C. This species
can be easily distinguished from the two other species with a
short auxiliary vein (*floridana* and *rostrifera*) by its yellow
rostrum.

I have taken, in the marshes on Long Island, near New York,
in autumn, several specimens which are somewhat larger and
darker in coloring; the thorax is brownish, sericeous with yellowish above, and with three dark brown stripes; the abdomen

is not paler on the under side, but uniformly brown; the stigma seems to be slightly longer; otherwise they agree with *D. brevivena*, and I am in doubt about their identity.

8. D. floridana, n. sp. ♂ and ♀.—Brunnea, fronte albomicante, rostro brevi, fusco; antennis nigro fumis; venæ auxiliaris apex præfarcæ initio anterior; præfurcâ brevi; cellulâ discoidali apertâ.

Brown, front with a whitish reflection, rostrum short, brown; antennæ brownish-black; the tip of the auxiliary vein is anterior to the origin of the præfurca; the latter short; discal cell open. Long. corp. 0.2—0.3.

Head including rostrum and palpi brownish, antennæ black; front with a whitish yellow reflection. Ground color of the thorax dark tawny, almost concealed by the three brown stripes; the intermediate one moderately shining, the lateral ones pruinose with grayish; humeral region finely sericeous with yellowish; metathorax brown, sericeous with brownish-yellow; pleuræ sericeous with gray. Abdomen brown, genitals subferruginous. Halteres with a fuscous knob. Feet dark tawny, coxæ and basis of the femora yellow. Wings somewhat tinged with cinereous; stigma pale; venation like that of *D. brevivena* and *rostrifera*, only the distance between the tip of the auxiliary vein and the anbcostal cross-vein is nearly equal to the whole length of the stigma.

Hab. Florida; two male and three female specimens caught by me in the spring of 1858; a pair of them were in copulation.

9. D. distans O. S. ♂ and ♀.—Brunnea; humeris pleurisque pallidioribus; antennis palpisque nigris; venæ auxiliaris apex initio præfarcæ plus minusve oppositus; venula transversa subcostalis ab apice venæ auxiliaris remota; venula transversa quæ cellulam discoidalem a cellulâ basali primâ separat, parum arcuata; alæ immaculatæ; stigmate pallido.

Brown, humeri and pleura pale; antennæ and palpi black; tip of the auxiliary vein nearly opposite the origin of the præfurca; subcostal cross-vein at some distance from the tip of the auxiliary vein; the cross-vein, separating the discal cell from the first basal cell, is very little arcuated; wings immaculate; stigma pale. Long. corp. 0.23—0.3.

Syn. *Dicranomyia distans* O. Sacken, Proc. Ac. Nat. Sc. Phil. 1859, p. 211.

Palpi and antennæ black; joints of the flagellum subglobular; front and vertex grayish-brown. Thorax dark tawny, sericeous with yellowish and with brown stripes; the pleuræ with a sericeous, yellowish reflection. Halteres brownish, pale at the root; abdomen brown, genitals paler; feet brownish, coxæ paler. Tip of the auxiliary vein nearly opposite the origin of the præfurca; the subcostal cross-vein is at a distance from the tip of the auxiliary vein which is not much less than the length of the stigma; the cross-vein at the inner end of the discal cell is but very slightly arcuated; discal cell closed.

Hab. Florida.

This species is very like *D. stulta* in general appearance, but easily distinguished by the great distance between the subcostal cross-vein and the tip of the auxiliary vein. I brought six specimens from Florida with me (caught in March, 1858); but I have only two left now. The rostrum seems to be of a pale color; but I cannot perceive it distinctly.

10. D. stulta O. S. ♂ and ♀.—Brunnea, humeris pleurisque pallidioribus; antennis palpisque nigris; venula transversa subcostalis apici venæ auxiliaris approximata; venula transversa quæ cellulam discoidalem a cellula basali primâ separat, valde arcuata; ala immaculata, stigmate pallido.

Brown, humeri and pleuræ pale; antennæ and palpi black; subcostal cross-vein near the tip of the auxiliary vein; the cross-vein separating the discal cell from the first basal cell is strongly arcuated; wings immaculate, stigma pale. Long. corp. 0.22–0.3.

Syn. *Dicranomyia stulta* O. Sacken, Proc. Ac. Nat. Sc. Phil. 1859, p. 210.

Palpi and antennæ black; joints of the flagellum oblong; front and vertex grayish. Thorax yellowish tawny; stripes brown, more or less shining, almost confluent; the intermediate one extends over the collare and has sometimes a pale longitudinal line in the middle; the lateral ones are extended beyond the suture; scutellum and metathorax brown; halteres infuscated, pale at the base; feet brownish, pale at the base. Abdomen brown; forceps of the male but little paler; the rostriform appendage is small and has two erect bristles; ovipositor ferruginous. Wings somewhat tinged with grayish, stigma pale gray; the tip of the auxiliary vein is nearly opposite the origin of the second longitudinal vein; the cross-vein is very near its tip (the distance is slightly

variable); the cross-vein separating the discal cell from the first
basal cell is more arcuated than usual, and hence the inner end
of the discal cell is comparatively but little more distant from the
basis of the wing than the inner end of the submarginal cell;
discal cell closed.

Hab. Trenton Falls, N. Y.; Canada, &c.

Observation: The excision between the 4th and 5th joints of
the male tarsi is hardly perceptible in this species.

11. D. liberta O. S. ♂ and ♀.—Grisea, thorace fusco-vittato, palpis
et antennis nigris, stigma pallidum, juxta venulam transversam margi-
nalem infuscatum.

Gray, thorax striped with brown, palpi and antennæ black; stigma pale,
infuscated along the cross-vein. Long. corp. 0.25—0.36.

Syn. *Dicranomyia liberta* O. Sacken, Proc. Ac. Nat. Sc. Phil. 1859, p. 219.

Rostrum and palpi black; front and vertex gray; antennæ
black, with hairs of moderate length. Thorax gray, almost slate
color; a well-defined broad, fuscous intermediate stripe, sometimes with a pale line along its middle; lateral stripes abbreviated
before and extended beyond the suture behind; scutellum slightly
tawny on the margins; halteres pale, knobs dusky; feet dark
tawny, pale at the base, darker brown towards the tip of the
femora; tips of the tibiæ and of the tarsi brown. Abdomen
blackish-gray; forceps of the male paler; its structure is like
Tab. III, fig. 3. Wings hyaline, faintly tinged with gray; pale
at the basis; veins brownish; a faint cloud at the root of the
fourth vein; stigma oblong, pale, distinctly clouded along the
marginal cross-vein; the tip of the auxiliary vein is nearly
opposite the origin of the second vein (sometimes a little before
or beyond it); the subcostal cross-vein is not far from its tip;
discal cell closed.

In one of the specimens the discal cell is open, on one wing
only. In another specimen (a female) the intermediate one of the
three refus running from the discal cell to the margin, takes an
oblique direction and forms a fork with the anterior one of the
three veins; this is the case on both wings.

Hab. United States; seems to be common everywhere; I have
collected specimens in Mobile, Ala.; Dalton, Ga.; Washington,

D. C.; New York, etc. Wisconsin (Kennicott). The infuscated marginal cross-vein is a very good distinctive character of this species.

This species is apparently identical with a European one, a specimen of which is in my possession. I cannot determine the latter with any degree of certainty, but the description of *D. tristis* Schum. agrees tolerably well with it.

12. D. hæretica, n. sp. ♂ and ♀.—Cervina, thorace vitta fusca; antennæ nigræ; rostrum ochraceum; palpi fusci; ala cinerascentes, immaculata; præfurca initium apici venæ auxiliaris plus minusve oppositum.

Drab colored, thorax with a brown stripe; antennæ blackish, rostrum yellow, with brown palpi; wings with a grayish tinge, immaculate; the origin of the præfurca is nearly opposite the tip of the auxiliary vein. Long. corp. 0.3—0.35.

Head brownish, finely sericeous with yellowish; rostrum yellow, palpi brown; antennæ brownish-black. Thorax brownish, finely sericeous with brownish-yellow; this sericeous dust being the thickest on the sides, leaves a brown stripe in the middle; pleuræ brownish, or, in some specimens, pale; sericeous with yellowish; scutellum and metathorax brownish, likewise dusted with whitish-yellow. Stem of halteres pale towards the basis, knob brown; abdomen brown above, venter paler. The forceps of the male is rather large and conspicuous even in dry specimens; in fresh specimens the reniform lobes appear somewhat club-shaped at one end, that is, broader at the tip than in the middle; the upper valves of the ovipositor are remarkable for their extreme smallness. Coxæ and base of the femora yellowish; feet tawny, tip of the tibiæ slightly infuscated; tarsi brown towards the tip. Wings (Tab. I, fig. 3) with a slight brownish-gray tinge, veins brown; stigma pale (slightly infuscated along the cross-vein in one of the specimens from Fort Resolution). Tip of the auxiliary vein nearly opposite the origin of the second vein; subcostal cross-vein removed from this tip at a distance a little less than the length of the great cross-vein; the marginal cross-vein is near the tip of the first longitudinal vein, and is placed in such a manner that it looks as if the first longitudinal vein was incurved towards the second and connected with the costa by the cross-vein, the latter being often indistinct; the submarginal cell is about one-third longer than the prefurca (this relation is, however, variable in different specimens); the seventh longitudinal vein is faintly sinuated about the middle; the position of the great cross-vein, as well as the inclination of the vein which closes the discal cell on the inside, are variable.

Hab. Environs of New York, on the salt-marshes, common. Fort Resolution, H. B. T. (Kennicott).

D. harretica may be easily distinguished from *D. liberta* by the coloring of the thorax, the shortness of the valves of the ovipositor, the greater distance between the tip of the auxiliary vein and the cross-vein, and, in fresh specimens, by the club-shaped lobes of the male forceps. The teeth on the under side of the ungues are very small and difficult to perceive. The last tarsal joint is somewhat incrassated in the male and the interval between it and the preceding joint is excised. There is a European species, the name of which I do not know, and which closely resembles *D. harretica*.

13. D. halterata, n. sp. ♂.—Fusca; rostrum, palpi et antennæ nigra; halteres longiusculi; alæ pallide infuscatæ, immaculatæ, stigmate obscuriore; venula transversa subcostalis ab apice venæ auxiliaris longitudine stigmatis remota.

Brownish; rostrum, palpi, and antennæ black; halteres rather long; wings tinged with pale brownish, immaculate, stigma darker; the subcostal cross-vein is removed from the tip of the auxiliary vein at a distance equal to the length of the stigma. Long. corp. 0.3.

Head brownish, somewhat sericeous with yellowish; antennæ and palpi black. Thorax dull brown, hardly shining above; humeral region sericeous with yellowish; the usual stripes confluent; pleuræ brown, sericeous with grayish below the root of the wings and that of the halteres; scutellum and metathorax brown, sericeous with gray; halteres comparatively long, infuscated, their root pale. Abdomen brown, the genitals but little paler. Feet brown, coxæ brownish-yellow; tarsi almost black. Wings tinged with pale brownish; tip of the auxiliary vein nearly opposite the origin of the prefurca; the subcostal cross-vein removed back of this tip at a distance nearly equal to the length of the stigma; marginal cross-vein at the tip of the first longitudinal vein; discal cell closed.

Hab. Labrador (Mr. A. S. Packard, Jr.); four male specimens.

This species will be easily distinguished from *D. harctica* by its brown rostrum, the darker tinge of its wings and of its stigma, by the greater distance between the subcostal cross-vein and the tip of the auxillary vein; by its unusually long halteres, and in general by its darker coloring. I can perceive a tooth at the basis of the ungues. The excision at the basis of the last tarsal joint of the male is likewise distinct.

I possess a male specimen from Canada, the halteres of which are of the same length as those of *D. halterata*; the venation and coloring of the wings are likewise the same (the stigma is slightly paler); but the thorax is brownish ochraceous, except the space on the back, usually occupied by the stripes, which is brown. Is it not a paler variety of *D. halterata?*

§ 1. **D. badia** WALK. ♂ and ♀.—Fusca, abdominis fasciis pallidis; pedibus fuscis, femorum apice pallido, alis fusco-nebulosis; stigmate subquadrato, fusco.

Brown, abdomen with pale bands; feet brown, tip of the femora pale; wings clouded with brownish; stigma nearly square, brownish. Long. corp. 0.3—0.35.

Srx. *Limnobia badia* WALK., List, etc. I, p. 46.
      Dicranomyia humidicola O. SACKEN, Proc. Ac. Nat. Sc. Phil. 1859, p. 210.

Rostrum, palpi, and antennae dark brown; front and vertex grayish-brown. Thorax tawny with more or less confluent brown stripes; a faint yellowish, sericeous reflection in the humeral region; pleurae brown, with some paler spots; halteres pale, knob infuscated; coxae pale; feet tawny; a pale band at the tip of the femora. Abdomen tawny, with pale bands on the incisures; male forceps like Tab. III, fig. 2; ovipositor of the female ferruginous. Wings somewhat tinged with grayish and faintly clouded with brownish; a pale brown cloud at the origin of the praefurca; another, rounded one, at the inner end of the submarginal cell; the cross-veins likewise clouded; stigma brown, in the shape of an elongated square. Tip of the auxiliary vein generally a little beyond the origin of the praefurca, sometimes nearly opposite it, the cross-vein very near its tip.

Hab. Washington, D. C.; Trenton Falls; Connecticut; Canada.

Common in damp, shady situations, especially in hollows, having a spring at the bottom.

This species can always be easily recognized by the pale band at the tip of the femora. I have found some specimens near the Sharon Springs, N. Y., without any apparent brown clouds, except the stigma; but this pale band and the other characters undoubtedly refer it here.

15. D. morioides O. S. ♂ and ♀.—Thorace nigro, nitido, pleuris argenteo-micantibus; alis pallide infuscatis, stigmate fusco.

Thorax black, shining; pleurae with a silvery reflection; wings somewhat infuscated, stigma brownish. Long. corp. 0.3.

Syn. *Dicranomyia morio* O. Sacken (nec *Fab.*), Proc. Ac. Nat. Sc. Phil. 1859, p. 212.

Head black, front silvery; palpi and antennæ black; the last joint of the former ends in a slender, cylindrical prolongation, which might be taken for a fifteenth joint. Thorax black, shining above, silvery on the pleurae; halteres with a blackish knob; feet pale brown, coxæ pale. Abdomen brownish, margins of the segments more or less pale. Wings pale brownish, stigma darker brown. *Hab.* Trenton Falls, N. Y.

In 1859 I had identified this species with the European *D. morio* Fab. Since then I conceived some doubts about this identity (*Proc. Acad. Nat. Sci. Phila.* 1860, p. 17), but I have not had an opportunity as yet, for comparing a series of specimens from Europe and from North America. The latter seems to have somewhat darker wings, but by all means the discrepancy is hardly anything more than one of coloring. The peculiar structure of the last antennal joint has already been noticed by Melgen (Vol. VI, p. 274).

16. D. pubipennis O. S. ♂ and ♀.—Obscure brunnea; alis immaculatis, in regione apicali sparse pubescentibus; stigmate pallide infuscato; vena longitudinali prima in secundam (non in costam) incurvâ; vena auxiliari pone præfurcae initium extensâ.

Dark brown; wings immaculate, sparsely pubescent in the apical region; stigma pale brownish; the first longitudinal vein is incurved towards the second (and not towards the costa); the auxiliary vein is prolonged beyond the origin of the præfurca (Tab. I, fig. 2). Long. corp. 0.35—0.36.

Syn. *Dicranomyia pubipennis* O. Sacken, Proc. Ac. Nat. Sc. Phil. 1859, p. 211.

Head dark brown, antennæ and palpi black. Thorax dark brown, moderately shining and slightly pruinose with grayish above; stripes not distinct; some parts of the pleura and of the posterior portion of the thorax are reddish or yellowish-brown. Halteres with an infuscated knob; feet dark brown, femora tawny, paler at the basis; coxæ brownish-yellow. Abdomen brown; forceps paler; the upper valves of the ovipositor are very narrow, pointed, and nearly straight. Wings (Tab. 1, fig. 2) immaculate, somewhat tinged with grayish; stigma elliptical, pale brownish; the apex of the wing is finely and sparsely pubescent; in the marginal cell this pubescence begins a little before the stigma, and it occupies nearly the whole of the submarginal, posterior, and discal cells. The tip of the auxiliary vein is about one length of the stigma beyond the origin of the second longitudinal vein; the subcostal cross-vein is near its tip. The first longitudinal vein ends in the second, forming a regular arc of a circle; the cross-vein connects it with the costa. The discal cell of this species is often open (among twenty specimens caught by me in 1859 in the same locality, five had it open), and in such specimens, it is the *anterior* branch (and not the *posterior* one as usual) of the fourth longitudinal vein which is forked; in other words, the discal cell coalesces with the third, and not with the second posterior cell.

Hab. Washington, D. C., not rare in April and May; also further north.

The pubescence in the apical portion of the wing, as well as the forking of the anterior, instead of the posterior branch of the fourth vein are very good distinctive characters of this species.

17. D. globithorax, n. sp. ♂ and ♀.—Brunnea, capite antennisque nigro-fuscis, thorace gibbo; alis brevioribus, pallide infuscatis, immaculatis, stigmatis vestigio nullo; vena longitudinali primā in secundam (non in costam) incurvā; venā auxiliari pone præfurcam initium extensā.

Brown, head and antennæ brownish-black; thorax gibbous, wings rather short, slightly tinged with brownish, without spots; no vestige of a stigma; the first longitudinal vein is curved towards the second (not towards the costa); auxiliary vein prolonged beyond the origin of the præfurca. *Long. corp.* 0.2—0.22.

Head, including the palpi, brownish-black; joints of the flagellum short, subglobular, with a short, scattered pubescence.

Thorax strikingly gibbous, rising abruptly over the head; it is brown, almost opaque above, without distinct stripes; more tawny on the sides and posteriorly; halteres infuscated; feet brownish; coxæ and base of the femora pale; abdomen, including the male genitals, fuscous; ovipositor rather short; upper valves distinctly curved. Wings comparatively shorter and broader than in the related species, with a slight brownish tinge; no perceptible vestige of a stigma. The first longitudinal vein, instead of ending in the costa, is curved at its tip towards the second longitudinal vein and ends in it; thus the cross-vein is apparently placed between the first longitudinal vein and the costa; the tip of the auxiliary vein, with the subcostal cross-vein close by it, is nearly opposite the middle of the præfurca; the submarginal cell is not quite one-third longer than the first posterior; first and second basal cells of equal length.

I possess two specimens, a male from the White Mountains and a female from Washington, D. C.

This species will be very easily recognized by its gibbous thorax and the total absence of a stigma. One of my specimens has the discal cell closed, the other open; thus I am in doubt, what is the rule and what the exception.

14. D. rara, n. sp. ♀.—Brunnea, capite antennisque nigris; alis apud costam maculis tribus fuscis, quartâ ad apicem minore; venâ auxiliari pone præfurcam initium longe externâ.

Brown, head and antennæ black; wings with three brown spots near the costa; a fourth, smaller spot near the apex of the wing; auxiliary vein prolonged far beyond the origin of the præfurca. Long. corp. 0.23.

Head, including the rostrum and the palpi, black; antennæ black. Thorax pale brownish, with three darker stripes above; a conspicuous dark brown stripe runs from the collare across the pleuræ towards the metathorax; brown spots on the sternum, between the fore and the intermediate coxæ; halteres infuscated; abdomen brown, segments paler at the basis; ovipositor subferruginous; coxæ and femora pale tawny; the latter with a brown band before the tip; knees pale; tibiæ and tarsi brownish. Wings distinctly infuscated; a brown spot (sometimes preceded by a pale streak) at the origin of the second vein; a smaller one at the tip of the auxiliary vein; a rounded brown spot, included between two whitish ones, at the tip of the first longitudinal vein; a smaller one at the tip of the second longitudinal vein; cross-veins infuscated, as well as the tips of all the other longitudinal veins. Subcostal cross-vein at the tip of the auxiliary vein, which is distinctly beyond the middle of the præfurca; marginal cross-vein very near the tip of the first longitudinal vein; second basal cell a little shorter than the first.

Hab. New York; two female specimens.

19. D. defuncta O. S. ♂ and ♀.—Fusco-cinerea, thorace vittis tribus nigro-fuscis, intermedia duplice; pedes nigro-fusci, femora apicem versus annulo albido; alæ in cellulis omnibus seriatim fusco-maculata et punctatæ; vena auxiliari pone præfurcam initium mollius extensa.

Brownish-gray, thorax with three brown stripes, the intermediate double; feet blackish-brown, femora with a whitish ring towards the apex; wings with brown spots and dots arranged in rows in all the cells; the auxiliary vein is somewhat prolonged beyond the origin of the præfurca. Long. corp. 0.35—0.4.

Sys. *Dicranomyia defuncta* O. Sacken, Proc. Ac. Nat. So. Phil. 1859, p. 213.

Head cinereous, front and vertex almost black in the middle; rostrum, palpi, and antennæ fuscous; joints of the flagellum subglobular, with short verticils. Thorax cinereous with three brown stripes, the intermediate one divided in two by a pale longitudinal line; pleuræ variegated with brown; halteres pale with black knobs; coxæ cinereous, feet brown, base of the femora tawny; a very distinct whitish ring at a distance equal to its own width, from the tip of the femora. Abdomen blackish cinereous; posterior margins of the segments paler; genitals pale.. Wings with a grayish tinge, spotted with blackish-brown; subcostal cell infuscated at four intervals; several spots, forming a short transverse band, along the central cross-veins; series of small, round dots along the middle of the cells; a larger spot at the tip of the seventh longitudinal vein; stigma square.

Hab. Washington, D. C.; Trenton Falls; Maine; Canada. I have often found it alighting on rocks and stones over which a thin sheet of water was running.

The forceps of this species (Tab. III, fig. 1 and 1a) has more elongated, slender lobes than the typical *Dicranomyiæ*; no rostriform horny appendage is apparent. The ungues are large and have several notches on the under side, instead of the teeth, which characterize the *Limnobina*. The excision on the under side at the basis of the last tarsal joint of the male is distinct, although small.

●

The following species from California is not included in the dichotomical table of page 60.

29. D. marmorata O. S. ♂.—Cinereo-fusca, thorace vittis tribus fuscis; alis cinereo-nebulosis, stigmate quadrangulari, fusco; femorum apicibus infuscatis.

Grayish-brown, thorax with three brown stripes; wings clouded with cinereous; stigma quadrangular, brown; tip of the femora brown. Long. corp. 0.4.

Syn. *Dicranomyia marmorata* O. Sacken, Proc. Ac. Nat. Sc. Phil. 1861, p. 246.

Rostrum, palpi, and antennæ brown; joints of the latter subglobular, verticils short; front and vertex cinereous, darker in the middle; thorax cinereous, with three brown stripes; abdomen brownish cinereous, posterior margins of the segments pale; halteres pale; feet yellowish, tips of femora, of the tibiæ, and of the tarsi brown; wings subcinereous with some darker clouds and some hyaline bands and spots; a cloud at the origin of the præfurca, another, round one, at its tip; cross-veins also clouded; stigma obscure-cinereous, elongated, quadrangular; the hyaline spots are arranged in the following way: a small, rounded one in the anal angle; a band running across the basal portion of the two basal and the anal cells, and ending in the spurious cell near the posterior margin; a spot near the tip of the seventh longitudinal vein; a large irregular hyaline space in the central portion of the wing, inclosing the stigma and the two clouds of the præfurca, and extending more or less towards the posterior margin, across the discal and the posterior cells; its outline is very indefinite, and it is interrupted by clouded marks along the veins; a small hyaline mark at the tip of the wing, in the submarginal cell. The tip of the auxiliary vein almost corresponds to the origin of the præfurca; the subcostal cross-vein is a short distance before its tip; the discal cell is present (closed), and the great cross-vein corresponds to its base.

Hab. California; two male specimens (Mr. A. Agassiz). This species is related to *D. humidicola* O. S.

Gen. II. GERANOMYIA.

One submarginal cell; four posterior cells; a discal cell. Antennæ 14-jointed, submoniliform; joints not pedicelled. *Rostrum and proboscis prolonged*, longer than the head and thorax taken together; the short palpi are inserted about their middle. Feet slender; tibiæ without spurs at the tip; empodia indistinct or none; ungues with teeth on the under side. The forceps of the male is like that of *Dicranomyia*, and consists of two fleshy, movable lobes, with horny appendages and a horny style under them.

This genus is most closely allied to *Dicranomyia*, and is distinguished from it only by the enormously developed oral parts. These consist of a very long, subcylindrical epistoma, a still longer lingua, which is slender and pointed, and a labium divided in two branches at the tip, terminated by slender, flattened lobes; these branches are divergent and sometimes curled up in dry specimens. The short palpi (bi-articulate according to Mr. Curtis) are inserted about the middle of the proboscis to the anterior angles of the rostrum. This proboscis is principally used for sucking moisture and flowers.

Mr. Halliday (*Entomol. Magaz.* I, p. 154) described this genus in 1833, establishing it upon *G. unicolor*, a species found on the rocks and shrubs near the sea-shore in England and Ireland.

Mr. Curtis (*Brit. Entom.* 573, 1835) gave a beautiful plate and a description of this genus, which he very correctly distinguishes from *Rhamphidia*, by stating that the latter has 16- and not 14-jointed antennæ, and a rostrum of a different structure. The structure of the proboscis of *Geranomyia*, subjected to a careful dissection, is represented on the plate (the figure is reproduced in Walker's *Ins. Brit. Dipt.* III, Tab. XXVII, fig. 6, a, b). The second species, described by Mr. Curtis (*G. maculipennis*) was considered by later authors as a variety of *G. unicolor* (comp. Walker, l. c. 310).

G. unicolor has hitherto been found only in England; a second European species has been discovered in Austria and also called *G. maculipennis* (*Verh. Zool. Bot. Ges. in Wien*, 1864).

Macquart (*Dipt. Exot.* I, p. 62, 1838) described the same genus under the new generic name of *Aporosa*; he introduces two species, one from the Canary Islands, the other from Isle Bourbon. But the American continent seems to be much more abundant in *Geranomyia*. Mr. Loew (*Linn. Entom.* Vol. V, p. 391) published six species from Brazil, Chile, and the West Indies ; Mr. Walker (*List*, etc. Vol. 1), one from Jamaica and (*Dipt. Sound.* pt. V) one from Brazil; Dr. Philippi (*Verh. Zool. Bot. Ges. in Wien*, 1865, p. 597, Tab. XXIII, fig. 1) described four species from Chile under the new generic name of *Plettusa*; Mr. Bellardi (*Saggio*, etc. *Appendice*, p. 2) one from Mexico. As three species from the United States have been described below, this makes a total of twenty species, only four of which belong to the old world.

Macquart's *Aporosa* and Philippi's *Plettusa* being identical with *Geranomyia* and posterior to it in point of time, have to be given up as generic names.

The name *Geranomyia* is derived from γέρανος, a crane, and μυῖα, a fly.

Table for determining the species.

1 { Wings spotted.   1 rostrata *Say*.
   { Wings not spotted.   2

2 { The auxiliary vein ends in the costa nearly opposite the origin of the
      prefurca.   2 diversa *O. S.*
   { The auxiliary vein ends in the costa far beyond the origin of the
      prefurca.   3 canadensis *Westw.*

Description of the species.

1. G. rostrata Say. ♂ and ♀.—Alis fusco-maculatis et nebulosis. Wings with brown spots and clouds. Long. corp. 0.3.

Syn. *Limnobia rostrata* Say, Journ. Acad. Nat. Sc. Phil. III, p. 22, 6.—
, Wied. Auss. Zw. I, p. 35, 20.
Geranomyia rostrata O. Sacken, Proc. Ac. Nat. Sc. Phil. 1859, p. 207.

Front and vertex gray; proboscis and antennae black. Thorax grayish, often with a yellowish or brownish tinge; three more or less distinct brown stripes; pleurae with a hoary bloom; scutellum and metathorax brownish, with a grayish bloom; halteres with a dark brown knob; feet tawny, tips of the tibiae black, subclavate in appearance; tips of the tarsi infuscated. Abdomen brown, venter paler. Wings with five brown spots along the anterior margin; the cross-veins and the tips of all the veins along the apex and along the posterior margin are clouded with pale brown.

Hab. Washington, D. C.; New York; Massachusetts; Illinois; Canada. I have brought home a specimen from Cuba, which I believe to be the same species. It shows some slight differences, the most striking of which is, that the brown spot at the tip of the first longitudinal vein is limited posteriorly by the second longitudinal vein; whereas in my North American specimens, it crosses this vein and invades the inner end of the submarginal cell.

2. G. diversa O. S. ♂ and ♀.—Thorace cinereo, vittis tribus obscure fuscis; vena auxiliaris apice prefurcae initio plus minusve opposito.

Thorax gray, with three dark brown stripes; the tip of the auxiliary vein is nearly opposite the origin of the prefurca. Long. corp. 0.25—0.29.

Syn. *Geranomyia diversa* O. Sacken, Proc. Ac. Nat. Sc. Phil. 1859, p. 207.

Proboscis, palpi, and antennæ black; front and vertex grayish. Thorax with a grayish bloom above and with three well marked dark brown stripes; pleura, scutellum and metathorax hoary, their ground color brownish; halteres with a brown knob; feet tawny, coxæ and basis of the femora paler. Abdomen brown; male forceps paler. Wings slightly tinged with brownish; stigma very slightly darker; a slight, hardly perceptible nebulosity at the origin of the prefurca; the marginal cross-vein forms an obtuse angle, sometimes nearly a straight line, with the tip of the first longitudinal vein; the tip of the auxiliary vein is opposite the origin of the prefurca.

Hab. Trenton Falls, N. Y.

The proboscis of this species is much shorter than that of the two other species. The male of *Limnobiorhynchus braziliensis* Westw. (*Ann. Soc. Ent. de Fr.* 1835, p. 683) is a *Geranomyia*, which is not unlike *G. diversa;* the stripes of the thorax are likewise narrow and dark, and the position of the marginal cross-vein is the same. I have seen the specimen in Mr. Westwood's collection, without having subjected it to a close comparison with *G. diversa.*

3. G. canadensis Westw. ♂ and ♀.—Thorace pallide fusco, vittis tribus obscurioribus; vena auxiliari pone prefuram initium extensa.

Thorax pale brown, with three darker stripes; auxiliary vein extended beyond the origin of the prefurca. Long. corp. 0.25—0.28.

Syn. *Limnobiorhynchus canadensis* Westw. Ann. Soc. Entom. de Fr. 1835, p. 683.
Geranomyia communis O. Sacken, Proc. Ac. Nat. Sc. Phil. 1859, p. 207.

Head tawny, somewhat grayish on the front; antennæ blackish, under side of the first joint tawny; proboscis and palpi brown, the former paler at the basis. Thorax brownish, with three more or less dark brown stripes; pleuræ paler; metathorax brownish, with a hoary bloom; halteres infuscated, pale at the basis; feet tawny, tips of the femora, of the tibiæ, and of the tarsi brown. Abdomen brown, posterior margins of the segments paler; venter pale. Wings very slightly tinged; stigma brownish; the tip of the first longitudinal vein is incurved towards the second, the marginal cross-vein being apparently between it and the costa; the tip of the auxiliary vein is nearly opposite the middle of the præfurca.

Hab. Washington, D. C.; Upper Wisconsin River (Kenni-cott); Illinois (LeBaron).

The proboscis of this species is very long, at least once and a half the length of the thorax. I have seen the original specimen of *Limnobiorhynchus canadensis* Westwood, in the author's own collection; (compare the genus *Toxorrhina*.)

Gen. III. RHIPIDIA.

One submarginal cell; four posterior cells; a discal cell. Antennæ 14-jointed; *bipectinate, pectinate or subpectinate*; joints of the flagellum always distinctly pedicelled. Rostrum and proboscis short. Feet slender; tibiæ without spurs at the tip; empodia indistinct or none. The forceps of the male is like that of *Dicranomyia* and consists of two immovable, fleshy lobes, and a horny style on the under side (Tab. III, fig. 5 and 5*a*).

Rhipidia is principally distinguished from *Dicranomyia* by the structure of the antennæ. This structure is most prominent and peculiar in the male of *R. maculata* M.; the joints of the flagellum (except the basal and the terminal ones) emit in this species two, rather long, branches. In the two other North American species and in the second European species (*R. uniseriata* Schin.) the joints of the flagellum bear only a single branch, which is shorter than those of *R. maculata*. The females of all the species have a moniliform flagellum, that is, the single joints are separated by distinct pedicels; the joints of the basal half of the flagellum are somewhat projecting on the under side.

The auxiliary vein reaches more or less beyond the origin of the second longitudinal vein, and in this respect *Rhipidia* agrees with those North American *Dicranomyiæ*, which have spotted

6 July 1869.

wings (*D. rara, defuncta*). The subcostal cross-vein in all the
species known to me, is close by the tip of the auxiliary vein;
the marginal cross-vein close by the tip of the first longitudinal
vein. The slenderness of the feet, the structure of tho forceps of
the male, etc., remind one of *Dicranomyia* (compare tho forceps
of *R. maculata*, figured by me in *Stett. Ent. Z.* 1854, Tab. I, fig.
3, and that of *R. domestica* in the present volume, Tab. III, fig.
5, 5 a).

The genus *Rhipidia* (from ῥιπίς, a fan) was established by
Meigen, in 1818, for the only European species at that time
known. A second European species, *R. uniseriata*, has been
only very recently (1864) described by Dr. Schiner. Among tho
three North American species, one occurs also in Europe; the
other is very like the European *R. uniseriata*, and the third
seems to be common to the United States and to Brazil. A
Rhipidia from Caffraria exists in the Berlin Museum.

Table for the determination of the species.

1 { Wings with spots and clouds scattered over the whole surface.
            1 maculata *M.*
      Wings with some brown spots or clouds along the anterior margin
            only.   2

2 { Antennæ black.   2 fidelis *O. S.*
    { Antennæ with the two penultimate joints yellow. 3 domestica *O. S.*

Description of the species.

1. R. maculata M. ♂ and ♀.—Cinereo-fusca, thoracis vitta brunnea,
alis maculis majoribus in margine antico, punctis et maculis minoribus
in cellulis omnibus, fuscis; antennæ maris bipectinatæ.

Grayish-brown, thorax with a brown stripe; wings with larger brown spots
along the anterior margin and with smaller spots and dots in all the
cells; antennæ of the male bipectinatæ. Long. corp. 0.3—0.4.

Syn. *Rhipidia maculata* Meigen, I. p. 153; Tab. V, fig. 9–11.—O. Sacken,
Proc. Ac. Nat. Sc. Phil. 1859, p. 219.

Front and vertex gray; rostrum, palpi, and antennæ black;
joints of the flagellum (except the basal and the terminal ones)
bipectinate in the male; in the female, these joints project distinctly on the under side. Thorax brownish, pruinose with gray
above; a broad brown stripe in the middle; lateral stripes somewhat indistinct; halteres pale; feet tawny; coxæ and base of the

femora pale; tip of the latter and of the tibiœ brown. Abdomen
brown. Wings with a grayish tinge, densely covered with pale
brown spots and smaller dots; several larger spots along the
anterior margin; numerous dots in all the cells; cross-veins
clouded.

Hab. Europe and North America; principally the northern
regions of the latter. White Mountains, N. H.; Trenton Falls,
N. Y.; Washington, D. C.; Maine (Packard); Hudson's Bay
Territory (Kennicott); Illinois (Id.). This insect occurs twice
in the year, in the spring and in autumn; it is more rare towards
the south.

A female specimen in my possession has the spots along the
anterior margin larger and the nebulosities on the cross-veins
darker; the smaller dots in the cells, on the contrary, are not so
dense as usual, leaving large hyaline intervals between them.

2. R. fidelis O. S. ♂ and ♀.—Cinereo-fusca, thoracis vittâ brunneâ;
alis in margine anteriore fusco-nebulosis; antennæ maris unipectinatæ.

Grayish-brown; thorax with a brown stripe; wings with brownish clouds
along the anterior margin; antennæ of the male unipectinate. Long.
corp. 0.2.

Syn. *Rhipidia fidelis* O. Sacken, Proc. Ac. Nat. Sc. Phil. 1859, p. 209.

Rostrum, palpi, and antennæ blackish; the flagellum of the
latter (beginning with its second joint) is short unipectinate in
the male, and only moniliform in the female; thorax brownish,
pruinose with gray above, a broad brown stripe in the middle;
lateral stripes less distinct. Halteres pale; feet brownish, femora
pale at the basis, darker at tip. Abdomen brown; male genitals
paler. Wings with a pale brownish tinge, excepting a large
whitish region, embracing the præfurca and the stigma; in this
region, however, the stigma itself, a round spot at the origin of the
præfurca, another one at the inner end of the submarginal cell,
and a small dot at the tip of the auxiliary vein are brown; a
narrow margin along the apex of the wing is likewise whitish.

Hab. Sharon Springs, N. Y.; Illinois. I possess only two
specimens.

The European *R. uniseriata* Schin. is remarkably like this
species, but the apex of the wings is altogether dark.

2. R. domestica O. S. ♂ and ♀.—Antennæ nigræ, articulis flagelli reniformibus, subpectinatis; penultimo et antepenultimo flavis.

Antennæ brown, joints of the flagellum reniform, subpectinate; the penultimate and antepenultimate joints yellow. Long. corp. 0.3—0.35.

Syn. *Rhipidia domestica* O. Sackes, Proc. Ac. Nat. Sc. Phil. 1859, p. 208.

Front and vertex cinereous; rostrum and palpi brown; eyes almost contiguous; in living specimens dark green above and purple below; antennæ black; penultimate and antipenultimate joints yellow; flagellum moniliform; its joints reniform. Thorax yellowish-brown, sericeous, when viewed in a certain light; the thoracic stripes (a double intermediate one and broad lateral ones) occupy the posterior part of the mesonotum; the anterior part shows a brown line in the middle, which is expanded in front, and several brown dots on the humeri; two brown stripes on the pleuræ, one running from the collare, backwards; the other along the base of the coxæ. Halteres tawny, with a dusky spot on the knob; feet tawny; coxæ and basis of the femora pale; tips of the femora, of the tibiæ, and of the tarsi brown. Abdomen brownish; lateral margins of the segments darker; forceps tawny (Tab. III, fig. 5 and 5a). Wings tinged with pale brownish; first and fifth longitudinal veins yellowish; the others brownish; five brown spots along the first longitudinal vein, more or less expanded on both sides of this vein in the shape of clouds; the third spot (counting from the root of the wing) is connected with a cloud at the origin of the præfurca; the fifth is a round spot at the tip of the first longitudinal vein; it is connected with a cloud, surrounding the stigma, the centre of which is pale; a pale cloud at the inner end of the submarginal cell; tips of all the longitudinal veins and all the cross-veins clouded; pale, indistinct clouds in some of the cells.

Hab. Washington, D. C., not rare; Palisades, New Jersey. I have seen in the Berlin Museum a specimen from Brazil, which I believe to be the same species.

Gen. IV. LIMNOBIA.

One submarginal cell; four posterior cells; a discal cell. The marginal cross-vein is sometimes at the tip of the first longitudinal vein, but often at some distance anterior to this tip, crossing the stigma; the tip of the auxiliary vein is usually far beyond the origin of the præfurca. Antennæ

14. (often apparently 15.) jointed. Feet comparatively strong; tibiæ without spurs at the tip; empodia indistinct or none; ungues with several teeth on the under side, giving them a pectinate appearance. The forceps of the male consists of two horny, movable hooks, and a horny style under them (Tab. III, fig. 6 and 7).

This genus is closely allied to *Dicranomyia*, but can be easily distinguished by the structure of the forceps of the male, and, in most cases, by the greater length of the auxiliary vein, which extends far beyond the origin of the præfurca and ends nearly opposite the inner end of the submarginal cell. The European *L. macrostigma* is the only species I know of, the auxiliary vein of which extends but very little beyond the origin of the præfurca; but the marginal cross-vein of this species is situated about the middle of the stigma and at some distance from the tip of the first longitudinal vein, which is never the case among the *Dicranomyiæ*.

The first longitudinal vein of *Limnobia* is generally also longer than that of *Dicranomyia*; its tip is usually nearly opposite the middle of the submarginal cell; sometimes (as in *L. parietina*) far beyond the middle. The discal cell is closed in all the species which I have had occasion to examine. The marginal cross-vein is either at the tip of the first longitudinal vein, or at some distance from the tip. In the first case it often occurs that the first longitudinal vein appears incurved towards the second, and that the cross-vein seems to be placed between it and the costa (this same structure occurs among the *Dicranomyiæ*). A more detailed comparison between the venation of *Limnobia* and *Dicranomyia* has been given above on page 67.

The *Limnobiæ* are generally larger and more strongly built than the *Dicranomyiæ*; their rostrum and palpi are somewhat longer; the joints of the flagellum more elongated, especially towards the tip; the verticils longer; the feet stouter, often more hairy; but all these characters are not of an absolute value.

The ungues of *Limnobia* have several distinct, and very striking teeth on the under side, which give them a pectinate appearance; in some species they reach to the middle of the unguis, in others they extend almost to the end.

The colors of the *Limnobiæ* are for the most part bright and striking, with well defined stripes on the thorax, bands on the feet, and spots on the wings; they form, in this respect, a contrast with the usually dull coloring of the *Dicranomyia*.

The last antennal joint of this genus often shows a cylindrical prolongation, sometimes slightly elevate at the tip, which, even in living specimens, looks like a fifteenth joint. That this is not a real joint seems to be proved by the circumstance that closely allied species differ with regard to its structure; one species may appear to have 15-jointed antennæ, whereas in the next one only 14 joints can be counted.

The larvæ of this genus live in decaying vegetable matter, especially in wood and fungi. Stannius (*Beitrâge*, etc. p. 202) found the larva of *Limnobia xanthoptera* (a species related to the North American *L. triocellata*) in an *Agaricus*; the larva was wrapped in a sheath of earthy matter, rough on the outside, smooth and shiny on the inside; it went underground for transformation. Van Roser (*Verz. Würt. Dipt.*) discovered the larva of *L. annulus* (closely allied to *L. cinctipes* Say) in decayed wood; they are like an earth-worm in size, as well as in color, and line their burrows with a kind of silken web.

Limnobia may be subdivided in two groups, defined by the position of the marginal cross-vein.

The first group, having the cross-vein close by the tip of the first longitudinal vein, contains large, very characteristic species, the typical *Limnobiæ*. A remarkable parallelism exists in this group, between the species from Europe and from North America. *L. annulus* Lin. is closely allied to *L. cinctipes* Say; *L. quadrinotata* Meig. is analogous to *L. solitaria*; and *L. xanthoptera*, although belonging to a somewhat different type, is represented in North America by *L. triocellata*.

In the second group, the marginal cross-vein is at some distance from the end of the first longitudinal vein, and more or less approximated to the middle of the stigma. The ovipositor of the females of this group is more long, slender and pointed than the ovipositor in the first group; the short, curved shape of the latter being more like the ovipositor of *Dicranomyia*. Four North American species belong to this group, two of which have clouded, and the two others almost immaculate wings. In Europe, this group is more abundantly represented, and there is a number of handsome species with more or less pictured and clouded wings, which, as far as known, have no representatives in North America (such are the European *L. flavipes* Meig., *nubeculosa* M., *sylci-cola* Schum., *nigropunctata* Schum. etc.).

The name *Limnobia* (from λίμνη, lake, swamp, and βίος, I live), as originally introduced by Meigen (1818), embraced all the brevipalpous *Tipulidæ*, with the exclusion of *Erioptera, Anisomera, Trichocera*, and *Rhipidia*. Macquart afterwards confined it to the species with four posterior cells. The genus, in its present limitation, dates from the time of the separation of *Dicranomyia* by Stephens in 1829; it has continued, however, in the principal works published since (especially those of Zetterstedt and Walker), to be received in Meigen's wide acceptation. My definition of *Limnobia*, in 1859, was coincident with the whole section *Limnobina; Rhipidia, Geranomyia, Dicranomyia*, and *Limnobia*, in the narrowest sense, were treated as subgenera.

Table for determining the species.

1 { The marginal cross-vein is at the tip of the first longitudinal vein.[1] 3
{ The marginal cross-vein is some distance back of the tip of the first longitudinal vein. 6

2 { Femora with one or more brown bands before the tip. 3
{ Femora without brown bands, brown at the tip only. 5 tricellata O. S.

3 { Knob of the halteres pale at the tip. 4
{ Knob of the halteres altogether infuscated. 5

4 { Femora with two brown bands and a pale band between them; a ring-like spot at the end of the first longitudinal vein. 1 cinctipes Say.
{ Femora with three brown bands and two pale ones between them; the brown spot at the tip of the first longitudinal vein is entire, not ring-like. 2 immatura O. S.

5 { A series of more or less numerous (from two to eight) brown dots along the first basal cell. 3 solitaria O. S.
{ Four large, dark, almost equidistant brown spots in the first basal cell. 4 hudsonica O. S.

6 { Wings clouded with brown. 7
{ Wings immaculate (or with a few small brown dots near the anterior margin only). 8

7 { Posterior cells clouded in the middle. 6 parietina O. S.
{ Posterior cells not clouded in the middle. 7 indigena O. S.

[1] Whenever the structure occurs that the first longitudinal vein is incurved towards the second, whereas the cross-vein seems to be placed between it and the costa, the cross-vein is to be considered as being at the tip of the first longitudinal vein.

{ Wings with pale brown dots at the tip of the auxiliary vein, the origin
8 {   of the præfurca, and at both ends of the stigma.   ♂ triatigma *O. S.*
{ Wings entirely immaculate.   ♀ sociabilis, n. sp.

Description of the species.

1. L. cinctipes Say.   ♂ and ♀.—Thoracis vittis quatuor, femorum
annulis duobus fuscis : halterum capitulo pallido, ad basin fusco ; alæ
fusco-maculatæ et nebulosæ ; venula transversalis marginalis juxta
apicem venæ longitudinalis primæ sita,[1] ocello fusco inclusa.

Thorax with four brown stripes, femora with two brown bands ; halteres
with a pale knob, which is infuscated at the basis ; wings spotted and
clouded with brown ; the marginal cross-vein is at the tip of the first
longitudinal vein ; a brown, ring-like spot passes over it.   Long. corp.
0.3—0.4.

Syn. *Limnobia cinctipes* Say, Journ. Ac. Nat. Sc. Phil. III, 21, 4.—Wiedemann, Aus. Zw. 1, 82, 15.—O. Sacken, Proc. Ac. Nat. Sc. Phil.
1859, p. 214.

Rostrum and palpi infuscated ; antennæ brown, more or less
ferruginous at the basis (usually the first three joints) ; front
yellowish-cinereous ; vertex with a large brown spot, divided in
two by a yellow line. Thorax yellow with four dark brown
stripes ; the intermediate ones separated by a narrow yellow line ;
in well-preserved specimens, these stripes are covered with a
grayish bloom, except in the middle of the intermediate ones and
at the anterior end of the lateral ones, where the color is velvety-
black ; humeri yellow, with a small brown dot ; the remaining
portions of the thorax are yellow, more or less spotted with
brown ; halteres pale, with a brown spot at the basis of the knob ;
feet yellow ; femora with two brown bands before the tip, which
is yellow ; tarsi infuscated beyond the tip of the first joint.
Abdomen ferruginous-yellow, with brown bands across the posterior half of the segments ; the bands on the anterior segments
interrupted ; venter darker towards the tip in the male ; genitals
pale ferruginous. Wings somewhat yellowish, with brown spots
and clouds ; four spots along the anterior margin ; the first at the
inner end of the basal cells ; the second at the origin of the præ-

---

[1] The structure where the first longitudinal vein is incurved towards the
second and the cross-vein is apparently placed between it and the costa,
generally occurs in this species and the four following ; this cannot prevent
us from considering the cross-vein as being at the tip of the first vein.

fures; the third, double spot, at the tip of the auxiliary vein and
at the lower end of the submarginal cell; the fourth, ring-like one,
at the tip of the first longitudinal vein; cross-veins infuscated;
a pale brown band crosses the cells of the apical portion of the
wing; several irregular pale brown clouds in the cells along
the posterior margin, leaving some pellucid spots alongside of
the margin.

Hab. Missouri (Say); Washington, D. C., end of April;
Illinois (Kennicott); Massachusetts (Scudder).

In general appearance this species is very like the European
L. annulus Lin.; but there are unmistakable differences in the
details. My female specimen shows no brown bands on the abdominal segments; this is undoubtedly accidental, as Wiedemann,
in describing a female, mentions them.

2. L. immatura O. S.   ♂ and ♀.—Thoracis vittis quatuor, femora
annulis tribus fuscis; halterum capitulo apice pallido; alis fusco-
maculatis et nebulosis, venula transversalis marginalis juxta apicem
vena longitudinalis prima sita, maculis fusca integra inclusa.

Thorax with four brown stripes, femora with three brown bands; the knob
of the halteres is pale at the tip; wings spotted and clouded with brown;
the marginal cross-vein is at the tip of the first longitudinal vein and is
included in a brown, entire (not ring-like) spot.   Long. corp. 0.4—0.5.

Syn. *Limnobia immatura* O. Sacken, Proc. Ac. Nat. Sc. Phil. 1859, p. 214.

Very like the preceding species, but showing the following
differences: It is smaller in size; the femora, besides the two
brown bands *beyond* the middle, have a third one *in* the middle;
it is pale, although distinct, especially on the anterior pair; the
lateral edges of the abdomen are black, but there are no black
stripes on the posterior portion of the segments; the spot at the
tip of the first longitudinal vein is entire, not ring-like; the
gray band at the tip of the wing and the dilated clouds along
the posterior margin are much darker; on the humeri there is a
large subtriangular brown spot, almost occupying the whole space
which is yellow in *L. cinctipes*; the pleura are darker; the basis
and the tip of the halteres are pale, the whole intermediate space
being dusky.

Hab. Washington, D. C., in May; Upper Wisconsin River
(Kennicott); Maine (Packard).

In this species, the fork formed by the subcostal cross-vein with the tip of the auxillary vein, usually has the posterior branch (ending in the first longitudinal vein) distinctly longer than the anterior one (ending in the costa).

8. L. solitaria O. S. ♂ and ♀.—Thorax vittâ mediâ pallidâ, fusco marginatâ; halterum capitulo infuscato; alæ fusco-maculatæ et nubulosæ, in cellulâ basali primâ serie punctorum fuscorum; venula transversalis marginalis juxta apicem venæ longitudinalis primæ sita.

Thorax with a pale intermediate stripe, margined with brown; knob of the halteres infuscated; wings spotted and clouded with brown; a series of brown dots in the first basal cell; the marginal cross-vein at the tip of the first longitudinal vein. Long. corp. 0.4—0.5.

Syn. *Limnobia militaris* O. Sackes, Proc. Ac. Nat. Sc. Phil. 1859, p. 215.

Rostrum and palpi infuscated; front with a yellowish cinereous reflection; vertex infuscated, with a yellow line in the middle; antennæ brown; first joint yellow; the two or three following yellowish at the basis, infuscated at the tip. Thorax yellow.; in the middle a pale yellowish stripe margined with brown; these brown margins are more or less broad, so as to invade sometimes nearly the whole stripe, except a yellowish line in the middle; two lateral brown stripes, extended beyond the suture behind; scutellum and metathorax pale yellowish, sericeous, both with lateral brown spots; halteres with brown knobs; femora with a brown band at the tip, preceded by a pale one; tibiæ and tarsi yellowish tawny, the former infuscated at the tip, the latter beyond the tip of the first joint. Abdomen yellowish-ferruginous; an indistinct brown band, formed by a series of spots, in the middle of the back; genitals pale; male forceps like Tab. III, fig. 6; the oripositor has the horny transverse piece, to which the upper valves are fastened, very broad and stout; this causes the basal portion of the valves to appear more divergent. Wings yellowish, with brown spots and clouds; an oblique spot extends from the inner end of the stigma to the inner end of the submarginal cell; the posterior end of the stigma is likewise infuscated; a series of brown dots begins with one at the inner corner of the first basal cell and extends more or less far along the middle of this cell; they are more or less numerous; sometimes eight or nine, reaching the inner end of the submarginal cell, sometimes only two or three at the inner end of the basal cell; the spot nearest to the cloud at the origin of the præfurca is often the

largest of them; there is a pale brownish band across the apical portion of the wing and some clouds along the posterior margin.
Hab. Trenton Falls, N. Y.; White Mountains, N. H.; Maine (Packard); northwestern regions of the Hudson's Bay Territory (Kennicott).

In the five male specimens which I have before me, the auxiliary vein ends in the costa a little beyond the inner end of the stigma, and the cross-vein is somewhat anterior to the tip of this vein. Thus, the fork formed by them has its anterior branch longer than the posterior one (the opposite is the case in most specimens of *L. immatura*). The two female specimens in my possession do not show these characters; both branches of the fork, above alluded to, are of the same length, and the anterior one does not reach beyond the inner end of the stigma.

4. L. hudsonica O. S. ♀.—Thorax vittis quatuor; halteres capitulo fusco; alae fusco maculatis et nebulosae; maculis obscure fuscis; in cellula basali primâ maculâ quatuor magnae, fere aequidistantes; venula transversa marginalis juxta apicem venae longitudinalis primae sita.

Thorax with four brown stripes; knob of the halteres brown; wings with brown spots and clouds; the spots dark brown; the first basal cell contains four large, nearly equidistant spots; the marginal cross-vein is at the tip of the first longitudinal vein. Long. corp. 0.5.

Syn. *Limnobia hudsonica* O. Sacken, Proc. Ac. Nat. Sc. Phil. 1861, p. 289.

Head blackish above, with a cinereous bloom; vertex with a yellow line in the middle; rostrum and palpi brown; antennae brown; first joint yellowish-ferruginous; the two following likewise, but more or less marked with brown. Thorax brownish-yellow, with four brown stripes; the intermediate ones are separated by a yellowish line, which is gradually widened anteriorly; pleurae mixed with yellowish and brown; halteres with a brown knob. Abdomen reddish-yellow, apparently with brownish bands on the posterior segments. Wings with deep brown spots along the anterior margin; the first is at the inner end of the two basal cells; its hindmost tip, which is in the second basal cell, is connected with a second spot in the first basal cell; the third spot, at the origin of the praefurca, is trapezoidal, its oblique sides being somewhat emarginate; the fourth forms an oblique band between the inner end of the submarginal cell and the anterior margin; the fifth and last is at the posterior end of the stigma.

The remaining portion of the wing is clouded with brown, as in the three preceding species, only these clouds are darker.

Hab. Slave Lake, H. B. T. (Kennicott).

I have only a single female, the feet of which are broken off and the abdomen somewhat injured in its coloring. The infuscated knob of the halteres and the coloring of the intermediate stripe of the thorax prove the relationship of this species to *L. solitaria.* The structure of the antennae, the joints of which are comparatively shorter and stouter in *L. hudsonica,* and that of the ovipositor, which is not so broad at the basis, prove to my satisfaction that this is not a darker variety of *L. solitaria.* The anterior branch of the fork, formed by the tip of the auxiliary vein with the subcostal cross-vein, is longer than the posterior one.

In the *Proc. Acad. Nat. Sci. Philad.* 1861, p. 290, I have tried to establish differences between the four above described, closely allied species, based upon the shape of the fork formed by the tip of the auxiliary vein with the subcostal cross-vein. These differences are not entirely reliable, however, as I have had occasion to convince myself since. I possess, moreover, several northern specimens of a doubtful character, which prove either that the number of the species belonging here will have to be enlarged, or that the typical forms of the species, such as I have described them, undergo considerable modifications.

5. L. triocellata O. S. ♂ and ♀.—Flavo-ferruginea, thorace lineis et punctis nigris; alis flavescentes, ocellis tribus parvis fuscis; venula transversa marginalis juxta apicem primae longitudinalis sita.

Yellowish-ferruginous, thorax with black lines and dots; wings yellowish, with three small brown eye-like spots; marginal cross-vein at the tip of the first longitudinal vein. Long. corp. 0.35—0.4.

Syn. *Limnobia triocellata* O. Sacken, Proc. Ac. Nat. Sc. Phil. 1859, p. 216.

Rostrum and palpi brown; antennae pale ferruginous-yellow; front slightly hoary; vertex yellow. Thorax ferruginous-yellow, shining above; collare long, with a longitudinal brown stripe in the middle; on the mesonotum, two short, brown lines near the collare and four brown spots before the suture; a brown dot on the humerus; pleurae yellow, slightly hoary, with two or three brown dots between the fore coxae and the root of the wings; between the thoracic suture and the scutellum, two brown lines in the middle and a dot on each side; metathorax with brown

marks in the four corners; halteres pale, with brown knobs; feet
ferruginous-yellow, hairy; tips of the femora and last joints of the
tarsi brownish. Abdomen ferruginous-yellow, margins of the segments brown. Wings tinged with yellow; subcostal cell more
saturate yellow; a brown ring at the origin of the præfurca;
another, smaller one at the inner end of the subcostal cell; a
third, sometimes indistinct one, at the posterior end of the
stigma; the anterior end is also marked with a brown spot; a
brown shade along the margin of the wing, between the stigma
and the apex; tips of the longitudinal veins clouded; a small
brown cloud at the inner end of the first basal cell. Tip of the
auxiliary vein opposite the inner end of the submarginal cell;
the cross-vein at this tip.
Hab. Washington, D. C.; Trenton Falls, N. Y.; Upper Wisconsin River (Kennicott). July, August.

6. L. parietina O. S. ♂ and ♀.—Fuscescens, thorace fusco-vittato;
alis longis, venus apicem latis; earum tubulis, strigis et maculis pallido
fuscis; stigmate pallido, longo; venulis transversa marginali ab auxiliaris et primæ longitudinalis apicibus æque distans.

Brownish, thorax with brown stripes; wings long, broad towards the apex;
with pale brown clouds, streaks, and spots; stigma long, pale; the
marginal cross-vein at an equal distance from the tips of the auxiliary
and of the first longitudinal veins. Long. corp. 0.6—0.65.

Syn. *Limnobia parietina* O. Sacken, Proc. Ac. Nat. Sc. Phila. 1861, p. 239.

Head, rostrum, and palpi dark brown; antennæ pale, joints
of the flagellum brown at the basis. Thorax yellowish, sericeous,
with three brown stripes; the intermediate one is divided in two
by a longitudinal pale, sometimes hardly apparent line; scutellum,
metathorax, and pleurae brownish; halteres infuscated, whitish at
the tip; feet tawny, tip of the femora brown; a pale band before
it; tarsi brown. Abdomen brownish, posterior margins of the
segments and a longitudinal stripe along the middle of the back,
pale. Wings with clouds on all the cross-veins and with pale
brown irregular clouds, spots, and streaks in almost all the cells;
in the submarginal and the second posterior cells, these clouds
assume the shape of an inverted V; a trace of a similar figure is
visible in the third posterior cell. The stigma is very long, pale;
the marginal cross-vein is a little anterior to its middle, and nearly
in the middle of the distance between the tip of the auxiliary and

that of the first longitudinal vein. The outline of the wing is
peculiar, as it is hardly narrowed at all towards the apex.

Hab. Trenton Falls, N. Y.; on fences, in September, numerous
male and female specimens.

7. L. indigena O. S.   ♂ and ♀.—Flavescens; thorace vittis, abdomine fascia fascis; alis fusco-nebulosis; venula transversa marginali ab apice venæ longitudinalis primæ remota.

Yellowish, thorax with brown stripes, abdomen with brown bands; wings
clouded with brown; the marginal cross-vein at some distance from the
tip of the first longitudinal vein. Long. corp. 0.4—0.45.

Syn. *Limnobia indigena* O. Sacken, Proc. Ac. Nat. Sc. Phil. 1859, p. 215.

Head black, front with a silvery reflection; antennæ and palpi
black; first joint of the flagellum nearly twice the length of the
second. Thorax pale brownish-yellow, shining, with three dark
brown stripes, the intermediate one is double and does not quite
reach the transverse suture; scutellum dark brown with a yellow
line in the middle; metathorax brown; pleuræ with a brown
stripe, running from the basis of the wings to the intermediate
coxæ; a large brown spot anterior to the basis of the halteres;
the latter pale yellow, faintly infuscated in the middle of the
stem; feet yellowish-tawny, with two brown bands on the femora
and a pale one between them; tip of the tibiæ and the tarsi infuscated. Abdomen brown; base of the second and of the following segments with a broad yellow band; forceps of the male like
Tab. III, fig. 7. Wings tinged with yellowish, stigma brown;
central cross-veins clouded with brown; three brown clouds form
an interrupted and more or less distinct band, in the middle of
the first basal cell, on the fifth longitudinal vein and across the
anal and axillary cells; veins in the apical portion of the wing
all margined with fuscous; the marginal cross-vein is anterior to
the middle of the stigma.

Hab. Maine (Packard); Upper Wisconsin River (Kennicott);
Washington, D. C.; New York. May, June.

8. L. tristigma O. S.   ♂ and ♀.—Ferrugineo-flava, capite nigro,
thoracis vittâ fuscâ; alis flavescentibus immaculatis, nebulis quatuor
marginalibus parvis, pallido fuscis; venula transversa marginali ab
apice venæ longitudinalis primæ remota.

Ferruginous-yellowish, head black, thorax with a brown stripe; wings

yellowish, immaculate, with four small brown clouds along the anterior
margin; the marginal cross-vein at some distance from the tip of the
first longitudinal vein. Long. corp. 0.4.—0.45.

812. *Limnobia tristigma* O. Sacken, Proc. Entom. Soc. Phil. 1859, p. 216.

Head, rostrum, and palpi black, front slightly hoary; the first
antennal joint black at the root, yellow towards the tip; the following four or five joints pale yellow; the remainder of the joints
infuscated at the basis. Thorax pale ferruginous; a broad brown
stripe extends over the collare and the anterior part of the mesonotum; halteres yellow, slightly brownish at the tip; feet yellowish-tawny; femora with two brown bands, one beyond the middle,
the other near the tip. Abdomen yellow. Wings yellowish;
stigma pale, infuscated at both ends; a small rounded cloud at
the tip of the auxiliary vein; another one, but much paler, at the
origin of the præfurca; the stigmatical cross-vein is in the middle
of the stigma, at some distance from the tip of the first longitudinal vein.

Hab. Near Chicago, Ill., in July, 1859, five male and six female
specimens.

This species is somewhat like the European *L. tripunctata*
Fab.; only in the latter the marginal cross-vein is infuscated,
and not the two ends of the stigma; the three clouds are also
much darker than in *L. tristigma*.

D. L. sociabilis, n. sp. ♀.—Ochracea, fronte et abdomine supreme
infuscatis; thorace vitta fusca; alis immaculatis; venula marginali
transversa ab apice venæ longitudinalis mediæ remota.

Ochraceous, front and the abdomen above, infuscated; thorax with a brown
stripe; wings immaculate; the marginal cross-vein is at a moderate
distance from the tip of the first longitudinal vein. Long. corp. 0.35.

Head yellow; rostrum and palpi likewise; front and a part
of the vertex infuscated; antennæ yellow. Thorax ochraceous-
yellow, shining above, with a broad brown stripe extending over
the collare and the middle of the mesonotum; vestiges of lateral
stripes, coalescing with the intermediate one; scutellum and metathorax brownish in the middle. Halteres brownish-ochraceous,
paler at the base. Abdomen brownish above, yellow on the under
side; ovipositor with remarkably straight upper valves. Wings
yellowish, immaculate; the marginal cross-vein is a little beyond

the middle of the stigma, and hence nearer the tip of the first
longitudinal vein than in the preceding species.

Hab. Illinois (Kennicott); a single female. The feet are
wanting and the thorax is somewhat injured by the pin; but the
species can never be mistaken for any other.

———————

The following species from California has not been included in
the dichotomical table on page 87 :—

10. L. californica O. S. ♀.—Thoracis vittis quatuor fuscis ; alis
fuscescentibus, pallide fenestratis, margine antico maculis quatuor fuscis.

Thorax with four brown stripes ; wings brownish, with some subhyaline
spaces ; anterior margin with four brown spots. Long. corp. 0.7—0.8.

Syn. *Limnobia californica* O. Sacken, Proc. Ac. Nat. Sc. Phil. 1861, p. 268.

Front and vertex brown ; under side of the head yellow ;
rostrum, palpi, and antennæ brown ; two basal joints of the latter
yellow. Thorax yellowish, mixed with brown ; the two intermediate thoracic stripes are narrow, parallel ; at their anterior
end, they coalesce with the brown margin of the mesonotum,
which is broadest at the humeri ; pleuræ, scutellum, and metathorax more or less tinged with brownish ; basis and tip of the
halteres pale, the intermediate portion infuscated ; femora brownish ; a yellow band before the tip, which is black ; tibiæ ferruginous-brownish, brown at the tip ; tarsi ferruginous-brownish at
the basis, the remainder brown. Wings with a uniform brownish
tinge ; four large brown spots along the anterior margin ; the
first at the inner end of the first basal cell ; the second, somewhat
trapezoidal in shape, at the origin of the præfurca ; both do not
cross the first longitudinal vein, and do not, therefore, reach the
anterior margin ; the second is limited posteriorly by the fourth
longitudinal vein ; the third spot is double, consisting of an
oblique spot which begins at the margin, just beyond the tip of
the auxiliary vein and coalesces with a round spot at the inner
end of the submarginal cell ; the fourth spot is at the tip of the
first longitudinal vein ; it is semi-oval and is inclosed between
the costa and the second longitudinal vein ; there are several
subhyaline spots on the surface of the wing ; a large angular one,
beginning about the middle of the anal cell and reaching the

posterior margin at the tip of the seventh longitudinal vein; in
the second basal cell (near the great cross-vein); in the discal
cell; at the tip of the wing and on both sides of the fourth brown
spot; a subbyaline longitudinal streak crosses the second brown
spot in the first basal cell, and the round spot at the inner end
of the submarginal cell is encircled in pale. The subcostal cross-
vein is almost in one line with the tip of the auxiliary vein.

Hab. California (Mr. Alex. Agassiz). A single male.

This species belongs to the relationship of *L. cinctipes* and
immatura, but is easily distinguished by its larger size and by
its brownish wings, marked with subbyaline spots.

Gen. V. TROCHOBOLA.

One submarginal cell; four posterior cells; a discal cell; the tip of the
auxiliary vein is far beyond the origin of the second longitudinal vein;
the marginal cross-vein is some distance anterior to the tip of the first
longitudinal vein; *a supernumerary cross-vein connects the sixth and seventh
longitudinal veins* (wing, Tab. I, fig. 4). Antennæ 14-jointed. Feet slender;
tibiæ without spurs at the tip; empodia individual; ungues with teeth on
the under side.

Trochobola is most closely allied to the *Limnobiæ* of the
second group (those with the marginal cross-vein removed from
the tip of the first longitudinal vein); like these species, it has
pictured wings, brown bands on the femora, a long auxiliary
vein, etc. But it is easily distinguished from them by the
presence of a supernumerary cross-vein. The antennæ have less
elongated joints, and look almost moniliform; the feet are more
slender than in the majority of the *Limnobiæ*; the structure of
the male forceps is somewhat intermediate between *Limnobia*
and *Dicranomyia*; the fleshy lobes of the latter are somewhat
reduced in size here and the rostriform appendage is comparatively larger. (A figure of this forceps has been given by me in
the *Stett. Entom. Zeitschr.* 1854, Tab. I, fig. 1; it represents the
forceps of the European *T. annulata* Lin.)

The number of species belonging to this genus is small, they
have a remarkable distribution all over the world, and they all
(as far as known) have the same eye-like spots on the wings. *T.
annulata* Lin. (*imperialis* Lw.) and *T. cæsarea* O. S. (perhaps
only a variety of the former), occur in northern Europe. *T.
argus* Say, is almost identical with the former. I have seen, in

the British Museum, numerous specimens of *Trochobola* from New Holland, Van Diemen's Land, and New Zealand, showing that they are quite common there; one of them, marked *Limnobia tessellata* White, which I examined, showed precisely the same distribution of the spots on the wings as *T. imperialis* or *argus*; I did not notice, however, whether the other specimens belonged to the same species or not.

In the *Proc. Philad. Entomol. Soc.* 1865, p. 226, I had proposed for this group the name of *Discobola*, which, being preoccupied, is replaced here by *Trochobola* (from τροχός, a wheel, and βάλλω, I throw).

1. **T. argus** Say. ♂ and ♀.—*Fuscano-flavida*; alis fusco ocellatis.

Brownish-yellow, wings with ocellate brown spots (Tab. I, fig. 4). Long. corp. 0.25—0.3.

Syn. *Limnobia argus* Say, Long's Exped. Append. p. 358.—Wiedemann, Auss. Zw. I, p. 33, 17.—O. Sacken, Proc. Ac. Nat. Sc. Phil. 1859, p. 217.

Head, rostrum, palpi, and antennae black; thorax yellowish with three brown stripes above; the intermediate double; pleuræ with two brown stripes; halteres with a brown band across the stem; knob likewise brown; abdomen brownish, genitals paler; feet yellowish; femora with a brown band at some distance from the tip; tip of the tibiæ and last joints of the tarsi infuscated. Wings yellowish or whitish, with brown, ocellate spots especially along the anterior and posterior margins; the centre of these spots, forming the pupil of the eye, is likewise infuscated; these centres are mostly placed at the origin or at the tip of the longitudinal veins, or upon cross-veins: thus a complete ocellus has the origin of the præfurca for its centre; a double one surrounds, as centres, the inner end of the submarginal cell and the small cross-vein; other centres of less complete ocelli are the tip of the seventh longitudinal vein and the supernumerary cross-vein, existing there; likewise the tip of the sixth vein and the inner end of the fifth basal cell; the apical portion of the wing contains several more ocelli, more or less distinctly marked in different specimens and giving that portion of the wing a variegated appearance.

Hab. Northwestern Territory (Say); Nova Scotia (British

Museum); Trenton Falls, N. Y.; Maine (Packard); Massachusetts (Scudder); Orange, N. Y.

This species is somewhat variable in its size, the intensity of the coloring, and the distinctness of the spots on the wings. I possess a specimen from Fort Simpson, H. B. T. (Kennicott), which is altogether brownish; the thorax is brown, somewhat yellowish sericeous above, without any apparent stripes; halteres brownish, pale at the basis only; the ocellate spots on the wings are the same as usual, but much darker and somewhat broader, thus imparting a darker coloring to the whole wing. The European *T. annulata* Lin. (*imperialis* Loew, *Linn. Entom.* V, p. 703, Tab. II, fig. 14–15) is hardly more distinct from *T. argus*, than some of the varieties of the latter are one from another. A closer observation will have to teach us what to make of these modifications of the same typical form.

Section II. LIMNOBINA ANOMALA.

One submarginal cell; normal number of the antennal joints sixteen.

This group is meant to be an artificial one, and for this reason I do not add anything to its short character. The brevipalpous *Tipulidæ* with a single submarginal cell and the antennæ of which, at the same time, count 16 joints, never fail to show, as far as hitherto observed, very striking peculiarities of structure, requiring their separation from the very compact and natural section of the true *Limnobina* with fourteen-jointed antennæ.

Thus the genera *Dicranoptycha, Orimarga, Atarba, Teucholabis,* and *Styringomyia* have distinct empodia; a character altogether foreign to the *Limnobina;* moreover, each of these genera possesses characters in the venation, in the structure of the forceps of the male or of the antennæ, which abundantly justify its separation from the *Limnobina.*

Rhamphidia, Toxorrhina, Elephantomyia, Antocha, Elliptera, and *Thaumastoptera* have no distinct empodia; nevertheless, their structural peculiarities are such, that the expediency of their separation from the *Limnobina* will not be disputed.

The link connecting these genera is purely artificial; but experience has proved that the establishment of this group, proposed by me in 1859, is very useful in the system, by collecting under one head a number of genera which would not find a fitting position in any other section. The genera belonging here have but a very limited number of species; most of them are comparatively rare, and, for this reason, as yet little known. Large additions to this group are therefore to be still expected, and these additions may develop links of relationship, not suspected now, as much between already known genera, as even with some of the other sections of the *Tipulidæ brevipalpi.*

Whether the absence of spurs at the tip of the tibiæ, which distinguishes all the known genera of *Limnobina anomala*,[1] is an indication of some degree of relationship, is as yet uncertain. Until future discoveries disclose the hidden links of relationship between these genera, we can perceive a distinct connection between three genera only, *Rhamphidia, Elephantomyia,* and *Toxorrhina*, which I have, for this reason, united in the subsection *Rhamphidina*, treated separately at the end of this paragraph. The genera *Dicranoptycha, Orimarga, Elliptera,* and *Antocha* show a certain obscure relationship to each other, especially in the venation. *Atarba* and *Teucholabis* seem to be isolated forms. A character worthy of notice in several genera belonging to the *Limnobina anomala* is the tendency of the veins near the costa to coalesce with each other. The first and second veins are very closely approximated in *Elliptera* and *Dicranoptycha*; in *Antocha* the first longitudinal vein coalesces very early with the costa, and in *Toxorrhina* the second vein seems to be entirely absorbed by the first; the latter portion of the first is coalescent with the costa. A similar coalescence is observable in *Styringomyia*. In the present state of our knowledge we cannot judge yet of the importance of these analogies.

Eleven genera constitute this group at present; three of which belong to the subsection *Rhamphidina*. Of the remaining eight genera two (*Dicranoptycha* and *Antocha*) are common to Europe and to North America; three have been found as yet only in Europe (*Orimarga, Elliptera, Thaumastoptera*); two only in America (*Teucholabis* and *Atarba*), and one is found included in amber and copal (*Styringomyia*).

Subsection RHAMPHIDINA.

One submarginal cell (none in *Toxorrhina*); four posterior cells; a discal cell; no marginal cross-vein; normal number of antennal joints sixteen (through the coalescence of the basal joints of the flagellum, 15 or 12). Tibiæ without spurs at the tip. Ungues smooth on the under side. Empodia indistinct or none.[*] Rostrum conspicuously prolonged.

The absence of any vestige of a marginal cross-vein, however unimportant it may appear as a character, acquires its significance by its constancy and its concomitance, in the three genera, with

---

[1] Except perhaps *Atarba*, about which I am in doubt.

a prolonged rostrum. In other respects, the venation of *Rhamphidia* and *Elephantomyia* is very like that of *Limnobia*; but the smooth ungues of both genera and the number of antennal joints of *Rhamphidia* (the same number existing in *Elephantomyia*, only atrophied) exclude them from among the *Limnobina*.

The most remarkable circumstance, connected with these genera, is their geographical distribution. *Rhamphidia* alone is common to Europe and America; *Toxorrhina* occurs in North and South America, and *Elephantomyia* has hitherto been found in North America only. But the principal prevalence of *Rhamphidia* and *Elephantomyia* seems to have taken place in the period of the amber fauna. According to Mr. Loew (*Bernstein u. Bernsteinfauna*, p. 87) four species of *Rhamphidia* and three of *Elephantomyia* (not distinguished by him from *Toxorrhina*, compare below in these two genera) have been already discovered in amber; a large number, considering the very fragmentary character of our knowledge of the amber fauna, and the small number of the species of these genera in the present age.

Being in possession of a lump of copal, from Zanzibar, in which a specimen of *Styringomyia* is included, I take occasion to give a description of this genus, to complete the statements of Mr. Loew in the *Dipterologische Beiträge*, I. p. 8. This author discovered his specimen in the same substance; another species had been previously found by him in amber (Loew, *Bernst. und Bernsteinfauna*, p. 31 and 38). The name of the genus is apparently derived from συριγξ, a kind of tree-gum.

Styringomyia Loew.—One submarginal cell, the peculiar, subtriangular shape of which depends on the abnormal course of the first and second longitudinal veins, as the former coalesces with the costa before the middle of the anterior margin: the latter, originating from the first vein a little before this point of convergence, is suddenly incurved towards the costa a little beyond the middle of the anterior margin; the auxiliary vein is not perceptible; four posterior cells; a discal cell. Feet comparatively short, stout, hairy. Tibiae without spurs at the tip; empodia distinct. Antennae 16-jointed.

The subjoined figure of the wing is copied from that of Mr. Loew. My specimen is but very little different: the second vein is still more abruptly turned towards the costa, its latter section assuming the appearance of a cross-vein; the præfurca is almost in one line with the third longitudinal vein; the second posterior cell is square at the basis and not attenuated; a trace of a brownish

Fig. 2.

cross-band is distinctly perceptible along the central cross-veins; the cross-veins at the basis of the two intermediate posterior cells are likewise infuscated. The following details not being distinctly visible in my specimen are copied from the description of Mr. Loew: "Palpi short, first joint short-cylindrical, the second a little longer, somewhat incrassated, ovate; the third of about the same length, more slender, cylindrical, the last joint perceptibly longer than the preceding, styliform; the whole palpi are beset with stiff, scattered hairs. The antennæ are not quite as long as head and thorax taken together; first joint elongated-cylindrical, the second pyriform, not very stout; the 14 joints of the flagellum are ovate, of diminishing length and stoutness, beset with short hairs and with longer verticels near the basis. The ovipositor is very short and ends in two sharp points."

The resemblance of the venation of *Styringomyia* to that of *Toxorrhina* is very striking, and shows itself in the course of the first and of the second longitudinal veins. If we suppress the section of the latter vein which runs towards the costa, we obtain a venation almost exactly similar to that of *Toxorrhina*. Whether this resemblance is indicative of relationship I am not prepared to say.

Gen. VI. RHAMPHIDIA.

One submarginal cell; four posterior cells; a discal cell; no marginal cross-vein. The tip of the auxiliary vein is at some distance beyond the origin of the second vein; the subcostal cross-vein is close at this tip. Rostrum elongated, but shorter than the thorax; last joint of the palpi elongated. Antennæ 16-jointed. Tibiæ without spurs at the tip; empodia indistinct; ungues smooth. The forceps of the male very like that of *Elephantomyia*.

The rostrum of the European *R. longirostris* is longer than the head and about equal to the distance between the collare and the root of the wings; that of the North American species is but slightly longer than the head. The palpi are inserted at its tip; their two first joints are very short, the third but little longer, the fourth linear, slender, about as long as the first three taken together; when at rest, its tip, pointing backwards, reaches but very little beyond the root of the first joint (observed on the N. A. species, when alive; Meigen's Tab. LXV, fig. 8, gives a correct idea of the palpi). Front narrow; eyes almost contiguous on the under side of the head. The antennæ, when bent backwards, hardly reach the root of the wings; flagellum somewhat incrassated at the basis, its joints subcylindrical, short, becoming more elongated towards the tip; verticils moderately long. Collare somewhat broad, prolonged in a short, but distinct neck. Thoracic suture deep. Feet long, slender, very finely pubescent; the interval between the two last tarsal joints is excised on the under side in the male. Wings moderately long and broad, but comparatively smaller in the American species; the tip of the auxiliary vein is opposite the inner end of the submarginal cell; in some specimens the subcostal cross-vein is obsolete; in such cases the auxiliary vein ends in the first longitudinal and not in the costa; the second longitudinal vein originates about the middle of the length of the wing; the præfurca is less than half of the whole length of the second vein and very gently arcuated, nearly straight; the third longitudinal vein is arcuated, which causes the submarginal cell to be much broader at the tip than at its inner end; the latter is, in some specimens, in contact with the discal cell, the small cross-vein being obliterated; this happens with the European, as well as with the North American species; the majority of the specimens, however, have a short, but distinct cross-vein; the discal cell is nearly square; the fifth, sixth, and seventh longitudinal veins are nearly straight; the stigma is oval, distinctly marked, but there is no trace of a marginal cross-vein.

The close relationship between *Rhamphidia* and *Elephantomyia* is evident; the shorter and stouter rostrum and the longer palpi of the former are the only important differences. The venation, including the absence of the marginal cross-vein, is almost the same; the forceps has the same structure; even the coloring of the North American species is remarkably like that of *E. westwoodi*.

In the preceding description I have compared the European

R. longirostris and the North American *R. flavipes* Macq., not having seen the one or two other species which are said to occur in Europe (compare Schiner, *Fauna Austr.* Vol. II, p. 558). In the Berlin Museum I have seen a Brazilian species and another remarkable species, without indication of the locality, the tarsi of which are white. These species agree with the typical one in the absence of the marginal cross-vein.

Four species are recorded by Mr. Loew (*Bernst. und Bernsteinfauna*, p. 37) as occurring in the Prussian amber. This would prove that this genus was much more abundantly represented in that fauna than it is now. I have not seen these species, and am not sure whether they belong to *Rhamphidia*, within the sense of my definition of it.

The genus *Rhamphidia* (from ῥαμφος, rostrum) was introduced by Meigen, in 1830 (in his VIth vol.); one year earlier, however, Mr. Stephens proposed for the European *R. longirostris* the generic name of *Leptorhina* (*Stephens, Catal.* etc. 1829), which has never been in use since. Still earlier, in 1825, Saint Fargeau (*Encyclopédie Méthodique, Insectes,* Vol. X, p. 585) proposed for this genus the name *Megarhina,* which he subsequently changed to *Helius* (in the Index to the same volume, p. 831). The claims of the name given by Meigen, strengthened as they are by long usage, cannot well be disputed.

1. R. flavipes Macq.   ♂ and ♀.—Femorum, tibiarumque apicibus obscure fuscis; alarum apice infuscato.

Tip of the femora and of the tibia dark brown; apex of the wings clouded with brown. Long. corp. 0.27—0.24.

Syn. *Rhamphidia flavipes* Macq. Dipt. Exot. 1e Suppl. p. 17 (1855).
Rhamphidia prominens Walk. Dipt. Saunders. p. 435 (1856).
Rhamphidia brevirostris O. Sacken, Proc. Ac. Nat. Sc. Phil. 1859, p. 222.

Head grayish-brown, rostrum but little longer than the head, brown; palpi brown; antennae brown at the base, flagellum paler. Thorax ochraceous, or brownish, with the usual stripes more or less distinctly marked; halteres pale, sometimes slightly brownish; feet pale yellow; tips of the femora and of the tibiae dark brown, almost black; tips of the tarsi also darker. Abdomen ochraceous or brownish; the anterior part of the segments darker; the genitals brownish. Wings hyaline, infuscated at the tip; stigma well marked, brown; costal and first longitudinal veins yellowish; the other veins brown (compare the generic character for more details about the venation).

Hab. Washington, D. C., in May; New York; White Mountains, N. H.; Wisconsin (Uhler); Illinois (Walsh); South Carolina (Mus. Berol).

This species varies in its coloring from ochraceous to brownish; Mr. Macquart drew his description from a dark specimen, whereas I had a light-colored specimen before me, when I described this species under a different name in 1859. I have since then recognized my error. Mr. Walker's *R. prominens*, some slight discrepancies in the description notwithstanding, is certainly the same species.

Gen. VII. ELEPHANTOMYIA.

One submarginal cell; four posterior cells; a discal cell; no marginal cross-vein; the tip of the auxiliary vein is at some distance beyond the origin of the second longitudinal vein; the subcostal cross-vein is close at this tip (Tab. I, fig. 5). *Rostrum almost as long as the body, very slender, filiform; the elongated, but minute palpi are inserted at its tip.* Antennæ apparently 16 jointed; all the joints of the flagellum are provided with verticils. Tibiæ without spurs at the tip. Empodia indistinct. Ungues smooth. The forceps of the male consists of the usual basal pieces with two horny, claw-shaped appendages each (Tab. III, fig. 9, one-half of the forceps of *E. westwoodi*).

The eyes are large, glabrous, leaving a very narrow, linear front between them above, and a somewhat broader space below. The rostrum is quite as long as the body in the male, and comparatively shorter in the female, on account of the greater length of its abdomen; it is straight in the living specimens, but becomes arcuated in the dead ones; it is finely pubescent and perfectly linear in its shape, from its root to the tip. The palpi are inserted close by this tip; they are attenuated at their basis. Not having had an opportunity to examine these palpi under a compound microscope, on living specimens, I refer to the observations and the fine figures published by Mr. Loew in *Linn. Entom.* Vol. V, p. 400, Tab. II, fig. 19, 20, 21. They are taken from three fossil species, found in amber, which apparently belong to the genus *Elephantomyia*. The palpi of *E. westwoodi* resemble Mr. Loew's fig. 20 most.

The antennæ, if bent backwards, would hardly reach the root of the wings; the first joint is comparatively shorter than usual; the second is rounded; the basal joint of the flagellum is elongated and stout, being apparently formed by the coalescence of two joints; the following joints are subcylindrical, more elongated towards the tip of the antennæ and beset with rather long verticils. Collare well developed; its neck short; thoracic suture well marked. The feet are long and slender, finely pubescent; the ungues are somewhat broad at the basis; the usual excision on the under side between the two last tarsal joints is apparent in the male. Wings moderately long and broad (Tab. I, fig. 5); tip of the auxiliary vein nearly opposite the inner end of the submarginal cell; the second longitudinal vein originates a little beyond the middle of the length of the wing; the præfurca is arcuated, short, not more in length than about one-third of the remaining portion of the second vein; the latter is nearly parallel to the third vein, and both are arcuated; thus the submarginal cell is of nearly equal breadth; the first posterior is only a little shorter than the submarginal; the discal cell is nearly square; the great cross-vein is usually opposite its middle; the fifth, sixth, and seventh veins are nearly straight; the stigma is oval, distinctly marked, and there is no trace of a marginal cross-vein.

The ovipositor of the female has rather long, narrow valves; the upper ones are very slightly arcuated.

This genus (the name from ἐλέφας, elephant, and μυῖα, fly) was introduced by me in the *Proc. Acad. Nat. Sci. Philad.* 1859, p. 220, and based upon a species which, at that time, I believed to be one described by Mr. Westwood, but which proved afterwards to be new. This is the only living species of the genus at present known; but the three species included in amber and mentioned by Mr. Loew as *Tanorrhinæ* (*Linn. Entom.* Vol. V), apparently belong to this genus.

Observation.—The statements of Mr. Loew (l. c. p. 394) about the "perfect agreement in the generic characters" (vollständige Uebereinstimmung in den generischen Merkmalen) between these fossil species and *Tanorrhina fragilis* from Porto Rico rests upon an oversight of the important difference between them: the absence of the submarginal cell in the latter. I have been able to ascertain this from the drawings of the fossil *Elephantomyia*, which Mr. Loew kindly showed me; but I have not seen the specimens themselves. The drawings of which I had a glimpse, showed a wing like *Elephantomyia*, that is, with a submarginal cell. Further in-

formation about the three fossil species may be gathered from the article
in the *Linnæa*. As Mr. Loew believed the antennæ of his specimens of
Tœorrhina fragilis to be injured at the tip (he could count only 2+10
joints, which is the real number, whereas he expected that they should
have 3+13, like the fossil species), he introduces the description of the
antennæ of the fossil species thus (l. c. p. 400): "I found the antennæ
of two of the fossil species 3+13 jointed, while I could count only 12
joints on the flagellum of the third; all the species have the two joints
of the scapus short and stout; the first joint of the flagellum likewise is
rather large and stout, more or less egg-shaped, the following joints are
of a similar shape, but smaller; afterwards they become more slender
and gradually more elongated; besides some very short hairs, the joints
of the flagellum have sparse verticillate hairs, which, in all the species,
become perceptibly longer on the last antennal joints." Thus, the fossil
species, like *Elephantomyia*, have 13-jointed antennæ (an unusual number,
as we know, among the *Tip. brevipalpi*); the third joint is strikingly
increased, and, as I have shown above, represents the coalescence of two
joints; the fossil species, like *Elephantomyia*, have verticils on all the
joints, whereas in *Tœorrhina*, only the two last joints are provided with
long hairs; the rest of the description of the antennæ of the fossil species
applies equally well to the antennæ of *Elephantomyia*. Another passage
is likewise important: "The venation (of *Tœr. fragilis*) is also peculiar in
several respects; I advert especially to the direction of the veins in the
vicinity of the root of the wing and to the connexion between the antepenultimate and the penultimate longitudinal veins; the latter does not
take place in the fossil species in a similar degree; in these species the
first longitudinal vein does not coalesce towards its end with the costa (as
it does in *T. fragilis*) and the great cross-vein is farther removed from the
root of the wing." If we compare the statement of these differences
between *T. fragilis* and the fossil species with the differences existing
between the *Tœorrhina*, described below, and the *Elephantomyia westwoodi*,
we will find them confirmed in every particular. What is called the connexion between the 5th and 6th longitudinal veins, will be shown below
(in the genus *Tœorrhina*) to be merely apparent, and to arise from the
close approximation between the basal portions of these veins (compare
Tab. I, fig. 6, the wing of *Tœorrhina*). This appearance does not exist
in *Elephantomyia* (Tab. I, fig. 5), which, like Mr. Loew's fossil species, has
the two veins more divergent. The peculiar course of the first longitudinal
vein, coalescing towards its end, with the costa, will also be described
under the head of *Tœorrhina*; in *Elephantomyia westwoodi*, as in the fossil
species, the mode of junction of the first and second veins is the ordinary
one. The great cross-vein, in both *Tœorrhina* described by me, is either
at the very basis of the discal cell, or before it; in *Elephantomyia*, it is
opposite the middle of the discal cell; again a point of agreement with
Mr. Loew's statement about the fossil species. The principal difference,
however, between the venation of *T. fragilis* and the fossil species, consisting in the absence of a submarginal cell in the former, is not mentioned

In Mr. Loew's comparison; but, as stated above, I have in this respect also confirmed the agreement of *Elephantomyia* with the fossil species.

The foregoing examination can, I think, leave no doubt about the generic identity of *Eleph. westwoodi* with the fossil species. Several years ago, I communicated to Mr. Loew specimens of my *Elephantomyia* for comparison. If he has discovered any difference between them and the fossil species, sufficient to place them in different genera, he will probably mention this difference in his forthcoming work on Amber-diptera.

1. E. westwoodi O. S. ♂ and ♀.—Ochraceus, femorum apice fusco, segmentis abdominis fusco-marginatis; stigmate alarum infoscato.

Ochraceous, tip of the femora brown, margins of the abdominal segments infuscated; stigma brownish. Long. corp. 0.3—0.35.

Syn. *Elephantomyia canadensis* O. Sacken (two Westw.), Proc. Ac. Nat. Sc. Phil. 1859, p. 221; the synonymy given there has to be stricken out.

Head yellow; rostrum finely pubescent; antennæ yellowish, with black verticils; basal joints, especially the second, more or less infuscated. Thorax yellow; a more or less distinct brown stripe runs along its middle and down the collare; in some specimens this stripe is obsolete; halteres pale; feet yellow; femora brown at the tip. Abdomen yellow; posterior margins of the segments brown; a more or less distinct brown stripe along the middle of the back; the last segment brown in the male; forceps tawny. Wings with a faint brownish tinge; a slight nebulosity along the apical margin (for more details compare the generic character).

Hab. Trenton Falls, N. Y., where I found this species in great numbers. At that time I took it for *Limnobiorhynchus canadensis* Westw., as the description of this species (*Ann. Soc. Entom. de Fr.* 1835, p. 683) agrees very well with the present one. But Mr. Westwood's species, which I have seen since in his own collection, is a *Geranomyia*, my *G. communis*; the *Elephantomyia* thus proving to be new, I dedicated this remarkable species to the author of an entomological work which is, as yet, without a rival for completeness, excellence of execution, and corresponding usefulness.

Gen. VIII. TOXORRHINA.

No submarginal cell; a discal cell, and four posterior cells; no marginal cross-vein. Rostrum very long, longer than head and thorax taken together;

palpi exceedingly minute, inserted at its tip. Antennæ very short, 12-
jointed: basal joint of the flagellum very stout; *the two apical joints only
are provided with long hairs.* Thorax elongated, extended anteriorly into a
long, cylindrical neck; mesonotum strongly projecting over the collare.
Tibiæ without spurs at the tip. Empodia indistinct or none.

The head is proportionally small; the antennæ are 12-jointed,
hardly longer than the head; the first joint is very short, and
still shorter in the male than in the female; the second is longer
and much stouter than the first, obconical; the third is increas-
sated, although less stout than the second joint; it seems to
represent the coalescence of several joints; it is more or less
rounded in the male, and more elongated, almost conical in the
female; the remainder of the antenna is filiform; the two apical
joints in the male are elongated, slender, and considerably longer
than the preceding joints, a difference which is not so striking in
the female; the intermediate joints are cylindrical, those nearer
to the stout basal joint of the flagellum are sometimes very short
and broader than long; the two joints of the scapus bear some
short bristles; the pubescence of the flagellum is almost imperceptible; the two apical joints only bear some long bristles, very
characteristic for the genus. The front is narrow in *T. magna*
and broader in *T. muliebris;* the eyes are slightly emarginate
on the inside, to leave room for the insertion of the antennæ and
very closely approximated, almost contiguous, on the under side
of the head. The palpi, inserted at the tip of the rostrum, are
exceedingly minute, and their joints seem to be almost coalescent;
they seem to be very like those of *Elephantomyia* (compare, as
to the structure of the palpi of this genus, Mr. Loew's figures,
Linn. Entom. V, Tab. II, fig. 12, 20, 21). The rostrum is
slender, perfectly linear, with an almost imperceptible pubescence;
both species described below have it about once and a half the
length of the head and thorax taken together.

The thorax is rather long, and remarkable for the great and unusual development of the mesosternum, in consequence of which
the fore coxæ are at a considerable distance from the intermediate
ones; the collare is entirely concealed under a projecting gibbosity of the mesonotum; on the under side, the prothorax is
extended into a long, narrow, cylindrical neck, to which the head
is fastened; the metathorax is also much developed, rather long
and horizontal. The feet are long and slender; their pubescence

hardly perceptible; the last joint of the tarsi of the male shows on the under side, at the basis, the excision characterizing the male sex in many genera. The tibiæ have no spurs at the tip, and the empodia are imperceptible.

The wings (Tab. 1, fig. 6, wing of *T. magna*) are rather short for the size of the body, and not broad.

The first longitudinal vein is short and joins the costa very early and very soon beyond the origin of the second longitudinal vein; the mode of this junction of the first vein with the costa is also peculiar; instead of running parallel to the costa and then taking a sudden turn towards it (as in most *Tipulidæ brevipalpi*), the first vein gradually converges towards the costa and finally coalesces with it, so that, beyond their junction, the costa becomes much stouter. The auxiliary vein is very closely approximated to the first longitudinal and ends in the costa almost opposite the origin of the second vein; the subcostal cross-vein is not far from its tip; there is no vestige of a marginal cross-vein. *There is no submarginal cell, as the second longitudinal vein does not emit any other vein;* the first posterior cell follows immediately after the marginal cell. The fourth vein starts, as usual, from the fifth, very near the basis of the wing, being slightly arcuated at its origin, and connected at this place with the first vein by a small, but very distinct cross-vein. A thickening of the alar membrane almost always exists at this place in the *Tipulidæ*: sometimes it assumes the appearance of a vein; in the present case, however, this cross-vein is particularly distinct, because the origin of the fourth vein is a little more distant than usual from the basis of the wing. Of the two branches of the fourth vein, the posterior one is forked, and a cross-vein between this fork and the anterior branch closes the discal cell.

The sixth vein is very closely approximated to the fifth for more than one-third of its course, and then suddenly diverges at so acute angle from it; in some specimens the basal portions of these veins are so near each other as to appear coalescent; a careful examination, however, proves that they run alongside of each other. The seventh vein is nearly straight.

The forceps of the male, as far as its structure can be ascertained on a dry specimen, seems to be somewhat like that of *Elephantomyia*, that is, it consists of a pair of subcylindrical basal pieces, to which two pairs of ensiform, horny appendages are attached. The ovipositor of the female has long, slender, almost imperceptibly arcuated valves.

The relationship of *Toxorrhina* with *Elephantomyia* and *Rhamphidia* is evident, and principally indicated by the prolonged rostrum, common to the three genera, the absence of the marginal cross-vein, and the structure of the feet.

Toxorrhina is easily distinguished from *Elephantomyia* by the venation of the wings, the submarginal cell of which is wanting; by the structure of the antennæ, which are 12-jointed and have some longer bristles on the apical joints only, whereas *Elephantomyia* has long verticils on all the joints, and by the structure of the thorax, the collare being entirely concealed under the projecting gibbosity of the mesonotum, the mesosternum being anomally developed, and the metathorax also rather large and horizontal.

The venation of *Toxorrhina* is unique among the *Tipulidæ*, and it is not easy to decide the disappearance of which veins has brought it about. The wing of *Elliptera* (Tab. 1, fig. 10) may afford an explanation. If we imagine that the first and second veins of *Elliptera*, already very closely approximated, coalesce with each other, we obtain a venation not unlike that of *Toxorrhina*. In this case what we have called above the second vein, would in reality be the third. Whether this explanation is the true one, I do not pretend to decide, but it is worthy of notice that several genera among the *Limnobina anomala* show a tendency towards the coalescence of the veins near the costa (*Antocha, Styringomyia,* etc.; compare above, p. 101).

The genus *Toxorrhina* was for the first time described and figured by Mr. Loew in 1851 (*Linnæa Entomologica*, Vol. V, p. 400, Tab. II, fig. 17). The pamphlet on the amber fauna, published a year earlier, contains a mere mention of the generic name, without description. The article in the *Linnæa* describes *Toxorrhina fragilis*, from Porto Rico, and, by way of illustration, introduces a mention of the fossil species, assuming their generic identity. The latter, however, as I have shown in the preceding genus, are, to all appearances, *Elephantomyiæ*, as they possess a submarginal cell, verticils on all the joints of the flagellum, etc.[1]

[1] Dr. Schiner (*Reise, etc. der Novara, Diptera,* p. 33) doubts the propriety of using the name *Toxorrhina* for *T. fragilis* and the other living species, instead of leaving it with the fossil species, for which it was origi-

In 1865 (*Proc. Philad. Ent. Soc.* 1865, p. 227) I published two North American *Toxorrhinæ*, and gave a detailed description of the generic character.

The genus *Limnobiorhynchus* Westw. (*Annales de la Soc. Entom. de France*, 1835, p. 683; the description has been reproduced) was intended. He says: "If Loew introduced this genus for several amber Diptera, which are provided with a submarginal cell, the circumstance that he *afterwards* added to it a species from Porto Rico, which has no such cell, does not prove that the absence of this cell is a characteristic mark of the genus, etc." It seems to me that the question, to which of the two genera does the name *Toxorrhina* rightfully belong? to *T. fragilis* and congeners or to the three fossil species? must be answered by another very natural question, to which of the two does Mr. Loew's description of *Toxorrhina* apply? *Toxorrhina* has been merely named and not described in the pamphlet *Bernstein und Bernsteinfauna*, 1860; it has been described in the following year only, in the *Linnæa*. This description applies to *T. fragilis* only, and not to the three fossil species. The circumstance that these fossil species are provided with a submarginal cell, the circumstance upon which Dr. Schiner's argument rests, has up to this day never been mentioned by Mr. Loew in print; on the contrary, he says expressly that these species are *absolutely similar to T. fragilis, with regard to their generic characters* (Mr. Loew's expressions have been quoted above, p. 107); in other words, destitute of a submarginal cell. As late as in 1861, in a lecture held before the meeting of the German naturalists in Königsberg (*Ueber die Dipternfauna des Bernsteins*), Mr. Loew says: "Among the amber Diptera I also found three species of a Tipulidæous genus, which I called *Toxorrhina*; it is remarkable . . . . *for the abnormal venation of its wings*. Afterwards I became acquainted with a living representative of the same genus," etc. Can it be affirmed, after that, that Mr. Loew introduced the genus *Toxorrhina* for certain species provided with a submarginal cell? He would not have very thoroughly examined the amber species, as he overlooked the presence of that cell; *T. fragilis*, on the contrary, he described and figured correctly. There can be no doubt, I think, that the latter is to be considered as the type of the genus. When I discovered *Elephantomyia*, I had no other source of information about *Toxorrhina* but the above quoted description. In consequence, I drew an elaborate statement of the differences between *Toxorrhina* as I found it described and my specimens (*Proc. Acad. Nat. Sci. Philad.* 1859, p. 231), and called the latter *Elephantomyia*.

My purpose, in publishing this somewhat lengthy explanation, is to justify the course I have adopted, which, owing to the intricacy of the question, has been misunderstood; and I hope that the eminent dipterologist, whose collaboration I have enjoyed now for twelve years in the publication of the North American Diptera, will not take offence if, in this instance, my views are not in accordance with his.

8 July 1868.

duced by me in *Proc. Philad. Entom. Soc.* 1865, p. 231) must be abandoned. I have had the opportunity to see the original specimens in Mr. Westwood's cabinet. The genus, as I had anticipated in the *Proc. Philad. Ent. Soc.* (l. c.) is founded upon the males of one genus and the females of another; the males are *Geranomyiæ* and the female is a *Toxorrhina*; hence it came that the genus was described as having a submarginal cell in the male and none in the female. *Limnobiorhynchus brasiliensis* Westw. (♂) is a *Geranomyia*; the female is a *Toxorrhina*, very similar to the male in coloring, and thus mistaken for the same species. *Limnobiorhynchus canadensis* Westw. (♂) is my *Geranomyia communis*; the female is not described.

Toxorrhina seems to be exclusively confined to the American continent. Besides the two species, described below, and the two others, mentioned above (*T. fragilis* Loew, from Porto Rico, and *T. brasiliensis* Westw. from Brazil), I am not aware of any species having been described.

The name *Toxorrhina* is derived from τόξον, a bow, and ῥίς, nose, in allusion to the long rostrum, which is arcuated in dried (but not in living) specimens.

Description of the species.

1. T. magna O. S. ♂ and ♀.—Thorax fusco-flavescens, vittis tribus fuscis, frontis angusta; alis immaculatis.

Thorax brownish-yellow, with three brown stripes; front narrow; wings immaculate. Long. corp. 0.5—0.6 (without the proboscis).

Syn. *Toxorrhina magna* O. Sacken, Proc. Phil. Entom. Soc. 1865, p. 232.

Head yellowish-cinereous; front narrow, brownish in the middle; antennæ brown; proboscis brown, about once and a half the length of the head and the thorax taken together. Thorax pale brownish-yellow, with three not very dark brown stripes; the intermediate one is rather broad; its sides are parallel and very well defined; beyond the suture, the thorax, including the scutellum and metathorax, is covered with a dense gray bloom; pleuræ brownish-yellow, with a cinereous bloom. Abdomen reddish-brown. Coxæ yellow; feet brownish-tawny; tips of the tibiæ and the tarsi, except the basis of the first joint, brown. Wings hyaline; costal veins yellowish-tawny, the other veins brown; the tip of the auxiliary vein is almost exactly

opposite the origin of the second vein; section of the second
vein, posterior to the small cross-vein, arcuated; the great cross-
vein is at the very basis of the discal cell; the cross-vein separating the discal from the first basal cell is very oblique; no
vestige of a stigma (Tab. I, f. 6).

Hab. New Jersey, in July (Cresson); a male and a female
specimen.

2. T. muliebris O. S. ♀.—Obscure cinerea, fronte latiori, vitta
thoracis obscuris, pedibus pallidis, alis immaculatis.

Dark cinereous, front rather broad, stripes of the thorax blackish, feet pale
tawny, wings immaculate. Long. corp. 0.3.

Syn. *Toxorrhina muliebris* O. Sacken, Proc. Phil. Entom. Soc. 1865, p. 233.

Head blackish or dark gray; occiput and occipital orbits
cinereous; antennæ brownish; basal joints darker; proboscis
pale brown. Thorax blackish-gray; the usual three stripes are
still darker, almost black; they occupy the greater part of the
mesonotum; the latter shows, especially on the sides, a yellowish
bloom; metathorax blackish, with a gray bloom. Feet, including
the coxæ, yellowish; tarsi infuscated from the tip of the first joint.
Abdomen blackish; forceps of the male reddish-yellow. Wings
hyaline; no vestige of a stigma; costal and first longitudinal
veins tawny, the other veins darker brown; the tip of the auxiliary vein is very slightly beyond the origin of the second vein;
the section of the second vein, posterior to the small cross-vein,
is strongly arcuated; the cross-vein at the inner end of the discal
cell is very oblique; the great cross-vein is a little before the
discal cell.

Hab. Princeton, Mass. (Scudder); a single male specimen.

This species is distinguished from the preceding by its much
smaller size, its darker and more gray coloring, and its comparatively broader front. Whether the position of the great cross-
vein, which in *T. muliebris* is before the discal cell, is also to be
reckoned among the constant characters of the species, is uncertain, as I have but a single specimen. The joints of the flagellum
of this species immediately following the stout basal joint, are
very short and crowded together; they are more elongated in *T.
magna*. The color of the only specimen in my possession is
somewhat injured by moisture, especially about the head.

Gen. IX. DICRANOPTYCHA.

One submarginal cell; four posterior cells; a discal cell; the first longitudinal vein very long, its tip is not very far back of the tip of the wing; the submarginal and the posterior cells also elongated; *a distinct fold, originating from about the middle of the sixth longitudinal vein, runs along the middle of the anal cell towards the posterior margin* (Tab. I, fig. 6). Wings elongated, strongly iridescent; veins pubescent. Feet long, pilose; tibiae without spurs at the tip; empodia distinct; ungues smooth. Antennae 16-jointed, of moderate length. The forceps of the male consists of the usual basal pieces, with claw-shaped or hook-shaped horny appendages (Tab. III, fig. 12, one-half of the forceps of *D. sobrina*; Tab. III, fig. 11, forceps of *D. nigripes*).

Rostrum short, epistoma transverse, stout; lips rather fleshy; palpi short, second joint short, stout, the third a little longer, the fourth not much longer than the third. Eyes glabrous, front rather broad; on the under side of the head, the eyes are contiguous. The antennae, when bent backwards, reach the root of the wings in the male; they are a little shorter in the female; second joint stout; four or five basal joints of the flagellum short cylindrical; the following ones more elongated, slightly increased at the basis; verticils moderately long. Collare moderately developed, the head closely applied to it; thoracic suture deeply marked. Feet long, rather stout, pilose; empodia large and distinct; no spurs; the anal excision exists on the under side between the two last tarsal joints in the male. The appendages of the male forceps of *D. sobrina* are double on each side; a horny, pointed, unguiform piece, and a more lamelliform, coriaceous, curved piece, with a brush of short hairs at the tip; the forceps of *D. nigripes* (Tab. III, fig. 11) has a somewhat similar structure; only the horny appendages are longer and form a double curve (for more details, compare the explanation of the plates at the end of this volume). Upper valves of the ovipositor are of moderate length, arcuated, somewhat flattened, and rather blunt at the tip. The wings (Tab. I, fig. 8, wing of *D. sobrina*) are elongated and comparatively narrow; the auxiliary vein reaches considerably beyond the origin of the praefurca, and ends in the costa a short distance beyond the inner end of the submarginal cell; the subcostal cross-vein is close by its tip; the first longitudinal vein runs very far towards the apex of the wing; its tip is nearer to this apex than to the tip of the auxiliary vein; the marginal cross-vein is somewhat back of this tip, at a distance which is a little shorter than the great cross-vein; the stigma is indistinct, forming an elongated streak on both sides of the first longitudinal vein; the origin of the second vein is before the middle of the length of the wing; the præfurca, very slightly arcuated at its basis, is generally short, much less than half the length of the submarginal cell; this early origin of the præfurca, its shortness, and the length of the wing, necessitate an unusually long submarginal cell; its sides (second and third veins), are nearly parallel and generally arcuated; the first posterior cell is a little shorter than the submarginal; the discal cell has the shape of a parallelogram; the fold in the anal cell is especially perceptible when the wing is held against the light; it assumes then the appearance of a vein, which disappears before reaching the posterior margin; the three last longitudinal veins are nearly straight. The venation varies but little in the species which I have examined; the difference principally consists in the length of the præfurca. The veins are always finely pubescent; the costa is also more hairy than usual, and sometimes, in the male sex, bears a conspicuous fringe of dense and comparatively long hairs. The wings have a rather striking iridescence, which, as in *Antocha*, seems due to the great density and minuteness of the microscopic pubescence of the surface; although transparent, they have a dull appearance, and are always tinged with grayish or yellowish.

Besides the three species described below, I possess one from California and two occur in Europe. The prevailing colors seem to be dull grayish or yellowish, without any well-marked stripes or bands.

The presence of empodia and the structure of the mouth remind of *Limnophila*, from which, however, *Dicranoptycha* is abundantly distinguished by the want of a second submarginal cell and of spurs on the tibiæ. No immediate relationship can yet be pointed out, except perhaps the European genus *Orimarga*.

The name of this genus, established by me in 1859, is derived from δίκρανος, fork, and πτυχή, fold, in allusion to the fold in the anal cell.

Description of the species.

1. D. germana O. S. ♂ and ♀.—Fuscaneo-ochracea; alis fulvo-flavidis, opalisantibus; præfurca cellulä discoidali multo longior.

Brownish-ochraceous; wings with a fulvous tinge, opalescent; the prefurca is much longer than the discal cell. Long. corp. 0.4—0.45.

Syn. *Dicranoptycha germana* O. Sacken, Proc. Ac. Nat. Sc. Phil. 1859, p. 217.

Head yellowish-cinereous; palpi brown; antennæ tawny at the
basis, darker towards the tip. Thorax brownish-ochraceous,
mesonotum above, especially posteriorly, the scutellum and the
metathorax with a more or less distinct brownish-gray bloom;
lower part of the pleuræ somewhat hoary; halteres ochraceous.
Feet ferruginous-tawny, clothed with black hairs; tips of the
tibiæ infuscated; last joints of the tarsi brownish. Abdomen
brownish-ochraceous, more or less dark; in the male, the last segment is sometimes brown; forceps ochraceous. The wings are
of a saturate, fulvous tinge, with a peculiar bluish, opalizing
reflection; the veins are fulvous and distinctly pubescent; if
viewed obliquely, the veins appear yellow on bluish ground. The
prefurca is about once and a third the length of the discal cell;
the latter is more than twice as long as it is broad; its inner end
is sometimes straight, sometimes oblique and arcuated.

Hab. Trenton Falls, N. Y., where I found this species to be
very common in July, 1858.

The description is drawn from dry specimens; among the notes
which I took from living ones, I find the following character
mentioned: "Abdomen yellow, with five brown spots along the
margins, at the incisures." One of the specimens has a stump
of a vein near the origin of the prefurca.

2. D. sobrina O. S.   ♂ and ♀.—Fuscano-cinerea, alis subbivernis;
prefurca cellula discoidali non longior.

Brownish-cinereous, wings subcinereous; prefurca not longer than the
discal cell (Tab. 1, fig. n). Long. corp. 0.4—0.45.

Syn. *Dicranoptycha sobrina* O. Sacken, Proc. Ac. Nat. Sc. Phil. 1859, p. 218.
Dicranoptycha sororcula O. Sacken, l. c.

Head yellowish-gray; palpi brown; antennæ brownish; two
basal joints paler; the first with a whitish bloom (in some specimens these joints are more infuscated). Thorax gray, with a
yellowish-brown bloom above, indicative of the ordinary stripes;
the latter are more or less distinctly marked; pleuræ hoary,
halteres pale; feet tawny, densely clothed with a moderately
long, black pubescence; fore femora sometimes brown, except at

the basis; the intermediate and hind ones brown at the tip only (sometimes the feet are altogether of a pale coloring). Abdomen blackish-cinereous, venter paler; genitals yellow. Wings with a pale cinereous tinge, iridescent; there is, in some specimens, a slightly more brownish tinge along the anterior margin between the tip of the first longitudinal vein and the apex of the wing; the costa is clothed with black hairs which, in the male, are much longer and form a dense, conspicuous fringe; all the veins are clothed with moderately long hairs; præfurca very short, hardly longer, sometimes evidently shorter, than the discal cell.

Hab. Washington, D. C. Immature specimens of a paler coloring, with uniformly pale feet, and without any trace of a darker tinge near the apex of the wing, often occur.

I possess some specimens from Georgia and Pennsylvania the males of which bare no conspicuous fringe of hairs along the costa; the pubescence of their costa is not perceptibly longer than that of the female; the two basal joints of the antennæ seem to be more intensely yellow. This is what I formerly described as *D. sororcula;* but I doubt now that it is a distinct species, and place it among the synonyms, until further observation proves the contrary.

3. D. nigripes O. S. ♂.—Ferruginoso-ochracea, s-morum apice nigro; alis fulvescentibus; præfurca cellula discoidali non longior.

Ochraceous, with a reddish, ferruginous tinge; tip of the femora blackish; wings yellowish; præfurca not longer than the discal cell. Long. corp. 0.4.

Syn. *Dicranoptycha nigripes* O. Sacken, Proc. Ac. Nat. Sc. Phil. 1859, p. 218.

Head cinereous, antennæ black; two basal joints ferruginous-yellow; rostrum brownish, palpi black. Thorax reddish-yellow; pleuræ, metanotum beyond the suture, scutellum, and metathorax with a strong hoary bloom; metathorax darker at the basis; halteres pale; coxæ and basis of the femora yellowish-ferruginous, the remainder of the feet is clothed with a dense, black pubescence, which almost entirely conceals the tawny ground color; tip of the femora black, with a yellow band before it, especially distinct on the front part. Abdomen brownish-yellow; the segments of the venter, from the third to the seventh, have transverse black spots in the middle. Wings tinged with brown-

ish-yellow, which color is more saturate, almost ferragioous, along
the anterior margin; there is a fringe of black hairs along the
costa, between the tip of the first longitudinal vein and the apex
of the wing; the surface of the wing is slightly infuscated along
this fringe; veins finely pubescent; the discal cell is at least
three times longer than it is broad; the præfurca is not longer
than this cell.

Hab. Dalton, Ga.; a single male specimen, taken by me in
1859.

Some remarks about the male forceps of this species (Tab. IV,
fig. 11) will be found in the description of the plates of the male
genitals, at the end of this volume.

Gen. I. OBIMARGA.

One submarginal cell; four posterior cells; *discal cell open, coalescent
with the second posterior cell; great cross-vein about the middle of the wing,
and hence, the fourth posterior cell very long* (Tab. I, fig. 9). Tibiæ without
spurs at the tip; empodia distinct. Antennæ 16-jointed. Basal pieces
of the male forceps elongated, slender, with horny, slender, claw-shaped
appendages at the tip; upper valves of the ovipositor small, slender,
pointed.

Rostrum projecting, cylindrical, much shorter than the head;
eyes large, glabrous; front comparatively narrow. Collare extended in a somewhat elongated neck; mesonotum moderately
convex, rather narrowed anteriorly; mesosternum very long.
Feet long and slender, apparently glabrous (the pubescence
being microscopic); the usual excision between the two last
tarsal joints, on the under side, exists here in the male. Abdomen elongated, narrow. Wings elongated, rather narrow (Tab.
I, fig. 9). The auxiliary vein ends in the costa a little distance
anterior to the inner end of the submarginal cell and at a considerable distance beyond the origin of the second longitudinal
vein (this distance being more than one-third of the breadth of
the wing); the tip of the auxiliary vein is stout and runs
obliquely into the costa which, at and beyond that point, seems
to be slightly incrassated; the subcostal cross-vein immediately
precedes the tip of the auxiliary vein; the first longitudinal vein
reaches far beyond the tip of the auxiliary vein and ends in the
costa at a point which is distinctly nearer to the apex of the wing
than to the tip of the auxiliary vein; the second longitudinal vein

Issues from the first at about the middle of the length of the wing; the prefurca is angularly bent near its basis (in my specimens even with a vestige of a stump of a vein); its remaining portion is nearly straight, the length of this portion being about two-thirds of the submarginal cell; the portion of the second longitudinal vein which is beyond the origin of the third, is very gently arcuated; the marginal cross-vein is at about the middle of the distance between the tip of the first longitudinal vein and the inner end of the submarginal cell; the stigma is indistinct, forming an elongated streak on both sides of the first longitudinal vein, between the tip of the auxiliary vein and the marginal cross-vein; the first posterior cell is a good deal shorter than the submarginal, as the small cross-vein is about opposite the middle of the distance between the inner end of the submarginal cell and the marginal cross-vein; the veins inclosing the first posterior cell are straight, parallel, converging at the tip only; the inner end of the second posterior cell is not quite in one line with the small cross-vein, but projects a little towards the basis of the wing; the third posterior cell is short, petiolate (and hence, it is the posterior branch of the fourth vein which is forked); the fourth posterior cell is nearly twice the length of the second, as the great cross-vein is removed to the middle of the wing, a little beyond the origin of the second vein; fifth longitudinal vein nearly straight; the seventh, for nearly one-half of its length, runs so closely along the sixth, that they appear coalescent; beyond this, however, the seventh vein diverges from the sixth and runs in a nearly straight line towards the margin of the wing.

The venation of this genus along the anterior margin has an unmistakable resemblance to that of *Dicranoptycha;* they have in common the great distance between the tips of the auxiliary and of the first longitudinal vein, the length of the latter, the shape and position of the stigma, and the position of the marginal cross-vein; both have distinct empodia. The differences (absence of a discal cell and unusual position of the great cross-vein in *Orimarga*) are obvious; but these differences notwithstanding, I incline to believe that the place of the present genus is next to *Dicranoptycha.* We ought not to overlook at the same time the remarkable analogy in the structure of the thorax of *Orimarga* and of *Toxorrhina:* in both the same oblong shape, comparatively narrow, when viewed from above, a long neck, and a remarkable development of the mesosternum. Such analogies are to be kept in view, till further discoveries point out their true significance.

The foregoing description has been prepared from two specimens found in Germany, and which I owe to Mr. Loew's communication. They belong, if I am not mistaken, to *Limnobia alpina* Zett. (*Dipt. Scand.* X, p. 389, 69); two other species described by the same author (l. c. 70, 71)—*L. virgo* and *juvenilis*—apparently belong to the same genus. A species similar to, or identical with the one I have now before me, has been seen by me in Mr. Bellardi's collection in Turin; I believe that it was taken in the north of Italy. No American species has as yet been discovered.

The name of this genus, introduced here for the first time, is derived from δριμαργος, meaning *extravagantly fond of mountains.*

Gen. XI. ELLIPTERA.

One submarginal cell; four posterior cells; discal cell open, coalescent with the third posterior cell; praefurca straight, very closely approximated to the first longitudinal vein (Tab. 1, fig. 10). Antennæ 16-jointed. Tibiae without spurs at the tip; empodia not distinct. Forceps of the male rather elongated.

As I have not seen this interesting European genus, I borrow the description partly from its author, Dr. Schiner, partly from a written communication of Mr. Loew; the description of the venation I prepare from specimens of wings which I have before me:[1]—

Head rounded, transverse, rather closely applied to the thorax; rostrum very short; antennæ of moderate length, 16-jointed; first joint short cylindrical, second globose; the third rounded oval, but little longer than broad; the following joints almost globose, with short hairs. Front broad; eyes glabrous, rounded. Thorax gently convex; collare distinct, but short; transverse suture distinct; metathorax well developed; abdomen narrow, the two halves of the forceps long and narrow, leaving an open space between them when closed; ovipositor short, arcuated at the tip. Feet long and slender; tibiae without spurs at the tip (the pubescence, as it reaches the tip has sometimes the appearance of spurs, which do not exist); empodia indistinct. Wings folded flat over the body, when at rest.

[1] Several wings were kindly sent to me by Dr. Schiner in a letter.

The auxiliary vein hardly reaches beyond the middle of the wing; the subcostal cross-vein is at a considerable distance from its tip (about three lengths of the great cross-vein); the costa is distinctly incrassated between the tip of the auxiliary vein and the apex of the wing; the tip of the first longitudinal vein is at about the middle of the distance between the two last-named points; the tip of the second longitudinal vein is again at about the middle of the distance between the tip of the first vein and the apex of the wing. The origin of the second longitudinal vein is a short distance beyond the subcostal cross-vein, and at a considerable distance before the tip of the auxiliary vein; the latter distance is more than double the length of the great cross-vein; the præfurca, starting at an exceedingly acute angle, runs very close by the first vein; beyond the origin of the third vein the interval between the first and second veins is a little greater; no marginal cross-vein is perceptible; the stigma is rather long. The third vein has its origin not far from the middle of the distance between the tip of the auxiliary and that of the first longitudinal vein; its first segment forms a sharp curve, almost a quarter of a circle, being sometimes provided at this place with a stump of a vein; its latter segment is gently arcuated. First posterior cell shorter than the submarginal; its inner end almost in a line with the third posterior cell, which is coalescent with the discal cell; the second posterior cell is about half the length of the first; the great cross-vein is almost in one line with the inner end of the third posterior cell, sometimes a little anterior to it; the fifth vein is gently arcuated beyond the great cross-vein; the sixth and seventh veins are nearly straight; the anal angle of the wing is moderately projecting.

The foregoing description applies to the wing of *Elliptera omissa* Schin. But Mr. Loew informs me that he has discovered a second species, the venation of which is somewhat different; the auxiliary vein is longer; and the subcostal cross-vein is nearly opposite the inner end of the submarginal cell.

Elliptera omissa is blackish in coloring, and has, according to Dr. Schiner, somewhat the appearance of *Dicranomyia morio* F. (or *morioides* O. S.); it is not rare in Austria.

The most remarkable feature of the venation of this genus is the course of the second vein, which is so much approximated to the first, as if to foreshadow an absolute coalescence. The position of the subcostal cross-vein is also unusual. The incrassation of the costa beyond the junction of the auxiliary vein is likewise observable in *Orimarga*, *Toxorrhina*, and *Antocha*. There is perhaps a certain relationship between *Elliptera* and *Orimarga*; but the latter has distinct empodia, which the former, according to all accounts, has not. On the other hand, the course of the second vein, the shape of the wing, and the absence of empodia somewhat remind us of *Antocha*.

Elliptera (from ἔλλειψις, I omit, perhaps on account of this genus having been overlooked so long) has been first introduced by Dr. Schiner, in 1863 (*Wiener Entomol. Monatschr.* Vol. VII, p. 223, and also *Fauna Austr. Diptera*, II, p. 559).

Gen. XII. ANTOCHA.

One submarginal cell; four posterior cells; a discal cell; auxiliary vein indistinct, being clearly applied to the first longitudinal vein; the latter convergent towards the costa and finally coalescent with it; the second longitudinal vein, at its origin, forms an acute angle with the first longitudinal; anal angle almost square (Tab. I, fig. 11). Wings with a milky tinge. Antennae 16-jointed, rather short. Tibiae without spurs at the tip. Empodia indistinct. Ungues with small teeth on the under side, at the basis. Forceps of the male with comparatively small claw-shaped horny appendages (Tab. III, fig. 10, forceps of *A. saxicola*, from above).

Rostrum cylindrical, somewhat projecting; palpi slender, rather prolonged, although shorter than the head; first joint elongated, second and third shorter; last joint somewhat elongated. The antennae, if bent backwards, would not reach the root of the wings; basal joint short; joints of the flagellum subglobular, last joint more elongated; the flagellum is beset with short hairs and, on the under side, with a delicate pubescence; no distinct verticils. Eyes glabrous, almost contiguous on the under side of the head; front narrow. Collare but moderately developed; thoracic suture deep. Knobs of the halteres rather large. Feet comparatively short, moderately stout; tibiae without spurs at the tip; empodia indistinct; the ungues have small teeth on the under side, near the basis, like those of *Dicranomyia*; the last tarsal joint of the male is excised on the under side in the interval between it and the preceding joint. The comparatively broad wings are distinguished by the shape of their anal angle, which is that of a rectangle with a rounded point; the course of the auxiliary and first longitudinal veins is peculiar; the former is closely approximated to the latter and therefore rather indistinct; the latter, instead of running parallel to the costa and then turning suddenly towards it (as it usually does), gradually merges into the costa, which is increased beyond their junction.[4] The marginal cross-vein is feebly marked, although perceptible. The origin of the second longitudinal vein is like that of *Erioptera*, that is, before the middle of the length of the wing and at a very acute angle; the praefurca is perfectly straight and quite as long as the remainder of the second vein, or longer; the submarginal cell is by one half longer than the first posterior; the latter is square at its inner end, the small cross-vein being comparatively long; discal cell small, almost square; its inner end is oblique, arcuated; owing to the shortness of the first posterior cell, the discal cell is unusually near the tip of the wing; the three last longitudinal veins are nearly straight. The stigma is elongated, its outline rather indefinite.

The wings of the species described below have a peculiar milky-whitish tinge; they are distinctly iridescent, when held obliquely towards the light. Besides, they show another peculiarity: It requires a magnifying power of 150 to discover the microscopic pubescence on their surface; so magnified, they appear covered with black dots, emitting very short hairs (much less power is required to show the pubescence on the wings of most of the other *Tipulidae*). The forceps of the male (Tab. III, fig. 10) has, on the anal basal pieces, a double claw-shaped appendage, which, as well as I could perceive, consists of a horny and of a soft part, closely joined. The ovipositor is of moderate length, somewhat arcuated.

The peculiar venation and the milky white tinge of the wings, the shape of the anal angle, etc., render this genus easy of recog-

---

[4] In order to ascertain this peculiarity of the venation with more precision, I compressed a wing of *A. varicula* between two glass plates. This straightens the fold usually existing in the *Limnobia* between the costal and first longitudinal veins and shows the course of the auxiliary vein with greater distinctness; in this case this vein appeared separated from the first longitudinal by a narrow interval far above one-third of its length only; beyond that both veins ran close along side of each other, till both united with the costa. Under such circumstances there was evidently no room for a subcostal cross-vein.

sition. The manner in which the first longitudinal vein joins the costa reminds us of *Taxorrhina*; otherwise the genus stands isolated, and no immediate relationship can be pointed out. The absence of distinct empodia and the presence of small teeth on the under side of the ungues constitute a leaning towards the *Limnobina*, which is balanced, however, by the structure of the forceps, etc.

Antocha was introduced by me in the *Proc. Acad. Nat. Sci. Philad.* 1859, p. 219. Since then, the only species (*A. opalizans*) has been found to occur in Europe also (comp. Schiner, *Fauna Austriaca*, *Diptera*, Vol. II, p. 559).

The name of the genus is derived from its principal character, the proximity of the auxiliary and the first longitudinal veins (ἄντοχη, close approximation, connection).

Description of the species.

1. **A. opalizans** O. S. ♂ and ♀.—Ochraceous vel cinerea, thoracis vittis infuscatis; halteres capitulo fusco; alis opalisantes, basi pallida.

Ochraceous or gray, stripes of the thorax infuscated; knob of the halteres brown; wings opalescent, pale at the basis. Long. corp. 0.22—0.32.

Syn. *Antocha opalizans* O. Sacken, Proc. Ac. Nat. Sc. Phil. 1859, p. 220.
Antocha saxicola O. Sacken, l. c.

Variable in size and coloring. Head grayish-brown; rostrum yellowish, sometimes infuscated; palpi and antennæ brown; the first joint of the latter sometimes yellowish. Thorax either ochraceous, or brownish-gray, with some yellowish spots on the humeri and pleura; in both cases with darker, more or less distinct stripes; halteres pale, with a more or less brown knob; feet tawny, more or less dark, according to the general coloring of the specimen; coxæ and base of the femora generally paler. Abdomen brownish or grayish-brown; the genitals often, but not always, yellow. Wings (Tab. I, fig. 11) with a whitish, somewhat milky tinge, opalescent; the veins at the basis of the wings pale yellow; the other veins more or less dark brown; stigma colorless.

Hab. Europe and North America. I possess specimens from Dalton, Ga.; Washington, D. C.; Trenton Falls, N. Y.; Montreal, Can.; Lake Winnipeg, H. B. T. (Kennicott); Illinois (Le Baron). The specimens from the north are generally larger. This species has been noticed in Europe only since it was discovered and described by me in North America; it occurs near running water, and I observed the gray variety (*A. saxicola*, olim) in large numbers, in May, 1859, on mossy stones in a creek, near Washington, D. C., performing a singular, sideways walk along tho water's edge, probably for the purpose of oviposition; some of them were in copulation. I have no doubt now that *A. saxicola* is only a variety of *A. opalizans*; I have received larger specimens of it from the north, and I understand that this variety also occurs in Europe.

Gen. XIII. ATARBA.

One submarginal cell; four posterior cells; a discal cell; no marginal cross-vein; tip of the auxiliary vein nearly opposite the origin of the second vein; the subcostal cross-vein at a distance from this tip which is a little shorter than the great cross-vein (Tab. I, fig. 13). Rostrum short. Antennæ 16-jointed, *rather long*. Tibiæ without spurs at the tip (!); empodia distinct; ungues smooth. The large forceps of the male consists of two elongated subcylindrical basal pieces, each bearing a double horny, claw-shaped appendage.

Eyes glabrous; front rather narrow; rostrum but little projecting; palpi rather long, especially the last joint. Antennæ rather long, reaching beyond the basis of the abdomen, when bent backwards; first joint short, not much longer than the second; joints of the flagellum elongated, cylindrical, gradually decreasing in length; they are clothed with a dense pubescence; a single, somewhat longer hair is perceptible on each segment, above the pubescence; the antennæ of the female are but little shorter than those of the male. Collars short—the head being rather approximated to the mesothorax. Thoracic suture distinct. Feet of moderate length, comparatively stout, finely pubescent; empodia distinct. The forceps of the male is large and not unlike Tab. IV, fig. 29, in appearance, only more hairy; the basal pieces leave an open interval between them, even when the forceps is closed; the ends of the claw-shaped appendages are distinctly blid, showing that they consist of two closely approximated horny pieces; there is a short stump in the place of the anal style of the *Limnobina* (one of my specimens has a long curved aculeus projecting on the under side; in the other male specimen this organ is apparently concealed internally). As the specimen, which I believe to be a female, has its abdomen broken off, I cannot describe the ovipositor.

Wings (Tab. I, fig. 13, wings of *A. picticornis*) of moderate
length and breadth; anal angle somewhat projecting; veins with
a hardly perceptible pubescence. The tip of the auxiliary vein
and the origin of the second longitudinal vein are a little beyond
the middle of the length of the wing; no trace of a marginal
cross-vein; the prefurca is short and arcuated (less than one-
third of the remaining portion of the second vein); third longitudinal vein gently arcuated; the first posterior cell a little
shorter than the submarginal; its sides nearly parallel; the
discal cell is not much longer than broad; the great cross-vein
is in a line with the inner end of the discal cell; fifth vein
slightly arcuated beyond the great cross-vein; the sixth and
seventh veins are nearly straight.

I do not perceive any spurs on the tibiae in the three specimens
which I have before me; but most of their feet are broken off,
and I believe formerly to have seen spurs on the middle pair
of feet, which is lost now. The question about the spurs is
therefore left doubtful.

The general appearance of the body is not unlike *Limnobia*,
only the antennae are comparatively longer. The genus can be
easily recognized by its long antennae and the absence of a
marginal cross-vein.

The name of this new genus is derived from ερεβος, fearless.

Description of the species.

1, A. **picticornis**, n. sp. ♂.—Ferrugineo-flava; antennarum flagelli
articulis singulis dimidio apicali infuscatis.
Reddish-yellow; the latter half of the single joints of the antennal flagellum
infuscated. Long. corp. 0.2—0.25.

Ochraceous yellow, with a more or less reddish tinge. Head
yellow, front and vertex with a grayish reflection; palpi infuscated at the tip; antennae yellow; the single joints of the flagellum pale brown at the tip, this brown gradually gaining ground
in the subsequent joints till the last joints are almost entirely
brown. Thorax reddish-yellow, shining above; pleura with a
very slight hoary reflection; halteres ferruginous-yellow; feet
yellow, tarsi brownish towards the tip. Abdomen yellow;
penultimate segment dark; forceps yellow, the horny claw-shaped
appendages black. Wings with a pale yellowish tinge; veins
yellow.

Hab. Delaware (Dr. Wilson); District Columbia (?). I am not quite sure of the latter locality.

Observation. I have for comparison two males and a specimen without abdomen, which is probably a female, as its antennæ are somewhat shorter.

Gen. XIV. TRICHOLABIS.

One submarginal cell; four posterior cells; a discal cell; *first longitudinal vein very short*, its tip being but little beyond the middle of the length of the wing, nearly opposite or not much beyond, the inner end of the submarginal cell (Tab. I, fig. 12). Wings vary hyaline, stigma rounded. Antennæ 16-jointed. Rostrum cylindrical, distinctly prolonged, although shorter than the head. *Collare prolonged in a narrow, linear neck.* Feet rather stout, hairy; tibiæ without spurs at the tip; empodia distinct, but small. Genitals of the male hairy on the outside; forceps with large, horny appendages and an anal style (Tab. III, fig. 9).

Eyes glabrous, more or less remote above, almost contiguous below. Palpi short, inserted at the tip of the short, cylindrical rostrum; last joint very short. The elongated, neck-like collare, although shorter than the head, is a very striking feature of this genus. Antennæ of moderate length; if bent backwards, they would not quite reach the basis of the wings; scapus of the usual structure; flagellum with oblong or rounded, well-separated joints, clothed with a short pubescence and with verticils, which are a little longer than the pubescence.

Feet of moderate length, comparatively short and rather stout, clothed with a rather long and dense pubescence; ungues apparently smooth; empodia small, but very distinct.

The forceps of the male consists of two oblong lobes, somewhat like those of *Dicranomyia*: large horny appendages on their under side; anal style distinct (Tab. III, fig. 9, represents the forceps of *T. complexa* from above; fig. 9 a, one-half of it, from below); in dried specimens none of these organs are perceptible. The tip of the abdomen is hardly incrassated, but always hairy. The valves of the ovipositor are of moderate length, slender, arcuated.

The wings (Tab. I, fig. 12, wing of *T. complexa*) are comparatively short, often broad; they are very transparent and the microscopic pubescence, common to all the wings of Diptera, seems to be more coarse and scattered here, as a moderate mag-

nifying power shows it distinctly. The stigma is short and
rounded. The tip of the maxillary vein is about the middle of
the length of the wing; the subcostal cross-vein at a moderate
distance before this tip; the tip of the first longitudinal vein is
at a comparatively short distance beyond the tip of the maxillary
vein, almost opposite the tip of the sixth longitudinal vein, and
but little beyond the inner end of the submarginal cell. The
second longitudinal vein originates before the middle of the
length of the wing; the præfurca is gently arcuated, and (in
both species which I have before me) of nearly the same length
with the remaining portion of the second vein, or a little shorter.
The marginal cross-vein, placed very near the end of the first
longitudinal vein, divides the marginal cell in two nearly equal
halves; this cross-vein is almost in a line with the inner end of
the submarginal cell and with the small cross-vein; the third
longitudinal vein is arcuated; the discal cell somewhat elongated,
its inner end narrowed; the great cross-vein is nearly opposite
the small one; the fifth longitudinal vein is straight; the sixth
nearly so; the seventh gently arcuated.

The two species which I have before me (a North American
and a Mexican one) have nearly the same venation; only in the
North American species the discal cell projects on the inside
of the cross-veins, whereas in the Mexican one the marginal
cross-vein and the inner ends of the submarginal, first posterior,
discal, and fourth posterior cells are all in one line. The venation
of *T. simplex* Wied., as figured by that author (*Auss. Zw.* I, Tab.
VI, b, fig. 8) is nearly the same, only the marginal cross-vein is
a little beyond the inner end of the submarginal cell, and not in
a line with it. The wing of *Rhamphidia scapularis* Macq.
(*Dipt. Exot.* I, 1, Tab. X, fig. 1), which is undoubtedly a *Teucholabis*, has the same venation; even the peculiar curve or ear,
formed by the first longitudinal vein before joining the costa, and
which is likewise perceptible in the two species before me, is
correctly represented by Macquart.

The peculiarity of the venation of *Teucholabis* consists in the
shortness of the maxillary and the first longitudinal veins; the tip
of the latter, for instance, is not much beyond the inner end of
the submarginal cell; whereas, in the other *Tipulidæ*, it is usually
more or less far beyond this end. The marginal cross-vein, being
near the tip of the first vein, is thus naturally brought in one line

with the inner end of the submarginal cell. The comparative
length of the cells in the apical half of the wing and the corresponding shortness of the two basal cells, are among the striking
characters of this genus. The stoutness of the veins and the
clearness of the membrane of the wing are likewise characteristic.

Teucholabis seems to be peculiar to the American continent,
at least no species belonging to it has as yet been discovered in
Europe. Besides the North American species described by me,
the following species, by former authors, belong here:—

Limnobia simplex Wied. *Auss. Zw.* I, p. 549, from Brazil. I
have seen the original specimen in Mr. Loew's collection.

Limnobia flavithorax Wied., from Brazil, according to Dr.
Schiner, who also describes a new species—*T. spinigera* (*Reise*,
etc. *der Novara, Diptera,* p. 44).

Rhamphidia scapularis Macq. *Dipt. Exot.* I, 1, Tab. X, fig. 1;
likewise from Brazil, is, to all appearances, a *Teucholabis.*

I have seen several specimens from Mexico in Mr. Bellardi's
collection. In drawing the generic character I had, besides *T.
complexa,* a male specimen from Mexico before me, which I owe
to the kindness of Mr. Bellardi. Its wings are somewhat narrower than those of *T. complexa.*

This genus, first established by me in 1859 (*Proc. Acad. Nat.
Sci. Philad.* p. 223), for the North American *T. complexa,* and
now corroborated by the comparison of several other species, is
very easily distinguishable by its neck-like collare, its broad, clear
wings, and the peculiarities of its venation. No immediate relationship can be pointed out.

The name is derived from τεύχω, weapons, and λαβίς, forceps,
in allusion to the horny processes of the male forceps.

Observation. Besides the South American and Mexican species
mentioned above, as belonging to *Teucholabis,* I have seen in Mr.
Bellardi's Mexican collection two forms, closely related to this
genus, but which may perhaps be separated from it. One of them
is distinguished by the presence of a supernumerary cross-vein
at the extremity of the second longitudinal vein, dividing the
marginal cell in two parts, and by the shortness of the first
posterior cell, in consequence of the submarginal cell being in
immediate contact with the discal cell. The 16-jointed antennæ,
the development of the collare, the stoutness and pubescence of
the feet, the shortness of the first longitudinal vein and of the

auxiliary vein, the course of the second longitudinal vein, the position of the marginal cross-vein, the hairy appearance of the male forceps, and finally the general appearance and coloration of the body, render evident its close relationship to *Teucholabis.*[1]

The other form is at once conspicuous by its rostrum, which is much more elongated than is the case in *Teucholabis,* and gives it the appearance of a *Rhamphidia.* This resemblance, however, is entirely superficial; the venation of the wings, as well as the structure of the body, very plainly shows that these insects are most closely allied to *Teucholabis.* The *Rhamphidia chalybeiventris* Loew (*Wien. Entomol. Monatschr.* 1861, p. 38), from Cuba, is not a *Rhamphidia,* but belongs to this form of *Teucholabis.*

Description of the species.

1. **T. complexa** O. S.   ♂ and ♀.—Obscure ochracea, thoracis vittis tribus brunneis; alis hyalinis, stigmate subrotundo, fusco.

Brownish-ochraceous, thorax with three brown stripes; wings hyaline, stigma rounded, brown.   Long. corp. 0.25—0.27.

Syn. *Teucholabis complexa* O. Sacken, Proc. Ac. Nat. Sc. Phil. 1850, p. 223.

Head dark brown, with a hoary bloom on the front; antennæ and palpi black; the former with oblong joints on the flagellum.

[1] This volume was already in press, when, through the kindness of Dr. Schiner, I received his work on the Diptera of the Voyage of the "Novara" (*Reise d. Oesterr. Fregatte Novara, etc. Zoologischer Theil; Diptera;* Wien, 1868); it contains a detailed description, with figures, of the new genus *Paratropesa,* the generic characters of which had been published some time earlier (*Verz. Zool. Bot. Ges. in Wien,* 1866). *Paratropesa* (type: *P. singularis* Schin., from Colombia, South America) is evidently the above-mentioned form of *Teucholabis,* of which I have had a glimpse, in 1865, in Mr. Bellardi's collection. The comparison of what I say about it, as I find it among my notes, with Dr. Schiner's description shows, that we agree in the interpretation of the veins forming the submarginal and first posterior cells; but that we disagree in the interpretation of the anterior branch of the second vein, which I considered as a supernumerary cross-vein. Such an interpretation permits me to retain the genus among those with a single submarginal cell, as its relationship to *Teucholabis* seems otherwise evident to me. *Paratropesa* is undoubtedly a good genus, and I am glad to have had the opportunity to identify it before the issue of the present volume. Dr. Schiner's description of *Paratropesa* will be found in the Appendix II, at the end of this volume.

Thorax brownish-ochraceous, with three brown stripes; the intermediate one begins at the collare; the lateral ones are abbreviated
before and extended beyond the suture behind; scutellum yellow,
metathorax more or less brown in the middle, yellow on the sides;
pleure yellow, with a more or less distinct brown stripe, running
from the collare to the base of the halteres; the latter pale.
Feet pale yellowish; tips of the femora and of the tibiæ brown;
last joints of the tarsi brown. Abdomen brown, posterior margins
of the segments a little paler; male forceps tawny. Wings (Tab.
I, fig. 12) hyaline, veins brown, costal and subcostal tawny;
anterior margin distinctly hairy; stigma brown, rounded, near the
tip of the first longitudinal vein. (For the further description
of the venation compare the generic characters.)

Hab. Washington, D. C.; Trenton Falls, N. Y., in June;
Illinois (Mr. Kennicott). . A specimen from Georgia, in the
Berlin Museum, seems to belong here.

One of my specimens, a male, shows a slight difference in the
venation; the latter portion of the second longitudinal vein is
more straight, and the cross-vein, closing the discal cell, is a
little nearer to the apex of the wing, which changes the shape
of the discal cell. The original description of this species was
drawn from four specimens; I have only two left at present.

Gen. XV. THAUMASTOPTERA.[1]

Not having seen this European genus, I translate the following
description by Mr. Mik, from the *Verh. Zool. Bot. Gesellsch. in
Wien*, 1866, p. 302. The appended woodcut is copied from a
figure in the same volume:—

Head rounded, transverse, somewhat flattened; occiput rather
strongly developed; rostrum moderately prolonged; palpi four-
jointed, the two last joints of equal length, more slender than
the two first; front broad in both sexes; antennæ rather short,
16-jointed; first joint cylindrical, of the length of the rostrum,
the second cyathiform, transverse, the following joints oblong,
setulose, somewhat verticillate, gradually diminishing in size; the
last joints indistinct. Eyes round, glabrous. Thorax convex,
gibbose, projecting over the narrow collare; transverse suture
distinct; scutellum narrow; metathorax well developed. Abdo-

[1] Θαυμαστός, wonderful; πτερόν, wing.

men with seven segments, short; the forceps with stout, obtuse
appendages; ovipositor long, with a gently arcuated tip. Feet
long and slender; the tibiæ without spurs; empodia indistinct;
ungues smooth. Wings comparatively long; longitudinal veins
pubescent, the margin fringed with hairs; the auxiliary vein ends
in the costa about the middle of the length of the wing; second
longitudinal vein not forked, connected by a cross-vein with the
first longitudinal vein; third longitudinal vein not forked; the

Fig. 3.

fourth longitudinal vein is
forked a short distance from
the small cross-vein; its principal branch runs straight
to the margin; the anterior
branch is forked; the branches
of this fork are longer than
the petiole; fifth and sixth veins straight; the seventh is somewhat sinuated; no discal cell; the subcostal cross-vein is very
near the origin of the præfurca; the great cross-vein is in the
middle of the wing, quite far from the branching of the fourth
vein; hence, the second basal cell is almost half as long as the
first; the anal angle of the wing rounded, but little projecting.

Type of the genus T. calceata Mik, found near Görtz, in
Illyria. The author describes it as a very delicate, pale yellow
species, about 0.2 lin. long, with dark brown tips of the femora
and of the tibiæ, looking like Erioptera imbuta Meig. It is on
the author's authority that I leave this genus among the Limnobina anomala, to which he refers it.

Section III. ERIOPTERINA.

Two submarginal cells; four (very seldom five) posterior cells; discal cell sometimes closed, but very often open. Normal number of the antennal joints sixteen. Eyes glabrous. Tibiae without spurs at the tip; empodia distinct; ungues smooth on the under side.

The *Erioperina* hold an intermediate position between the *Limnobina* and the *Limnophilina*. Like the latter, they have two submarginal cells and 16-jointed antennae and distinct empodia; but, like the former, they have no spurs at the tip of the tibiae. Similar to all the spurless *Tipulidae*, they have only four posterior cells; *Cladura* is the only exception, the only tipulideous insect to me known which has no spurs at the tip of the tibiae and nevertheless five posterior cells. Besides the characters enumerated at the head of this paragraph, the typical *Erioperina* (the genera *Rhypholophus*, *Erioptera*, and *Trimicra*) have some striking peculiarities of the venation in common. The subcostal cross-vein is placed at a very considerable distance before the tip of the auxiliary vein; the second longitudinal vein originates nearer than usual to the root of the wing, and the prefurca forms, at its basis, a very acute angle with the first longitudinal vein (compare Tab. I, fig. 14–20, and Tab. II, fig. 1). In the other genera, these typical characters gradually disappear. Already in *Symplecta*, closely related as it is to the three former genera, the prefurca is gently arcuated at its basis. *Gnophomyia* loses another important character; its subcostal cross-vein is only at a moderate distance from the tip of the auxiliary vein. *Goniomyia*, owing to the presence of a second submarginal cell, and the absence of spurs at the tip of the tibiae, has to be placed among the *Erioperina*; but its immediate relationship has, for a long time, seemed doubtful to me. I believe now that *Psiloconopa*, the European representative of *Gnophomyia*, forms the transition between

Goniomyia and the typical *Erioptcrina*. That *Cryptolabis* belongs here will hardly be questioned. *Cladura*, with its five posterior cells, looks exactly like the *Limnophilina*; its resemblance would be complete if it had spurs at the tip of the tibiæ.

Chionea has been hitherto placed at the end of the *Tipulidæ*, as an anomalous group, without any distinct relationship. The strict application of the characters upon which the classification adopted by me is based, points out its place very clearly. *Chionea* has no spurs at the tip of the tibiæ, which would locate it either among the *Erioptcrina* or among the *Limnobina*. Its distinct empodia and smooth ungues determine its location among the former. If we compare *Chionea* with the European *Trimicra pilipes* we cannot but be struck by the analogies between them; the same incrassated male forceps; the same stout, hairy feet; and even the anomalous structure of the antennæ of *Chionea* is foreshadowed in *Trimicra* in the abrupt reduction of the size of the three last antennal joints. *Chionea* has therefore to be placed next to *Trimicra*, and is closely allied to *Erioptera*.

The review of the genera of *Erioptcrina* just given shows that, upon the whole, this section is less homogeneous than any other (except the *Limnobina anomala*). The link connecting some of the genera, like *Cladura*, for instance, with the typical forms, is apparently artificial; a *Limnophila* with the spurs of the tibiæ so short as to appear obsolete, would, to all appearances, approach *Cladura*. The same remark may be applied to the *Limnophila* with four posterior cells, and *Gnophomyia*; the former may have obsolete spurs; they would then be hardly distinguishable from the *Erioptcrina*. Is the distinction between those genera, based upon the presence or absence of spurs on the tibiæ, the expression of a real fact in nature or only an artificial subdivision? I believe this distinction to be a real one, although I confess that it would be very desirable to discover some more characters to support it. The male forceps of both *Gnophomyia* and *Cladura* is very different from that of most *Limnophilina*; still, it would be necessary to show that it is more cognate to the forceps of the *Erioptcrina*. Here, as in many other cases, the discovery of new forms may help to solve these difficulties.

Besides the characters of the *Eriopterina* which have already
been enumerated, there is one which deserves to be mentioned
here. In this group of *Tipulidæ* the *anterior* branch of the
fourth longitudinal vein is quite frequently forked, while the
posterior branch is simple, and thus, when the discal cell is open,
it coalesces with the *third* and not with the second posterior cell.
We find this structure in two North American *Eriopteræ* (*E.
caloptera* Say, and *parva* O. S.), three North American and
several European *Rhypholophus*; in all the *Goniomyiæ*, which
have no discal cell, and in the European *Psiloconopa lateralis*
Macq. (*flavolimbata* Hal.). Among the other *Tipulidæ* this
structure is rare (compare the Introduction, page 33).

I am not aware that any genus of *Eriopterina*, foreign to
Europe and North America, has been published, unless *Lachnocera*
Philippi (*Verh. Zool. Bot. Ges. in Wien*, 1865, p. 615, Tab. XXIII,
fig. 5), from Chile, belongs here. The venation of this genus is not
unlike that of *Goniomyia*; it also reminds of a *Limnophila* with
four posterior cells. The statements of the author are not complete enough to admit of any certain conclusion. The translation
of the description is given in the Appendix.

The following new genus, from Mexico, is in Mr. Bellardi's
collection, in Turin:—

Sigmatomera, nov. gen. (from σίγμα, the letter s, and μέρος,
part).

Two submarginal cells, four posterior cells, and a discal cell; the tip
of the auxiliary vein is not much beyond the basis of the second submarginal cell; the subcostal cross-vein is at a moderate distance from
this tip; tibiæ without apparent spurs; empodia small; antennæ (♂)
16-jointed, more than once and a half the length of the head and the
thorax taken together; joints subreniform, nodose; eyes (♂) very large,
convex, almost contiguous on the upper as well as on the under side
of the head.

The very large, convex, apparently bare eyes, come almost in
contact on the front; they are separated by a small triangle above
the antennæ, and by a very narrow, linear space above this
triangle. The rostrum is rather short, and shows the general
structure of the *Limnophilina*—two stout lips being visible
below the oblong epistoma. The palpi are of moderate length,
and the last joint is more prolonged than is generally the case
among the *Limnophilina*. The antennæ remind of those of

Nephrotoma. The first joint is very short, the second almost
rudimental; the third joint (first joint of the flagellum) is more
than four times the length of the first and second taken together;
it is subcylindrical, with a rounded projection on the under side
near the tip; the fourth joint has about four-fifths of the length
of the third; it has almost the shape of a recumbent S; it is
attenuated at the basis and in the middle, whereas the intermediate parts are incrassated, as also the tip of the joint which
projects distinctly on the under side; the following joints (from
the fifth to the fifteenth) have exactly the same shape as the
fourth, only they very gradually decrease in length and this
peculiar shape becomes less and less distinct; the sixteenth and
last joint is subcylindrical and almost rudimental. The joints of
the flagellum are densely clothed with a delicate down; each of
them bears two longer hairs on the upper side near the basis, and
two similar, only shorter hairs, on the projecting sinuosities of the
under side.

The collare is narrow and but little developed. The thorax
has on the upper side, between the transverse suture and the
scutellum, a pair of peculiar pits or impressions, originating on
each side near the root of the wing and running towards the
middle (I do not know whether they were not accidental in the
described specimen). I cannot say anything positive about the
male genitals, except that they do not give to the tip of the abdomen a club-shaped appearance. The feet (the specimen had only
a single anterior foot left) are very long; their pubescence is short
and not at all striking. No spurs are perceptible at the tip of the
tibiæ. The last joint of the tarsi of the male has no excision on
the under side.

The wings are rather long and moderately broad. The marginal
cross-vein is very little before the tip of the first longitudinal vein.
The stigma is inclosed between the subcostal and marginal cross-
veins. The origin of the second longitudinal vein is rather before
the middle of the anterior margin; the præfurca forms a straight
line with the third longitudinal vein; first submarginal cell shorter
than the second; the latter very square at its basis, nearly of the
same length with the first posterior; the discal cell somewhat
elongated.

The coloring of the only species I have seen is yellow (it will
be published shortly in Mr. Bellardi's work on Mexican Diptera).

en. XVI. RHYPHOLOPHUS.

Two submarginal cells; four posterior cells; discal cell present or absent. Wings pubescent on the whole surface (Tab. I, fig. 14, wing of *R. nubilus*; fig. 15, *R. rubellus*). The second longitudinal vein originates at a more or less acute angle, before the middle of the anterior margin; the subcostal cross-vein is a considerable distance (two or three lengths of the great cross-vein) anterior to the tip of the auxiliary vein. Antennæ 16-jointed. Tibiæ without spurs at the tip; ungues smooth on the under side; empodia distinct.

This genus is closely allied to *Erioptera* and distinguished from it by the wings, which are densely pubescent on the whole surface. As in *Erioptera*, the intermediate pair of feet is usually the shortest here; however this character is less striking in *R. nubilus*. The antennæ of some species are longer than usual in the male sex and the joints of the flagellum are elongated, strongly pedicelled, and pubescent (the genus *Ormosia* Rondani is founded upon this character). The structure of the forceps of the male varies in different species, and the study of these variations would probably afford an insight into the true affinities between the species. I have not had the necessary opportunities for the study of these parts on living specimens. The principal modification in the venation of the wings in this genus consists in the presence or absence of a discal cell; when it is absent, we generally find that the anterior branch of the fourth vein is forked (as in Tab. I, fig. 15); this constitutes the genus *Dasyptera* of Dr. Schiner; but this is not always the case; sometimes, as in *R. holotrichus*, it is the posterior branch of the fourth vein which bears the fork. The course of the seventh longitudinal vein is also variable; sometimes it is nearly straight (*R. innocens*); sometimes arcuated at the basis in such a manner that its first half runs very near the sixth longitudinal vein (*R. nigripilus*); sometimes arcuated in the opposite direction, with the concavity towards the sixth vein; in this case the tip of the seventh vein is approximated to the tip of the sixth, and the auxiliary cell is broader in the middle than at the end. This is the case with *R. holotrichus*, and reminds of a similar course of the seventh vein in *Erioptera* (subgenus *Erioptera*).

Dr. Schiner, in subdividing the genus *Erioptera*, adopted two genera for the species the wings of which are hairy on the whole surface: *Rhypholophus*, with a discal cell, and *Dasyptera*, with-

out discal cell, and with the *anterior* branch of the fourth vein
forked. This subdivision, according to my opinion, is not satisfactory. I possess a North American species (and European
species of the same kind may also occur) which has no discal cell,
but the *posterior* branch of the fourth vein of which is forked.
Such a species would neither be a *Rhypholophus*, nor a *Dasyptera*. We might enlarge the character of *Dasyptera* and admit
in it all the species without a discal cell. But in the family of
Tipulidæ we have abundant evidences of the fact, that the mere
presence or absence of the discal cell, if unsupported by other
characters, has but very little systematic value. Moreover, in the
genus *Erioptera* itself, we have the proof, that a discal cell may
be formed by the forking of either the *anterior* or the *posterior*
branch of the fourth vein (compare in that genus the subgenera
Acyphona and *Mesocyphona*). Therefore, a subdivision based
upon the mere presence or absence of a discal cell would not be a
natural one. The comparison of the structure of the forceps of
the males, in connection with the venation and with the structure
of the antennæ, would alone enable us to arrange the species of
the present genus in natural groups. Not having species enough
for such a distribution, nor having had an opportunity to study
the structure of the male forceps of many species, I am unable
to point out their natural affinities. As to an actual subdivision
in genera, I do not see any necessity for it at present; in adopting
the two genera *Rhypholophus* and *Erioptera*, based upon the
nature of the pubescence of the wings, we have done enough, I
think, for any purpose of systematic distribution.

The structural affinities between *Rhypholophus* and *Erioptera*
are very great. Besides the difference in the nature of the pubescence, I am not able to point out any character, peculiar to one
of these genera and foreign to the other; this may be partly
owing to our as yet very imperfect knowledge of these genera.
The coloring of *Rhypholophus* is decidedly more dull than that
of *Erioptera*; gray and grayish-brown are the prevailing colors
in it.

The generic name of *Rhypholophus* has been first proposed by
Kolenati for a single species, discovered by him in Austria
(*Wiener Entom. Monatschr.* 1860, p. 398). It was retained for
the same species by Dr. Schiner, in his *Fauna Austriaca*. In
. the present work the definition of the genus has been enlarged,

so as to embrace all the *Erioptera* the wings of which are pubescent on the whole surface.

Table for determining the species.

1 {
Discal cell closed, or, if open, it coalesces with the second posterior cell. 2
Discal cell open; it coalesces with the third posterior cell (Tab. 1, fig. 15). 5
}

2 {
Wings variegated with gray or brown. 3
Wings uniformly colored. 4
}

3 {
Wings clouded with gray. 1 nubilus *O. S.*
Wings spotted with brown in all the cells. 2 innocens, n. sp.
}

4 {
Four basal joints of the antennæ pale. 3 nigripilus, n. sp.
Antennæ altogether blackish. 4 holotrichus, *O. S.*
}

5 {
Thorax reddish, with a distinct black line in the middle. 5 rubellus, n. sp.
Thorax gray, without any distinct stripe. 6
}

6 {
Knob of the halteres yellow; wings with a conspicuous stigmatical spot. 6 medgenii *O. S.*
Knob of the halteres infuscated; stigmatical spot not conspicuous. 7 monticola, n. sp.
}

Description of the species.

1. R. nubilus O. S. ♂ and ♀.—Cinereus, vitta thoracis distincta, fusca; alis griseo nebulosis, cellulâ discoidali clausâ; venis longitudinalibus sextâ et septimâ versus apicem subparallelis.

Gray, thorax with a distinct brown stripe; wing clouded with grayish: discal cell closed; sixth and seventh longitudinal veins subparallel towards the tip. Long. corp. 0.23—0.27.

Syn. *Erioptera nubila* O. Sacken, Proc. Ac. Nat. Sc. Phil. 1859, p. 227.

Brownish-gray; a distinct, narrow brown stripe over the thorax; thorax sparsely, abdomen densely clothed with rather long, soft, pale yellowish hairs; antennæ brownish-black, paler at the basis of the flagellum, with short verticils; palpi black; halteres pale, slightly infuscated at the base of the knob, the tip of which is clothed with a short golden-yellow pubescence; feet brownish, coxæ and basis of the femora paler; knees pale; femora with an indistinct brownish band before the tip; wings (Tab. 1, fig. 14) grayish-white, with gray nebulosities; they form two more or less marked bands across the apical portion of the wings; a third band passes over the cross-veins; a cloud in the first basal cell; another in the axillary, and some nebulosities in the spurious

cell; stigma large, brown, square; all the veins dark brown;
discal cell present; the seventh longitudinal vein is situated in
the middle; its latter portion is rather approximated to the sixth
vein; the great cross-vein is usually before the middle of the
discal cell.

Hab. Washington, D. C.; Trenton Falls, N. Y. Occurs commonly in the spring and in autumn, and may be seen in copulation
at both seasons.

R. fascipennis Zett., evidently allied to *R. nubilus*, and originally found in Norway, has been also received from Greenland
(Stæger, *Grœnl. Antliater* in Krøjer's *Tidskrift*, etc. 1845, p.
355, 16); its description from Zetterstedt, *Dipt. Scand.* X, p.
3777, is reproduced in the Appendix I.

2. R. innocens, n. sp. ♂ and ♀.—Fuscano-cinereus, vittis thoracis
indistinctis; alarum cellulis omnibus crebre fusco-maculatis; cellulâ
discoidali clausâ; venis longitudinalibus sixtâ et septimâ divergentibus.

Brownish-gray; stripes of the thorax indistinct; all the cells on the wings
densely spotted with brown; discal cell closed; sixth and seventh longitudinal veins divergent. Long. corp. 0.2—0.25.

Brownish-gray; antennæ and palpi blackish; stripes of the
thorax very indistinct; abdomen grayish-brown; male forceps
reddish-brown, with strong, short, black horny appendages;
halteres somewhat infuscated; feet brownish; tip of the femora
darker. Wings grayish, with dense brown dots in all the cells;
several larger brown spots along the anterior margin; in the
intervals of these spots, the costal and first longitudinal veins
are pale yellow. Discal cell closed; the sixth and seventh longitudinal veins are throughout strongly diverging, and thus the
axillary cell is much broader at the tip than in the middle.

Hab. Washington, D. C., in April; New Jersey.

In some specimens the spots are less dense in some of the cells,
especially in the basal ones.

3. R. nigripilus, n. sp. ♂ and ♀.—Fuscano-cinereus; alis immaculatis; cellulâ discoidali clausâ; venis longitudinalibus sixtâ et septimâ
divergentibus; antennarum basi pallidâ.

Brownish-gray; wings immaculate; discal cell closed; sixth and seventh
longitudinal veins divergent; basis of the antennæ pale. Long. corp.
0.2—0.22.

Brownish-gray; palpi blackish; antennæ brown, four basal
joints pale yellow; flagellum of the male densely clothed with a
long, soft, pubescence; only a few verticillate hairs reach above
it; joints elongated, becoming longer towards the tip; flagellum
of the female with a much shorter pubescence, and hence, verticillate hairs more distinctly visible; thorax with a brownish tinge
above and an indistinct intermediate brownish stripe; two rows
of blackish hairs on the posterior part of the mesonotum; coxæ
grayish-brown; feet brown, with an appressed pubescence, which
appears golden-yellow in a reflected light; trochanters and basis
of the femora paler; knob of the halteres yellow; its basis and
the stem with a pale grayish tinge; abdomen grayish-brown;
horny appendages of the male forceps sharp, black. Wings uniformly gray, with a somewhat more brownish tinge in the region
of the stigma; seventh longitudinal vein approximated to the sixth
on its anterior half, strongly diverging beyond the middle, and
thus the axillary cell much broader at the tip than in the middle;
discal cell elongated, narrow; the inner end of the third posterior
cell is nearly opposite its middle; all the veins comparatively
slender.

Hab. Washington, D. C.   Two specimens.

L. R. kalotrichus O. S.   ♀.—Fuscanus; alis immaculatis; cellula
discoidali apertà, cum secundà posteriori confluens; venis sixtà et sep-
timà longitudinalibus convergentibus; antennis nigris.

Brownish; wings immaculate; discal cell open, confluent with the second
posterior cell; sixth and seventh longitudinal veins convergent; antennæ
black. Long. corp. 0.23.

Syn. *Erioptera kalotricha* O. Sacken, Proc. Ac. Nat. Sc. Phil. 1859, p. 224.

Palpi and antennæ blackish; thorax uniformly pale yellowish-
gray above, with some pale hairs; stripes hardly marked at all;
halteres yellowish; coxæ and basis of the femora brownish-
yellow; the remainder of the feet brown; abdomen grayish-
brown, with a pale, erect pubescence. Wings of a uniform pale
yellowish-brown color; veins not darker than the ground color;
a darker shade in the stigmatic region; discal cell open, confluent
with the second posterior cell; the latter portion of the seventh
vein is rather approximated to the sixth vein, in such a manner
that the axillary cell is not broader at the tip than in the middle.

Hab. Washington, D. C; three female specimens. One of them
has the discal cell closed on one of the wings.

I possess a male specimen which is related to *R. holotrichus*,
and very like it, but probably distinct: the discal cell is closed;
the veins are darker than the ground color; the antennæ are
densely pubescent on one side, and with longer verticils on the
other; joints subcylindrical, moderately long; thorax with two
brown lines on the hind part of the mesonotum, before the suture,
etc.

5. R. rubellus, n. sp. ♂ and ♀.—Thorace rubescente, linea intermedia fusca; alis immaculatis; cellula discoidali apertà, cum tertiâ
posteriori confluente.

Thorax reddish, with a brown line in the middle; wings immaculate;
discal cell open, confluent with the third posterior cell. Long. corp.
0.2—0.23.

Palpi brown; antennæ brownish, the very stout second joint
sometimes a little paler; if bent backwards they would hardly
reach the root of the wings; those of the male have nothing unusual in their structure; the pubescence is not very conspicuous,
and the verticils of moderate length; the antennæ of the female
do not differ much from those of the male. Thorax reddish-
yellow, sometimes with a grayish bloom; a dark brown stripe in
the middle; a row of pale yellow hairs (easily rubbed off) on each
side; halteres pale; their knob very slightly, often more distinctly,
infuscated; feet brownish, coxæ and base of the femora brownish-
yellow; knees pale. Abdomen brown, with pale yellow hairs;
the last segment and the genitals brownish-yellow; forceps of the
male rather large, its horny appendages black at the tip. Wings
(Tab. I, fig. 15) grayish, darker in the region of the stigma;
discal cell open, confluent with the third posterior cell; the latter
portion of the seventh longitudinal vein is approximated to the
sixth in such a manner that the axillary cell is not broader at the
tip than in the middle.

Hab. West Point, N. Y., in numbers; Delaware (Dr. Wilson).

6. R. meigenii O. S. ♂ and ♀.—Thorace vittis nullis; alis stigmate
obscuro fusco; venis crassis, fuscis; cellula discoidali apertà, cum tertiâ
posteriori confluente.

Thorax without stripes; wings with a dark brown stigma; veins stout

brown; discal cell open, confluent with the third posterior cell. Long.
corp. 0.2—0.23.

Syn. *Erioptera wrigesii* O. Sacken, Proc. Ac. Nat. Sc. Phil. 1859, p. 224.

Head grayish, rostrum and palpi brown; antennæ brownish;
those of the male, if bent backwards, would not reach much
beyond the root of the wings; the joints of the flagellum are
elongated, subcylindrical, with a long, soft pubescence; those of
the female bare the joints shorter, beset with verticils and scattered hairs, but without any conspicuous pubescence. Thorax
of a uniform, dull yellowish-gray; beset with yellow hairs on the
back, as well as on the pleuræ and on the halteres; the latter
with a yellow knob. Abdomen brown, with a soft, long, erect
yellowish pubescence; genitals of the male reddish-brown; horny
appendages black; feet brownish; coxæ and basis of the femora
paler; knees likewise somewhat pale. Wings brownish-gray,
shorter and comparatively broader than in *R. rubellus* and *R.
monticola*; veins much stouter, dark brown; stigma distinct,
brown; usually there is a clearer spot at the end of the first basal
cell; discal cell open, coalescent with the third posterior cell;
seventh longitudinal vein somewhat arcuated, approximated to
the sixth, in its latter portion, in such a manner that the axillary
cell is not much broader towards the tip than in the middle; the
great cross-vein is usually anterior to the inner end of the discal
cell.

Hab. Middle States; not rare.

7. **R. monticola**, n. sp. ♀.—Thorace vittis nullis; alis immaculatis; articulis antennarum maris elongatis, pedunculatis, longe pubescentibus; cellula discoidali apertâ, cum tertiâ posteriori confluente;
stigmate pallido.

Thorax without stripes; wings immaculate; joints of the antennæ of the
male elongated, pedicelled, and with a long pubescence; discal cell open,
confluent with the third posterior cell; stigma pale. Long. corp. 0.22?

Head and thorax brownish, with a bluish-gray bloom, somewhat concealing the ground color. The antennæ, if bent backwards, would reach some distance beyond the root of the wings;
the joints of the flagellum, beginning with the second, are
elongated and narrow, terminating in an elongated point, to
which is fastened the following joint; each joint bears, on both

10   August, 1868.

sides, a tuft of long and soft hairs; no verticils, above this pubescence, are apparent (there are only 13 joints on both antennæ of my specimen, but the tip may be broken off). Palpi blackish; halteres with a somewhat infuscated knob, paler at the root; feet brownish; coxæ and basis of the femora brownish-yellow. Wings uniformly grayish; the stigmatic region very slightly darker; veins brown, comparatively slender; discal cell open, confluent with the third posterior cell; seventh longitudinal vein slightly sinuated in the middle, feebly divergent from the sixth.

Hab. White Mountains, N. H.; a single male specimen, the abdomen of which is broken. The peculiar structure of the antennæ of this species will render it easily recognizable; they must be remarkable for their length, if those of my specimen are imperfect, as I have every reason to suppose they are. The size of this species is about equal to that of the preceding ones; it could not be accurately given, on account of the broken abdomen of my specimen.

Gen. XVII. ERIOPTERA.

Two submarginal cells; four posterior cells; discal cell present or absent. Wings pubescent along the veins only. The second longitudinal vein usually originates at a very acute angle, some distance before the middle of the anterior margin; the subcostal cross-vein is at a considerable distance (two or three lengths of the great cross-vein, or more) from the tip of the auxiliary vein. Antennæ 16-jointed. Tibiæ without spurs at the tip; ungues smooth on the under side; empodia distinct.

The rostrum is short; the palpi likewise; their two intermediate joints rather stout. Eyes glabrous, separated above by a broad front; almost contiguous on the under side of the head. The antennæ are generally short, with oval or oblong joints; in some species, the males have the antennæ longer than usual, reaching, if bent backwards, beyond the basis of the abdomen; in such cases the joints of the flagellum are elongated and pedicelled. Thoracic suture well marked, often deep and glossy at the bottom; the longitudinal suture, connecting it with the scutellum, is generally well marked. The feet are of moderate length, comparatively short, usually pubescent, sometimes conspicuously hairy; the intermediate pair (as it was already noticed by Meigen) is shorter than the two other pairs. *Erioptera* has this character in common with the allied genera *Rhypholophus, Trimicra, Sym-*

plecta, and *Gnophomyia*. The last joint of the tarsi somewhat projects above and beyond the ungues, not quite so much, however, as in *Trimicra*.

The forceps of the male consists, as usual, of two movable basal pieces, to which horny appendages are fastened, the number and shape of which are variable in different species; in some they appear like a pair of strong hooks (*E. venusta*, Tab. IV, fig. 10); in others several horny branches are visible on each side (*E. vespertina*, Tab. IV, fig. 20, *E. armata*, fig. 14).

The ovipositor of the female is of moderate length in some species and rather long in others. The upper valves are arcuated and pointed; the lower ones, likewise pointed, but less curved, sometimes reach only the middle of the upper ones with their tip, sometimes very nearly the end. The little horny projections noticed by Schummel at the basis of the upper valves of *Symplecta* (*Beiträge*, etc. p. 158), seem to be common to all the *Erioptera*.

The wings are more generally broad than narrpw; in some species, as in the European *E. atra*, they are shortened in the male, which apparently renders them unfit for flying. The pubescence along the veins is usually long enough to give to the whole wing a hairy appearance; in some species however (as in the North American *E. septemtrionis*, or the European *E. ciliaris* Schum.), it is much shorter, and such species might not be recognized for *Erioptera*, if the other distinguishing characters were overlooked. (More will be said about such cases under the head of *Trimicra*.) The venation shows considerable modifications in different species; the subdivisions of the genus are principally based upon these differences, which will be explained below.

Besides the North American and European *Erioptera* at present known, only three species from all the rest of the world have been published. They belong to Chile, and have been described by Blanchard and Philippi (Blanch. *Gay's Fauna*, VII, p. 343, and Philippi in *Verh. Zool. Bot. Ges. in Wien*, 1865, p. 616).

Mr. Loew (*Bernst. u. Bernsteinfauna*, p. 37) says that he recognizes eight well-defined species of *Erioptera* in amber; he does not describe them.

The name *Erioptera* (from ἔριον, wool, and πτερόν, wing) has been introduced by Meigen as early as 1803 (*Illiger's Magazin*, Vol. VI). In the first volume of his principal work (*Systemat. Beschr.* etc. Vol. I, p. 109) he mentions among the characters of the genus that "the wings are pubescent along the veins only." It must not be overlooked, however, that at the time of the publication of this volume he had not seen any of the species with the wings hairy on the whole surface. When he obtained such a species (*E. varia*, Vol. VI, p. 237) he included it in the same genus. Since Meigen, *Erioptera* has been understood by later authors (Macquart, Zetterstedt, Staeger, and Walker) in the same sense, that is, as including the species with the wings pubescent on the whole surface, as well as those pubescent along the veins only.

In 1833 Mr. Curtis (*British Entomol.* 444) proposed the adoption of the genus *Molophilus* for a species which he described as *Molophilus brevipennis*, but which later English entomologists unanimously considered as synonymous with *E. atra* Meig.[1] The characters upon which this genus was established (modified shape of abdomen and thorax, small size of the wings, and large size of the male forceps) do not warrant its retention in the sense of the author, but the name *Molophilus* may be well retained for the subgenus to which *E. atra* belongs.

In 1848 Mr. Rossi (*System. Verz.* etc. p. 12) proposed the generic name of *Cheilotrichia* for the European species having a discal cell (*E. imbuta* and *E. cinerascens*), however without nearer defining this new genus.

In 1860 Mr. Kolenati (*Wien. Entom. Monatschr.* Vol. IV) adopted the genus *Rhypholophus* for a new species, discovered by him in Austria. This name has been retained in the present volume, but in a more extended sense.

---

[1] The synonymy of *M. brevipennis* with *E. atra* M., admitted by all English authors (compare Westwood, Walker, etc.), is probably based upon a comparison of original specimens. If we hold on to Mr. Curtis's description only, this synonymy may appear doubtful. He (*Brit. Entom.* 157) mentions both *E. atra* and *E. marina* among the species found in England, although in the same article he speaks of *M. brevipennis* as a distinct species. In the description of this species he says that the wings are "straw-colored" at the basis; from the fact that the author, having both sexes before him, does not notice the difference in the length of their wings, one would infer that they are short in both, and this is not the case with *E. atra*, etc.

In the same year Mr. Rondani (*Prodr. Dipterologiæ Italicæ*, Vol. I) proposed a series of new generic names for ecrtain groups of the genus *Erioptera*. They have already been enumerated above (p. 12), but among that number *Ilisia* alone, with *Erioptera maculata* M. for type, has been described (*Mus. Cancetr.* III, p. 91, 1865). The description of the others is to be expected in the volume of Mr. Rondani's work which will treat of the *Tipulidæ*, and which, as far as I am aware, has not yet appeared. This circumstance, as well as my limited knowledge of tho European *Eriopteræ*, prevent me from entering in a detailed examination of this distribution.

In 1863 Mr. Lioy (*Atti Inst. Venet.*, 3d series, Vol. IX, p. 224) proposed the genus *Platyoma* (with *E. cineroscens* M. for type) for the *Eriopteræ* with a discal cell and with an increased second antennal joint.

Dr. Schiner (*Wiener Entomol. Monatschr.* Vol. VII, 1863, and *Fauna Austriaca, Diptera*, Vol. II, 1864) divided the genus *Erioptera* (in the broadest sense) in four genera, which may be tabulated thus :—

I. Wings pubescent on the whole surface.
    1. A discal cell . . . . . . **Rhypholophus.**
    2. No discal cell, and anterior branch of the fourth vein forked . . . . **Dasyptera.**
II. Wings pubescent along the veins only.
    1. The fork of the fourth longitudinal vein, and with it, the great cross-vein, are in their usual position; the posterior branch of the fourth longitudinal vein is forked . **Trichostioha.**
    2. The fork of the fourth longitudinal vein and with it, the great cross-vein, are much nearer to the root of the wing than the small cross-vein . . . . . **Erioptera.**

Under the head of the genus *Rhypholophus* (comp. p. 130) I have shown why Dr. Schiner's subdivision of the species of Sect. I ("wings pubescent on the whole surface") cannot be retained for the present. In the same way, the subdivision of Section II ("wings pubescent along the veins only") is inapplicable to the North American species. The definition of *Trichosticha*, as given by the author, excludes two North American species (*E. caloptera* and *parca*), and perhaps some European ones (*E. tænio-*

nota Zett. *Dipt. Scand.* X, p. 3781 ?) which have the *anterior* branch of the fourth vein forked. Whether we enlarge the genus, so as to admit these species, or whether wo leave it in the acceptation of the *Paula Austriaca*, *Trichosticha* will contain very heterogeneous elements. The genus *Erioptera*, in Dr. Schiner's limited acceptation, is a natural group, which I have retained below. It is to be regretted, however, that the author transferred to this group the name of *Erioptera*, which belongs much more legitimately to his genus *Trichosticha*, as containing Meigen's most numerous and typical species.[1]

In the *Proc. Acad. Nat. Sci. Philad.* 1859 (p. 225), I have indicated the principal groups of the North American *Eriopteræ*. They are substantially the same as those which have been more fully defined in the present publication. If I have retained them in the position of groups or subgenera, it is because, in my opinion, the characters which all those species possess in common constitute between them a link of affinity more important than the structural differences which some of them show. Even the genus *Rhypholophus*, as defined above, proves by the position of its subcostal cross-vein, the manner in which the second longitudinal vein originates, and, in some species, by the arcuated course of the seventh longitudinal vein, a strong affinity to the genus *Erioptera* in its present definition. If I have adopted these two genera, it is because the difference in the pubescence of the wings of both affords a ground of subdivision as simple as easily applicable to all the species at present known. But it remains to be shown yet, whether the difference in this character is indicative of some corresponding modifications in other organs. Another potent reason for not further subdividing the genus *Erioptera* in my case was, my unacquaintance with the European species, the rather small number of the North American ones, and the comparatively large number of subdivisions which they require. For all these reasons I have preferred to indicate the natural affinities existing between the North American *Eriopteræ*, and to distribute them in groups accordingly, leaving these groups in the position of subgenera.

[1] It may be said in favor of Dr. Schiner's nomenclature, that Meigen, in his earlier work (*Klassification*, etc. 1804), has figured *Erioptera atra* as if it was the type of the genus. In his principal work the species are arranged in a different order, and this figure is not reproduced at all.

The North American species, contained in the genus *Erioptera*, as defined above, may be distributed into the following groups:—

A. The præfurca ends in the second submarginal cell, which is longer than the first; the inner end of the discaл cell (or, when it is open, of the cell with which it coalesces) is on the same line with the small cross-vein (Tab. 1, fig. 16, 17, 18).

1. The *posterior* branch of the fourth longitudinal vein is forked (in other words, when the discal cell is open, it coalesces with the second posterior cell; when it is closed, the inner end of the third posterior cell is nearer the basis of the wing than the inner end of the second).

a. The seventh longitudinal vein is arcuated (converging towards the sixth) in such a manner, that the axillary cell is broader in the middle than near the margin of the wing (Tab. I, fig. 16): subgenus Erioptera.

The six species of this subgenus (*E. chlorophylla, straminea, vespertina, septentrionis, chrysocoma, villosa*) form a very natural group; their venation is exactly the same; their discal cell is open, coalescent with the second posterior cell; their third posterior cell is rather long; their male forceps seems to be built upon the same plan, and consists of two basal pieces, bearing several horny branches each (compare Tab. IV, fig. 20, the forceps of *E. vespertina*); their wings are immaculate, their feet without well-marked bands. Although the above named six North American species have the discal cell open, the mere fact of its being closed would not prevent a new species from being included in this group, if the agreement in the other characters was sufficient. The present group almost answers to Dr. Schiner's genus *Trichostícha*; but it seems to me that *Erioptera* is a more appropriate name for it, as it will probably include the majority of the species, as well as the most typical forms, of the genus *Erioptera* in the sense of Meigen's principal work.

b. The seventh longitudinal vein is straight, diverging from the sixth; hence the axillary cell is much broader near the margin of the wing than in the middle; discal cell closed.

* The fork of the posterior branch of the fourth longitudinal vein (containing the third posterior cell) has the usual structure, that is, consists of two gently arcuated branches (Tab. I, fig. 17): subgenus Acyphona.

The three species belonging here (*E. venusta, graphica,* and *armillaris*) are very closely allied. They have handsomely variegated wings, and bands on the feet differing from the ground color. The male forceps has a very different structure from that of the preceding and of the following groups: it has, on each of the basal pieces, a single, strong, hook-shaped horny appendage (Tab. IV, fig. 16, *a, b;* forceps of *E. venusta*). The lower valves of the ovipositor are as long as the upper ones.

     ** The fork of the posterior branch of the fourth longitudinal vein (containing the third posterior cell) has an angular anterior branch which emits a stump of a vein inside of the discal cell (Tab. I, fig. 18): subg-nus **Hoplolabia**.

Only a single North American species, *E. armata,* belongs to this group. Its forceps is entirely distinct in structure from that of the preceding group (Tab. IV, fig. 14 a, 14); its wings are likewise variegated with brown, but its feet are of a uniformly pale color.

    2. The *anterior* branch of the fourth longitudinal vein is forked (in other words, when the discal cell is open, it coalesces with the *third* posterior cell) ; when the discal cell is closed the inner ends of the second and third posterior cells are nearly in one line: subg-nus **Mesocyphona**.

E. caloptera Say, and *E. parva* O. S. belong here ; both are distinguished by the above-mentioned peculiarities in the venation, and their relationship is further proved by the resemblance in the coloring of their body. The position of the two brown stripes on the thorax is quite peculiar, and not to be found in the other *Erioptera;* the feet have dark bands. The forceps of *E. caloptera* is represented on Tab. IV, fig. 15. The discal cell of this species is generally, that of *E. parva* always open. When closed in the former species, the shape of the discal cell is such that the inner ends of the second and third posterior cells are in one line; this is far from being the case with the other *Erioptera* with a closed discal cell, as *E. venusta, graphica, armata,* etc. The shape of the discal cell in these latter species evidently shows that it is the *posterior* and not the *anterior* branch of the fourth vein which is forked.

    B. The *præfurca* ends in the first submarginal cell, which is longer than the second ; the inner end of the discal cell (or rather, as it is always open, of the second posterior cell), as well as the great cross-vein, are not in one line with the small cross-vein, but much nearer to the root of the wing (Tab. I, fig. 19): subgenus Molophilus.

The peculiarities of the venation of this group are: 1. That the second longitudinal vein emits the third, not from its main stem, as usual, but from its posterior branch (as in some species of *Amalopis*); hence the first submarginal cell is longer than the second; the latter, in all the species which I have seen, has its inner end in one line with the inner end of the first posterior cell, both inner ends being nearly square; the first submarginal cell has usually a somewhat rounded inner end, and the marginal cross-vein is but a short distance beyond it; in *E. ursina* nearly in one line with it; 2. That the first bifurcation of the fourth longitudinal vein takes place at a considerable distance before the small cross-vein, and that the great cross-vein is also removed backwards to a corresponding distance; the consequence is, that the inner ends of the second and fourth posterior cells are nearer to the basis of the wing than the inner ends of the first posterior and of the submarginal cells. The discal cell seems to be always open (this is the case with the North American species, as well as with the European species, which I find mentioned in the authors). The third posterior cell is rather long in most species, and has its inner end more or less opposite that of the first posterior cell; in *E. ursina*, however (and probably in the related European species), it is much shorter.

Dr. Schiner has retained the name of *Erioptera* for this sub-division, but this name is more properly applied to another group. As *Molophilus*, a generic name proposed by Mr. Curtis for a species of this group with very short wings, unfit for flying, cannot well be retained in this narrow sense, we may apply it to the whole group.

Table for determining the species.

1 {
  The præfurca ends in the second submarginal cell (Tab. 1, fig. 16, 17, 18).   **2**
  The præfurca ends in the first submarginal cell (Tab. I, fig. 19).   13
}

2 {
  The discal cell, when open, coalesces with the second posterior cell (Tab. I, fig. 16); when closed, the inner ends of the second and third posterior cells are not in one line, the inner end of the latter being anterior (Tab. I, fig. 17, 18).   **3**
  The discal cell, when open, coalesces with the *third* posterior cell; when closed, the inner ends of the second and third posterior cells are nearly in one line.   12
}

3 { Discal cell open; seventh longitudinal vein arcuated in such a manner that the axillary cell is broader in the middle than near the
margin (Tab. 1, fig. 16).   4
Discal cell closed; seventh longitudinal vein straight, diverging from
the sixth, and, hence, the axillary cell much broader near the
margin than in the middle (Tab. 1, fig. 17, 18).   9

4 { Knob of the halteres yellow.   5
Knob of the halteres infuscated.   1 septemtrionis O. S.

5 { Body and wings yellow or green.   6
Body and wings brown.   2 villosa O. S.

6 { Cross-veins not infuscated, feet yellow.   7
Cross-veins infuscated, feet conspicuously clothed with black hairs.
3 chrysocoma O. S.

7 { Front and humeri with sulphur yellow marks, the remainder of the
head and of the thorax being of a saturated reddish or brownish-
yellow.   4 vespertina O. S.
Whole body pale green or pale yellow.   8

8 { Body pale green.   5 chlorophylla O. S.
Body pale yellow.   6 straminea, n. sp.

9 { No stump of a vein inside of the discal cell; femora with brown
bands.   10
A stump of a vein inside of the discal cell (Tab. 1, fig. 19); femora
without brown bands.   10 armata O. S.

10 { Wings with a broad brown band and a large brown spot before it,
nearer the basis (Tab. 1, fig. 17).   7 venusta O. S.
Wings with a very narrow brown band and numerous brown spots
and marks.   11

11 { Prevailing color of the body and of the wings yellowish.
8 armillaris, n. sp.
Prevailing color of the body and of the wings brownish.
9 graphica O. S.

12 { Wings brownish, with numerous white spots.   11 caloptera Say.
Wings pale grayish, with small dark spots along the margin, at the
tip of the longitudinal veins.   12 parva O. S.

13 { Prevailing color of the body yellow.   13 pubipennis O. S.
Prevailing color of the body brown or black.   14

14 { Size from 0.2 to 0.25; color brown.   15
Size hardly 0.1; color black.   16 ursina O. S.

15 { Antennæ altogether brownish.   14 hirtipennis O. S.
Two basal joints of the antennæ yellowish.   16 forcipula, n. sp.

Description of the species.

A. The profurca ends in the second submarginal cell, which is longer than the first; the inner end of the discal cell (or, when it is open, of the cell with which it coalesces) is on the same line with the small cross-vein.

1. The posterior branch of the fourth longitudinal vein is forked.

a. Seventh longitudinal vein arcuated, converging towards the sixth (Tab. I, fig. 16) : subgenus Erioptera (compare above, page 151).

1. E. septemtrionis O. S. ♂ and ♀.—Fuscano-ochracea, alis immaculatis, venarum villosie perbrevi, halteres capitulo infuscato.

Brownish-ochraceous, wings immaculate, the pubescence of the veins very short, the knob of the halteres brown. Long. corp. 0.2—0.25.

Syn. *Erioptera septemtrionis* O. Sacken, Proc. Ac. Nat. Sc. Phil. 1859, p. 223.

Body ochraceous, more or less tinged with brownish; front infuscated in the middle; palpi brown; antennæ brownish, more or less pale at the basis; thorax brownish above, with more or less sulphur yellow in the humeral region; a brown stripe, more or less distinct, along the middle of the mesonotum and of the collare; pleuræ usually pale, with a brown stripe, running from the collare to the root of the halteres; in some specimens, the pleuræ are brownish; knob of the halteres dark brown; feet brownish-yellow; abdomen brownish above, venter paler. Wings immaculate; veins brownish, their pubescence very short, not long enough by far to reach from vein to vein and thus to cover the surface of the cells.

Hab. Maine (Packard); Sharon Springs, N. Y.; seems to be more common in the north. I possess a male from Washington, D. C., which is altogether brownish, humeri yellowish, forceps reddish; a female of very large size (locality uncertain) has the same dark coloring. I believe that they belong to E. septemtrionis, which can always be distinguished by the dark knob of the halteres and the short pubescence of the wings.

2. E. villosa O. S. ♂.—Fusca, alis fuscescentibus, conspicue fusco-villosulis, halteribus flavis.

Brown, wings brownish, with conspicuous brown hairs; halteres yellow. Long. corp. 0.25.

Syn. *Erioptera villosa* O. Sacken, Proc. Ac. Nat. Sc. Phil. 1859, p. 224

Brown; antennæ and palpi of the same color; a sulphur yellow
spot on the humeri, extending towards the root of the wings;
halteres yellow; their tip with a fine, silky, golden yellow pubescence; abdomen with a long, soft, pale brownish-yellow pubescence; genitals paler than the abdomen, yellowish-brown; the
horny appendages of the male forceps are pale, with their tips
only black. Feet brownish-yellow, rather stout, pubescent with
brownish hairs, which look golden in a reflected light. Wings
with a somewhat dusky tinge; pubescence of the veins long,
brown.

I possess a single male specimen, captured by myself in the
Middle States of the Union; the precise locality I am unable to
give.

8. F. chrysocoma O. 8. ♂ and ♀.—*Flava, alis flavescentibus,
punctis paucis fuscis; pedibus conspicue fusco-villosulis.*

Yellow, wings yellowish with a few brown dots; feet with a conspicuous
brown pubescence. Long. corp. 0.2—0.22.

Syn. *Erioptera chrysocoma* O. Sacken, Proc. Ac. Nat. Sc. Phil. 1859, p. 228.

Bright yellow; palpi brownish; antennæ brownish, basal joints
yellow; those of the male have a dense, even pubescence on one
side, and long verticils on the other. Thorax somewhat more
saturate-yellow above, in well-preserved specimens with obsolete
hoary lines, visible in a reflected light, and indicative of the
intervals of the ordinary stripes; halteres yellow; abdomen
slightly tinged with brownish above; male forceps yellow, the
horny appendages likewise; when the forceps is open, a pair of
internal horny appendages become perceptible, the tip of which
is black. The feet are rather stout, and clothed with long brown
hairs, which makes them look altogether brown; the basis of the
femora on the front feet and nearly the whole femora of the other
two pairs, except their tip, are yellow, and devoid of this brown
pubescence; the front feet are conspicuously elongated. Wings
with a yellowish tinge, purely yellow along the anterior margin,
and more brownish behind; the costa has a fringe of golden
hairs, especially towards the apex; small brown dots at the tip
of the first longitudinal vein and on the marginal cross-vein;
still smaller ones on the subcostal cross-vein and at the tips of all
the longitudinal veins; the central cross-veins are dark brown,

whereas the other veins are yellowish-brown; costa and first
longitudinal veins yellowish.

Hab. Washington, D. C., and farther north; not rare.

4. E. vespertina O. S. ♂ and ♀.—Ochracea, thorace superne
saturate rufo-fusca; humeris sulphureo-flavis; alis immaculatis; venis
pallidis; halteribus flavis.

Ochraceous, thorax of a saturate reddish-brown above; humeri sulphur
yellow; wings immaculate; veins pale; halteres yellow. Long. corp.
0.22—0.25.

SYN. *Erioptera vespertina* O. SACKEN, Proc. Ac. Nat. Sc. Phil. 1859, p. 226.

Ochraceous, with a slight brownish tinge; front sulphur yellow.
brown in the middle; rostrum yellowish, palpi brownish; antennae
brownish; two basal joints somewhat pale, but infuscated at the
tip; basis of the flagellum likewise pale. Thorax reddish-brown
above; the usual four stripes hardly indicated by faint, yellow,
dividing lines; pleura yellowish, very slightly hoary; humeri
sulphur yellow; halteres yellow; feet slender, brownish-yellow;
abdomen brownish-ochraceous; horny appendages of the male
forceps (Tab. IV, fig. 20) brown at the tip. Wings with a slight
grayish tinge; veins pale.

Hab. Washington, D. C.; Florida; Wisconsin (Kennicott);
not rare.

5. E. chlorophylla O. S. ♂ and ♀.—Pallide viridis tota.
Altogether pale green. Long. corp. 0.2—0.25.

SYN. *Erioptera chlorophylla* O. SACKEN, Proc. Ac. Nat. Sc. Phil. 1859, p. 226.

Body pale green; antennae, halteres, veins, genitals, etc. likewise; the eyes alone being black. The ovipositor of the female
is rather long; the upper valves but little curved (wing, Tab. 1,
fig. 16).

Hab. Middle States; not rare.

6. E. stramine a, n. sp. ♂ and ♀.—Pallide flava tota.
Altogether pale yellow. Long. corp. 0.3—0.23.

The whole body, including the wing-veins, is uniformly pale
yellow; the last tarsal joint slightly infuscated.

For a long time I took this species for a mere variety of *E.
chlorophylla*; but the upper valves of its ovipositor are shorter
and much more arcuated.

b. Seventh longitudinal vein straight, diverging from the sixth; discal cell closed.

* The fork of the posterior branch of the fourth longitudinal vein consists of two gently arcuated branches: subgenus Acyphona (compare p. 152).

7. F. venusta O. S. ♂ and ♀.—Alis flavescentibus, fasciis duabus fuscis; femora ante apicem annulo fusco.

Wings yellowish, with two brown bands; femora before the apex with a brown band. Long. corp. 0.23.—0.25.

Syn. Erioptera venusta O. SACKEN, Proc. Ac. Nat. Sc. Phil. 1859, p. 227.

Body brown; antennæ paler on their basal half; thorax reddish above, with a faint indication of a double stripe in the middle; genitals reddish-yellow; halteres and feet pale yellow; femora with a brown band before the tip; on the front femora there is an indication of a second band about the middle; wings (Tab. I, fig. 17) pale yellowish, with two brown bands; the first begins at the origin of the præfurca, is broadest in the middle, and reaches the posterior margin so as to include the tip of the seventh longitudinal vein; the other band lies almost entirely beyond the central cross-vein; it runs through from the anterior to the posterior margin; it is almost of equal breadth; it includes a pale spot at each end; in some specimens, the spot at the anterior margin is connected with the yellow of the apical portion of the wing; in this case a brown spot at the tip of the first longitudinal vein is isolated from the band; the cross-vein, closing the discal cell, is clouded; the tip of the anterior branch of the second vein and the tips of both branches of the fork which includes the third posterior cell, and the subcostal cross-vein are likewise clouded.

Hab. Middle States; common (I have seen specimens from New York, Virginia, Georgia, Illinois, Connecticut, etc.).

8. F. armillaris, n. sp. ♂ and ♀.—Alis flavescentibus, fascia media angusta et nebulis parvis in venarum initio et apice sitis, fuscis; femora pallida, fusco-annulata, vel fusca, pallido-annulata.

Wings yellowish, with a narrow brown band in the middle, and small brownish clouds at the origins and at the tips of the veins; femora pale, with brown bands or brown with pale bands. Long. corp. 0.23—0.25.

Body brown; antennæ paler on their basal half; thorax reddish above, with a faint indication of a double stripe in the middle;

genitals reddish-yellow; halteres yellow; feet pale yellow; the femora of some specimens are pale yellow, with a brown band before the tip; in other specimens they are dark brown, with a pale band; wings yellowish; a narrow brown band runs along the central cross-veins, and generally does not go beyond the great cross-vein; sometimes, however, it is connected with a cloud at the end of the anal cell; small brown clouds at the tip of all the veins (except the third), on the subcostal and the discal cross-veins, at the origin of the præfurca, and the inner end of the third posterior cell; the middle portion of the fifth longitudinal vein infuscated and surrounded by a more or less extended cloud, which sometimes expands so as to coalesce with the spots at the origin of the præfurca and at the tip of the seventh vein, and forms a band not unlike the inner band of *E. venusta.*

Hab. Trenton Falls, N. Y.; Washington, D. C., etc.

This species is in all respects similar to *E. venusta,* only the brown picture of the wings is less extended. If we imagine some of the spots more expanded, two bands, perfectly similar in shape to those of *E. venusta* will be formed. Still, although I have seen numerous specimens of *E. venusta,* I found its picture rather constant, and I have not observed any specimens with brown femora, as they occur in *E. armillaris.* The following species—*E. graphica*—shows also the most striking analogy to *E. armillaris* in the distribution of the spots on the wings; only the body as well as the wings is a shade darker brown. If *E. graphica* did not exist, I would feel less hesitation about uniting *E. armillaris* and *venusta;* but *E. graphica* is, to all appearances, nothing but a dark colored *E. armillaris,* and anybody would hesitate to consider *graphica* and *venusta* as the same species. I invite the attention of collectors to these three species.

9. E. graphica O. S. ♂ and ♀.—Fusca, alis fuscescentibus, fascia media angusta et nebula plurimis fusois; in margine antico majoribus, in postico parvis; femora fusca, annulo ante apicem pallida.

Brown, wings brownish, with a narrow brown band in the middle, and numerous brown clouds; larger ones along the anterior, smaller ones along the posterior margin. Long. corp. 0.25—0.37.

Syn. *Erioptera graphica* O. Sacken, Proc. Ac. Nat. Sc. Phila. 1859, p. 227.

Body brownish; antennæ paler at the basis; thorax yellowish-gray above, with a faint brown stripe, divided in two by a longi-

tudinal grayish line, in the middle; the sides of the mesonotum
and two stripes on the pleura, dark brown; abdomen brown;
halteres pale; femora dark brown, except the basis of the anterior
ones, and a pale band some distance before the tip; the tips of the
tibiæ and of the tarsi likewise infuscated; wings with a slight
brownish-gray tinge; a brown band runs along the central cross-
veins; broad at the anterior end, it soon becomes narrow; tips
of all the veins with small gray clouds; similar clouds on the
discal cross-vein, and at the inner end of the third posterior cell;
the clouds at the tip of the first and of the second longitudinal
veins are larger; the fifth longitudinal vein is infuscated and
clouded at the two intervals before the great cross-vein; the
cloud on the second infuscation, in connection with a large cloud
on the anterior margin and another cloud at the tip of the seventh
longitudinal vein, form an interrupted transverse band; the veins
are infuscated, wherever there is a cloud upon them; in the
intervals of the clouds the veins are yellowish.

Hab. Washington, D. C. Caught in numbers.

The position of the clouds is exactly like that in the preceding
species; only the tinge of the wings is darker, and the clouds
larger and darker. The coloring of the body of both species is
also very similar; only that of *E. graphica* is darker (compare
the observations at the end of the preceding species).

** The fork of the posterior branch of the fourth longitudinal vein (containing the third posterior
cell) has an angular anterior branch, which
emits a stump of a vein inside of the discal
cell: subgenus **Hoplolabis** (comp. p. 152).

18. **E. armata** O. S. ♂ and ♀.—Fumana; abdominis segmentorum
marginos postici pallidi; pedes pallidi; alæ fusco maculatæ; venæ
truncus abrupta, in cellulam discoidalem porrectus.

Brownish; hind margins of the abdominal segments pale; feet pale;
wings with brown spots; a stump of a vein inside of the discal cell.
Long. corp. 0.23—0.25.

Syn. *Erioptera armata* O. Sacken, Proc. Ac. Nat. Sc. Phil. 1859, p. 227.

Body brownish; thorax yellowish-gray above; stripes indistinct; knob of the halteres infuscated; abdomen brown, hind
margins of the segments pale; feet yellowish. Wings (Tab. I,
fig. 13) with five or six brown spots along the anterior margin;

the first, a small dot, is on the humeral cross-vein; the second at
the origin of the præfurca; it does not reach the costa; the third
runs from the costa, across the subcostal cross-vein to the præfurca; the fourth spot is large, and lies between the costa and
the inner end of the first submarginal cell; the fourth, equally
large, covers the tip of the first longitudinal vein; cross-veins
infuscated and clouded; tips of all the longitudinal veins, except
the third, with small brown clouds; the third posterior cell is
square at the inner end, and emits a long stump of a vein from
the angle of this square inside of the discal cell; in some specimens this stump reaches the opposite side of the cell, and thus
divides it in two.

Hab. Washington, D. C.; New York; Illinois (LeBaron);
Wisconsin (Uhe); usually in the spring.

The male forceps of this species (Tab. II, fig. 14, 14 a) is distinguished by long slender horny processes (compare the description in the explanation of the plates).

2. The *anterior* branch of the fourth longitudinal vein is forked (in
other words, when the discal cell is open, it coalesces with
the third posterior cell); when the discal cell is closed the
inner ends of the second and third posterior cells are nearly
in one line: subgenus **Mesocyphona** (compare p. 152).

11. E. caloptera SAY. ♂ and ♀.—Alis fuscatis, guttis, guttulisque
limpidis.

Wings brownish, with hyaline spots and smaller dots. Long. corp. 0.13—
0.25.

SYN. *Erioptera caliptera* SAY, Journ. Ac. Nat. Sc. Phil. III, p. 17, 1.
Erioptera caloptera WIED. Auss. Zw. I, p. 23, 1.
Erioptera caloptera O. SACKEN, Proc. Ac. Nat. Sc. Phil. 1859, p. 236.

Brownish-yellow, thorax with a whitish tinge above, and with
two distinct, dark brown stripes; similar stripes on the pleura;
one above, another in the middle, and a third, less distinct one,
along the coxæ; feet whitish, with a brown band before the tip
of the femora. Wings brownish (which color is more intense on
their anterior portion), covered with numerous white spots;
those along the margins are larger, especially on the anterior
one; those in the apical portion of the wing in the submarginal
and posterior cells (except the fourth) are smaller, numerous,
and crowded together; a hyaline band over the central cross-veins.

Hab. United States, common; occurs also in Cuba.

The discal cell of this species is sometimes closed, but generally open.

12. F. porva O. S.   ♂ and ♀.—Alis sublimpidis, nebulis in margine parvis novem vel decem obscuris.

Wings subhyaline, nine or ten small dark clouds along the margin. Long. corp. 0.15—0.2.

Syn. *Eriopera porva* O. Sacken, Proc. Ac. Nat. Sc. Phil. 1859, p. 227.

Brownish-yellow, thorax paler above, with two distinct dark brown stripes; similar stripes on the pleura; feet whitish, with an obscure band before the. tip of the femora. Wings with a grayish tinge; small gray clouds along the anterior and posterior margins, at the tips of all the longitudinal veins; those of the anterior margin somewhat larger; central cross-veins clouded. Discal cell open, coalescing with the third posterior cell.

Hab. Washington, D. C.; Orange, N. J., in June, not rare; Dalton, Ga. The coloring of its body is very like that of *E. caloptera*.

B. The prefurca ends in the first submarginal cell, which is longer than the second; the inner end of the discal cell (or rather, as it is always open, of the second posterior cell), as well as the great cross-vein, are not in one line with the small cross-vein, but much nearer to the basis of the wing (Tab. I, fig. 19): subgenus **Molophilus** (compare p. 153).

13. F. pubipennis O. S.   ♀.—Flava, fronte et humeris sulphureo-flavis; pedibus antlcis fuscis; alis immaculatis, costa et apice flavo-villosis.

Yellow, front and humeri sulphur-yellow; front feet brownish; wings immaculate, costa and apex with a golden-yellow fringe of hairs. Long. corp. 0.2.

Syn. *Eriopera pubipennis* O. Sacken, Proc. Ac. Nat. Sc. Phil. 1859, p. 228.

Body of a saturate yellow; front and margin round the thorax sulphur yellow; this margin, if viewed in a certain light, has a hoary reflection; mesonotum reddish-yellow; palpi brown; antennae pale, brownish at the tip; halteres pale yellow; fore feet brown, clothed with brown hairs; the two other pairs yellow, with the tips of the tibiae and the tarsi brown; wings grayish, thickly hairy; costa yellow, with a fringe of golden-yellow hairs, running also round the apex. The third posterior cell is somewhat longer than the first, nearly of the same length with the second marginal cell.

Hab. Washington, D. C.

The description is drawn from a number of female specimens. I possess several male specimens from Pennsylvania, which are somewhat darker in coloring; the antennæ are very long, but little shorter than the body; brown, basal joints yellow; the long cylindrical joints of the flagellum clothed with long hairs; the sulphur yellow on the front and the humeri is much less striking; the halteres are slightly brownish and the pubescence of the anterior margin of the wings has a more brownish tinge. I am uncertain whether these specimens belong to the same species.

14. E. hirtipennis O. S. ♀.—Fusca, griseo-pruinosa, antennis pallide fascia; also immaculata, pube nigrescente.

Brown with a grayish bloom, antennæ pale brown; wings immaculate, with a blackish pubescence. Long. corp. 0.3—0.25.

Syn. *Erioptera hirtipennis* O. Sacken, Proc. Ac. Nat. Sc. Phil. 1859, p. 228.

Rostrum and palpi brown; antennæ brownish or blackish; second joint generally slightly paler; joints of the flagellum short subcylindrical; front with a gray bloom and some scattered hairs, which, in a certain light, have a golden-yellow reflection. Thorax dull grayish-brown; stripes obsolete; in somewhat immature specimens a very indistinct pale longitudinal line is sometimes perceptible; humeri with an inconspicuous pale yellow spot; halteres brownish, their basis pale; abdomen grayish-brown, with a golden yellow pubescence; ovipositor ferruginous; feet blackish, coxæ and basis of the femora paler; wings immaculate, with a blackish pubescence; root of the wings pale.

Hab. Washington, D. C.; Maryland; the present description was drawn from four fresh specimens, which I found in Orange, N. J.

15. E. forcipula, n. sp. ♂ and ♀.—Fusca, mesonoto pallide fuscano, antennis fascia, basi pallidis; abdomen fuscum, genitalia flavida; also immaculata, pube fuscana.

Brown, mesonotum pale brownish, antennæ brown, pale at the basis; abdomen brown, genitalia yellowish; wings immaculate, with a brownish pubescence. Long. corp. 0.3—0.25.

Rostrum and p. 'pi brown; antennæ brown, two basal joints
pale yellowish; joints of the flagellum in the female rather
elongated, almost cylindrical; in the male they are shorter; front
brownish, with a gray bloom (the male has some yellow on the
vertex). Thorax pale brownish above; stripes generally obsolete
in front, sometimes visible on the posterior portion of the mesonotum; humeri with rather conspicuous sulphur-yellow spots;
halteres infuscated, except their basis, which is pale; feet brown,
coxæ and basis of the femora yellowish; abdomen brown, with
golden-yellow hairs; its tip, including the male forceps, is yellowish; horny appendages of the male dark brown; ovipositor ferruginous; wings immaculate, with pale veins and a brownish
pubescence.

Hab. South Orange, N. J.; three specimens.

This species is most closely related to the former, but will be
easily distinguished by its paler coloring, the yellowish basal
joints of its antennæ, the more elongated joints of the flagellum
in the female, the more distinct sulphur yellow spot on the
humeri, etc.

In both of these species the males seem to be comparatively
rare. Having found recently a male specimen of *E. forcipula,*
I examined its forceps, which has a very peculiar structure:
rather large, broad at the basis, showing several coriaceous
appendages, the outer ones linear, the inner ones somewhat
foliaceous; each half of the forceps bears a pair of brown horny
appendages, curved against each other, so as to form a separate
little forceps, which opens and shuts when the large forceps is in
motion.[1]

16. E. ursina O. S.   ♂.—Nigrescens, pilis longis nigris vestita.

Blackish, clothed with long black hairs.   Long. corp. 0.06.

Syn. *Erioptera ursina* O. Sacken, Proc. Ac. Nat. Sc. Phil. 1859, p. 226.

Grayish-black; the body, the veins, and the posterior margin
of the wings covered with long, black hairs, which appear golden
in a reflected light; halteres, antennæ, and feet black.   The
venation is peculiar and different from that of the two preceding

[1] *E. forcipula* has been added since this volume is in press; for this
reason it has not been comprised in the numerical data given on pages
35 and 36.

species; the marginal cross-vein is almost on one line with the
inner end of the first submarginal cell; the latter is but very
little anterior to the inner end of the second submarginal and
first posterior cells; the third posterior cell is much shorter than
the first (the venation can of course be perceived only when the
hairs are rubbed off).

Hab. Washington, D. C., and Maryland; forms clouds in the
spring near running waters. This species seems to be very like
the European *E. marina* Meig.; but I have had no opportunity
for a comparison.

Gen. XVIII. TRIMICRA.

Two submarginal cells; four posterior cells; a discal cell; the second
longitudinal vein originates, at a more or less acute angle, before the
middle of the length of the wing and a considerable distance (more than
the breadth of the wing) before the tip of the auxiliary vein; the subcostal cross-vein is at a considerable distance (three lengths of the great
cross-vein, or more) from the tip of the auxiliary vein; seventh longitudinal vein straight. Wings and their veins glabrous (Tab. II, fig. 1).
Antennæ 16-jointed; three last joints of the flagellum abruptly smaller. Tibiæ
without spurs at the tip; ungues small, smooth on the under side, inserted
under a projection of the last tarsal joint; empodia small, but distinct.
Forceps of the male with large, incrassated basal pieces, and a double
claw shaped horny appendage fastened to them on each side; ovipositor
with flattened, curved, pointed upper valves and short lower ones.

Rostrum and palpi short; eyes glabrous, separated above by a
moderately broad front and almost contiguous below. Antennæ
of moderate length, or rather short, as they would hardly reach
the root of the wings, if bent backwards; joints of the flagellum,
especially the basal ones, short, oblong or subcylindrical, with
moderate verticils; the three last joints of the antennæ are
abruptly smaller than the preceding ones (this peculiarity may
be perceived even in dry specimens). Feet comparatively long,
more or less clothed with hair, sometimes conspicuously hairy;
intermediate pair comparatively short; femora sometimes conspicuously incrassated at the tip. The position of the ungues
under a projection of the last tarsal joint, which likewise exists
in some degree in *Erioptera* and *Symplecta*, is particularly striking here. The forceps has very stout basal pieces, closely applied
to each other (and not with an open interval between them, as in
Symplecta). The wings (Tab. II, fig. 1) are rather long and

comparatively narrow. The venation has nothing abnormal, and strikes at once by the straight course and the parallelism of the veins ending in the apex of the wing, between the latter portion of the first longitudinal vein and the second posterior cell; hence the rather long first and second submarginal and first posterior cells have parallel sides and are narrow and linear. Discal cell subtriangular; the great cross-vein a little anterior to it; the auxiliary vein ends opposite the marginal cross-vein; the first longitudinal vein some distance beyond it; the origin of the second longitudinal vein is some distance before the middle of the anterior margin; the præfurca is straight, and its curvature near its origin is none or almost none; petiole of the first submarginal cell shorter than the great cross-vein; the marginal cross-vein is a trifle beyond the inner end of the first submarginal cell; the sixth as well as the seventh longitudinal veins are nearly straight. The stigma is almost imperceptible, hardly marked at all. The venation of the European *T. pilipes* and the North American *T. anomala* are exactly alike.

Trimicra forms a natural transition between *Erioptera* and *Chionea* on one side and *Symplecta* on the other. The position of its subcostal cross-vein and of the origin of the second longitudinal vein proves its relationship to *Erioptera*. *Symplecta* possesses the same characters, somewhat weakened however; its præfurca is more distinctly arcuated near its origin, and this origin is somewhat less near the basis of the wing; moreover it has, like *Trimicra*, the great cross-vein somewhat anterior to the discal cell. But although the sinuated course of the seventh longitudinal vein, and the structure of the male genitalia sufficiently distinguishes *Symplecta*, both genera are very closely allied. The European species, *Symplecta stictica* and *similis*, are very like *Trimicra* in outward appearance, but I have had no opportunity to examine the structure of their forceps. Among the *Erioptera* with short hairs along the veins some might perhaps be mistaken for *Trimicra*. But the pubescence of the wing-veins of this genus is much more minute, hardly perceptible; the seventh longitudinal vein runs straight to the posterior margin, the axillary cell being broadest near the margin; the inner ends of the second and third posterior cells are in one line, making it appear doubtful which of the branches of the fourth longitudinal vein is furcate. The *Erioptera* of the section

where the short pubescence occurs (subg. *Eriojtera* nob.) have
the seventh vein arcuated, its tip being approximated to the tip
of the preceding vein, the third posterior cell is longer than the
second, showing distinctly that it is the posterior branch of the
fourth longitudinal vein which is forked, etc. I have before me
a European *Eriopiera* of that kind (*Limnobia ciliaris* Schum.?),
the appearance of which, at first sight, is very deceptive, as its
venation in most points, and its coloring, are not unlike those
of *Trimicra.*

When I first established this genus (*Proc. Acad. Nat. Sci.
Philad.* 1861, p. 290) upon a small North American species, I
was not at all aware of the existence of the European *T. pilipes*
Fab., a much larger and more striking form, the true type of the
genus. All the characters, indicated by me at that time as dis-
tinctive of the genus, are to be found strongly marked in *T. pilipes.*
The genus *Gnophomyia* of the *Fauna Austriaca* (*Diptera*) is not
Gnophomyia O. S., but *Trimicra.*

Besides Europe and North America, *Trimicra* has been found
in Mexico, South America, South Africa, and Australia. I have
seen a species from Mexico in Mr. Bellardi's collection; one from
Montevideo in the Berlin Museum. *Limnobia hirtipes* Walk.
(*List.* etc., I, p. 60), from the Swan River, Australia, and *Gnophomyia inconspicua* Loew, from Caffraria (*Berl. Entom. Z.*
1866, p. 59), are *Trimicrae.* Dr. Schiner (*Reise d. Novara*, etc.,
pp. 42, 43) describes two species from the island of St. Paul (*T.
antarctica* and *T. st. pauli*), and one (*T. sidneyensis*) from Sidney.
Those species which I have seen, although coming from distant
parts of the world, are very much alike in coloring.

The name (from τρεῖς, three, and μικρός, small) alludes to the
small size of the terminal joints of the antennae.

Description of the species.

1. T. anomala O. S.—Fuscano-cinerea, thorace lineis tribus fuscis,
alis immaculatis, modice fuscescentibus; antennis nigris.

Brownish-gray, thorax with three brown lines, wings immaculate, somewhat tinged with brownish; antennae black. Long. corp. 0.3—0.35.

Syn. *Trimicra anomala* O. Sacken, Proc. Ac. Nat. Sc. Phil. 1861, p. 290.

Brownish-gray; vertex brownish in the middle, with a dark
line extended over the front; the latter yellowish on the sides,

along the orbits of the eyes; antennæ and palpi blackish-brown; the space occupied by the usual stripes on the mesonotum is brownish, with three dark brown lines; the intermediate one is especially distinct; the lateral ones are curved anteriorly and extended beyond the suture posteriorly; the humeral region is yellowish; pleuræ hoary below, with a brown stripe between the collare and the root of the halteres; metathorax brownish, with a hoary bloom; halteres yellowish, sometimes infuscated; feet brownish, tip of the femora broadly, tip of the tibiæ only a little infuscated; abdomen brown, the lateral margins, as well as those of the single segments, paler; forceps of the male reddish. Wings slightly tinged with brownish; cross-veins with hardly perceptible brownish clouds.

Hab. Washington, D. C.; New Rochelle, N. Y.; Newport, R. I.; in June, also in August and September; always near water.

Gen. XII. CHIONEA.

No wings. Antennæ 8-jointed, structure abnormal; feet stout, hairy; abdomen short; last segment very large, subglobular, inclosing the basis of the forceps; the latter comparatively large and strong, with strong claw-shaped appendages; ovipositor pointed; the upper and lower valves divaricated at the basis.

Head rounded, front convex; rostrum short; palpi with four short joints; first joint of the antennæ cylindrical, elongated; the second of equal length, club-shaped at the tip; the third short conical; the remainder of the antennæ slender, filiform, with three joints;[1] joints of the scapus pubescent, those of the flagellum with rather long verticils. Thorax comparatively small; the transverse suture visible at the sides only; scutellum short and broad; last abdominal segment very large, rounded on the under side, inclosing the basis of the forceps. Feet stout, comparatively long, hairy; coxæ large; the hindmost femora (according to Dr. Harris) are very thick and somewhat bowed in the males; tibiæ without spurs at the tip; empodia distinct; angues smooth; the fourth joint of the tarsi is somewhat incrassated on the under side, at the basis. Halteres short, with

[1] For the number of antennal joints I rely upon Dr. Schiner (*Fauna Austr. Dipt.* II. p. 573), who had seen living specimens. It seems to me that I can count four joints in the only specimen in my possession.

n large knob. " The body of the female ends in a sword-shaped
borer, resembling that of a grasshopper." (Harris.)

The relationship of *Chionea* has been discussed on p. 136.

These insects occur on snow in winter; the larvæ live underground, apparently upon vegetable matters, and have been described in detail by Braner (*Verh. Zool. Bot. Ver. in Wien. 1854*).

Chionea (from χιών, snow) *araneoides* has been described for
the first time by Dalman, in 1816 (*K. Vetensk. Acad. Handl. 1816,*
102; Tab. II, fig. 2). A second European species, *Ch. crassipes,*
has been described since by Boheman. Harris (*Ins. of Mass.
Injur. to Veget. 1841*) first mentioned the American species, *Ch.
valga.* Later, Mr. Walker described two North American
Chioneæ, Ch. aspera and *scita,* the former of which is probably
synonymous with *Ch. valga.* The descriptions of Mr. Walker's
species are reproduced in the Appendix I to this volume.

I have never had an opportunity to observe any species of this
genus alive, and possess only a single, somewhat mutilated specimen of one of the North American species. Partly from this
specimen, partly from Dr. Harris's and Dr. Schiner's statements
(*Fauna Austr. l. c.*) the foregoing generic description has been
drawn. Assuming that my specimen is *Chionea valga* Harr., I
describe it under this name.

Description of the species.

1. C. valga Harr. ♀.—Rufa, fuscescens, pedibus pallidioribus.
Brownish-red, feet paler. Long. corp. 0.22.

Syn. *Chionea valga* Harris, Ins. Injur. to Veget. 410. 1841.
  Chionea aspera Walker, List, etc. 1, p. 82.

Head brownish-red, in a reflected light the front and vertex
show a hoary bloom; palpi brown; front with an impressed
transverse line between the eyes; vertex broad, rounded, sparsely
clothed with erect, blackish, rather long hairs; the brownish antennæ are but little longer than the head, from the point of its
connection with the collare to the extremity of the labium (their
description is given above). Thorax reddish-brown (injured by
the pin in my specimen); halteres brownish-yellow. Abdomen
short, pubescent with yellowish, segments contracted (at least in
the dry specimen), so that the last joint, which is horny and subglobular, appears to be larger in size than the remainder of the

abdomen; the color of the abdomen is pale brownish; last joint reddish-brown, with brownish hairs, especially on its rounded under side; its upper side convex, with an open space below (fornicate); forceps large, reddish; horny appendages stout, claw-shaped, ending in a rather blunt point. Feet paler than the body, reddish-yellow, rather uniformly beset with long, black-ish hairs; the hairs on the under side of the first tarsal joint are shorter, but denser than those on the upper side; under side of the following joints with a microscopic pubescence; under side of the last joint not excised in the male; the length of the femora is equal to about three-quarters of the length of the body.

Hab. Massachusetts; Canada (Harris).

Gen. XX. SYMPLECTA.

Two submarginal cells; four posterior cells; discal cell closed; the second longitudinal vein originates before the middle of the length of the wing and at a considerable distance (about equal to the breadth of the wing) before the tip of the auxiliary vein; the subcostal cross-vein is at a considerable distance (three lengths of the great cross-vein or more) from the tip of the auxiliary vein; the seventh longitudinal vein is strongly bisinuated (Tab. I, fig. 20, wing of *S. punctipennis*). Wings and their veins glabrous. Antennae 16-jointed. Tibiae without spurs at the tip; ungues small, empodia distinct. The forceps of the male consists of two elongated subcylindrical basal pieces, with two blunt horny appendages attached to each of them (Tab. IV, fig. 21, forceps of *S. punctipennis*, from above). Ovipositor with curved, pointed upper valves and short lower ones.

The close relationship between this genus and *Trimicra* has already been pointed out under the head of the latter genus. However, the three terminal joints of the antennae are not abruptly smaller, the wings are somewhat broader, the second vein, after originating from the first, describes a gentle curve (and therefore does not form an acute angle with the first); the seventh longitudinal vein is bisinuated, not straight; the basal pieces of the forceps are subcylindrical, elongated, and not so much incrassated as in *Trimicra*, leaving a large interval, distinctly perceptible even in dry specimens, between them and the horny appendages. The structure of the feet is the same, and the ungues are also inserted under a slight projection of the last tarsal joint.

Meigen adopted this genus in 1830 (*Meig. Zweifl.* etc. VI. p.

282). Since then, it has been retained by all the subsequent authors. Its name (from σύν, with, and πλέκω, to connect) alludes, I suppose, to the supernumerary cross-vein of *S. punctipennis*. A little earlier than Meigen, in 1825, St. Fargeau (*Encycl. Méthod. Ins.* Vol. X, p. 585) proposed to call this genus *Helobia*. Meigen's name, as that given by the monographer of the order and consecrated by a long usage, ought not to be superseded.

Three European species are known; one of them, which has a supernumerary cross-vein in the first submarginal cell, occurs also in America (*S. punctipennis*). In this species it is the posterior branch of the fourth longitudinal vein which is forked; in the two other species (*S. similis* and *stictica*) it is the anterior one; this is indicated in each case by the shape of the discal cell. Like *Trimicra*, the three species of *Symplecta* have the great cross-vein anterior to the inner end of the discal cell, and rather oblique. The supposed new genus and species *Idioneura macroptera* Philippi (*Verh. Zool. Bot. Gesellsch.* 1865, p. 615, Tab. XXIII, fig. 4), is undoubtedly *Symplecta*, and not at all unlikely the same *S. punctipennis* M.

Description of the species.

1. **S. punctipennis** O. S. ♂ and ♀.—Cinerea, thorace vittis tribus fuscis; alis albicantibus, vena transversis obscure nebulosis; vena transversa supernumeraria in cellula marginali secunda.

Gray, thorax with three brown stripes, wings whitish, cross-veins clouded; a supernumerary cross-vein in the second marginal cell. Long. corp. 0.23—0.25.

Syn. *Limnobia punctipennis* Macq. Hist. Ent. Zw. Ins. I, p. 147; Tab. V, fig. 7.
Symplecta punctipennis Macq. I. c. VI, p. 283.
Symplecta punctipennis O. Sacken, Proc. Ac. Nat. Sc. Phil. 1859, p. 228.
Symplecta cana Walk. List, etc. I, p. 48.

Head gray, antennæ and palpi black; thorax gray, hoary on the pleura; three distinct brown stripes above; the lateral ones cross the transverse suture; knob of the halteres infuscated; feet brown; abdomen gray, darker above; wings (Tab. 1. fig. 20) with a whitish tinge; a supernumerary cross-vein about the middle of the first submarginal cell; the posterior branch of the fourth longitudinal vein is forked, and hence, the inner end of the third posterior cell is nearer the basis of the wing than the inner end

of the second ; the first is pointed, the latter square ; the great
cross-vein is some distance anterior to the discal cell ; all the
cross-veins, the origin of the prefurca, and the tip of the first
longitudinal vein are clouded with brownish-gray.

Common everywhere in the spring and in autumn. I possess
specimens from Washington, D. C. ; Mobile, Ala. ; New York ;
Canada ; Illinois (Kennicott). The supernumerary cross-vein of
the first submarginal cell is wanting in some specimens; the discal
cell is sometimes open.

Gen. XXI. GNOPHOMYIA.

Two submarginal cells ; four posterior cells ; a discal cell : the second
longitudinal vein originates somewhat before the middle of the anterior
margin, a considerable distance anterior to the tip of the auxiliary vein ;
prefurca very slightly arcuated at the basis, nearly straight; submostal
cross-vein at a small or moderate distance (hardly exceeding the length
of the great cross-vein) from the tip of the auxiliary vein ; seventh longitudinal vein nearly straight. Wings glabrous (except an almost microscopic pubescence in the apical cells of *G. luctuosa*). Antennae 16-jointed.
Tibiae without spurs at the tip; tarsi with distinct empodia. The forceps of
the male (Tab. IV, fig. 19, forceps of *G. tristissima* when open) consists
of two comparatively short basal pieces, and a pair of claw-shaped horny
appendages ; a second pair of horny appendages, below the first, is shorter
and stouter.

Body and feet rather stout ; the latter of moderate length,
their pubescence short ; femora slightly increased before the
tip. Front broad, very convex ; eyes glabrous, almost contiguous on the under side ; rostrum short ; palpi of moderate length ;
last joint somewhat elongated. Antennae 16-jointed ; when bent
backwards they reach a little beyond the root of the wings in
both sexes ; joints of the flagellum elongated, subcylindrical in
G. tristissima ; short, subglobular in *G. luctuosa ;* verticils much
longer in the former than in the latter. Collare somewhat
elongated in *G. tristissima ;* short and stout in *G. luctuosa.*
Suture of the thorax distinct. The wings are rather broad in *G.
luctuosa ;* narrower in *G. tristissima* (Tab. II, fig. 5, wing of *G.
tristissima*). The marginal cross-vein is close by the inner end
of the first submarginal cell ; the great cross-vein is more or less
posterior to the inner end of the discal cell ; the latter elongated ;
the fifth, sixth, and seventh longitudinal veins are nearly straight
(more details about the venation and the differences between that

of the two North American species will be given below in the
description of these species). The horny appendages of the forceps of *G. tridissima* are remarkably slender, almost linear and
pointed; the corresponding appendages of *G. luctuosa* seem to
be shorter. The ovipositor of the female (*G. tridissima*) has the
upper valves of moderate length and breadth (Tab. IV, fig. 19,
o); incrassated and arcuated on *the under side* at the basis,
which gives a peculiar appearance to their manner of attachment;
the lower valves are very short, reaching but little beyond the
basis of the upper pair.

Closely allied as *Gnophomyia* is to *Trimicra* and *Symplecta*,
it may at once be distinguished by the position of the subcostal
cross-vein, which is much nearer to the tip of the auxiliary vein
than is the case in those genera; by the position of the great
cross-vein, which is not anterior to the inner end of the discal
cell; by the structure of the forceps of the male, etc. Both
North American species are altogether black; the knob of the
halteres of one of them only is yellow. I have seen two South
American *Gnophomyiæ* in the Berlin Museum, one of which is
the *Limnobia nigrina* Wied. *Auss. Zw.* II, p. 87. A handsome
species from the Cape, with brown wings, banded with white (in
the same museum), is either a *Gnophomyia*, or closely related to
this genus.

The genus *Gnophomyia* (from γνόφος, darkness, and μυῖα, fly)
was introduced by me in the *Proc. Acad. Nat. Sci. Philad.* 1850,
p. 223. The genus described under this name in the *Fauna
Austriaca* is *Trimicra* (comp. above, page 167).

A genus closely allied to the present one is *Psiloconopa* (from
ψιλός, glabrous, and κώνωψ, gnat). It was established by Zetterstedt, in 1840 (*Fauna Lapponica*, p. 847, and later. *Dipt. Scand.*
X, p. 4007), upon a single species (*P. meigenii*), found in the
northern parts of Sweden. The genus has hardly been noticed
since, although several other species occur in Europe. The
typical species, *P. meigenii*, I have not seen, but have before me
an apparently undescribed species from Germany, larger than *P.
meigenii*, and distinguished by the frequent absence of the marginal cross-vein. Of another, smaller species, I have a single
specimen from the north of Italy. It has no marginal cross-vein
and its discal cell is open, coalescing with the *third* posterior
cell. There is but little doubt that this species is the *Erioptera*

lateralis Macq. Hist. Natur. Dipt. II, p. 653 (syn. Limnobia
flavolimbata Hal. in Walker's Ins. Brit. Dipt. III, p. 304). The
two species which I have before me otherwise agree in their
venation, and differ in it from Gnophomyia: the anterior branch
of the second longitudinal vein is short and oblique, almost like
that of Goniomyia, thus modifying the shape of the first submarginal cell (it seems, however, that in P. meigenii, which I
have not seen, the first submarginal cell has the same shape as in
Gnophomyia); the petiole of this cell is longer; the marginal
cross-vein seems to be usually wanting. The abdomen of the
German species is more club-shaped at the tip than that of Gnophomyia, and the forceps has a different structure. Again, the
three European species agree among themselves in their coloring;
they have yellow stripes on the sides of the thorax and a yellow
scutellum, besides some other yellow marks peculiar to some of
them. The known American species of Gnophomyia are altogether dark in their coloring, except the halteres of G. tristissima,
which are yellow.

Psiloconopa supplies, in my opinion, the missing link between
the Eriopterina and the genus Goniomyia, the link for which I
have been looking unsuccessfully in the Proc. Acad. Nat. Sci.
Philad. 1859, p. 230. This has become particularly evident to
me, since I have seen Psiloconopa lateralis Macq., the venation
of which (short first submarginal cell, oblique anterior branch of
the second vein, open discal cell, coalescent with the third
posterior cell) very forcibly reminds of Goniomyia. The prevalence of yellow in the coloring of Psiloconopa increases the
probability of the relationship of these two genera. My knowledge of Psiloconopa is not sufficient to enable me to decide
upon the degree of this relationship; but at the same time, I
have seen enough of this genus to convince me that it would be
premature to unite it with Gnophomyia.

Description of the species.

1. G. luctuosa O. S.   ♂.—Atra, halteribus atris; alis obscure in-
fumatis.

Black, opaque; halteres black; wings smoky blackish. Long. corp. 0.32.

Syn. Gnophomyia luctuosa O. Sacken, Proc. Ac. Nat. Sc. Phil. 1859, p. 224.
    Limnobia nigricula Walker, Trans. Ent. Soc. Lond. V, n. s. part VII,
    p. 66.

The whole body, including the halteres, of a deep, opaque black; velvet black on the thorax. Wings smoky, nearly black; costal cell still darker; stigma hardly distinct; a short, almost microscopic pubescence in the apical portion of the wings; the venation is somewhat different from that of the following species; the anterior branch of the second longitudinal vein is almost imperceptibly arcuated; the posterior branch and the third vein are quite straight; the petiole of the first submarginal cell (that is, the distance between its inner end and the tip of the præfurca) is not much longer than the distance between the tip of the præfurca and the small cross-vein. The forceps of the male is hairy; the horny appendages seem to be somewhat stouter than in the following species; the joints of the flagellom, at least the four or five basal ones, are short, not much longer than broad, with a delicate, short pubescence on the under side.

Hab. Florida; I caught a single male, in March, 1858. That Mr. Walker's *L. nigricola* has been published later than 1859, appears from the circumstance that Mr. Bellardi's work, published in that year, is quoted by him in the same paper (page 2d).

2. G. tristissima O. S. ♂ and ♀.—Nigra, pedibus piceis; halteres capitulis flavis; alis subhyalinis, stigmate oblongo, obscuro.

Black, feet blackish-brown; knob of the halteres yellow; wings subhyaline, stigma oblong, dark. Long. corp. 0.25—0.35.

Syn. *Gnophomyia tristissima* O. Sacken, Proc. Ac. Nat. Sc. Phil. 1859, p. 224.

Body black, but little shining; mesonotum more gibbose than in *G. luctuosa*; a slight hoary reflection on the lower part of the pleuræ and sometimes on the front; feet dark brown, coxæ black; stem of the halteres brown, knob yellow; wings (Tab. II, fig. 5) slightly tinged with brownish-gray; stigma blackish, elongated, divided longitudinally in two halves by the first longitudinal vein; the marginal cross-vein, usually placed at the inner end of the first submarginal cell, is sometimes a little posterior to it; both branches of the second longitudinal vein and the third vein are arcuated; the petiole of the first submarginal cell is longer here than in *G. luctuosa*; whereas the small cross-vein is close by the origin of the third vein. The forceps (Tab. IV, fig. 19) and the ovipositor (fig. 19 a) have been described above.

Not rare; Washington, D. C.; New York; Virginia; Upper Wisconsin River (Kennicott).

Gen. XXII. PHILOCONOPA.

This European genus being but imperfectly known by me, I
have to confine myself to the remarks already given about it in
the genus *Gnophomyia* (compare p. 173).

Gen. XXIII. GONIOMYIA.

Two submarginal cells; *the first very short, subtriangular,* owing to the
shortness and the oblique direction of the anterior branch of the second
longitudinal vein (Tab. II, fig. 4, wing of *G. subcinerea*; fig. 2, *G. sulphurella*); no marginal cross-vein; four posterior cells; discal cell open or
closed; when open, it is coalescent with the *third* posterior cell; wings
glabrous. Antennæ 16-jointed, rather short. Feet long, slender; tibiæ
without spurs at the tip, tarsi with distinct empodia. Forceps of the male
with several branches and linear appendages (Tab. IV. fig. 17, forceps of *G.
blanda*; fig. 18, of *G. cognatella*). Ovipositor of the female slender, acuated.

Rostrum and palpi short; the joints of the latter nearly of
equal length. The antennæ, if bent backwards, would not reach
beyond the root of the wings; the joints of the flagellum are
short subcylindrical or oval, verticillate; in *G. sulphurella* the
basal joints in the male are strongly incrassated. The feet are
more or less pubescent; sometimes this pubescence is hardly perceptible. The wings vary in length; they are comparatively
short in *G. sulphurella* (Tab. II, fig. 2), and longer in *G. subcinerea* (Tab. II. fig. 4) and *blanda*. The venation has many
striking peculiarities; the tip of the auxiliary vein is nearly
opposite the origin of the second longitudinal vein, often a little
before or a little beyond it; never so much beyond it as in the
other *Eriopterina*; the subcostal cross-vein is at this very tip (*G.
subcinerea, cognatella, sulphurella*), or quite near it (*G. blanda*).
The præfurca originates about the middle of the anterior margin;
it is more or less arcuated; the first submarginal cell is very short;
its petiole being long and its inner end being posterior to the tip
of the first longitudinal vein, or at the utmost, nearly opposite
this tip (*G. blanda*); the anterior branch of the second longitudinal vein is short, running obliquely towards the costa and
reaching it at a short distance beyond the tip of the first longitudinal vein, or at this very tip (*G. blanda*); this course of the
anterior branch of the second longitudinal vein gives to the first
submarginal cell a triangular shape; the marginal cross-vein is

wanting in all the species to me known; the relative length of the
second submarginal and of the first posterior cells is somewhat
variable; they are of equal length in *G. sulphurella;* the submarginal is a trifle longer in *G. cognatella* and *subcinerea;* a
good deal longer in *G. blanda;* the discal cell is open in some
species and closed in others; this character is in some measure
even variable within the same species, and therefore not entirely
reliable; whenever the discal cell is open, it coalesces with the
third posterior cell,[1] and thus it becomes apparent that it is the
anterior branch of the fourth longitudinal vein which is forked;
fifth, sixth, and seventh veins nearly straight; the latter sometimes slightly curved before the tip. The veins almost glabrous,
except in some rare cases, when they show a more distinct,
although very short pubescence.

These delicate insects are distinguished by the frequent occurrence of a peculiar sulphur yellow in their coloring, and in this
respect the European and the American species agree with each
other. They are not numerous—four or five being known in
Europe, and four having been discovered in America. The
peculiar shape of the first submarginal cell distinguishes them
easily; and if we add to that the relative position of the tip of the
auxiliary vein to the origin of the second vein (so different from
the other *Eriopterina*), the absence of the marginal cross-vein
(at least in all the species known to me); the coalescence of the
discal cell with the *third* posterior cell, whenever it is open; and
the peculiar structure of the male forceps, visible even in dry
specimens, we will have sufficiently characterized the genus.
The majority of the European species have the forceps of an
analogous structure; one or two of them seem to be different;
I have not seen the species of the latter kind and have therefore
no opinion about them.

In speaking of the genus *Psiloconopa* (compare above, p. 174)
I have alluded to the possible relationship between it and *Goniomyia,* especially apparent in the European *P. lateralis* Macq.;
this discovery seems to resolve the doubts which I formerly enter-
tained (*Proc. Acad. Nat. Sci. Philad.* 1859, p. 230) about the
location of *Goniomyia* among the *Eriopterina.*

[1] Exceptions are merely individual; thus I have seen a specimen of *G.
subcinerea,* the discal cell of which was coalescent with the second posterior
cell.

12   Sept. 1868.

By all means the position of *Goniomyia*, as proved by its
characters, is on the extreme limit of the group of *Eriopterina*,
and this view is strengthened by the following circumstance: The
smallness of the first submarginal cell seems to foreshadow its
entire disappearance; and indeed, I possess two specimens where
this disappearance actually takes place through the obliteration
of the branch of the second longitudinal vein. One of these
specimens resembles *G. sulphurella* very much; it is hardly
possible that it is an accidental abnormity[1] of a specimen of this

[1] While this volume was in press, I have found a second specimen of the
same kind, and have had the opportunity to examine it when it was still
alive. It is not an accidental abnormity, but a new species closely allied
to *G. sulphurella*. Although a new genus might be easily formed upon
this species, I prefer to leave it in the genus *Goniomyia*, until more species
of the same kind are made known. Thus *Goniomyia* will contain species
with two and with one submarginal cell, just as *Limnophila* contains species
with five and with four posterior cells.

Goniomyia manca, n. sp. ♂.—Flava, sulphureo maculata, halteribus sulphureo-flavis; ala cellula submarginali unica.

Yellow, marked with sulphur yellow, halteres sulphur yellow; wings with
a single submarginal cell. Long. corp. 0.2.

Rostrum yellowish, palpi brown; front brownish in the middle; two
basal joints of the antennae yellowish, considerably infuscated; the first
is small; the second much larger than the first, rounded; flagellum blackish, slender, with long verticils (somewhat similar to those of *G. sulphurella*), which give the flagellum a feather-like appearance. Thorax yellow,
pale brownish above with faintly indicated stripes and a slight gray bloom;
collare and upper part of the pleura sulphur yellow; the remainder of the
pleura with a hoary bloom; halteres with a sulphur yellow knob. Abdomen and male forceps yellow. Feet yellowish-tawny; the tips of the
femora, tibiae, and tarsi hardly darker. Wings immaculate, with a slight
grayish tinge; the venation is precisely like that of *G. sulphurella* (Tab.
II, fig. 3), except that the *posterior* branch of the second longitudinal vein
is obliterated; thus the second longitudinal vein, shortly before its tip,
takes a sudden turn towards the anterior margin, in consequence of which
the submarginal cell is trumpet-shaped, that is, very considerably narrower
at its inner than at its outer end. The discal cell is closed.

The forceps of the male (which I have examined on a living specimen)
belongs to the same type of structure as those of the other species of
Goniomyia, but the structure is more simple than that of the two species
the forceps of which I have figured (Tab. IV, fig. 17 and 16). There are
two lateral, elongated, subcylindrical (digitiform) lobes, converging, but

species; the specimen is too imperfectly preserved to allow a close comparison. The other specimen, however, belongs to a species which is manifestly distinct from all known *Goniomyia*, but which, at the same time, shows the characters of this genus in a most striking manner; the venation (except the absence of the first submarginal cell) resembles that of *G. sulphurella*, but the auxiliary vein is much shorter; the marginal cross-vein is absent; the discal cell is open and coalesces with the third posterior cell; the costa has a remarkable whitish tinge; otherwise the coloring and the general appearance of the insect are those of *Goniomyia*. The structure of the male forceps would be decisive as to the relationship of this species; but the specimen is a female.

The name of this genus occurs for the first time in Meigen, Vol. I, p. 146, as *Gonomyia*. Megerle sent him *L. tenella* under that generic denomination, which, however, Meigen did not adopt. It was revived afterwards by Mr. Stephens in his *Catalogue*, etc. (1822), and by Mr. Curtis in his *Guide* (1837), in connection with the same species, but without any definition. I have defined the genus in the *Proc. Acad. Nat. Sci. Philad.* 1859, p. 229, and described the four North American species belonging to it. In 1864 Dr. Schiner (*Fauna Austriaca, Dipt.* Vol. II, p. 543) gave this genus a wider definition by admitting in it some species which, according to my opinion, it is better to separate, and which now form the genus *Empeda*.

As the name of this genus is probably derived from γωνία, angle, in allusion to the shape of the fork of the second longitudinal vein, I propose to amend it in *Goniomyia*.

Table for the determination of the species.

1 {	Wings spotted.	4 blanda O. S.
	Wings not spotted.	2

---

not lapping over each other in repose; immediately above and parallel to them is a single, long, horny style, the tip of which reaches beyond the tip of the lobes; below the lobes, some small, black, horny organs are perceptible.

Hab. South Orange, N. J., June 30, 1868; a single specimen.

The first longitudinal vein in my specimen comes to an abrupt termination before reaching the costa.

> 2 { Femora with a distinct brown band before the tip ; knob of the halteres
>   lemon yellow.   1 sulphurella *O. S.*
>   { Femora without brown band.   3
> 3 { Antennæ orange at the basis.   2 pugnatella *O. S.*
>   { Antennæ entirely black.   3 subobscurea *O. S.*

Description of the species.

1. G. sulphurella O. S. ♂ and ♀.—Sulphureo-flava, fusco-varie-
gata; antennis basi aurantiacis, in mare verticillis longis; femoribus
annulo fusco; cellula discoidali (in speciminibus typicis) clausa.

Sulphur yellow, variegated with brown; antennæ orange yellow at the
basis; those of the male with long verticils; femora with a brown
band; discal cell (in normal specimens) closed. Long. corp. 0.2—0.25.

Syn. *Gonomyia sulphurella* O. Sacken, Proc. Ac. Nat. Sc. Phil. 1859, p. 230.

Front and vertex sulphur yellow, infuscated in the middle;
proboscis, palpi, and antennæ brown; basal joints of the latter
orange yellow; flagellum of the male incrassated at the base and
slender beyond it, with long, feathery verticils; that of the female
filiform with short verticils; collare sulphur yellow; mesonotum
light brown, yellow along the margins; scutellum yellow with a
brown line in the middle; metathorax yellowish, infuscated in the
middle; pleuræ yellow above; a yellow stripe, margined with
brown, runs from the fore coxæ backwards; halteres yellow;
knob lemon yellow; coxæ pale yellow; femora slightly incrassated at the tip, with a yellow band beyond the middle and a
brown band near the tip, which is yellow; anterior pair of femora
darker, their tip brown; tibiæ tawny, infuscated at the tip; tarsi
fuscous. Abdomen of the male lemon yellow; base of the segments brown, genitals yellow; abdomen of the female brownish;
posterior margins of the segments yellow, genitals ferruginous.
Wings (Tab. II, fig. 2) slightly gray, pale at the base, stigma
pale; origin of the præfurca a little posterior to the tip of the
auxiliary vein, strongly arcuated; the remainder of the course
of the second vein is parallel to the first; the distance between
the tips of the two branches of the second longitudinal vein is
nearly equal to the distance between the tip of the anterior
branch and that of the first longitudinal vein; the inner ends of
the second submarginal, first posterior, discal, and fourth posterior cells are nearly on one line; the third vein is arcuated,

strongly converging towards the anterior branch of the fourth
vein; discal cell closed in the majority of tho specimens.

Common, in summer; Washington, D. C.; Trenton Falls, N Y,
etc. Among fifteen specimens which I had before me, when I
first described this species, only one had the discal cell open.

2. G. coxualella O. S. ♂ and ♀.—Sulphureo-flava, fusco variegata,
antennis basi aurantiacis, in mare dense pubescentibus, verticillis brevibus; pedibus unicoloribus; cellula discoidali aperta.

Sulphur yellow, variegated with brown; antennæ orange yellow at the
basis, densely pubescent and with short verticils in the male; feet unicolorous; discal cell open. Long. corp. 0.2—0.25.

Syn. *Gonomyia coxualella* O. Sacken, Proc. Ac. Nat. Sc. Phil. 1859, p. 230.

Very like the preceding, but easily distinguished by the following characters: The antennæ of the male are covered on every
joint with a short, dense pubescence, which, being interrupted at
the articulations, makes the antennæ appear moniliform; the
halteres (both stem and knob) are infuscated; the pleuræ are
yellow, with a brown stripe; the feet are uniformly pale tawny,
only the tips of the tarsi darker; the discal cell is open (at least
in the normal specimens); the inner angle of the marginal cell is
more acute, the præfurca running obliquely from the first longitudinal vein; the anterior branch of the second longitudinal vein
is more oblique, and therefore somewhat longer; the distance
between the tips of both branches of this vein is about twice the
length of the distance between the tip of the anterior branch and
that of the first longitudinal vein; the third vein is straight,
although, in its whole course, somewhat converging towards the
anterior branch of the fourth; the second submarginal cell is
somewhat longer than the first posterior. The forceps of the male
(Tab. IV, fig. 18) has a somewhat different structure from that of
G. sulphurella.

Hab. Washington, D. C. I had seven specimens.

3. G. subcinerea O. S. ♂ and ♀.—Sulphureo-flava: mesonoto
cinereo-fusco; antennis nigris; pedibus unicoloribus; cellula discoidali
(in speciminibus typicis) clausa.

Sulphur yellow; mesonotum grayish-brown; antennæ black; feet unicolorous; discal cell (in the normal specimen) closed.

Syn. *Gonomyia subcinerea* O. Sacken, Proc. Ac. Nat. Sc. Phil. 1859, p. 231.

Rostrum yellow, palpi brown; antennæ black; those of the male bare moderately long verticils; thorax sulphur yellow; mesonotum grayish-brown; pleuræ without any brown stripes, uniformly yellow; halteres very slightly infuscated; feet pale tawny Wings (Tab. II. fig. 4) comparatively longer than in the preceding species; the discal cell is closed in normal specimens; the tip of the auxiliary vein is a little posterior to the origin of the præfurca; the interval between the tip of the first longitudinal vein and the anterior branch of the second vein is five or six times shorter than the interval between the tips of the two branches of the second vein; the inner end of the second submarginal cell is pointed, very little anterior to the inner end of the first posterior cell; the third vein is straight and very little convergent with the anterior branch of the fourth; the inner end of the marginal cell (angle of the præfurca) almost acute; the inner ends of the first and fourth posterior, and of the discal cell, nearly in one line. Abdomen brown above; margins of the segments yellow; venter and forceps of the male yellow; the latter with linear, hairy, slightly dusky appendages.

Hab. Trenton Falls, N. Y.; Washington, D. C. Among twelve specimens, the discal cell is open in one only.

4. G. blanda O. S.   ♂ and ♀.—Alæ stigmate et marginis anterioris parte apicali fuscis; venulis transversis infuscatis; venæ longitudinalis secundæ rami anterioris apex cum apice venæ longitudinalis primæ coincidens.

Wings with the stigma and the apical portion of the anterior margin infuscated; cross-veins clouded; the tip of the anterior branch of the second vein is coincident with the tip of the first longitudinal vein. Long. corp. 0.25—0.28.

Syn. *Gonomyia blanda* O. Sacken, Proc. Ac. Nat. Sc. Phil. 1859, p. 231.

Rostrum gray, margined with yellow above; front and vertex gray, margined with yellow along the eyes; antennæ brown; two basal joints yellow. Thorax gray above, with two approximated brownish stripes in the middle; two hardly distinct lateral stripes; scutellum brownish, gray in the middle; metathorax brownish; pleuræ pale yellow, slightly hoary; halteres dusky, with dark knobs; feet pale yellow, pubescent; tips of the femora, of the tibiæ, and the whole of the tarsi dark brown; abdomen grayish-brown; lateral and posterior margins of the segments yellow;

venter yellow ; male forceps yellow, with black horny appendages
(Tab. IV, fig. 17). Wings with the cross-veins and the inner
ends of the basal cells, and of the second submarginal and second
posterior cells clouded ; the stigma and the portion of the anterior
margin between it and the tip are blackish; the præfurca, strongly
arcuated at the basis, is parallel, during the remainder of its course,
to the first longitudinal vein ; the tip of the anterior branch of the ,
second longitudinal vein is coincident with the tip of the first
longitudinal vein; the origin of the præfurca is a little anterior
to the tip of the auxillary vein; the second submarginal cell is
longer than the first posterior ; generally there is a stump of a
vein near the origin of the præfurca, and an indication of a second
stump at the inner end of the second posterior cell; discal cell
open; the great cross-vein is a considerable distance before the
inner end of the discal cell.

Hab. Washington, D C.; Trenton Falls, N. Y.; South Carolina (Berlin Museum).

Gen. XXIV. EMPEDA.

Two submarginal cells; the first rather short, owing to the shortness
and the oblique direction of the anterior branch of the second longitudinal
vein ; a distinct marginal cross-vein connecting the first and second longitudinal veins is inserted a considerable distance before the inner end of
the first submarginal cell ; four posterior cells ; discal cell closed or open :
when open, it coalesces with the second posterior cell. Wings glabrous.
Antennæ 16(?)-jointed. Tibia without spurs at the tip, tarsi with distinct
empodia.

This genus is undoubtedly allied to *Goniomyia*, as the general
appearance, the coloring, and in part also the venation of the
species show. Dr. Schiner (*Fauna Austriaca, Diptera*, II, p. 542)
gave a wider definition to *Goniomyia*, so as to embrace this group
of species also. I think, however, that it is sufficiently distinct, to
be introduced as a separate genus, leaving *Goniomyia* with its
former definition (as adopted by me in 1859). *Empeda* differs
from *Goniomyia* in the following characters : 1. The marginal
cross-vein is present ; but owing to the shortness of the anterior
branch of the second longitudinal vein, it is not this branch, but
the petiole of the first submarginal cell, which the cross-vein
connects with the first vein; the cross-vein is thus placed between
the origin of the third longitudinal vein and the fork of the

second, and nearer to the former than to the latter. (Compare the figures of the wings of the European species *nubila* and *flava* in *Schummel's Beiträge*, etc. Tab. II, fig. 4 and 5, which, in regard to the position of the cross-vein, are in perfect agreement with the American species.) 2. The auxiliary vein is longer than in *Goniomyia*, that is, it extends beyond the origin of the second longitudinal vein to a distance which is equal to half the breadth of the wing, or a little shorter; the cross-vein is very near its tip (this, according to the same figures of Schummel, is also the case with the European species). 3. Whenever the discal cell is open, it coalesces with the *second*, not with the *third* posterior cell (the latter is the case in *Goniomyia*); in other words, it is not the *anterior* branch of the fourth longitudinal vein, but the *posterior* one, which is forked (this again is distinctly mentioned by Schiner, l. c. p. 511, lines 4 and 11 from the bottom, for the European species, and figured by Schummel). 4. The forceps of the male has a different structure; I am unable to describe it, not having observed it on any living specimen, but even dry ones show plainly that the forceps has a more simple structure, and none of the numerous branches which distinguish the forceps of *Goniomyia*.

Besides the single North American species, described below, three European species undoubtedly belong here: *Limnobia dilata* Zett. (Schiner); *Limn. flava* Schum.; *Limn. nubila* Schum.

The name of this new genus is derived from ἔμπεδος, steady, unshaken.

Description of the species.

1. E. stigmatica, n. sp. ♂.—Fuscana, halteribus pallidis, alis immaculatis; cellula discoidalis aperta, cum secunda posteriori confluens.

Brownish, with pale halteres, immaculate wings, and an open discal cell coalescent with the second posterior cell. Long. corp. 0.2.

Dull brownish; antennæ black; in the male, with rather long verticils; a sulphur yellow spot on the humeri; halteres pale yellow; forceps of the male reddish-brown; feet tawny. Wings nearly hyaline; veins brown; stigma very slightly tinged with brown; the tip of the auxiliary vein is nearly in the middle of the distance between the origin of the præfurca and the marginal cross-vein; the distance between the tip of the first longitudinal

vein and the tip of the anterior branch of the second is distinctly
shorter than the distance between the tips of both branches
of the second vein; third and fourth veins somewhat converging; discal cell open, confluent with the second posterior
cell (for more details about the venation compare the generic
characters).

Hob. Trenton Falls, N. Y. A male specimen; another one,
which is injured, has only the thorax and the wings left.

Gen. XIV. CRYPTOLABIS.

Two submarginal cells; *the inner marginal cell is short and almost triangular* (Tab. II, fig. 11), owing to the shortness and the very oblique course
of the prefurca; the origin of the latter is a little beyond the middle of
the length of the wing; four posterior cells; *discal cell open*; the posterior
branch of the fourth longitudinal vein is forked. Wings glabrous, except
an almost microscopic pubescence in the apical portion of the wing. Antennæ 16-jointed. Tibiæ without spurs at the tip; empodia distinct.
Forceps of the male with very small horny appendages; *ovipositor of the
female without any apparent horny valves.*

The body is short and stout; the antennæ, if extended backwards, would not quite reach the root of the wing; joints of the
flagellum oval, with rather long, verticillate hairs. Rostrum
short; palpi with subcylindrical joints of nearly equal length.
Feet rather short and stout, strongly pubescent; those of the
intermediate pair much shorter than the hind ones; tibiæ slightly
increased towards the tip; ungues very small; empodia distinct.
Thoracic suture distinct. Wings (Tab. II, fig. 11) comparatively
short and broad; the auxiliary vein ends a little beyond the origin
of the second longitudinal vein; the rather indistinct subcostal
cross-vein is at a distance from the tip of the auxiliary vein, which
is equal to about one and a half the length of the great cross-vein;
owing to the shortness of the prefurca, the subcostal cross-vein
is a little anterior to the origin of the latter; the branches of the
second vein and the third vein are straight, the two latter nearly
parallel; the veins separating the first, second, and third posterior
cells are gently arcuated; the second submarginal cell is equal in
length to the first posterior cell; the discal cell being open, coalesces with the second posterior cell. The inner marginal cell
(included between the prefurca and the marginal cross-vein) is
not elongated, as usual, but has the shape of an almost equilateral

triangle; this is due to the shortness and the oblique course of the
præfurca, the origin of which is a little beyond the middle of the
length of the wing; the tip of the præfurca almost coincides with
the origin of the third longitudinal vein. The portion of the fifth
vein beyond the great cross-vein is at an obtuse angle with the
previous course of this vein; the sixth longitudinal vein is gently
arcuated; the seventh nearly straight. The forceps of the male
(Tab. III, fig. 13 from above, fig. 13 a from below) has two small
horny appendages which, in the state of repose, are closely
applied to the under side of the fleshy basal pieces; hence, and
owing to their smallness, they are indistinct. The ovipositor of
the female is soft, obtuse, without any apparent horny lamels
(Tab. III, fig. 13 b, side view; 13 c, from above). This structure
of the ovipositor renders the recognition of the sexes very difficult
in dried specimens.

The genus *Cryptolabis* (from ꭓρυπτός, concealed, and λαβίς,
forceps) has been introduced by me in 1859 (*Proc. Acad. Nat.
Sci. Philad.* p. 224), for a single species which I discovered in
Virginia. No other species has been added to it since.

**1. C. paradoxa O. S. ♂ and ♀.—Thorace livide, nigro-vittato; an-
tennis nigris; pedibus basi pallidis; alis immaculatis.**

Thorax livid, with black stripes; antennæ black; feet pale at the basis;
wings immaculate. Long. corp. 0.1—0.13.

Syn. *Cryptolabis paradoxa* O. Sacken, Proc. Nat. Sc. Phil. 1859. p. 225.

Head blackish; palpi and antennæ black. The color of the
thorax is livid, but it is scarcely apparent between the black
stripes; the intermediate stripe is double; the lateral ones are
extended backwards beyond the suture; scutellum pale; metathorax dark; pleuræ blackish; halteres pale; feet hairy; coxæ
and base of the femora pale; the tips of the latter brown; tibiæ
brownish tawny, infuscated at the tip; the tarsi likewise. Abdomen blackish (often greenish in living specimens). Wings hyaline, without any apparent stigma; veins brown, costal and
auxiliary veins pale.yellow; the apical portion of the wings is
slightly pubescent along the middle of the cells.

Hab. White Sulphur Springs, Va. Twenty-one specimens
taken on the 30th of June, 1859.

Gen. XXVI. CLADURA.

Two submarginal cells (compare above, p. 34, the wing of *C. indirica*); *five posterior cells*, the second petiolate; discal cell closed; præfurca arcuated at its origin, which is very little anterior to the middle of the length of the wing, but a considerable distance anterior to the tip of the auxiliary vein (this distance being more than the breadth of the wing); subcostal cross-vein a short distance from the tip of the auxiliary vein; seventh longitudinal vein straight. Wings glabrous, except a short pubescence along the veins in the apical portion of the wing. Antennæ 16-jointed. Feet very long, pubescent; tibiæ without spurs at the tip; tarsi with distinct empodia; ungues smooth on the under side. The upper side of the last abdominal segment is horny, convex, having a rounded excision between two projecting points on its posterior margin (Tab. IV, fig. 2', forceps of *C. flavoferruginea*; *a*, horny convexity; *b*, excision); the forceps, inserted under the convexity, is large, and consists of a long, cylindrical basal joint and a horny branch upon it. Ovipositor with flattened, rather broad valves.

Rostrum and palpi short; last joint of the latter stout; front moderately broad, very convex above the eyes; the latter glabrous, almost contiguous on the under side of the head. The antennæ, if bent backwards, would reach the root of the wings; joints of the flagellum subcylindrical, slightly increasated at the base; verticils of moderate length. The wings are rather long and comparatively narrow; the veins, on their apical portion, show a short, but distinct pubescence. The tip of the auxiliary vein is somewhat beyond the inner end of the first submarginal cell; the latter is shorter than the second submarginal; its petiole is about equal in length to the interval between the subcostal and marginal cross-veins; the marginal cross-vein is in the middle of the distance between the subcostal cross-vein and the tip of the first longitudinal vein; the præfurca is strongly arcuated; the second submarginal and first posterior cells are of nearly equal length; in *C. flavoferruginea* the second submarginal cell is divided in two parts by a cross-vein in its middle; this is not the case with the other species, *C. indirica*; there are five posterior cells, the petiole of the second posterior cell is much shorter than this cell; the pentagonal shape of the discal cell plainly shows that it is the forking of the posterior branch of the fourth vein which forms one of its sides; the great cross-vein is posterior to the inner end of the discal cell; the fifth, sixth, and seventh longitudinal veins are almost straight. The presence of five

·

posterior cells, and the unusual size and structure of the male forceps, render the recognition of this genus very easy.

The position of the subcostal cross-vein near the tip of the auxiliary vein; the shape of the inner end of the marginal cell, which is broad and not pointed, and before all the presence of five posterior cells—these characters show that there is a wide interval between this genus and the typical *Eriopterina*. *Cladura* is placed in this section on account of the absence of the spurs at the tip of the tibiæ; its general appearance is that of *Limnophila*, and the only character which may be indicative of a relationship to the *Eriopterina* is the pubescence of the wing-veins, which is more distinct here than is usual among the *Limnophilina*.

Cladura (from κλάδος, branch, and οὐρά, tail, in allusion to the forceps of the male) was introduced by me in the *Proc. Acad. Nat. Sci. Philad.* 1859, p. 229. It has not been discovered in Europe, and besides the two North American species described below I know of no others.

Description of the species.

1. C. flavoferruginea O.S. ♂ and ♀.—Flavo-ferruginea; pleuris punctis, abdomen fasciis brunneis; in cellula submarginali secunda venula transversalis supernumeraria; venulæ transversæ omnes infuscatæ.

Ferruginous-yellow; pleure spotted, abdomen banded with brown; the second submarginal cell has a supernumerary cross-vein in the middle; all the cross-veins infuscated. Long. corp. 0.3—0.35.

Syn. *Cladura flavoferruginea* O. Sacks, Proc. Ac. Nat. Sc. Phil. 1859, p. 229.

Rostrum, palpi, and antennæ pale ferruginous; the two latter infuscated at the tip; mesonotum ferruginous, shining; a more or less apparent dark line in the middle; a brown spot on the humeri; pleure pale yellow; two brown spots between the humerus and the basis of the wing; a third one lower, about the middle of the pleure; scutellum and metathorax ferruginous; a small black dot on each side, between the latter and the basis of the halteres; these are pale; feet hairy, yellowish ferruginous; tips of the femora, of the tibiæ, and of the tarsi brown. Abdomen ferruginous; lateral margins of the segments brown, united by a pale brown band running across the middle of each segment; venter yellow; genitals ferruginous, shining. Wings yellowish; costa, first, and fifth longitudinal veins ferruginous; the other

veins brown; cross-veins and origin of the præfurca clouded with
brown; stigma pale; a supernumerary cross-vein about the middle
of the second submarginal cell.

Hab. Washington, D. C.; October, November. Compared
seven specimens; one of them has another supernumerary cross-
vein in the first submarginal cell; it is a little anterior to the
cross-vein of the second submarginal cell, and occurs on both
wings of the specimen.

2. C. indivisa O. S. ♂ and ♀.—Flava; pleuris punctis, abdomen
familia brunneis; cellula submarginali secunda integra.

Yellow; pleuræ spotted, abdomen banded with brown; the second submarginal cell is not divided by a supernumerary cross-vein. Long.
corp. 0.28—0.3,

Syx. *Cladura indivisa* O, Sacken, Proc. Ac. Nat. Sc. Phil. 1861, p. 291.

Somewhat smaller than the preceding, and paler in coloring;
origin of the præfurca and cross-veins but indistinctly clouded;
no supernumerary cross-vein in the second submarginal cell
(compare the wing of this species, on page 34); otherwise, the
coloring is like that of the preceding species.

Numerous specimens, caught at Trenton Falls, N. Y., in September, 1860; some of the specimens, probably recently excluded,
were pale, and without spots. Massachusetts (Scudder).

Section IV. LIMNOPHILINA.

Two submarginal cells; usually five, seldom four posterior cells; discal cell generally present; subcostal cross-vein posterior to the origin of the second longitudinal vein, usually closely approximated to the tip of the auxiliary vein (considerably distant from it in *Trichocera* only). Eyes glabrous (pubescent in *Trichocera*). Normal number of antennal joints sixteen.[1] Tibiae with spurs at the tip; empodia distinct; ungues smooth.

The contrast between the characters of the two sections of *Limnophilina* and *Limnobina*, has been explained under the head of the latter. This contrast shows itself, moreover, in another manner: While "the forms of *Limnobina*, belonging to the temperate regions of Europe and America, afford but little structural diversity, and their relationship is so great and evident that one is more tempted to unite them all in one genus, than to subdivide them in several" (compare above, p. 51), precisely the contrary is the case with the species of *Limnophilina*. The structural modifications they show are so numerous, that the desire to introduce new generic groups is restrained by the fear of adopting too many. At present, the section *Limnophilina* consists, properly speaking, of the single genus *Limnophila*; *Trichocera* is an aberrant form, singular in its structure as in its mode of life. *Epiphragma* and *Ulomorpha* are *Limnophilæ*, but sufficiently well-defined forms to be separated immediately, as several other forms will have to be separated, when better known (compare the genus *Limnophila* below).

The difference between the *Limnophilina* and *Eriopterina*, besides the presence of spurs at the tip of the tibiæ, consists in the following characters: The subcostal cross-vein in the majority

---

[1] This refers to the European and North American species; *Gynoplistia* Westw. has (♂) 16·, and (♀) 17-jointed antennæ; *Ctedonia* Phil. has 15–24 joints, etc.

of the *Eriopterina* is far anterior to the tip of the auxiliary vein, in the *Limnophilina* it is usually at its tip; the *Eriopterina*, with the exception of *Cladura*, have four posterior cells, the majority of the *Limnophilina* five; in the *Eriopterina* the discal cell is very often open; very rarely among the *Limnophilina*. *Cladura* (*Eriopterina*), with its five posterior cells, is very like the *Limnophilina*; on the other hand, the *Limnophilina* with four posterior cells are very like some *Eriopterina*, as for instance *Gnophomyia*; besides the presence or absence of spurs, no important structural difference has been discovered yet, in order to justify the present location of these forms on more than artificial grounds; nevertheless, such differences in all probability exist (compare also p. 138).

The difference between the *Limnophilina* and the *Amalopina* consists in the position of the subcostal cross-vein, and in the pubescence of the eyes of the latter. In both characters, *Trichocerra* shows an approach to the *Amalopina*. Another important difference is to be found in the structure of the penultimate posterior cell. In the *Amalopina* this cell (compare the Tab. II, fig. 14–18) is evidently formed by the fork of the *posterior* branch of the fourth vein. In the *Limnophilina* this cell looks in most cases as if its presence was merely due to a cross-vein, separating it from the discal cell; and indeed in the few abnormal specimens that came under my observation, in which the discal cell was open, it coalesced with the penultimate posterior cell, and not with the cell preceding it, as it always does in the *Amalopina*; in such specimens, the anterior branch of the fourth vein had a double fork, like *Dolichopeza* (compare Meigen, Vol. VI, Tab. 65, fig. 10, or Walker, *Ins. Brit. Dipt.* Tab. XXVIII, fig. 3 b). I have not met with any *Limnophilina* yet, which have the discal cell normally open (except the abortive form *Rhicnoptila*; compare p. 198). This peculiarity in the structure of the discal cell and of the penultimate posterior cell in *Limnophila* deserves to be noticed, although it has been too little observed yet to allow any general conclusions (compare the Introduction, p. 83).

The genera *Amalopis* and *Pedicia* have, in the majority of cases, the first submarginal cell longer than the second, in consequence of a peculiar structure of the fork of the second vein (as in Tab. II, fig. 14); which is never the case among the *Limnophilina*.

The *Limnophilina* are further distinguished by the position of the great cross-vein, which is generally farther beyond the inner end of the discal cell than is usually the case among the *Tip. brevipalpi*. In *Trichocera* this cross-vein is at the very end of the discal cell. Exceptions occur, however (compare the genus *Limnophila* at the end).

Several remarkable foreign forms of *Limnophilina* have been described, but as I have not had the opportunity to study them I will merely enumerate them here. (The descriptions of these genera, with the necessary remarks and quotations, are reproduced or translated in the Appendix II.)

Gynoplistia Westw. is a *Limnophila* with unipectinate antennæ in both sexes; several species have been described from Australia and South America. Mr. Westwood has even described one, *G. annulata*, from North America. The description is reproduced in the Appendix I.

Cledonia Philippi, from Chile, seems in no way distinct from a South American *Gynoplistia*; *Cloniophora* Schiner, from Australia, is established upon *Gynoplistia subfasciata* Walker, a species which shows some structural peculiarities.

Ceroxodia Westw. from Australia, seems also to belong to the *Limnophilina*; it has 32-jointed, pectinate antennæ.

Polymeria Philippi, with five species from Chile, may be one of the numerous forms of *Limnophila*, although the statements of the author are not complete enough to admit of any conclusion.

Lachnocera Philippi, from Chile, is either a *Limnophila* with four posterior cells, or perhaps a genus related to *Goniomyia* (Eriopterina). The densely pubescent antennæ of this genus remind of the antennæ of *Limnophila lenta* O. S., which has also four posterior cells and a venation not quite unlike *Lachnocera*.

The *Limnophilina* contained in the Prussian amber are quite numerous. Mr. Loew's pamphlet, *Bernstein und Bernstein-fauna*, 1850, merely gives the names of the genera and species, without descriptions, but owing to the author's kindness, I have had a glimpse at the specimens, which convinced me of the close analogy of some of them to North American forms. *Cylindrotoma longicornis* Lw. is a *Limnophila*, closely allied to *L. macrocera* Say, by its long, pubescent antennæ, its somewhat elongated last joint of the palpi, and its venation. *Cylindrot. brevicornis* Lw. is a *Limnophila* of the type of *L. tenuipes* Say; *Cylindr. succini* and *longipes* Lw. are likewise *Limnophila*. The genus *Tanymera* Lw. contains *T. gracilicornis*, which belongs to the relationship of the North American *Limnophila recondita* O. S. *Tanysiphyra* Lw. and *Critoneura* Lw. seem likewise to be *Limnophila*. The number genus *Trichoneura* Lw. is distinguished by the first longitudinal vein being incurved towards the second, and ending in it, almost as in the *Cylindrotomina*. I take it to be a *Limnophila* with four posterior cells; what appears to be the end of 'the first vein, is in reality the marginal cross-vein, whereas the real end of this vein, touching the costa, is visible, but feebly marked; this structure reminds of a similar one, often occurring among the *Limnobina* (compare Tab. I, fig. 2; the wing of *Dicranomyia pubipennis*), but not observed among the *Limnophilina*. The shortness of the auxiliary vein in *Trichoneura*, the course of the central cross-veins, the position of the great cross-vein, etc., remind of the wing of *Limnophila quadrata* (Tab. II, fig. 9), and convince me that *Trichoneura* is related to it.

Gen. XXVII. EPIPHRAGMA.

Two submarginal cells; five posterior cells; discal cell closed; subcostal cross-vein at the tip of the auxiliary vein; a supernumerary cross-vein between the costa and the auxiliary vein. Wings glabrous, handsomely pictured. Eyes glabrous. Antennae 16-jointed; two basal joints of the flagellum incrassated, almost coalescent. Tibiae with spurs at the tip; empodia distinct; ungues smooth.

The antennae, bent backwards, do not reach beyond the basis of the wings; basal joint elongated cylindrical, second joint short, cyathiform; third joint elongated, incrassated; a suture a little beyond its middle indicates that it consists of two almost coalescent joints; the following joints are elongated, slender, with rather long verticils. Collare moderately developed; thoracic suture deep. Feet rather strong; the spurs at the tip of the tibiae comparatively long and distinct. The wings (Tab. II, fig. 8, wing of *E. solatrix*) are broad and handsomely pictured in all the known species. The venation is nearly the same in the three species which I have before me: there is a strong supernumerary cross-vein between the costa and the auxiliary vein and the costa; the origin of the praefurca is very strongly arcuated, often with a stump of a vein; the petiole of the first submarginal cell is longer than the great cross-vein in *E. picta* and *fascipennis*; shorter than the

13 Sept. 1868.

great cross-vein in E. solatrix; the inner ends of the second submarginal, of the first posterior, and of the discal cells are nearly in one line; the fourth vein originates from the fifth somewhat farther than usual from the root of the wing, and its origin is very much arcuated. The abdomen has, a little before the middle of the segments, a transverse impressed line, smooth and shining at the bottom, interrupted in the middle, and of a darker coloring than the surface of the abdomen; these lines exist in several other genera, but are not so conspicuous as here. The forceps of the male is large, with an open space in the middle, even when it is closed; in structure it is not unlike that of the typical *Limnophila*; only both appendages fastened to the subcylindrical basal pieces seem to be of a horny texture; the inner one is flattened. The ovipositor is slender and arcuated.

Epiphragma (from επι, upon, and φραγμα, partition) was introduced by me as a subgenus of *Limnophila* in the *Proc. Acad. Nat. Sci. Philad.* 1859, p. 238. It is sufficiently well characterized, however, to be permanently separated from *Limnophila*. Besides one European (E. picta Lin.) and two North American species, I have seen a couple of South American ones in European collections; E. histrio Schiner, from Columbia, is one of them (*Reise d. Novara*, etc. p. 41).

1. **E. fascipennis** Say.   ♂ and ♀.—Alis maculis pallide fuscis, obscure fusco-marginatis, subrotundis, confluentibus, fascias formantibus.

Wings with pale brown spots, margined with dark brown, more or less rounded, confluent, and forming bands across the wing.   Long. corp. 0.45.

Syn. *Limnobia fascipennis* Say, Journ. Ac. Nat. Sc. Phil. III, 19, 1.—Wied. Auss. Zw. I, 31, 14.

Limnophila (*Epiphragma*) *pavonina* O. Sacken, Proc. Ac. Nat. Sc. Phil. 1859, p. 238.

Head brownish, with a yellowish, sericeous reflection; palpi brown; antennæ brownish; basal joint with a yellowish bloom; the two or three basal joints of the flagellum are reddish-yellow. Thorax brownish; the mesonotum has a broad chestnut brown anterior margin; the remainder of its surface, as well as the scutellum and the metathorax, are of an opaque yellowish-gray; the separations of the usual stripes are marked by pale brownish lines; pleuræ with a yellowish sericeous reflection; halteres pale, basis of the knob infuscated. Abdomen brownish, with a gray dust, forming two more or less distinct longitudinal stripes along the back. Feet yellowish tawny; femora with a brown band at the tip, sometimes with a second one, preceding it; tips of the tibiæ and of the tarsi brown. Wings with a pale brown picture, the margins of which are darker brown; the spots, taken singly, are more or less circular, but most of them are confluent, so as to form several bands across the wing. Two principal bands thus formed by confluent circular spots occupy the middle of the wing; one runs from the costa across the origin of the præfurca to the tip of the seventh vein; the other is broader and begins at the costa, includes the discal cell, and ends at the posterior margin on both sides of the tips of the fifth and sixth veins; a smaller brown picture fills the basal portion of the wing, and seven almost confluent round spots, the apical portion.

Hab. United States. I have seen specimens from Georgia (Berlin Museum), Maine (Packard), and Illinois (Kennicott), and have taken them abundantly in May and June near Washington, D. C., and in the White Mountains. A number of the specimens from the latter locality have the picture on the wings very pale, almost obsolete, and, at first sight, might be taken for a different species.

2. E. solatrix O. S. ♂ and ♀.—Alis picturâ irregulari fusco et testaceo mixtâ.

Wings with an irregular picture, which is brown, mixed with yellowish (Tab. II, fig. 8, wing). Long. corp. 0.45.

Syn. *Limnophila* (*Epiphragma*) *solatrix* O. Sacken, Proc. Ac. Nat. Sc. Phil. 1859, p. 232.

Head brownish, sericeous with yellowish; rostrum and palpi brown; antennæ brownish; basal joint dusted with gray; the second brown, the basal joint of the flagellum reddish-yellow. Thorax brownish; mesonotum of a handsome reddish-brown anteriorly, with somewhat darker stripes; the posterior part of the mesonotum, as well as the scutellum and the metathorax, are of a peculiar whitish or yellowish-white, with a sericeous reflection; pleuræ partly brown, partly sericeous with yellowish; halteres pale, a part of the knob brown; feet yellowish, with a brown band before the tip of the femora. Wings variegated with brown and tawny; the costal cell contains two angular brown

marks, besides the two infuscated cross-veins (humeral and supernumerary); a large spot is situated at the basis of the wing,
between the first longitudinal vein and the posterior margin; its
anterior part is tawny, the remainder brown; a brown band
begins at the posterior margin, before the tip of the seventh
longitudinal vein; it extends to the fourth vein, where it assumes
a tawny color and emits two branches; the posterior branch is
connected with the two angular marks in the costal cell; the
anterior branch expands into a large brown spot, occupying a
considerable portion of the marginal cell and emitting a branch
which runs along the central cross-velus, as far as the fifth vein;
the apical portion of the wing contains a band, running across
from the tip of the second longitudinal vein to the tips of the
fifth and sixth veins; this band emits a branch towards the apex
of the wing. All these bands are very irregular, and they vary
in extent in different specimens; those of the apical portion of
the wing are surrounded with irregular dots, streaks, etc.

Hab. Washington, D. C., in July and August. A Brazilian
specimen in the Berlin Museum seems to belong to this species.

Gen. XXVIII. LIMNOPHILA.

Two submarginal cells; usually five, seldom four posterior cells; discal
cell closed; subcostal cross-vein posterior to the origin of the second
longitudinal vein, usually closely approximated to the tip of the auxiliary
vein. Wings glabrous. Eyes glabrous. Antennæ 16-jointed. Tibiæ with
spurs at the tip; empodia distinct; ungues smooth.

The diversity of forms, comprised under this definition of
Limnophila, has already been alluded to above (p. 190). I have
not been able to introduce a satisfactory natural arrangement,
partly on account of the difficulty of the task, partly owing to the
limited materials at my disposal, especially with regard to the
European fauna. *Epiphragma* and *Ulomorpha*, two small, but
apparently well circumscribed genera, I have separated from
Limnophila; but it would be premature, I think, to do the same
with some of the other subdivisions, adopted by me in 1859.
Some American species, discovered by me since, do not exactly
answer the definitions of those subdivisions, as I understood them
at that time; often, the relationship is evident, but difficult to
define in a satisfactory manner. The present genus is therefore
left in an unfinished condition.

The difficulty consists in discovering the proper characters for a subdivision. Some characters, very striking at first sight, prove, upon comparison, to be of a secondary value. We find, for instance, a number of *Limnophilæ* which, in the male sex, have the antennæ much longer than in the female, and of a different structure. This would seem a good character for a subdivision. But we soon discover that *L. tenuipes* Say, with long antennæ in the male, is very closely related to the European *L. discicollis* Meigen, and to the North American *L. recondita*, which have short antennæ in both sexes, whereas it is much less related to some other species with long antennæ in the male sex. In the same way, the number of posterior cells is a character of a very secondary value for any subdivision above 'a specific one; I believe, for instance, that *L. quadrata*, with four posterior cells, is more related to *L. tenuipes*, which has five, than to some other species with four posterior cells. The presence of a cross-vein in the second basal cell, upon which Macquart has based his genus *Idioptera*, is not a sufficient character to be used, unsupported by others, for the establishment of a genus. The species which Macquart would have placed in this genus are more closely related to some species without such a cross-vein (to *L. poetica*, for instance), than to the subgenus *Ephelia*, which is also distinguished by this cross-vein.

The most reliable characters to guide us are those taken from the structure of the male forceps; but in order to be available, they must be supported by characters supplied by other parts of the organization. Those *Limnophilæ* which, like the subgenera *Dactylolabis*, *Prionolabis*, and *Ephelia*, have a forceps of a very peculiar structure, are the best entitled to a separation. The remaining *Limnophila*, with a forceps of the typical shape (Tab. IV, fig. 24, 25), would then form a still numerous genus, subdivided in groups, indicative of different degrees of relationship between the species. I have to confine myself for the present to an account more historical than critical, of the subdivisions hitherto adopted by other authors as well as by myself; I will add to it suggestions about some affinities which I perceive, but which are of too vague a nature yet as to be available immediately.

1. The subgenus *Prionolabis* O. S. (*Proc. Acad. Nat. Sci. Philad.* 1859, p. 239), has *Limnophila rufibasis* O. S. for type;

the outer appendages of the male forceps (Tab. IV, fig. 27, from above, open) are horny, large, strong, serrated on the inside; the inner ones (b b of the figure) are not parallel to the outer pair, and also different from the usual structure. The ovipositor of the female is long and remarkably straight; the feet rather stout, hairy; the antennae comparatively short in both sexes, stout, hairy; their verticils but little apparent; the wing-veins stout, often infuscated; the venation like Tab. II, fig. 3. The new species *Limnophila munda*, described below, shares most of the above characters, and may also be considered as a *Prionolabis*.

2. The subgenus *Dactylolabis* O. S. (*Proc. Acad. Nat. Sci. Philad.* 1859, p. 240). Type: *Limnophila montana* O. S. 'The forceps of the male (Tab. IV, fig. 26, from above, closed; 26 a from the side) has digitiform appendages of a soft texture, not horny, and not overlapping each other in repose; ovipositor of the female with short, rather broad upper valves, abruptly tapering towards the tip; feet very long, slender; wings usually spotted; both branches of the second vein and the third vein are long, rather straight; first submarginal cell very long; great cross-vein near the inner end of the discal cell (Tab. II, fig. 7); head narrowed posteriorly; collare broad; antennae comparatively short, verticils short, bristle-like. Since the adoption of this subgenus, Dr. Schiner has introduced it as a genus, including five or six European species; they are closely related to *D. montana*, and have the same spots or clouds on the cross-veins and at the origin of some of the veins, the intervals of the veins being without spots. One of the European species, *D. dilatata* Loew, is very large, and has the wings remarkably dilated anteriorly. The North American *Limnophila cubitalis*, of which I have seen only dried specimens, seems to have a forceps of a structure analogous to that of *Dactylolabis*; the ovipositor seems to be peculiar (compare the description of the species below); the venation and the structure of the antennae are not unlike those of *Dactylolabis*; but the feet are stouter, and the wings without any spots. If I had followed Dr. Schiner's precedence in adopting *Dactylolabis* as a genus, I would have been in doubt whether this species belongs to it or not. *Rhicnoptila* Now. (*Verh. Zool. Bot. Ges. in Wien*, 1867), specimens of which were kindly communicated to me by Dr. Schiner, is a *Dactylolabis* with somewhat shortive wings. The wings are shorter than the abdomen, rather narrow; the venation

Is that of *Dactylolabis*, with the following differences: the discal cell is open and coalescent with the fourth posterior cell; there is a supernumerary cross-vein in the first submarginal cell. The body is shorter and stouter, the feet stronger than in *Dactylolabis*. These differences notwithstanding, I do not think that the separation of *Rhicnoptila* from *Dactylolabis* is necessary. The only species, *R. wodzickii*, occurs in Austria.

3. The subgenus *Lasiomastix* O. S. (*Proc. Acad. Nat. Sci. Philad.* 1850, p. 233). Very long filiform antennæ in the male, about as long as the body, with a long, erect pubescence on the flagellum; palpi unusually long; forceps somewhat peculiar, etc. (compare below, the description of the species). Only a single North American species, *L. macrocera* Say, is known. The *Limnophila longicornis* Loew, contained in amber, seems to be related to this species.

4. Subgenus *Dicranophragma* O. S. (*Proc. Acad. Nat. Sci. Philad.* 1859, p. 240), distinguished by a cross-vein, connecting both branches of the second vein. The only North American species, *D. fuscovaria*, is a delicate, rather small species, with slender feet and broad wings, rounded posteriorly, and densely spotted with brown.

5. *Idioptera*, introduced as a genus by Macquart (*Hist. Natur. Dipt.* I, p. 91), has been adopted in Dr. Schiner's work (l. c. II, p. 549). It is principally based upon the presence of a supernumerary cross-vein in the second basal cell. The antennæ of the male are much longer than those of the female, filiform, pubescent; the body slender, the wings banded with brown, etc. Two European and one North American species are known; they are very closely allied, and the picture of their wings is nearly the same. The wings in the female of one of the European species are abortive.

6. *Ephelia*, a genus introduced by Dr. Schiner (l. c. II, p. 549), is likewise based upon the presence of a supernumerary cross-vein in the second basal cell; the antennæ are short in both sexes, the wings are rather broad and spotted with brown, the spots lying along the margin and on the veins. Two European and one American species are known. The forceps of the latter (Tab. IV, fig. 23) has the outer horny appendages stout, blunt, bifid at the tip, and therefore sufficiently distinct from the usual

type of the genus *Limnophila*. I have not had an opportunity to
examine the forceps of the European species.

7. *Poecilostola*, a genus adopted by Dr. Schiner (l. c. II, p.
551) for four European species of large size and with spotted
wings. No American species, belonging here, are known as yet;
and I have not had sufficient opportunity to study the European
species. *P. pictipennis* reminds of *Limnophila luteipennis* in
the structure of its head and thorax; *P. punctata* is quite different in this respect, and *P. barbipes* still more so. The above-
quoted species, it seems to me, show a leaning towards a *Prionolabis* on one side, and to the group of which *L. luteipennis* O. S.
is the type on the other. Like the latter group, the species of
Poecilostola have the pits on the humeral part of the mesonotum
very distinct, and also the corresponding blackish double dots on
the front part of the intermediate stripe of the thorax.

8. *Limnophila luteipennis* O. S., *L. contempta*, n. sp., and *L.
inornata*, n. sp., form a natural group, distinguished by the structure of the head, narrowed behind; a neck-like prolongation of
the collare; the venation (length of the second submarginal cell,
arcuated course of the posterior branch of the second vein, incurved tip of the seventh vein, etc., compare Tab. II, fig. 10, the
wing of *L. luteipennis*); the structure of the antennæ, the joints
of the flagellum of which are rather elongated, with distinct, but
moderately long verticils, etc. These species have very distinct
pits on the humeral part of the mesonotum, and a corresponding
double dot on the anterior part of the intermediate thoracic
stripe. Their forceps (Tab. IV, fig. 25, forceps of *L. luteipennis*,
half open) has nothing peculiar in its structure, and belongs to a
type rather common among the *Limnophilæ*. I have seen one
or two European species belonging to the same group.

9. *Limnophila tenuipes* Say, *imbecilla* O. S., *recondita* O. S.,
and the European *dieeicollis* Meig., are evidently allied; their
venation is the same; the inner ends of the second submarginal
and first posterior cells are in one line; the small cross-vein is
perceptibly arcuated; the first submarginal cell is short and has
a long petiole; the præfurca is long and forms a very straight
line with this petiole; the auxiliary vein is comparatively short,
and ends before the inner end of the second submarginal cell; the
marginal cross-vein is generally somewhat oblique, etc. The
joints of the flagellum are elongated, slender, with very long

vertlclls (the antennæ of *L. tenuipes*, ♂, are very long, filiform; compare the description of this species). The venation of this group resembles that of *L. quadrata* O. S. (Tab. II, fig. 9), although the latter has only four posterior cells, and this resemblance may be indicative of a relationship. The same remark, although in a lesser degree, may apply to the venation of the genus *Ulomorpha*.

Some general remarks on the venation of *Limnophila* may find their place here:—

1. The marginal cross-vein is apt to be very weakly marked in many species of *Limnophila*; but I have never found it absolutely wanting. I perceive it in two European specimens of *Idioptera*, although Dr. Schiner mentions the absence of this vein among the characters of the genus.

2. *Rhicnoptila* (compare above, page 198) is the only *Limnophila* with an open discal cell, which I have seen, and this exceptional case is evidently due to the abnormal and abortive condition of the whole wing. But it is worthy of notice that in *Rhicnoptila*, as well as in those single specimens of *Limnophila* in which the discal cell is adventitiously open, the anterior branch of the fourth vein bears a double fork, similar to that of *Dolichopeza*, the posterior branch having no fork at all. In the *Amalopina*, when the discal cell is open, each of the branches of the fourth vein has a fork (compare above, p. 191).

3. The great cross-vein in the genus *Limnophila* is very often nearer to the middle than to the inner end of the discal cell; in the subgenus *Dactylolabis*, however, it is usually near the inner end of this cell.

4. The venation is always somewhat variable in different specimens of the same species, which applies especially to the relative length of the petioles of the first submarginal and of the second posterior cells; also to the position of the great cross-vein, and of the marginal cross-vein. These variations ought to be taken into account in reading the descriptions of the species.

Several larvæ of *Limnophila* have been observed; those of *L. punctata* M. by Scheffer (in Rösel's *System. Verz. Oesterr. Ins.* p. 10), in decayed beech-wood; *L. (Epiphragma) picta* by Brenni, in oak-wood; *L. dispar* M. by Perris (*Ann. Soc. Entom. de Fr.* 1849, p. 331, Tab. VII, fig. 5), in dry stems of *Angelica sylvestris*·

Iris, in which the larva dug longitudinal burrows. The latter
larva is the only one which has been described and figured in
detail. It is cylindrical, glabrous, of a livid gray, with a horny,
black head; its structure is in no way distinguished from the
other larvæ of the *Tipulidæ*, as described in the Introduction to
this volume. I have already observed above (p. 4) that Mr.
Heeger's (*Sitzungsber. d. Wien. Acad.* Vol. XI) description of
the larva of *Limnophila platyptera* Macq. is evidently erroneous; the larva is apparently that of *Bolitophila*. I may also
remark here that *Limnobia platyptera* Macq. quoted by Dr.
Schiner (*Dipt. Austr.* II, p. 572), among the unknown species
of doubtful location, cannot well be anything else but *Limnophila hospes* Egger (l. c. p. 554).

Table for determining the species.

1	Five posterior cells.	2
	Four posterior cells.	26
2	A supernumerary cross-vein in the second basal or in the first sub-marginal cell.	3
	No supernumerary cross-vein in the second basal or in the first sub-marginal cell.	5
3	A supernumerary cross-vein in the second basal cell.	4
	A supernumerary cross-vein in the first submarginal cell.	20 fuscovaria O. S.
4	Antennæ of the male much longer than those of the female.	3 fasciolata O. S.
	Antennæ of the male not conspicuously longer than those of the female.	19 aprilina O. S.
5	Thorax shining black.	6
	Thorax not shining black.	7
6	Wings with large brown spots.	1 macrocera Say.
	Wings not spotted.	22 munda, n. sp.
7	Marginal cross-vein some distance from the tip of the first longitudinal vein.	8
	Marginal cross-vein at the tip of the first longitudinal vein, which is incurved immediately beyond it.	16
8	Inner end of the second submarginal cell considerably anterior to the inner end of the first posterior cell.	9
	Inner end of the second submarginal cell in a line with the first posterior cell, or almost so.	12
9	Petiole of the first submarginal cell three or four times shorter than this cell.	10
	Petiole of the first submarginal cell nearly as long as this cell.	16 ultima O. S.

10 { Wings with some indistinct clouds along the second longitudinal vein
     and on the central cross-veins.   13 lutelpennis O. S.
     Wings of a uniform coloring, without spots or clouds.   11

11 { Halteres yellow.   15 inornata, n. sp.
     Knob of the halteres brownish.   14 contempta, n. sp.

12 { Discal cell very much elongated, its inner end conspicuously anterior
     to the inner end of the first posterior cell.   11 areolata O. S.
     Discal cell of the ordinary size; its inner end not anterior to the inner
     end of the first posterior cell.   13

13 { Petiole of the first submarginal cell not longer than the great cross-
     vein.   14
     Petiole of the first submarginal cell distinctly longer than the great
     cross-vein.   15

14 { Petiole of the second posterior cell not longer than this cell.
                                                    5 tenuicornis, n. sp.
     Petiole of the second posterior cell three or four times longer than
     this cell.   17 brevifurca O. S.

15 { Thorax gray, with four brownish stripes (L. ultima).   9
     Thorax yellowish or brownish.   16

16 { Antennæ of the male much longer than those of the female; thorax
     brown above.   7 tenuipes Say.
     Antennæ of the same length in both sexes; thorax reddish or yellow-
     ish above.   17

17 { Thorax shining above.   6 recondita, n. sp.
     Thorax opaque above; front gray.   8 imbecilla O. S.

18 { Thorax gray, or brownish-gray.   19
     Thorax yellow, or brownish-yellow.   24

19 { Great cross-vein usually at the inner end of the discal cell.   20
     Great cross-vein nearer to the middle of the discal cell.   21

20 { Wings spotted with brown.   23 montana O. S.
     Wings immaculate.   24 cubitalis, n. sp.

21 { Hind tarsi white.   6 niveitarsis, n. sp.
     Hind tarsi not white.   27

22 { Wings spotted with brown.   3 unica, n. sp.
     Wings not spotted with brown.   23

23 { Fifth longitudinal vein and central cross-veins margined with narrow
     brown clouds.   21 rufibasis O. S.
     Wings unicolorous.   16 fratria, n. sp.

24 { Petiole of the first submarginal cell twice the length of the great cross-
     vein, and conspicuously arcuated.   10 toxoneura O. S.
     Petiole of the first submarginal cell not longer than the great cross-
     vein.   25

25 { Antennæ of the male more than twice the length of the thorax.
                                                    4 poetica, n. sp.
     Antennæ of the male shorter than the thorax. 13 adusta O. S.

26 { Body gray.   25 quadrata O. S.
     Body yellow.   26 lenta O. S.

Synoptical table of the species.[1]

I. *Five posterior cells.*

A. Antennæ of the male much longer than those of the female.

1 macrocera *Say.*	5 tenuicornis, n. sp.
2 unica, n. sp.	6 nivelitarsis, n. sp.
3 fasciolata *O. S.*	7 tenuipes *Say.*
4 pœtica, n. sp.	

B. Antennæ of the male not conspicuously longer than those of the female.

8 recondita, n. sp.	(Subg. **EPHELIA.**)
9 imbecilla *O. S.*	10 aprilina *O. S.*
10 toxoneura *O. S.*	(Subg. **DICRANOPHRAGMA.**)
11 areolata *O. S.*	20 inaeovaria *O. S.*
12 adusta *O. S.*	(Subg. **PRIONOLABIS.**)
13 lateipennis *O. S.*	21 rufibasis *O. S.*
14 contempta, n. sp.	22 manda, n. sp.
15 inornata, n. sp.	(Subg. **DACTYLOLABIS.**)
16 fratria, n. sp.	23 montana *O. S.*
17 brevifurca *O. S.*	24 cubitalis *O. S.*
18 ultima *O. S.*	

II. *Four posterior cells.*

25 quadrata *O. S.*	26 lenta *O. S.*

Description of the species.

I. *Five posterior cells.*

A. Antennæ of the male much longer than those of the female.

1. L. macrocera Say. ♂ and ♀.—Nigra, nitida; antennæ maris longitudine corporis, filiformes, pilosæ; alæ fusco maculatæ.

Black, shining; antennæ of the male as long as the body, filiform, beset with hairs; wings spotted with brown. Long. corp. 0.3—0.4.

Syn. *Limnobia macrocera* Say, Journ. Acad. Phil. III, p. 20, 2.—Wiedemann, Ausserr. Zw. I, 34, 19.

Cylindrotoma macrocera Macquart, Dist. Nat. Dipt. I, 106, 2.

Limnophila (Lasiomastix) macrocera O. Sacken, Proc. Ac. Nat. Sc. Phil. 1859, p. 234.

Head black, shining; front above the antennæ, and lower part of the head yellowish-ferruginous; rostrum and palpi black; antennæ black, except the basal joints, which are reddish; an-

[1] This arrangement is purely artificial and therefore provisional; compare p. 187.

tenuæ of the male as long or a little longer than the body, slender,
filiform; two basal joints short, the following elongated, cylindrical, of nearly equal length, clothed with soft, erect hairs; the
third and fourth joints have a small spine on the under side, at
the tip; antennæ of the female setaceous, not reaching much
beyond the basis of the wing; joints cylindrical, clothed with
sparse hairs; palpi unusually long, longer than the head; last
joint elongated. Thorax black, shining; pleuræ slightly hoary;
halteres pale yellow, the knob sometimes infuscated; feet dark
tawny; coxæ and basis of femora paler; tips of the femora, of
the tibiæ, and of the tarsi brown. Abdomen black; three or
four intermediate segments with pale ferruginous spots at the
basis (more distinct in living specimens); genitals ferruginous-
yellow.' Wings hyaline, spotted with brown; a spot at the inner
end of the basal cells; a large square one, between the first and
fifth longitudinal veins, across the origin of the præfurca; a third
one between the costa and the discal cell; the tip of the wing,
as well as the cross-veins, is clouded; petiole of the first submarginal cell very short, sometimes almost obsolete; the second
submarginal very little longer than the first posterior cell; the
marginal cross-vein is close at the tip of the first longitudinal vein.

Hab. United States; not common. I found male specimens
quite commonly on the 2d of July, 1859, near the so-called Salt-
pond, in southern Virginia (about twenty miles from the Mont-
gomery White Sulphur Springs). I caught this species in Florida,
in March, 1858. Quebec (Couper); Illinois (LeBaron).

The forceps of the male is like that of the typical *Limnophila*,
that is, the two pairs of movable appendages are subparallel;
the outer one is slender and pointed; the inner.one short, stout,
with the point turned upwards. (About the subgenus *Lasiomastix*, compare p. 199.)

N. B.—Say commits a mistake when he compares the venation
to Meig. I, Tab. V, fig. 7. Wiedemann quotes correctly Meig. I,
Tab. VI, fig. 3.

2. L. unica, n. sp. ♀.—Thorace cinereo, antennis fuscis, articulis
basalibus brevibus, rufis; alis stigmate obscure fusco, præfurcæ basi et
venulis transversis fusco-nebulosis; cellulis submarginali secundà et
posteriori primà subæque longis.

Thorax gray, antennæ brown, basal joints short, reddish; wings with a
dark-brown stigma; brownish clouds at the origin of the præfurca and

on the cross-veins ; second submarginal and first posterior cells nearly of the same length. Long. corp. 0.35.

Head yellowish-gray above; rostrum and palpi brown; antennæ brown, basal joints reddish; those of the female (the only sex I have before me) are longer than the head and the thorax taken together; the first joint is very short, not longer than the second; the joints of the flagellum are elongated, subcylindrical, with moderately long verticils in the middle. Thorax yellowish-gray, this color being produced, on the mesonotum, by a dense gray bloom, apparently upon a darker ground; pleuræ somewhat hoary ; halteres yellowish, with a faintly brownish knob. Abdomen brown, with short scattered yellowish hairs; ovipositor rather short, moderately ornated ; coxæ and femora tawny, tibiæ and tarsi brown. Wings with a brownish tinge ; stigma dark brown ; a pale brown cloud at the origin of the præfurca ; another one on the central cross-veins ; smaller clouds on the great cross-vein, and the cross-veins at the inner end of the third and fourth posterior cells. Tip of the auxiliary vein nearly opposite the inner end of the second submarginal cell; the petiole of the first submarginal cell is but little shorter than the upper branch of the second longitudinal vein ; the marginal cross-vein is at the tip of the first longitudinal vein, a short distance beyond the inner end of the first submarginal cell ; the second submarginal cell is only slightly longer than the first posterior ; the great cross-vein is opposite the middle of the discal cell ; the latter is elongated.

Hab. White Mountains, N. H. ; a single female.

The structure of the antennæ of the female renders it very probable that the male has much longer antennæ, and it is on this supposition that this species is placed among those with elongated male antennæ.

3. L. fasciolata n. sp. ♂.—Ferrugineo-flava, thorace cinerascente, antennis maris thorace multo longioribus, articulis elongatis, pubescentibus; alis fusco-fasciatis et maculatis; præfurca basi appendiculata ; venula transversa supernumeraria in cellula basali secunda.

Ferrugineous-yellow, thorax grayish ; antennæ of the male much longer than the thorax ; joints elongated, pulverulent ; wings banded and spotted with brown ; a stump of a vein at the origin of the præfurca ; a supernumerary cross-vein in the second basal cell.

Syn. *Limnophila fasciata* O. Sacken (non Schum.), Proc. Ac. Nat. Sc. Phil. 1859, p. 224.

Front and vertex brownish, with a gray bloom; rostrum and
pulpi brown; antennæ brownish, basal joints yellowish; those
of the male are much longer than the thorax; first joint rather
short; joints of the flagellum elongated, subcylindrical, densely
pubescent, and with a few verticils about the middle; thorax
brownish above, with a yellowish-gray bloom; pleuræ yellowish;
halteres with a brown knob; abdomen reddish-yellow, posterior
margins of the segments brown; last segment brownish; forceps
yellow. Wings almost hyaline, banded and spotted with brown
as follows: the inner end of the basal cells, the costal and subcostal cells, three large spots at the origin of the præfurca, on the
supernumerary cross-vein of the second basal cell, and at the tip
of the seventh vein; these spots are almost, but not quite in contact, and thus form an interrupted band; the first spot is connected
with the brown of the anterior margin; the brown stigma and a
series of spots along the central cross-veins form a second cross-
band; the apex of the wing is infuscated, and there are clouds
at the inner ends of the three intermediate posterior cells.
Marginal cross-vein near the tip of the first vein; præfurca with
a stump of a vein near its origin; the inner ends of the second
submarginal, first posterior, and the discal cells nearly in a line.

Hab. Massachusetts (Mr. Scudder); a single male.

My only specimen is somewhat injured, the feet and the tips of
the antennæ being broken. This species is very like the European
Limnophila (*Idioptera*) *pulchella* Meig. (syn. *L. fasciata* Schum.
non Linn. according to Dr. Schiner). It may be that they are
the same species, and it is upon this assumption that I introduced
the American species as *L. fasciata* Schum., in my former paper.
The European species has generally abortive wings in the female
sex (compare Schum. *Beitr.* etc. Tab. V, fig. 2). *L. fasciolata*
is closely allied to *L. portica*, and it would be unnatural to separate them on account of the presence of the supernumerary cross-
vein of the former. (About *Idioptera* compare p. 199.)

4. **L. portica**, n. sp. ♂.—Ferrugineo-flava, antennis fuscis, articulis
basalibus flavis; in mare thorace plus quam duplo longioribus, articulis
elongatis, pubescentibus; ala immaculata, stigmate pallido infuscato,
præfurca basi appendiculatâ.

Reddish-yellow, antennæ brown, basal joints yellow; in the male the antennæ are more than twice the length of the thorax; joints elongated,

pubescent; wings immaculate; stigma pale brownish; a stump of a
vein near the origin of the præfurca. Long. corp. 0.35.

Head reddish-yellow, with a grayish bloom on the front; palpi
brown; antennæ more than twice the length of the thorax, brown,
two basal joints yellowish, the second somewhat infuscated; joints
of the flagellum elongated, cylindrical, clothed with a dense, delicate pubescence; a few short verticils about the middle of the
joints. Thorax reddish-yellow, somewhat shining above, sometimes with faintly-marked brownish stripes; pleuræ with an opaque
yellowish bloom; halteres with a brownish knob. Feet tawny;
tips of the femora and of the tibiæ brown. Abdomen yellow;
last segment brown; forceps yellow. Wings with a faint pale
brownish tinge; stigma pale brown; a faint, small pale brown
cloud at the origin of the præfurca (sometimes obsolete); marginal cross-vein at the tip of the first longitudinal vein; petiole
of the first submarginal cell about the length of the great cross-
vein; this cell is very narrow in its basal half, broader towards
the tip; the inner end of the second submarginal cell very little
anterior to the inner ends of the first posterior and of the discal
cells; the petiole of the second posterior cell is nearly of the same
length with the cell itself (sometimes longer); the great cross-
vein is a little anterior to the middle of the discal cell; there is a
stump of a vein near the origin of the præfurca.

Hab. Milton, Mass., May 18th (Mr. Scudder); four male
specimens.

5. **L. tenuicornis,** n. sp. ♂ and ♀.—Nigrescens, cinereo-pollinosa,
antennis nigris, in mare thorace multo longioribus, articulis elongatis,
pubescentibus; in feminâ longitudine thoracis; halteres capitulo infuscato, abdomen cum forcipe nigro-fusci; alæ immaculatæ, stigmate pallido.

Blackish, with a grayish pollen, antennæ black, those of the male much
longer than the thorax, joints elongated, pubescent; those of the female
of the length of the thorax; halteres with a brownish knob; abdomen
and forceps blackish-brown; wings immaculate, stigma pale. Long.
corp. 0.28—0.32.

Head black, clothed with a gray bloom; rostrum and palpi
brown; antennæ black; those of the male, if bent backwards,
would reach the second abdominal segment; joints of the flagellum elongated, slightly attenuated at both ends, clothed with a

delicate, dense pubescence; a few verticillate delicate hairs about
the middle of each joint; antennæ of the female shorter than
those of the male; bent backwards, they would reach the end of
the thorax; the flagellum is clothed with scattered hairs, and
shows no vestige of a pubescence, except on the underside of the
joints near the basis. Ground-color of the thorax brownish-black,
clothed with a grayish bloom; the space usually occupied by the
stripes has less of this bloom, and is therefore darker, somewhat
shining, clothed with a short, delicate, erect, yellowish-gray
pubescence; the stripes are not well defined, although their
general outline is marked by the more dense gray bloom surrounding them. Halteres pale, knob brownish. Coxæ yellow,
the front ones brownish at the extreme basis; feet brown, femora
yellowish towards the basis. Abdomen blackish-brown; venter
yellowish, except at the tip, where it is brown; forceps brownish-
black; ovipositor elongated, slender, gently curved. Wings with
a slight pale brownish tinge; stigma colorless; tip of the auxiliary vein a little before the inner end of the second submarginal
cell; præfurca arcuated near the origin, otherwise quite straight;
petiole of the first submarginal vein short; the marginal cross-
vein is about the middle of the distance between the tip of the
first longitudinal vein and the inner end of the first submarginal
cell; the inner ends of the second submarginal and first posterior
cells are nearly in one line; the inner end of the discal cell is
slightly anterior to them; the great cross-vein is nearly opposite
the middle of the discal cell; petiole of the second posterior cell
usually shorter than the cell itself; fifth longitudinal vein arcuated
at the tip; the apex of the wing is finely pubescent.

Hab. White Mountains, N. H., in July. Three male and one
female specimen.

G. L. niveitarsis, n. sp. ♂ and ♀.—Thorace nigro, cinereo-pol-
linoso; antennis nigris, in mare thorace multo longioribus, articulis
elongatis, pubescentibus; in feminâ thorace brevioribus; abdomen fuscescens, forceps in mare flavus; tarsi postici albi; alæ immaculatæ;
stigmate pallide fuscescente.

Thorax black, with a gray pollen; antennæ black, much longer than the
thorax in the male; shorter than the thorax in the female; abdomen
brownish; forceps of the male yellow; hind tarsi white; wings immaculate; stigma with a pale brownish tinge. Long. corp. 0.25.

14   Sept. 1868.

Head black; front broad, with a gray, almost silvery reflection; antennæ of the male more than double the length of head and thorax taken together; first joint very short; joints of the flagellum long, cylindrical, clothed with a dense, delicate pubescence; the verticils are hardly perceptible; the antennæ of the female, when bent backwards, would hardly reach the root of the wings; joints short, oval, the basal ones of the flagellum truncate at the end; with scattered hairs and inconspicuous verticils among them. Ground color of the thorax black, clothed above with a yellowish-gray pollen, and therefore but faintly shining; stripes hardly marked; pleuræ somewhat hoary; halteres yellowish. Coxæ yellow; feet brownish-tawny, pubescent; femora and tibiæ, towards the tip, brownish; hind tarsi, except the tip, white. Abdomen brown (in some specimens mixed with yellowish); male forceps yellow. Wings with a faint brownish tinge; stigma pale brownish; tip of the auxiliary vein nearly opposite the inner end of the second submarginal cell; petiole of the first submarginal cell about equal in length to the great cross-vein; marginal cross-vein faintly marked, close by the tip of the first longitudinal vein; inner end of the second submarginal cell somewhat anterior to the inner end of the first posterior cell; in some specimens the inner end of the third posterior cell is almost pointed, the cross-vein separating it from the discal cell being very short; in other specimens, however, this is not the case; great cross-vein nearly opposite the middle of the discal cell, somewhat variable in its position.

Hab. Delaware (Dr. Wilson); Maryland (Cresson). Three male and one female. The tip of the abdomen of the female is broken off.

7. **L. tenuipes** Say. ♂ and ♀.—Brunnea, humeris pleurisque ochraceis; antennis maris thorace multo longioribus, articulis elongatis, pubescentibus; alis immaculatis, pallide infuscatis.

Brown, humeri and pleura ochraceous; antennæ of the male much longer than the thorax; joints elongated, pubescent; wings immaculate, with a pale brownish tinge. Long. corp. 0.3—0.4.

Syn. *Limnobia tenuipes* Say, Journ. Acad. Nat. Sc. Phil. III. p 21, 8.
Limnobia humeralis Wied. (non Say), Auss. Zw. I, p. 34.
Limnophila tenuipes O. Sacken, Proc. Ac. Nat. Sc. Phil. 1859, p. 235.

Rostrum ochraceous, palpi dark brown; front brownish, with a gray bloom; antennæ brown, paler at the basis; those of the male about once and a half the length of the thorax, filiform; joints subcylindrical, elongated, clothed with a dense pubescence; a few verticillate hairs on each joint of the flagellum; the antennæ of the female are shorter than those of the male, but longer than the thorax; joints elongated; no pubescence, but long verticils. Thorax brown above, this color occupying the space of the ordinary stripes, which are not otherwise marked; humeri and pleuræ ochraceous; scutellum and metathorax brown; the knob of the halteres is more or less infuscated; feet long, slender, dark tawny, pale at the basis, darker at the tips of the femora and of the tibiæ; coxæ ochraceous. Abdomen brown, venter paler. The tip of the auxillary vein is some distance anterior to the inner end of the second submarginal and first posterior cell, which are in one line; the marginal cross-vein is some distance anterior to the tip of the first longitudinal vein, close by the inner end of the first submarginal cell; the præfurca is long, straight, in one line with the petiole of the first submarginal cell, which is rather long, longer than the great cross-vein; the small cross-vein is arcuated; the great cross-vein is usually about the middle of the discal cell. The wings are slightly tinged with brownish; the stigma is more or less brown; sometimes quite pale.

Hab. United States; not rare. Washington, D. C., Savannah, Ga.; Canada (Couper); Illinois (LeBaron).

Say's descriptions of *L. tenuipes* and *L. humeralis* are so much alike that the choice between them was somewhat difficult in identifying the present species. Still, the words in the description of *L. tenuipes*, "antennæ long" and "wings dusky," determined my choice. Wiedemann took both for synonyms; but Say denies this synonymy in a manuscript note, which I discovered in a copy of Wiedemann's work, in the library of the Academy of Natural Sciences in Philadelphia. That Wiedemann's *L. humeralis* is the present species, results from his comparing it to *L. discicollis* Meig. And, indeed, these species are most closely allied, with the only exceptions that the European species is slightly larger, and that the antennæ of the male are like those of the female, and not at all elongated and pubescent as those of *L. tenuipes*. The coloring and the venation of both species are precisely the same.

B. Antennæ of the male not perceptibly longer than those of the female.

5. **L. recondita, n. sp.** ♂ and ♀.—Flavo-ferruginea, nitens, antennis utrinsque setra longitudine mediocri, verticillis longis; alis fusco-flavescentibus, stigmate concolori; petiolo cellulæ submarginalis primæ longo; cellulis submarginali secundâ et posteriori primâ æque longis.

Yellowish-red, shining, antennæ of moderate length in both sexes; verticills long; wings with a yellowish-brown tinge; stigma of the same color; the petiole of the first submarginal cell is long; the second submarginal and first posterior cells are of the same length. Long. corp. 0.35—0.4 (sometimes smaller).

Head yellowish-red or brownish, front shining, with some black hairs; palpi brown; first joint of the antennæ, and sometimes the basis of the second, yellowish; the remainder of the antennæ brownish, gradually darker towards the tip; first two or three joints of the flagellum rounded, the following elongated; verticills long; bent backwards, the antennæ would hardly reach the basis of the wings. Thorax yellowish-red, or reddish-yellow, in some specimens brownish-red; it is more or less shining above and on the pleuræ; the humeri are not perceptibly paler than the rest of the mesonotum; the pleuræ but slightly paler, also shining; halteres pale, sometimes faintly brownish. Feet yellowish-tawny, faintly infuscated at the tips of the femora, of the tibiæ, and of the tarsi. Abdomen reddish- or yellowish-brown; forceps of the male of the same color; ovipositor long, slender, very slightly arcuated. Wings with a yellowish-brown tinge; stigma not darker; tip of the auxiliary vein slightly anterior to the inner end of the second submarginal cell, which is in one line with the small cross-vein; the latter gently arcuated; præfurca as long as the first posterior cell, straight, in one line with the petiole of the first submarginal cell; this petiole is as long as the anterior branch of the second vein; the oblique marginal cross-vein is close at the basis of this anterior branch; the great cross-vein (slightly variable in its position) is usually about the middle of the discal cell.

Hab. New York, Pennsylvania, Georgia, etc. Twenty specimens.

The renation of this species is almost exactly like that of *L. tenuipes* Say; the long verticills of the antennæ, the length of the ovipositor, etc., prove the relationship of these species, the difference in the length of the male antennæ notwithstanding. The size of this species is somewhat variable. In some specimens the præfutra has a stump of a vein near its origin.

9. L. imbecilla O. S. ♂ and ♀.—Pallide ochracea, fuscescens, opaca, fronts cinerascente; antennis utrinsque sexus longitudine mediocri, verticillis longis; alis pallide fusco-flavescentibus, stigmate concolori; petiolo cellulæ submarginalis primæ longo; cellulis submarginali secundâ et posteriori primâ æquæ longis.

Pale brownish-ochraceous, opaque, front grayish; antennæ of both sexes of moderate length, with long verticils; wings with a pale yellowish-brown tinge; stigma concolorous; the petiole of the first submarginal cell is long; the second submarginal and first posterior cells are of the same length. Long. corp. 0.33—0.38.

Syn. *Limnophila imbecilla* O. Sacken, Proc. Ac. Nat. Sc. Phil. 1859, p. 237.

This species is remarkably like the preceding in all the important characters; it is slightly smaller, and the wings are narrower; besides these, the only striking differences consist in the coloring. The body is entirely opaque; the front is gray; the thorax pale yellowish, of a more saturate color above; pleuræ and metathorax slightly hoary; the first joint of the antennæ is brownish, with a gray bloom above, the basis of the flagellum paler; the wings have a slight yellowish-gray tinge. All the other characters, including the structure of the antennæ and the venation, are like those of *L. recondita*.

Hab. Trenton Falls, N. Y.; Maryland (Cresson). In one specimen the stigma is faintly brownish. The indicated differences, notwithstanding, it is not impossible that this species is only a variety of the preceding.

10. L. toxoneura O. S. ♂ and ♀.—Pallide ochracea, fuscescens; antennis utrinsque sexus longitudine mediocri, fuscis; alis subhyalinis, stigmate pallide infuscato; petiolo cellulæ submarginalis primæ longo, conspicue arcuato; cellulis submarginali secundâ et posteriori primâ subæquæ longis.

Pale ochraceous, brownish; antennæ in both sexes of moderate length, brown; wings subhyaline; stigma pale brownish; petiole of the first submarginal cell long, conspicuously arcuated; second submarginal and first posterior cells almost of the same length. Long. corp. 0.3—0.35.

Syn. *Limnophila toxoneura* O. Sacken, Proc. Ac. Nat. Sc. Phil. 1859, p. 236.

Front grayish; palpi infuscated; rostrum yellowish; antennæ
brown; basis of the third joint pale; joints of the flagellum
elongated-elliptical; verticills moderate. Thorax brownish-yellow with two pale brown stripes, which become paler near the
collare, where they communicate with a brown spot near the
humerus; they extend beyond the suture posteriorly; pleuræ
pale, sometimes with a pale brown stripe; halteres pale, slightly
infuscated; feet pale tawny, tips slightly infuscated. Abdomen
brownish; ovipositor arcuated, of moderate length. Wings
slightly tinged with grayish; stigma faintly infuscated; marginal
cross-vein at the tip of the first longitudinal vein; præfurca gently
arcuated, rather short, not longer than the petiole of the first submarginal cell; this petiole is conspicuously arcuated; the branches
of the second vein are nearly parallel, except at the basis; the
second submarginal cell is only a trifle longer than the first posterior; the second posterior cell rather long, in comparison to its
petiole (the relation between them is variable); the great cross-
vein is usually opposite the middle of the discal cell.

Hab. Trenton Falls, N. Y.

This species is easily distinguished by the arcuated petiole
of its first submarginal cell.

11. L. areolata O. S.   ♂ and ♀.—Ochracea: alæ subhyalinæ, immaculatæ; cellula discoidali elongatâ; ejus angulus interior et præfurca infimum ab alæ basi fere æquæ distantiæ; cellulæ submarginalis
secunda et posterior prima longissimæ; præfurca brevis.

Ochraceous; wings subhyaline, immaculate; discal cell elongated; its
inner end not much more distant from the basis of the wing than the
origin of the præfurca; the second submarginal and the first posterior
cells are very long; præfurca short. Long. corp. 0.27—0.32.

Syn. *Limnophila areolata* O. Sacken, Proc. Ac. Nat. Sc. Phil. 1859, p. 237.

Ochraceous yellow, antennæ, except the basal joint, slightly
infuscated; front sometimes with a yellowish-gray bloom; knob
of the halteres more or less infuscated; abdomen brownish above,
venter pale; forceps ochraceous; ovipositor long, slender, very
slightly curved; feet yellowish, the latter part of the tibiæ and
the tarsi, except at the basis, brownish; sometimes the tibiæ are
altogether yellowish. The antennæ, if bent backwards, would
not reach much beyond the root of the wings; the joints of the
flagellum are about twice longer than broad, gradually becoming

more slender towards the tip; the verticils are of moderate
length. Wings subhyaline, with a slight yellowish or brownish
tinge; velas somewhat pubescent; those near the costa yellowish,
the other veins brownish; stigma pale, sometimes very slightly
infuscated; the most striking character of the venation is the
shape of the discal cell (Tab. II, fig. 6); it is long and narrow;
its inner end reaches the middle of the length of the wing,
and is but little more distant from the basis of the wing than
the origin of the præfurca; the second submarginal and first
posterior cells are also very long, and have their inner ends exactly in one line, at a distance beyond the inner end of the discal
cell, which is about equal to the great cross-vein or longer; the
length of these cells causes the præfurca to be very short, distinctly shorter than the discal cell; the petiole of the first submarginal cell is about equal to the præfurca in length, or a little
longer; this cell is elongated, sometimes angular at its inner end;
the marginal cross-vein is very faint, about the middle of the
distance between the tip of the first longitudinal vein and the
inner end of the first submarginal cell; the subcostal cross-vein
is at a distance from the tip of the auxiliary vein, which is a
little shorter than the length of the great cross-vein; great cross-
vein more or less near the middle of the discal cell, often a little
beyond it.

Hab. Trenton Falls, N. Y.; Maryland; Washington, D. C.
Not rare in May and June.

12. L. adusta O. S.   ♂ and ♀.—Flava, thorace ferrugineo, nitido,
    fronte cinerea; præfurca brevi, arcuata; alarum margine apicali in-
    fuscato.

Yellow, thorax reddish, shining, front gray; præfurca short, arcuated;
    apical margin of the wings clouded with brown.   Long. corp. 0.3—0.5.

Syn. *Limnophila adusta* O. Sacken, Proc. Ac. Nat. Sc. Phil. 1859, p. 225.

I possess a series of specimens, varying considerably in their
size and in the coloring of their wings, but having the following
characters in common:—

Head gray, opaque above; rostrum brownish-yellow, palpi
brown; antennæ short in both sexes, yellowish, basal joint sometimes darker; verticils of moderate length, black; basal joints
of the flagellum elongated-elliptical, becoming more long and

slender towards the tip. Thorax reddish-yellow, shining above,
sometimes with a faint longitudinal brown line in the middle;
pleuræ paler yellow, with a hardly perceptible yellowish bloom,
which is also perceptible beyond the suture above; halteres with
a more or less infuscated knob. The auxiliary vein is nearly
opposite the inner end of the second submarginal cell; its tip has
the appearance of being incurved towards the first longitudinal
vein, whereas the cross-vein seems to be placed between it and
the costa; the præfurca is arcuated at its origin, and remarkably
short, not longer than one-third of the length of the second submarginal cell; petiole of the first submarginal cell of moderate
length, sometimes but little longer than the small cross-vein, sometimes about the length of the great cross-vein; first submarginal
cell gradually tapering towards its inner end; second submarginal
cell a little longer than the first posterior; marginal cross-vein at
the tip of the first longitudinal vein, and not far from the middle
of the anterior branch of the second vein; great cross-vein usually
about the middle of the discal cell; seventh longitudinal vein
slightly sinuated in the middle, and somewhat curved in the
opposite sense at the tip. The tip of the wing, between the
stigma and the apex, is more or less distinctly clouded with
brown along the margin. The ovipositor of the female is moderately long, slender, perceptibly arcuated.

The specimens vary in the following characters:—

The larger specimens have a yellowish abdomen, brownish
along the lateral margins only; the feet are yellowish; femora
with a distinct brown band before the tip; tip of the tibiæ brown;
wings with a yellowish tinge; stigma dark brown; a narrow
brown cloud runs along the fifth longitudinal vein and the central
cross-veins; a brown mark at the origin of the præfurca; the
cloud at the tip of the wing is dark and very well marked.

A series of smaller specimens have a brownish abdomen, and
brownish-tawny feet, except the coxæ and the basis of the femora,
which are pale; the wings have a very pale tinge, and have no
clouds, except the more or less faint apical cloud and the more
or less infuscated stigma; the latter is sometimes quite pale.

Between these extremes, gradations in size and coloring occur,
which compel the describer to unite all these forms into one
species, until further observation brings more light upon the
subject.

Hab. United States; I have seen specimens from most of the Middle and Northern States; as far south as Georgia, west as Northern Illinois and the Upper Wisconsin River, and north as Maine (Mr. Packard). The specimen from Maine is one of the largest and most clouded upon the wings; a series of specimens from Delaware, Pennsylvania, and Maryland are small, with pale-colored wings.

13. L. inteipennis O. S. ♂ and ♀.—Fuscana, thorace lineâ mediâ fuscâ, pleuris cannoentibus; alis fusuanis, nebulis obsoletis paucis obscuris; cellola submarginalis secunda posteriori primâ conspicue longior; longitudinalis septimae spina incurva.

Brownish, thorax with a brown line in the middle, pleura grayish; wings brownish with a few obsolete clouds; second submarginal cell considerably longer than the first posterior; seventh longitudinal vein incurved at the tip. Long. corp. 0.28—0.3.

Syn. *Limnophila inteipennis* O. Sacken, Proc. Ac. Nat. Sc. Phil. 1859, p. 236.

Head narrowed posteriorly, meeting a neck-like prolongation of the collare; front and vertex brownish-gray; rostrum and palpi brown; antennae brown; first joint grayish above; basis of the third joint pale; joints of the flagellum rather short, becoming more slender towards the tip; verticils moderate. Thorax opaque, brownish above, gray on the sides; stripes nearly obsolete, but a brown longitudinal line in the middle always distinct. Halteres with a dusky knob. Feet tawny; tips of the femora very faintly, tips of the tibiae and of the tarsi more distinctly infuscated. Abdomen yellowish-brown; venter paler; forceps brownish-yellow; ovipositor of moderate length, gently arcuated. Wings (Tab. II, fig. 10) tinged with brownish; there are faint brownish clouds at the origin of the praefurca, the inner end of the second submarginal cell, and on the marginal cross-vein (other clouds, on the cross-veins, at the inner end of the second posterior cell, and at the tips of the sixth and seventh longitudinal veins are almost obsolete, and generally invisible except in fresh specimens); veins brown; first longitudinal ferruginous; praefurca of moderate length, straight, except at the basis; petiole of the first submarginal cell about half the length of the praefurca, gently arcuated; marginal cross-vein about the middle of the distance between the inner end of the first submarginal cell and the tip of the first longitudinal vein; branches

of the second longitudinal vein, especially the posterior one,
arcuated; second submarginal cell longer than the first posterior,
by a distance about equal to the length of the great cross-vein;
second posterior cell short, in comparison to its petiole; seventh
longitudinal vein conspicuously curved at the tip.

Hab. United States; common in the vicinity of Washington,
D. C., from the earliest spring through the greatest part of the
summer.   Florida (in March); South Carolina; Massachusetts
(Mr. Scudder).

The forceps of this species is represented on Tab. IV, fig. 25;
the inner pair of appendages is ciliated.

I possess a specimen without petiolated (second) posterior cell
on both wings.   A stump sometimes occurs at the origin of the
prefurca.

This species, together with *L. inornata* and *contempta*, form a
separate group, distinguished by the structure of the antennæ,
the shape of the head, which is narrowed behind; the neck-like
prolongation of the collare, the venation (length of the second
submarginal cell, arcuated course of the posterior branch of the
second vein, seventh vein incurved at the tip), etc.   All these
species have very striking pits or impressions on the humeri,
smooth, and as if horny, at the bottom; in front of the mesonotum, where the intermediate thoracic stripe reaches the collare,
there are two small, closely approximated dots with a shining
surface.   These marks are either black or brown, and somewhat
different in size in the different species.   In *L. luteipennis* they
are shining brown and very distinct.   Similar pits on the humeri
exist in many other species and in different sections (compare the
Introduction, p. 29), but they are particularly well marked in the
above-mentioned three species, and also in *L. fratria.*

14. L. contempta, n. sp.   ♂ and ♀.—Fuscana, thorace concolore,
vittis obsoletis, pleuris canescentibus; alis dilutissime fusco tinctis,
unicoloribus; cellula submarginalis secunda posteriori primâ conspicue
longior, longitudinalis septima apex incurvus.

Brownish, thorax of the same color, with obsolete stripes, pleuræ with a
hoary bloom; wings tinged with pale brown, unicolorous; second submarginal cell considerably longer than the first posterior; seventh longitudinal vein incurved at the tip.   Long. corp. 0.21—0.25.

Head grayish-brown, narrowed posteriorly; rostrum and palpi

brown; antennæ brown, third joint pale at the basis; flagellum
with subcylindrical joints, gradually becoming more slender; the
ten joints before the tip are almost linear; verticils moderate.
Thorax pale brownish, opaque; two brownish stripes above are
hardly perceptible; pleuræ somewhat hoary. Halteres brownish,
paler at the basis; feet pale tawny, tips of the tarsi brownish.
Wings with a pale brownish tinge; stigma pale, seldom very faintly
clouded; veins pale brown; the venation is similar to that of *L.
luteipennis* and *inornata.* Abdomen brown; forceps yellowish.
Hab. Middle States; four specimens.

This species is smaller than *L. luteipennis* and *inornata;* of a
more dull, brownish color; the veins of the wings are paler, etc.
The impression on the humeri and the double dot in front of the
mesonotum near the collare, are small, brownish, but distinct.

15. L. inermata, n. sp. ♂.—Fuscana, thorace griseo, melanoto
medio infuscato; alis fuscano-flavescentibus, unicoloribus; cellula submarginalis secunda posteriori primā conspicue longior; longitudinalis
septima apex incurvus.

Brownish, thorax gray, metanotum brownish in the middle; wings tinged
with brownish-yellow, unicolorous; second submarginal cell considerably longer than the first posterior; seventh longitudinal vein incurved
at the tip. Long. corp. 0.3.

Head narrowed posteriorly, meeting a neck-like prolongation
of the collare; rostrum and palpi brown; front and vertex gray,
with black hairs; antennæ brown; basal joint grayish above; the
third joint (the first of the flagellum) is a little longer than broad,
cylindrical, attenuated at the basis, which is pale; the second
joint of the flagellum is of a similar shape, very slightly shorter;
the third is again somewhat shorter and more slender; the fourth
and the following joints are linear, slender; verticils moderately
long. Thorax bluish-gray on the pleuræ; mesonotum opaque, infuscated in the middle, in the location of the usual intermediate
stripe; brownish-gray on the sides; collare and metathorax gray;
halteres yellow. Abdomen brownish; venter paler; forceps
reddish-yellow. Coxæ reddish-yellow, with a very slight gray
bloom; yellowish at the base, becoming gradually brown towards
the tip; (this brownish-tawny; their tip brown; tarsi brownish.
The length of the feet is comparatively greater than in *L. luteipennis.* Wings tinged with brownish-yellow; stigma pale; a

very faint shade on the marginal cross-vein; otherwise the wing
is unicolorous; auxiliary and first longitudinal veins reddish; the
other veins brown; præfurca of moderate length, straight, except
at the basis; petiole of the first submarginal cell about half the
length of the præfurca, distinctly longer than the great cross-
vein, gently arcuated; marginal cross-vein somewhat nearer to
the inner end of the first submarginal cell than to the tip of the
first longitudinal vein; branches of the second longitudinal vein,
especially the posterior one, arcuated; second submarginal cell
longer than the first posterior by a distance which is a little
shorter than the great cross-vein; seventh longitudinal vein
curved at the tip.

Hab. Massachusetts (Mr. Packard); a single male specimen.

This species is very like *L. luteipennis* in its general appearance,
but is easily distinguished by its unicolorous wings; the thorax,
although brownish above, has not the distinct brown line in the
middle, which is very striking in *luteipennis;* the size is somewhat larger; the feet are considerably longer; in *L. luteipennis,*
the fore tarsi of the male are about 0.22 long, in *L. inornata*
about 0.83; the head of the latter species is of a purer gray, the
pleuræ more bluish-gray; the second submarginal cell is a little
shorter. The only specimen in my possession has the second
posterior cell much longer than its petiole, and the great cross-
vein very near the inner end of the discal cell. The impressions
on the humeri and the double dot in front of the mesonotum are
very distinctly marked, black, shining.

16. L. fratria, n. sp. ♂.—Fuscana, thorace cinereo, mesonoto pallide
infuscato; antennarum flagelli articulis usque ad apicem brevibus; alis
unicoloribus, subhyalinis, parum fuscano tinctis; cellula submarginalis secunda posteriori primâ modice longior.

Brownish, thorax yellowish-gray, mesonotum somewhat brownish; joints
of the flagellum short to the very apex; wings unicolorous, subhyaline,
very faintly tinged with brownish; second submarginal cell moderately
longer than the first posterior. Long. corp. 0.3.

Head yellowish-gray, with blackish hairs; rostrum and palpi
brown; antennæ pale brownish; first joint cylindrical; the second
rather large, rounded; all the joints of the flagellum are not much
longer than broad, rounded, gradually diminishing in size towards
the tip (not at all linear, like those of *L. luteipennis* and *inor-*

nata); verticils moderate. Thorax opaque, of a dull yellowish-
gray; mesonotum yellowish-brown, grayish along the margins;
stripes almost obsolete; pleuræ and metanotum hoary gray.
Halteres yellow; knob somewhat infuscated. Feet yellowish-
brown; the tips of the femora, of the tibiæ, and the tarsi darker;
abdomen brownish; tenter paler; forceps reddish-yellow. Wings
unicolorous, with a very slight brownish tinge; the stigma but
faintly clouded along the marginal cross-vein, which is very near
the tip of the first longitudinal vein and rather distant from the
inner end of the first submarginal cell; the petiole of the latter
is of about the same length with the distance between the tip of
the præfurca and the small cross-vein, and distinctly shorter than
the great cross-vein; the second submarginal cell is therefore but
little longer than the first posterior; præfurca nearly straight;
seventh longitudinal vein very gently bisinuated.

Hab. Northern States; a single male specimen. (I have lost
the label with the precise locality; the specimen is caught by
me, and therefore either in the State of New York, or in New
Hampshire.)

This species has a superficial resemblance to *L. inornata*, but
is easily distinguished by the different structure of the antennæ,
which might almost be called submoniliform; by the much
shorter second submarginal cell, the proximity of the marginal
cross-vein to the tip of the first longitudinal vein, and the much
shorter feet and tarsi. The impressions on the humeri and the
double dot in front of the mesonotum are black, and very distinct.
The second posterior cell, in my only specimen, is shorter than
its petiole, and the great cross-vein is a little beyond the middle
of the discal cell.

17. L. brevifurca O. S. ♂.—Fuscana, thorace concolore, vittis obsoletis, alis dilutissime fusco tinctis, unicoloribus; cellula submarginalis
secunda et posterior prima subæque longæ; posterior secunda perbrevis,
petiolo longissimo.

Brownish, thorax of the same color, stripes obsolete; wings faintly tinged
with brownish, unicolorous; second submarginal cell of almost the same
length with the first posterior cell; second posterior cell very short, with
a very long petiole. Long. corp. 0.27.

Syn. *Limnophila brevifurca* O. Sacken, Proc. Ac. Nat. Sc. Phil. 1859, p. 227.

Head brownish-gray, antennæ and palpi brown; joints near the basis of the flagellum not longer than broad, somewhat more elongated and slender towards the tip; verticils comparatively short. Thorax grayish-brown; an obsolete pale brown double stripe above; halteres pale at the basis; knob slightly infuscated; feet dark tawny, slightly infuscated at the tips of the femora and of the tarsi; coxae and basis of the femora pale. Abdomen brownish; forceps paler. Wings faintly tinged with brownish; stigma very slightly darker; the second submarginal cell only a trifle longer than the first posterior; the second posterior is five or six times shorter than its petiole; the petiole of the first submarginal cell is distinctly shorter than the great cross-vein; marginal cross-vein very faint, about the middle of the distance between the tip of the first longitudinal vein and the inner end of the first submarginal cell; great cross-vein about the middle of the discal cell; seventh longitudinal vein straight, except the extreme tip, which is a little curved.

Hab. Washington, D. C., in April. I had eight male specimens when I first described this species. A number of them were swarming round a spring, in the woods. One of the specimens has a faint indication of an adventitious cross-vein in the middle of the first basal cell. The black pits on the humeri are well marked, but the double dot in the front of the mesonotum is obsolete.

18. **L. ultima** O. S.   ♂ and ♀.—Grisea, thorace vittis quatuor fuscis; alis hyalinis, immaculatis; antennis fuscis, articulis flagelli basalibus quatuor coalescentibus, incrassatis; cellula submarginalis secunda primá posteriori parum longior; vena longitudinalis septima recta.

Gray, thorax with four brown stripes; wings hyaline, immaculate; antennae brown; the four basal joints of the flagellum are coalescent, incrassated; second submarginal cell but little longer than the first posterior; seventh longitudinal vein straight. Long. corp. 0.25—0.33.

Syn. *Limnophila ultima* O. Sacken, Proc. Ac. Nat. Sc. Phil. 1859, p. 238.

Head and thorax of a pure gray; antennae and palpi brown; the antennae, if bent backwards, would hardly reach the basis of the wings; the four first joints of the flagellum are short and almost coalescent, forming an elongated almost conical body, which is stouter than the remainder of the antenna; the following joints are elongated, subcylindrical; joints rather short. The thorax has four distinctly-marked brown stripes; the intermedi-

ate ones are approximated. Halteres pale; the tip sometimes
slightly infuscated; feet brownish-pubescent; spurs very short.
Abdomen grayish-brown; forceps of the same color. Wings
almost hyaline, distinctly broader in the female than in the male;
stigma pale; first submarginal cell very short, being about equal
in length to its petiole; the latter is gently arcuated, and very
long (about four-fifths of the length of the præfurca); the second
submarginal cell is very little longer than the first posterior; the
small cross-vein is somewhat oblique; the discal cell is somewhat
elongated, the cross-vein at its inner end is straight; the petiole
of the second posterior cell is usually longer than this cell; the
seventh longitudinal vein is perfectly straight. The marginal
cross-vein is a little before the tip of the first longitudinal vein,
a little beyond the middle of the stigma; but as the length of the
first submarginal cell is somewhat variable, the marginal cross-
vein, which is usually inserted a little before its inner end (that
is, between the petiole and the first vein), is sometimes close by
this end; in some specimens even, although rarely, a little beyond
it (that is, between the anterior branch of the second vein and
the first vein). The position of the great cross-vein is also very
variable; a little beyond the inner end of the discal cell; or
opposite this inner end, or even a little before it.

Hab. Washington, late in October; Maine (Packard); Canada;
the northwestern regions of Hudson's Bay Territory, and also on
the Yakon River in Allaska (Kennicott).

The forceps of this species (Tab. IV, fig. 24) is distinguished
by the great length of the basal pieces, and the comparative
smallness of the horny appendages; this peculiarity is perceptible
even in dry specimens. The ovipositor of the female is long,
gently curved. The black humeral pits are distinctly perceptible;
but there are no dots on the front part of the mesonotum.

19. L. aprilina O. S.   ♂ and ♀.—Cinerascens, abdomine fusco,
pedibus testaceis; alis ad costam sex or septem-maculatis; venis transversis nebulosis; venulâ transversâ supernumerariâ in dimidio cellulæ
basalis secundæ.

Grayish, abdomen brown; feet tawny; wings with six or seven brown
spots near the costa; cross-veins clouded; a supernumerary cross vein
in the middle of the second basal cell. Long. corp. 0.25.

Syn. *Limnophila aprilina* O. Sacken, Proc. Ac. Nat. Sc. Phil. 1859. p. 235.

Head cinereous; palpi black, short, especially the three last joints; antennæ brownish-tawny, basal joints darker; they are short in both sexes; when bent backwards, they would not reach beyond the root of the wings; joints of the flagellum subglobular or short-oval; those of the male are clothed on the under side with a dense pubescence; verticils distinct, moderately long. Thorax yellowish-gray, with indistinct brownish stripes, the intermediate double; halteres with a brown knob, sometimes pale; feet with a comparatively long pubescence, tawny, coxæ and basis of the femora paler; tips of the femora and extreme tips of the tarsi sometimes slightly infuscated. Abdomen brownish, margins of the segments darker. Wings with brown spots along the anterior margin: the first and smallest at the humeral cross-vein; the second between it and the origin of the præfurca; the third on the latter; the fourth at the tip of the auxiliary, the fifth at the tip of the first longitudinal vein; there are smaller spots or clouds at the tips of all the longitudinal veins, except the third; all the cross-veins and the inner end of the first submarginal cell are also clouded with brown; the first and fifth longitudinal veins, in the intervals of the brown spots, are usually yellow. The petiole of the first submarginal cell is rather long, longer than the great cross-vein; præfurca angular at its origin; sometimes provided with a stump of a vein; second submarginal cell distinctly longer than the first posterior; a supernumerary cross-vein in the middle of the second basal cell; the seventh longitudinal vein is gently sinuated in the middle and incurved at the tip.

Hab. Washington, D. C., in the spring; White Mountains, N. H.

The male forceps of this species (Tab. IV, fig. 23) is somewhat peculiar; the horny appendages are short, stout, obtuse, provided with a deep notch at the tip (l. c. fig. 23a). The ovipositor is very long and slender, gently arcuated. This species belongs to the genus *Ephelia* Schiner (compare p. 109), and is very much like an unnamed European species (perhaps *guttata* Macq. ?).

I possess a couple of specimens with comparatively shorter and broader wings, larger and darker spots; the horny appendages of their forceps (as I have noticed upon a fresh specimen), although also cleft, are less blunt at the tip and more elongated. I do not think that such specimens are specifically distinct.

20. L. fuscovaria O. S. ♂ and ♀.—Cinerascens, abdomine fusco, pedibus pallidis; alis latis, dense fusco-punctatis; ad costam maculis majoribus fuscis; venula transversa supernumeraria in cellula submarginali prima.

Grayish, abdomen brown, feet pale; wings broad, densely dotted with brown; larger brown spots along the costa; a supernumerary crossvein in the first submarginal cell. Long. corp. 0.2‥.—0.3.

SYN. *Limnophila* (*Dicranophragma*) *fuscovaria* O. SACKEN, Proc. Ac. Nat. Sc. Phil. 1859, p. 240.

Head gray, proboscis and palpi brown; antennæ pale, brownish towards the tip, with moderately long verticils; when bent backwards, the antennæ would hardly reach the basis of the wings; joints of the flagellum short, subglobular, becoming more elongated and slender towards the tip. Thorax grayish, with three narrow brown lines; the intermediate one, which is paler, begins in two black dots near the collare; pleura with two brown stripes; brown spots near and on the coxæ; halteres pale, with the tip slightly dusky; feet pale, pubescent; tip of the tarsi a little darker. Abdomen brown, paler on the margins of the segments; lateral margins darker; forceps pale; ovipositor ferruginous, long, slender, nearly straight. Wings very broad, variegated with numerous little brown dots; five larger, nearly square brown spots along the anterior margin; a supernumerary cross-vein connects both branches of the second vein, near the tip of the anterior one; petiole of the first submarginal cell not longer than the small cross-vein; the inner end of this cell rather broad, not pointed; præfurca somewhat angular near the basis; second posterior cell short, with a long petiole.

Hab. Washington, D. C., and farther north; as far as Quebec (Couper); not rare.

In the *Proc. Acad. Nat. Sci. Philad.* I have proposed for this species the subgeneric name of *Dicranophragma* (compare p. 199).

21. L. rufibasis O. S. ♂ and ♀.—Cinerea, halteribus pallidis, alis pallide fusco-flavescentibus, stigmate fusco; venulis centralibus et vena longitudinali quinta fusco-nebulosis; pedibus fuscis, femorum basi ferruginea.

Yellowish-gray, halteres pale, wings pale brownish-yellow, stigma brown; central cross-veins and fifth longitudinal vein clouded with brown; feet brown, basis of the femora ferruginous. Long. corp. 0.4—0.47.

SYN. *Limnophila* (*Prionolabis*) *rufibasis* O. SACKEN, Proc. Ac. Nat. Sc. Phil. 1859, p. 239.

15 Sept. 1868.

Head yellowish-gray, palpi and antennæ brown; basis of the
flagellum sometimes faintly rufescent; the antennæ in both sexes,
if bent backwards, would not reach beyond the root of the wings;
joints of the flagellum not much longer than broad, somewhat
more elongated towards the tip, clothed with scattered hairs, but
without verticils. The ground-color of the thorax above is a
shining black, but it is almost completely hidden under a thick
gray dust; stripes obsolete; pleuræ gray; halteres pale yellow.
Coxæ gray; feet rather stout, brownish-tawny; femora somewhat
reddish, except the tip, which is brown; tip of the tibiæ and the
tarsi brown. Abdomen grayish-brown; horny parts of the
genitals ferruginous and brown. Wings tinged with brownish-
yellow, yellow at the root; stigma oblong, brown; central cross-
veins, origin of the præfurca, and fifth longitudinal vein slightly
clouded with brown; all the veins brown, except those near the
costa, which are yellowish; the marginal cross-vein is very near
the tip of the first longitudinal vein, although not quite close at
it; it is about the middle of the anterior branch of the second
longitudinal vein; the petiole of the first submarginal cell is of a
variable length, but generally shorter than the great cross-vein
(the figure, Tab. II, fig. 8, represents one of the shortest); the
second submarginal cell is but slightly longer than the first
posterior cell.

Hab. Washington, D. C.; New York; Massachusetts, etc.
Found in woods, round stumps of trees.

The size of this species is somewhat variable; the wings are
more yellowish in the larger specimens, and more grayish in the
small ones. The male forceps (Tab. IV, fig. 27) has a pair of
large, flat, horny appendages, serrated on the inside; and a second
pair of shorter and broader appendages, independent of the first
(fig. 27, *b*); the number of indentations of the large appendages
varies according to the size of the specimen. The ovipositor of
the female has long, rather straight, slender valves. I have proposed for this species the subgeneric name of *Prionolabis*, principally on account of the peculiar structure of the forceps (compare
p. 197).

23. I. **munda**, n. sp. ♂ and ♀.—Nigra, thorace nitido, alis pallide
fuscescentibus, stigmate fusco; pedibus intercoutibus, femorum tibiarumque apicibus fuscis.

Black, thorax shining, wings with a pale brownish tinge; stigma brown; feet yellowish, tips of the femora and of the tibiæ brown. Long. corp. 0.23—0.3.

Head black, covered above with a brownish-gray bloom, and hence opaque; rostrum and palpi brown; antennæ brown, clothed with moderately long hairs, but without verticils; when bent backwards, they would reach but little beyond the root of the wings; the joints of the flagellum are short, somewhat obconical, becoming cylindrical towards the tip. Thorax black and shining above; pleuræ opaque; halteres yellowish, knob faintly brownish. Abdomen blackish-brown, the male forceps reddish-black. Coxæ yellowish; feet brownish-yellow, clothed with a rather long, black pubescence; femora and tibiæ infuscated at the tip; tarsi brown. Wings with a slight brownish tinge, yellowish near the root; veins brown, except those near the costa, which are yellowish; stigma brown; cross-veins faintly clouded with brownish; petiole of the first submarginal cell not longer than the great cross-vein; second submarginal cell but slightly longer than the first posterior.

Hab. White Mountains, N. H., in July; not rare. I have seven male and two female specimens.

The venation of this species is very like that of *L. rufibasis* (Tab. II, fig. 3). The forceps of the male is also somewhat like that of the latter species; the outer horny appendage is elongated and curved; the inner one stout and short (compare Tab. IV, fig. 27, forceps of *L. rufibasis*). The ovipositor of the female has long, slender, and rather straight valves. The relationship of the two species is evident, and *L. munda* may be also considered a *Prionolabis*.

22. L. montana, O. S. ♂ and ♀.—Thorace cinereo; vittis quatuor fuscis; alis fusco-maculatis.

Thorax gray with four brown stripes; wings spotted with brown. Long. corp. 0.35—0.4.

Syn. *Limnophila (Dactylolabis) montana* O. Sacken, Proc. Ac. Nat. Sc. Phil. 1859, p. 240.

Head gray; rostrum and palpi brown; antennæ brown, four basal joints grayish; they do not reach much beyond the basis of the wings in both sexes; joints of the flagellum elliptical, clothed in the male with a dense, microscopic pubescence; verti-

cils short, bristle-like. Thorax yellowish-gray above, with four
brown stripes, the intermediate ones approximated; the lateral
ones extend over the suture behind; pleuræ, scutellum, and metathorax grayish; halteres pale; feet very long and slender, dark
tawny, tips of the femora and of the tibiæ darker; tarsi brown.
Abdomen brownish-gray; forceps likewise; ovipositor ferruginous. Wings (Tab. II, fig. 7)[1] with four or five brown spots
along the anterior margin; the third one is usually prolonged in
the shape of a band, over the central cross-veins as far as the fifth
longitudinal vein; the fifth spot, at the tip of the anterior branch
of the second vein, is often wanting; the posterior end of the
discal cell, and the inner end of the second posterior cell are
likewise spotted with brown. Marginal cross-vein at the tip of
the first longitudinal vein; anterior branch of the second vein
arcuated, almost angular, near the basis; petiole of the first submarginal cell about the length of the great cross-vein; second
submarginal cell only a trifle longer than the first posterior;
discal cell elongated.

Hab. United States. It is a common species, and occurs
in abundance especially in rocky localities, alighting upon the
stone; I found it in this situation along the Hudson River Rail-
road, near New York, in abundance.

The spots vary in intensity as well as in size; those at the tip
of the second vein and at the inner end of the second posterior
cell are among the first to disappear; the other brown marks are
apt to become very pale, almost obsolete. I possess a couple of
specimens with an adventitious cross-vein in the first submarginal
cell, opposite the marginal cross-vein. Another specimen has an
adventitious cross-vein in the marginal cell, near the inner end
of the first submarginal cell.

The forceps of the male of this species is very peculiar;
instead of the usual horny appendages, it has a pair of elongated,
digitiform, soft appendages, which do not overlap each other in
repose (Tab. II, fig. 26 and 26a). The ovipositor has short,
rather broad upper valves, abruptly tapering towards the tip.
The structure of the forceps and of the antennæ, and the peculiar
venation, have induced me to propose for this species the subgeneric name of *Dactylolabis* (compare above, p. 198).

---

[1] The figure shows only the veins and not the spots.

24. L. cubitalis, n. sp. ♂ and ♀.—Cinerea, fuscescens, thorace fusco-quadrivittato, pedibus testaceis, alis immaculatis, stigmate concolore, petiolo cellulæ submarginalis primæ brevissimo; venula transversa marginali ad apicem longitudinalis primæ sita.

Brownish-gray, thorax with four brown stripes, feet yellowish-tawny, wings immaculate, stigma colorless, petiole of the first submarginal cell very short; marginal cross-vein near the tip of the first longitudinal vein. Long. corp. 0.37—0.4.

Head gray, with short black hairs on the front; antennæ brownish, with short verticils; bent backwards, they would hardly reach the root of the wings. Thorax gray, somewhat brownish above, with four brown stripes; pleuræ of a lighter gray; halteres yellow; feet yellowish-tawny; tip of the tibiæ and tarsi brownish; basis of the coxæ grayish; the feet are rather stout and clothed with a somewhat conspicuous blackish pubescence. Abdomen grayish-brown, male forceps brownish-tawny; ovipositor ferruginous. Wings immaculate, with a pale yellowish tinge; veins pale brownish, except the first longitudinal and the auxiliary veins, which are yellowish: the stigma is hardly perceptible and entirely colorless. The petiole of the first submarginal cell is about the length of the small cross-vein; the anterior branch of the second longitudinal vein forms an almost right angle near its origin; the præfurca originates at an almost acute angle; the second submarginal cell is only slightly longer than the first posterior cell; the great cross-vein is near the inner end of the discal cell.

Hab. Virginia, Ohio; a male and a female specimens.

The forceps of the male, as far as can be judged from dry specimens, resembles that of *L. montana;* the venation also reminds of this species, especially the abrupt angle, formed by the anterior branch of the second vein at its origin, the position of the great cross-vein, etc. The ovipositor of the female is very peculiar, if that of the only female in my possession can be considered as normal: the upper valves are of moderate length and hardly arcuated at all; each one is connected on the under side with a membrane, which seems to be the prolongation of the valve. The dry specimen of course does not convey a correct idea of this structure. *L. cubitalis* is certainly related to *L. montana,* but I am uncertain whether it is to be considered as a *Dactylolabis.*

11. *Four posterior cells.*

24. L. quadrata O. S. ♂ and ♀.—Cinerea, abdomine fuscescente,
antennis palpisque fuscis; pedibus flavis, femorum, tibiarum, tarso-
rumque apicibus fuscis; alis immaculatis, stigmate pallido, cellulis
posterioribus quatuor.

Yellowish-gray, abdomen brownish; antennae and palpi brown; feet yellow; tips of the femora, of the tibiae, and of the tarsi brown; wings
immaculate, stigma pale; four posterior cells. Long. corp. 0.28—0.32.

Syn. *Limnophila quadrata* O. Sacken, Proc. Ac. Nat. Sc. Phil. 1859, p. 241.

Front and vertex yellowish-gray; palpi and antennae brown;
basal joints of the flagellum a little paler; antennae of moderate
length; verticils rather long. Thorax dark yellowish-gray; without distinct stripes; pleurae slightly hoary;·halteres pale; feet
yellowish; coxae and base of the femora pale yellow; tips of the
femora, of the tibiae, and of the tarsi brown. Abdomen brownish;
genitals yellow; ovipositor slender, long, slightly curved. Wings
(Tab. II, fig. 9) faintly tinged with pale brownish; stigma colorless; veins brownish. The auxiliary vein ends a little before the
inner end of the second submarginal cell; the subcostal cross-vein
is close by its tip; the praefurca is long, straight, hardly arcuated
at its origin; the petiole of the first submarginal cell is longer
than the great cross-vein; the anterior branch of the second vein
is oblique; the marginal cross-vein is at the inner end of the first
submarginal cell, and somewhat oblique; the inner ends of the
second submarginal, first posterior, and discal cells are nearly in
one line; there are only four posterior cells; the great cross-vein
is about the middle of the discal cell.

Hab. New York, Virginia, Maryland, etc. May, June.

The ground color of the head and thorax of this species is a
shining black, but it is concealed under a gray dust or bloom,
which renders it opaque.

Although this species has only four posterior cells, while *L.*
recondita, imbecilla, tenuipes, etc. have five, there are abundant
signs of a relationship between them. Except the different
number of posterior cells, the venation is very much alike: a
long, straight praefurca, forming a straight line with the posterior
branch of the second vein; the oblique anterior branch of this
vein, with the cross-vein near its origin; the inner ends of the
second submarginal, the first posterior, and discal cells almost in

one line; the small cross-vein gently arcuated; the end of the fifth
vein strongly arcuated; the long verticils of the antennæ, the
comparatively long feet, etc.

26. L. lenta O. S.   ♂ and ♀.—Ochracea, fronte cærescuis; antennæ
maris densæ pubescentes; alæ immaculatæ; cellulis posterioribus
quatuor.

Ochraceous, front grayish; antennæ of the male densely pubescent; wings
immaculate; four posterior cells. Long. corp. 0.27—0.32.

Syn. *Limnophila lenta* O. Sacken, Proc. Ac. Nat. Sc. Phil. 1859, p. 241.

Ochraceous yellow; palpi and antennæ (except the basal joints
of the latter), brownish; the antennæ of the male, if extended
backwards, would reach a little beyond the root of the wings; the
joints of the flagellum are elongated-elliptical, and each of them
is clothed on both sides with a dense pubescence; the verticils
are but little longer than this pubescence; in the female there is
no conspicuous pubescence, and for this reason the verticils,
although short, are more distinct. The front and vertex are
grayish, the former even with a slight silvery reflection. Thorax
ochraceous yellow, opaque above, without apparent stripes;
halteres yellow; abdomen yellowish; feet pale yellow; tips of
the tarsi, sometimes also the extreme tips of the tibiæ, infuscated.
Wings subhyaline, with a faint yellowish tinge; veins yellowish
or yellowish-brown; stigma pale, sometimes faintly infuscated at
the cross-vein. Præfurca comparatively short (not much longer
than the anterior branch of the second vein), strongly arcuated
at its origin; petiole of the first submarginal cell about the length
of the great cross-vein; the marginal cross-vein is usually between
the inner end of the first submarginal cell and the tip of the first
longitudinal vein; anterior branch of the second vein oblique;
the inner ends of the second submarginal, the first posterior, and
the discal cells are nearly in one line; only four posterior cells.

Hab. Virginia, Maryland; Illinois (Kennicott).

In the male forceps of this species the usual falciform appendages are less parallel and more diverging at the tip, when in
repose, than in the other species. The shape of the first submarginal cell, the arcuated small cross-vein, etc. of this species
may indicate a slight degree of relationship to *L. quadrata;* but
the course of the præfurca, the structure of the antennæ, etc. are
different.

Gen. XXIX. ULOMORPHA.

Two submarginal cells; four posterior cells; discal cell closed: subcostal cross-vein near the tip of the auxiliary vein; wings finely, but densely pubescent. Eyes glabrous. Antennæ 16-jointed. Tibiæ with spurs at the tip; empodia distinct; ungues smooth.

Rostrum short, palpi of moderate length, last joint slender, but not much longer than the preceding; front moderately broad. Antennæ 16-jointed; those of the male, if bent backwards, would nearly reach the end of the thorax; those of the female are shorter; first joint cylindrical, comparatively short; the second short, as usual; the third oval, rather stout; the following joints slender, linear, with rather long verticils; those of the male with a dense pubescence on the under side of the flagellum. Collare moderately developed. Feet moderately long and stout; hairy. Spurs of the tibiæ small, but distinct. Wings clothed with a short, moderately dense, almost microscopic pubescence, which is evenly spread over the whole surface; it is not woolly, like the pubescence of Eriopterα, and does not affect much the transparency of the wing. The subcostal cross-vein is near the tip of the auxiliary vein; the præfurca has its origin a little before the middle of the wing; this origin is slightly arcuated and sometimes with a stump of a vein; the marginal cross-vein is rather faint, and placed at a considerable distance before the tip of the first longitudinal vein; the first submarginal cell is almost as long as the second, its petiole being very short, and in some specimens obsolete; the inner ends of the second submarginal, the first posterior, and the discal cells are almost in one line; there are four posterior cells; the second has its inner end more or less attenuated; the portion of the fifth longitudinal vein, lying beyond the great cross-vein, is arcuated; the great cross-vein in most specimens has the appearance as if it was too short for the distance it has to cross over; it strains the two veins which it connects; the vein on the hind side of the discal cell shows this strain very plainly, appearing angular at the point of intersection with the cross-vein.

The structure of the antennæ and the venation (the presence of only four posterior cells notwithstanding) seems to point to a relationship with Limnophila rotundata and its group; perhaps also to L. quadrata. The external resemblance of Ulomorpha

to *Ula* is great, and has suggested the name of this new genus
(*Ula*, and ρορτή, form); still, they are easily distinguished by the
position of the subcostal cross-vein, the structure of the ovipositor, which is more elongated and straight in the present
genus than in *Ula*; by the glabrous eyes of *Ulomorpha*, its
shorter palpi, etc. At present, only one species is known; but
it seems possible that *Limnophila pilicornis* Zett. *Dipt. Scand.*
X, p. 8885, No. 61, is an *Ulomorpha*.

Description of the species.

1. U. pilosella O. S. ♂ and ♀.—Pallide fusca, antennis, palpis, et
fronte fuscis; abdomine et halterum capitulo infuscatis; alis immaculatis, pallide fusco tinctis.

Pale brown, antennæ, palpi, and front brown; abdomen and knob of the
halteres brownish; wings immaculate, tinged with brown. Leng. corp.
0.3—0.35.

Syn. *Limnophila pilosella* O. Sacken, Proc. Ac. Nat. Sc. Phila. 1859, p. 242.

Rostrum yellowish, palpi brown; front and vertex infuscated
in the middle, grayish on the sides, clothed with black hairs;
antennæ brownish. Thorax pale brownish, without any apparent
stripes above; pleuræ yellowish; halteres pale at the base; the
knob infuscated; feet tawny, tips of the femora faintly infuscated; tips of the tarsi brown. Abdomen brown, venter paler;
valves of the ovipositor long, slender, pointed, nearly straight.
Wings tinged with brownish; stigma colorless.

Hab. Trenton Falls, N. Y.; Sharon Springs, N. Y.

Gen. XXX. TRICHOCERA.

Two submarginal cells; five posterior cells; a discal cell; the subcostal
cross-vein at a considerable distance from the tip of the auxiliary vein
(about equal to the breadth of the wing), although posterior to the origin
of the second vein; seventh longitudinal vein very short, strongly arcuated,
abruptly incurved towards the anal angle (Tab. II, fig. 13). Tibiæ with spurs
at the tip; empodia distinct. *Eyes pubescent; distinct ocelli on the sides
of the frontal tubercle;* antennæ setaceous, 16-jointed, but joints very indistinct. Male forceps with elongated, fleshy, digitiform appendages;
ovipositor of the female reversed, that is, with the convex side above and
the concave below.

Rostrum and proboscis short; palpi somewhat prolonged, the
last joint elongated, attenuated in the middle, and thus showing

the appearance of two joints. Eyes large, very convex, pubescent, separated above by a very broad front; two ocelli are
distinctly visible on each side of a gibbosity immediately above
the antennæ; the latter are considerably longer than the head
and the thorax taken together, setaceous, very slender, finely
pubescent; first and second joints very short; the third and the
following subcylindrical, elongated, gradually becoming more
slender; in dry specimens the joints of the flagellum, except the
basal ones, are indistinct; in living specimens, under the microscope, the antennæ appear 16-jointed.[1] The thoracic suture is
well marked; the interval between it and the scutellum shows a
smooth depression, and no trace of the longitudinal furrow usually visible there. Feet slender, with an almost imperceptible
pubescence. Wings (Tab. II, fig. 18, wing of *T. bimacula* Walk.)
rather broad; the tip of the auxiliary vein is nearly opposite the
tip of the fifth longitudinal vein; the subcostal cross-vein is at a
distance from the tip of the auxiliary vein, which is nearly equal
to the breadth of the wing; the tip of the first longitudinal vein
is nearly opposite the posterior branch of the first fork of the
fourth vein; the second longitudinal vein originates before the
middle of the length of the wing; the subcostal cross-vein is at a
distance beyond it, which is a little longer than the great cross-
vein; the præfurca, gently arcuated at its basis, is comparatively
long, but little shorter than the second submarginal cell; the first
submarginal cell is shorter than the second, its petiole being
about equal in length to the great cross-vein; the marginal cross-
vein is a little beyond the inner end of the first submarginal cell;
the second submarginal and first posterior cells are of equal
length; the discal cell is somewhat elongated, projecting inside
of the small cross-vein; the great cross-vein is opposite the
further end of the discal cell; the fifth longitudinal vein is angularly broken at the great cross-vein; sixth vein straight; seventh
very short, arcuated, incurved to the anal angle. The forceps of
the male consists of the usual two subcylindrical basal pieces,
each of which, instead of any horny organs, bears a movable,
elongated, cylindrical, fleshy appendage; these appendages, when

---

[1] This number has been for the first time correctly stated by Mr. Westwood in the explanation to Tab. XXVI, fig. 8, of Walker's *Ins. Brit. Dipt.*
Vol. III; in former works it was given incorrectly or not mentioned at all.

at rest, are porrected, slightly inclined towards each other, leaving a considerable open space between them. The ovipositor
of the female is distinguished from all the ovipositors of the
Tipulidæ by being reversed; that is, having the convex side of
the arcuated valves above and the concave side below.[1]

The Trichoceræ appear in swarms during sunny autumn and
winter days; their larvæ live in decaying vegetable matters, and
have been described and figured by Perris (Ann. Soc. Entom. de
France, 2e sér. Vol. V, 1847, page 37; Tab. I, No. III).

The pubescence of the eyes is a character which, so far as
observed, belongs among the Tipulidæ, to the Amalopina alone.
Trichocera is the only exception. Further, this genus, and perhaps also Pedicia, seem to be the only ones among the Tipulidæ,
which have ocelli. Trichocera is, moreover, abundantly distinguished by the position of the great cross-vein, at the further
end of the discal cell, the course of the seventh longitudinal
vein, the flat depression between the thoracic suture and the
scutellum, and the structure of the ovipositor. Nevertheless, its
position among the Limnophilina has nothing unnatural. The
structure of the forceps alone would be sufficient to separate
Trichocera from the Amalopina, which always have a strong,
branched horny forceps. Trichocera is represented by five species
in Europe. Only one species (T. ocellata Walk. Dipt. Saunders.
p. 433; East Indies) from any other part of the world, besides
America, has been described. Two fossil species have been found
by Mr. Loew, in the Prussian amber (Loew, Bernst. u. Bernsteinfauna, p. 37); they are very like the European species, and
show only slight differences in the venation.

The name is derived from θρίξ, hair, and κέρας, horn.

Four species of Trichocera, peculiar to North America, have
been described (T. bimacula Walker, gracilis, Walker, brumalis
Fitch, and scutellata Say[1]). Moreover, two European species
have been mentioned as occurring in North America: T. maculipennis Meig. by Sturger, and T. regelationis Lin. by O. Fabricius.

[1] It is very singular that this striking peculiarity has been entirely
overlooked by previous authors, even by those who, like Walker and
others, pretend to describe the ovipositor. That the pubescence of the
eyes has not been noticed, is easier to explain; likewise the presence of
ocelli. Meigen alone saw the latter (Meigen, Vol. I, p. 211), but his statement has been overlooked since.

[1] The descriptions of these species are reproduced in the Appendix I.

The small number of *Trichocerae* which I have before me for comparison, may be grouped thus:—

I. Wings with two brown clouds, one near the origin of the præfurca, the other on the small cross-vein.

   1. Knob of the halteres not infuscated; thorax with a yellowish-gray bloom above, and with rather distinct brown stripes; the petiole of the first submarginal cell is about three times the length of the distance between the inner end of this cell and the marginal cross-vein (Tab. II, fig. 13); the latter not perceptibly clouded with brown; wings comparatively narrow; long. corp. about 0.21. Very common everywhere . . . . . bimacula *Walt.?*

   2. Knob of the halteres distinctly infuscated; wings broader than in the preceding species; the thorax is of a paler yellowish-gray and the stripes less distinct, although visible; the petiole of the first submarginal cell is but little longer than the interval between the inner end of this cell and the marginal cross-vein; the latter with a distinct brown cloud; long. corp. 0.25. A single female specimen, from Canada . . . maculipennis *Mrig.*, or nov. sp.?

II. Wings with a single faint brown cloud on the small cross-vein.

   3. The petiole of the first submarginal cell is about twice the length of the distance between the inner end of this cell and the marginal cross-vein; the wings are rather broad, almost hyaline; the thorax brownish, with a yellowish-gray bloom; stripes almost obsolete, hardly visible; knob of the halteres brown; the great cross-vein is a little before the posterior end of the discal cell; a single male specimen; long. corp. 0.18 . . . . . Spec. nova?

III. Wings unicolorous.

   4. Thorax brownish, with a yellowish-gray bloom, and with tolerably well marked brownish stripes; wings with a very faint yellowish tinge; the petiole of the first submarginal cell is equal in length to the distance between the inner end of this cell and the marginal cross-vein; the great cross-vein is at the posterior end of the discal cell, or very near this end; halteres with brownish knobs; long. corp. 0.21 . . . . . Spec. nova?

6. Thorax of a purer gray than any of the preceding species; the two brown stripes are very faintly marked on the front part of the mesonotum only; wings clearer byaline than in the preceding species; venation as in the preceding species; stigma very faintly infuscated; halteres with a brown knob; long. corp. about 0.2 . . brumalis *Fitch ?*

The small materials in my possession do not allow me to attempt the description of the apparently new species. At the same time, the existing descriptions are too incomplete or too incorrect to admit of a positive identification. The description of *T. bimacula* Walker, for instance, is such as to render it very doubtful whether the species given above under that name is really Walker's species; the character, "abdomen with alternate tawny and brown rings," is not visible in my specimens.

A large number of specimens and a comparison with the European species will be necessary to those who will attempt the description of the North American species.

Section V. ANISOMERINA.

Two submarginal cells (only one in *Cladolipes*); three, four, or five posterior cells; discal cell closed or open; subcostal cross-vein near the tip of the auxiliary vein, posterior to the origin of the second vein. Eyes glabrous. *The normal number of the antennal joints is six in the male and not more than ten in the female.* Tibiæ with spurs at the tip; empodia distinct; ungues generally smooth.

This section is easily distinguished by the aberrant number of antennal joints. In other respects, the most numerous genus of the family, *Eriocera*, is exceedingly like the *Limnophilina* in its venation and the structure of its male forceps. The species of *Eriocera* and *Penthoptera*, have either five or four posterior cells, a character which, in this section, seems to have no higher importance than for the distinction of species. In *Anisomera* and *Cladolipes* the posterior cells are reduced to the unusual number of three; to which, in the latter genus, is added the disappearance of the first submarginal cell.

These differences in the venation notwithstanding, strong links of affinity unite these genera. The male has six-jointed antennæ, which, in some species, are much longer than those of the female, sometimes more than twice the length of the body; while in otherwise closely allied species the antennæ of both sexes are short and nearly of the same length. These modifications in the relative length of the antennæ occur in the three principal genera of this section, *Anisomera*, *Penthoptera*, and *Eriocera*. The female antennæ are short, and the structure of their apical portion is such as to leave the number of the joints, composing it, somewhat uncertain, especially in dry specimens. On living female specimens of *Eriocera* and *Penthoptera* I have distinctly counted ten joints.

The ovipositor of *Anisomera* has a peculiar structure; the valves are short and blunt, the upper ones much shorter than the lower ones. The same structure occurs in *Eriocera longicornis*. The other *Eriocera*, as well as *Penthoptera*, have the ovipositor of the usual structure.

Eriocera and some forms related to it are abundantly represented in the warmer regions of Asia, Africa, and America; the genera *Pterucusmius* Walk., *Physcerania* Jllgot, *Oligomera* Dulesehall, and *Evaniopiera* Godrin, are either synonymous with *Eriocera* or related to it. The other genera of this section have not been discovered yet outside of the temperate regions of Europe and North America.

The genus *Bertea* Rondani (*Atti d. Sc. Natur. di Milano*, II, p. 56, with figures), for which this author establishes a separate family, *Berteidæ* (comp. above, p. 12), is based upon a single specimen found under beech leaves. Its wings are abortive, very short, without any apparent venation; it has a tubercle on the front with two or three indistinct ocelli (the author himself, however, was not certain about the correctness of this statement); the antennæ are twelve-jointed, the third joint being cylindrical and about twice the length of the first and second joints taken together, while the other joints of the flagellum are rounded. If I mention this genus here, it is because the tubercle on the front and the length of the third antennal joint may indicate a relationship of *Bertea* to the *Anisomerina*; however, the above-quoted description does not furnish the necessary data for any positive conclusion.

Gen. XXXI. ANISOMERA.

Two submarginal cells; three posterior cells; discal cell open; subcostal cross-vein near the tip of the auxiliary vein (Tab. II, fig. 12). Tibiæ with spurs at the tip; empodia distinct. Eyes glabrous, front with a large gibbosity behind the antennæ; the latter 6-jointed, sometimes with a rudimental seventh joint at the tip, in the male; in the female they have the same number of joints, but the sixth has often the appearance of being subdivided in three, four, or five joints. Ovipositor of the female short, obtuse; upper valves shorter than the lower ones.

Head large and broad; rostrum and palpi short; the latter (according to Walker and Schiner) have joints of an equal size; front very broad, frontal gibbosity bituberculate; eyes very remote on the upper as well as on the under side of the head. Antennæ six-jointed in the male, the third joint being the longest;

they are filiform or subfiliform, and vary in length in different species; in some, they are longer than the body, in others about half the length of the body; again in others shorter than the thorax. The antennæ of the female are always shorter than those of the male, apparently likewise 6-jointed; the last joint, however, shows transverse divisions, which have often the appearance of three, four, or five additional joints.[1] The antennæ of both sexes are pubescent, but without verticillate hairs. The head is closely applied to the short collare, which receives it in a kind of excavation; this character, distinctly apparent in the only North American species, is also common to all the European ones (Loew, l. c.). Thoracic sutures deeply marked. Feet more or less long and stout, spurs of the tibia and empodia distinct; ungues usually smooth. (The European *A. longipes* has, according to Loew, a distinct and rather strong tooth on the under side of the ungues of the hindmost feet; this is probably the angular projection of the stout basal portion of the ungues, which occurs also in *Eriocera* and looks like a tooth, although it is quite distinct from the teeth on the ungues of the *Limnobina*.) The wings of the North American *A. megacera* are much shorter and narrower in the male than in the female; but this does not seem to be the case with the European species (Mr. Loew often mentions the wings of the female as being like those of the male). The venation of *A. megacera* (Tab. 11, fig. 12) shows the following characters: the auxiliary vein ends in the costa nearly oppo-

[1] Hence the disagreement between authors as to the number of the antennal joints of the female. Westwood (in the explanation of Tab. XXVI of Walker's *Ins. Brit. Diptera*) calls the antenna of a female *Anisomera* 10-jointed; this would be in conformity with the antenna of the females of *Eriocera* and *Penthoptera*, upon which I have counted ten joints on living specimens. The only fresh female specimen of *A. megacera*, which I have had the opportunity to examine, had several subdivisions of the last joint, but they were not sufficiently distinct to be counted; a dry specimen shows three such subdivisions; a dry European specimen which I have before me (perhaps *Pervacera*?), shows four or five. Mr. Loew, in his article, *Ueber die bisher beschriebenen europäischen Anisomera*-Arten (in the Zeitschrift für die gesammten Naturwissenschaften, Nov. 1863), calls the antenna six-jointed in both sexes, sometimes with a more or less developed seventh joint; the latter species, according to this author, belong to the number of those which have short antennæ in the male sex. I will have frequent opportunities to quote Mr. Loew's article, and give therefore its title in full.

the the inner end of the second submarginal cell (a little anterior
to it); the subcostal cross-vein is very near its tip; the tip of
the first longitudinal vein is nearly opposite the tip of the
posterior branch of the fourth longitudinal vein; the marginal
cross-vein is a very short distance anterior to this tip; the second
longitudinal vein originates about the middle of the length of
the wing, or a little before it (in the female); prefurca long,
almost equal in length to the second submarginal cell, or somewhat longer (in the female); its course is straight; the fork of
the second vein is very short, as in *Goniomyia*, and hence, the
first submarginal cell is triangular; the petiole of this cell is
many times longer than the cell, and has the marginal cross-vein
about its middle; the second submarginal cell, which is somewhat arcuated in shape, is longer than the first posterior; the
inner ends of the three posterior cells are often nearly in a line;
sometimes, however, the inner end of the second posterior cell
projects inside of this line; the fourth vein is in a straight line
with its posterior branch; the anterior branch (inclosing the
second posterior cell) is angular at the inner end; as neither of
the branches is forked, there can be only three posterior cells and
no discal cell; the three last longitudinal veins are nearly
straight. The European species have, in the main, an exactly
similar venation (compare the figures in Meigen, Vol. I, Tab.
VII, and Walker, *Ins. Brit. Dipt.* Tab. XXVI, fig. 9). The
species differ, however, in one point only: the length of the first
submarginal cell; in some species, this cell is longer than its
petiole, and in such cases the marginal cross-vein connects the
first longitudinal vein with the anterior branch of the second,
and not with the petiole. It seems that among the European
species a short first submarginal cell and a marginal cross-vein
inserted about the middle of its petiole, are characters usually
connected with short antennæ in the male (compare Loew, l. c.
p. 411); but the American *A. megacera* proves that this is not
an invariable rule; although this species has a very short first
submarginal cell, the antennæ of the male are much longer than
the body.

The male forceps does not seem to have anything unusual in
its structure; it consists of the ordinary basal pieces, with horny
appendages; I have not had the opportunity to observe it upon
living specimens. The ovipositor of the female is remarkable for

the shortness of its valves; the upper pair is always shorter than the rather obtuse lower pair.

Anisomera is, among all the *Tipulidæ*, the only genus which has three posterior cells (and this venation is still more reduced in the genus *Cladolipes* Loew, which has only one submarginal cell). Nevertheless, the relationship of *Anisomera* to *Eriocera* (with its four or five posterior cells) cannot be called in doubt. The anomalous structure of the antennæ, the great length which they frequently attain in the male, the structure of the head and of the feet prove this relationship.

Hitherto I have discovered only one North American species of *Anisomera*; it is distinguished by the considerable length of its antennæ. Mr. Loew enumerates nine European species. One of them, *A. fuscipennis*, has been proposed, by Mr. Curtis (*Brit. Entom.* 539; 1836), for the type of a separate genus, *Peronecera* (from σπείρα, a button, and κέρας, horn, in allusion to the rudimental joint at the tip of the antennæ). This genus, also adopted by Loew, is based solely upon the number of antennal joints, which is seven in the male and nine in the female (this is Mr. Loew's statement; Mr. Curtis says seven (♂) and eight joints (♀)). The antennæ are short in both sexes, and not much longer in the male than in the female. According to Mr. Loew, *Peronecera* is closely related to those *Anisomeræ* with short male antennæ, which have a rudimental seventh joint. Such species have but a limited power of flying, as they seem to jump rather than to fly (Loew, l. c. p. 414). Mr. Loew mentions but a single species of *Peronecera*; Mr. Curtis, besides this same species, describes another one, *P. lucidipennis*, n. sp.

The species of *Anisomera* occur along the banks of streams; the larvæ (according to Van Roser (*Verz. Würt. Dipt.* p. 262) live in the sand of these banks (or perhaps in the vegetable detritus found there?).

The first species belonging to this genus was described by Latreille, in 1809 (*Genera Crust. et Ins.* IV, p. 260), under the generic name of *Hexatoma*.

Meigen, in 1818, rather arbitrarily changed the name of *Hexatoma* in *Nematocera*, on the ground that he had been compelled to alter the name of his own genus *Heptatoma* (Tabanidæ) in *Hexatoma* (Meig. Vol. I, p. 209). At the same time he adopted

the genus *Anisomera*, of which he had received a drawing and
description; the latter by Wiedemann.

In 1830 Meigen (Vol. VI, p. 291) recognized the identity of
Nematocera and *Anisomera*, and dropped the former name.

Curtis (*Brit. Entom.* 689), in 1836, introduced the genus *Peronecera*, already mentioned above.

A detailed account of all the European species and the history
of each, has been given by Mr. Loew in his often quoted article.
The coloring of the European species seems to be rather uniform:
blackish-gray, with darker stripes on the thorax; the only known
American species agrees in this respect with them.

The name *Anisomera* is derived from ἄνισος, unequal, and μέρος,
part, in allusion to the structure of the antennæ.

Description of the species.

1. A. megacera O. S.   ♂ and ♀.—Obscure cinerea, nigrescens;
thorace vittis tribus obscuris; antennæ maris corpore toto longiore;
feminæ thorace breviore; venula transversa marginalis pedunculo
cellulæ submarginalis primæ inserta.

Dark gray, blackish; thorax with three dark stripes; antennæ of the male
longer than the whole body; those of the female shorter than the thorax;
marginal cross-vein inserted on the pedicle of the first submarginal cell.
Long. corp. 0.27—0.3.

Syn. *Anisomera megacera* O. Sacken, Proc. Ac. Nat. Sc. Phil. 1859. p. 242.

Head dark gray, almost blackish in the middle; palpi and antennæ black; the latter, in the male, nearly once and a half the
length of the body, finely pubescent; basal joints short; flagellum
filiform; first joint very long (if bent backwards, it would reach
the basis of the abdomen); the second and third also elongated,
although somewhat shorter than the first; the remaining portion
of the antennæ is a little shorter than the third joint of the
flagellum. The antennæ of the female are short (bent backwards, they would hardly reach the root of the wings); the third
joint is the longest; the sixth is very short, almost rudimental.
Thorax dark gray, with a yellowish reflection; a brownish,
cuneiform intermediate stripe, with a faint pale longitudinal line
in the middle; the two lateral stripes are much abbreviated in
front, and extended beyond the suture behind; a soft, short,
hardly perceptible yellowish pubescence between the stripes;
halteres more or less dusky; feet brownish, femora somewhat

darker at the tip. Abdomen blackish; male forceps likewise.
Wings with a slight grayish tinge; the marginal cross-vein is
inserted a little before the middle of the petiole of the first submarginal cell.

Hab. Washington, D. C.; Maryland; early in the spring, near
running water. I have had six males and three females.

Gen. XXXII. CLADOLIPES.[1]

*A single submarginal cell; three posterior cells; no discal cell; subcostal
cross-vein near the tip of the auxiliary vein. Tibiæ with spurs at the
tip; empodia distinct; ungues smooth. Eyes glabrous; front convex, but
without projecting gibbosity. Antennæ (in the female) 6-jointed. Ovipositor very long, narrow, pointed, somewhat arcuated towards the tip.*

This genus (which I have not seen) has been established by
Mr. Loew, in 1865 (in the article quoted above on page 240, in
the foot-note), upon the female of a species from Greece. It
differs from *Anisomera* in the absence of the fork of the second
vein, and, consequently, the presence of only one submarginal
cell. The antennæ of the female resemble those of *Anisomera*
in being without verticillate hairs. Although, in an artificial
arrangement, *Cladolipes* would have to be placed among the
Tipulidæ with a single submarginal cell, it is evidently related
to *Anisomera*.

Cladolipes simplex Loew, the species alluded to, is of the
size of an ordinary *Anisomera* and altogether blackish, including
the wings.

Gen. XXXIII. ERIOCERA.

*Two submarginal cells; four, sometimes five posterior cells; a discal
cell; the subcostal cross-vein a short distance back of the tip of the auxiliary vein; the first submarginal cell shorter than the second. Tibiæ
with spurs at the tip; empodia distinct. Front with a more or less striking gibbosity behind the antennæ; antennæ 8-jointed in the male, sometimes enormously prolonged, sometimes not much longer than those of the
female; antennæ of the female ten-jointed, comparatively short. Male
forceps with a pair of elongated, subcylindrical basal pieces, each bearing
two appendages, one of which is claw-shaped, horny; the other coriaceous, bipoi (Tab. IV, fig. 29, forceps of E. spinosa; fig. 28, that of E.
fuliginosa).*

---

[1] From κλάδος, a branch, and λείπω, I omit.

Head rather large; front broad, with a more or less conspicuous, often bituberculate gibbosity behind the basis of the antennæ; epistoma short, transverse, often concealed under the basal joints of the antennæ; lips of the proboscis large, projecting; the palpi rather long, often as long as the head; the two first joints are generally prolonged, and the fourth is still longer; the third being usually the shortest; however, these proportions vary somewhat in different species. *E. wilsonii* has comparatively short palpi; the first two joints seem to be prolonged, but the fourth is short. Eyes glabrous, remote above and below. The antennæ of the male are of two kinds: either very long, and much longer than in the female; or short, and not perceptibly longer than in the female. The long ones again, vary in their length, the nature of their pubescence, and their structure; those of *E. spinosa* and *E. longicornis* are the longest, being more than twice the length of the body; they are similar in structure; the scapus consists of a subcylindrical, rather stout basal joint, and a very short, annuliform second joint; the flagellum is filiform, gradually attenuated towards the end; the first joint is about as long as the thorax; the second is a little longer than the first; the third is about equal to the second and third taken together, and the fourth is still longer than the third; the joints of the flagellum are beset on their under side, at rather regular intervals, with strong, spine-like bristles, which gradually become softer and more hair-like towards the end of the antenna; the upper side of the flagellum is glabrous. The antennæ of *E. wilsonii* are about once and a half the length of the body; the first joint of the flagellum is a little longer than the second; the whole flagellum on both sides is evenly and delicately pubescent, the pubescence being intermixed, towards the end of the antenna, with some scattered longer hairs. The male antennæ of the short kind, if bent backwards, would not reach beyond the roots of the wings (this is the case with *E. fuliginosa*); they are rather coarsely hairy, but without verticils; the scapus has the ordinary structure; the first joint of the flagellum is the longest. The antennæ of all the female *Eriocerae* are very much like those of the latter kind of males, and not perceptibly shorter; a subcylindrical basal joint; a short second one; the third joint (first joint of the flagellum) is the longest. In dry specimens four joints of the flagellum can be more or less distinctly counted; beyond this, the female antenna is usually wriukled and shranken; but in fresh specimens I have counted (in *E. longicornis* Walk.) eight joints of the flagellum, which would make the female antenna ten-jointed.

The head is, as in *Anisomera*, closely applied to the collare, which is narrow. The thoracic suture is well marked. The feet are long and usually rather stout; *E. longicornis* has a remarkable character in the great shortness of the two anterior pairs of femora, which are not much over half the length of the posterior ones; this character is much less striking in the other species; it is to be remarked, however, that the two anterior pairs of femora seem to be rather inconstant in their length, in *E. longicornis*, as well as in *E. spinosa*. In *E. spinosa* and *E. longicornis* the last joint of the tarsi of the male is excised at its basis on the under side, and also hollowed out and hairy in the middle of its under side; this character is not perceptible in *E. wilsonii*. Some of the species (for instance *E. spinosa*) have a small projecting tooth at the extreme basis of the ungues, on the under side; but it is difficult to perceive among the hairs which clothe the tarsi.

The venation of the wings is exactly like that of some *Limnophila*. The auxiliary vein, the tip of which is more or less opposite the inner end of the second submarginal cell, has the subcostal cross-vein a short distance back from its tip. The marginal cross-vein is a short distance anterior to the tip of the first longitudinal vein; its relative position to the inner end of the first submarginal cell depends on the length of the latter; sometimes the cross-vein is inserted at this very inner end, sometimes beyond this point. Praefurca long, straight, arcuated at its basis only. The inner end of the first submarginal cell, in all the species which I have before me, is pointed, its petiole is either a little shorter than the great cross-vein, or much longer; the second submarginal cell likewise varies in length, its inner end (which is also pointed) projects more or less inside of the small cross-vein towards the basis of the wing. It follows from this that the first posterior cell is, in most cases, shorter than the second submarginal; in some cases they are subequal. The discal cell is more or less square; the section of the fifth longitudinal vein lying beyond the great cross-vein is generally, but not always, at an angle with the anterior portion of the vein; the sixth and seventh veins are straight. Three North American species have

four posterior cells (*E. longicornis, wilsonii,* and *fuliginosa*);
one species has five (*E. spinosa*)

The forceps of the male is not unlike that of the typical *Limnophila*, that is, it consists of two elongated, subcylindrical basal pieces with a horny unguiform and an obtuse, apparently coriaceous appendage, attached to each (compare, for the details, the description of the figures, Tab. IV, figs. 28 and 29). The ovipositor of the female consists of two elongated, pointed, rather narrow, nearly straight or gently curved upper valves, and a pair of lower ones, which are shorter. But the female of *E. longicornis* (provided what I have before me is really the female of this species) has the ovipositor of an entirely different structure, and exactly similar to that of *Anisomera*. It is short, blunt, and somewhat directed upwards (at least in dry specimens); its upper valves are shorter than the lower ones. I have not seen the female of *E. wilsonii.*

The relationship between *Eriocera* and *Anisomera* appears: in the abnormal structure of the antennæ, their frequent extraordinary length in the male, and aberrant structure in the female; the peculiar shape of the collare; the very unusual structure of the ovipositor of the latter genus, which structure occasionally reappears in *Eriocera.*

Every one of the four North American *Eriocera* at present known shows peculiarities of structure which, in some of the other sections of the *Tipulidæ*, would have been sufficient for a generic separation; here, these same characters do not seem to have any other but a specific value. In order to compare the principal of these characters, we may tabulate them as follows:—

A. Antennæ of the male very long and much longer than those of the female.
  1. Antennæ of the male glabrous on the upper side, and with a series of bristles, inserted at regular intervals on the under side (**ARRHENICA** O. S., olim).
    a. Five posterior cells . . . . . . **E. spinosa.**
    b. Four posterior cells . . . . . . **E. longicornis.**
  2. Antennæ of the male finely pubescent on both sides.
    a. Four posterior cells . . . . . . **E. wilsonii.**
B. Antennæ short in both sexes.
    a. Four posterior cells . . . . . . **E. fuliginosa.**

The two species of the first group (*E. spinosa* and *longicornis*) are most closely allied, which is proved by the analogous structure of their antennæ, and the resemblance of the coloring and of the whole bearing of the insects. Nevertheless, one has four and the other five posterior cells, which shows the secondary importance of this character in the present group. The two other species have four posterior cells.

No true *Eriocera* has been discovered in Europe yet (the closely allied genus *Penthoptera*, however, occurs both in Europe and in North America). But in the warmer latitudes of Asia, Africa, and America, *Eriocera* seems to be one of the most abundantly represented genera of *Tipulidæ brevipalpi*. I was struck with this in looking over the principal collections in Europe; some of the species, however, may be more related to *Penthoptera*. The following historical account of the genus *Eriocera* contains the list of species described by former authors, as far as I have been able to ascertain their relationship.

Wiedemann's *Limnobia basilaris, acrostacta*, and probably *mesopyrrha*, all from Java; *L. caminaria, erythrocephala*, and *nigra*, from Brazil, are *Erioceræ*.

The genus *Eriocera* (from ἔριον, wool, and κέρας, horn) was first introduced by Macquart in the *Diptères Exotiques*, etc. Vol. I, p. 74, Tab. X, fig. 2. This author was struck by the abnormal number of antennal joints of *Limnobia nigra* Wied., and founded the genus principally upon this character; but that he did not realize the true character of the genus he was establishing, results from the fact, that in the same volume (l. c. p. 67) he describes *Eriocera erythrocephala* Wied. and *Eriocera acrostacta* Wied. as *Cylindrotoma*, upon the ground of the cylindrical shape of the joints of the flagellum; the abnormal number of antennal joints he explains away in both cases by the supposition that the ends were broken off. Moreover, he had another *Eriocera*, likewise with four posterior cells (*E. bituberculata*, from Brazil), but the antennæ of the specimen were entirely broken off; this species he placed, on account of its four posterior cells, in the genus *Limnobia* (l. c. p. 72). He had done the same in his earlier work, with his *Limnobia diana*, from Bengal (*Hist. Natur. Dipt.* I, p. 107), which is likewise an *Eriocera* with four posterior cells. His *Limnophila bicolor*, from Bengal, *Dipt. Exot.* Vol. I (antennæ also broken), is apparently an *Eriocera*, put among the *Limnophilæ* on account of its five posterior cells; whether his *Limnobia sumatrensis* (*Dipt. Exot. Suppl.* 4e) likewise belongs here is less certain; it has four posterior cells.

In the same year with Macquart's *Eriocera*, the genus *Eranioptera* (*E. fasciata* Guér., from Brasil) was published by Mr. Guérin (*Voyage de la Coquille; Zoologie*, Texte II, 2, p. 287; Tab. XX, fig. 2, Insectes). The volume of the letter-press, as appears from the date of Mr. Guérin's preface, was issued in 1838; the volume of the plates, however, must have appeared much earlier. On the plate the new genus was named *Caloptera*, but as this name had been used by another author in the interval which elapsed before the publication of the text, Mr. Guérin changed it in *Evanioptera*. In the mean time Mr. Westwood, who had seen the plate representing *Caloptera*, identified with it a species from Nepaul, which he described (*Ann. Soc. Entom. de Fr.* 1835, p. 681) as *Calopitera nepalensis.*[1] *Evanioptera* is an *Eriocera* with four posterior cells.

Pterocosmus, a genus introduced by Mr. Walker (*List*, etc. 1, p. 78), in 1848, is based upon some Asiatic *Eriocerae*, mostly of dark coloring, with dark and banded wings. Seven species from the Sunda Islands, China, and Nepaul have been described by Mr. Walker, in the above-quoted work, and in the *Journ. Proc. Lin. Soc. Zool.* I, p. 105, 1857.

Oligomera Doleschall, published in 1857 (*Tweede Bidrage*, etc. p. 11, Tab. VII, fig. 3), is likewise a genus based upon a species of *Eriocera* (*O. javensis*), from Java. It has four posterior cells, and the antennæ of the male are short, eight-jointed; the joints of the flagellum are said to be of nearly equal length.

Limnobia albonotata Loew, from Mozambique, described in the work on Mr. Peters' voyage to that country, is an *Eriocera.*

Physecrania Bigot (*Ann. Soc. Entom. de France*, 1859, p. 123, Tab. III, fig. 1), is an *Eriocera* with short antennæ in the male and five posterior cells. It shows some peculiarities which may perhaps justify a generic separation, but it has nothing in common with *Cylindrotoma*, the author's statement notwithstanding. The species *P. obscura* Bigot, is from Madagascar.

---

[1] It was a mistake on my part when I stated in the *Proc. Acad. Nat. Sci. Philad.* 1859, p. 246, that *Evanioptera* probably belongs to the same section with *Amalopis.*

In 1859 (*Proc. Acad. Nat. Sci. Philad.* 1859, p. 343) I described the North American *Eriocera fuliginosa*, which has short antennæ in both sexes. At the same time I founded the genus *Arrhenica* for two other species, *E. spinosa* and *E. longicornis*, both distinguished by the enormous length of the antennæ of the male, and by the structure of these antennæ, the under side of which is beset with a row of erect, spine-like bristles. The only species of *Eriocera* I had seen at that time was *E. fuliginosa*, which, on account of its short male antennæ, I recognized as the true *Eriocera* Macq. Since then, a more extensive knowledge of the species of this group convinced me of the fact that *Arrhenica* stands in the same relation to the *Erioceræ* with short male antennæ, as the *Anisomeræ* and *Penthoptera* with long male antennæ stand to the species of these genera with short antennæ. If a larger number of species, distinguished by the same characters as the two above-mentioned ones, is discovered, the name *Arrhenica* may be used for them as a subgeneric name; but there is no necessity to maintain it at present as a separate genus.

In 1863 (*Wiener Entom. Monatschr.* VII, p. 230, and afterwards in the *Fauna Austr. Diptera*, Vol. II, p. 534), Dr. Schiner proposed the genus *Penthoptera*, based upon a peculiar form of *Eriocera*, represented by two species in Europe, to which I have since added one from the United States.

The foregoing historical account shows how abundant in species the genus *Eriocera* is, and how little is known about them. *Eriocera* from all parts of the world have been described at different times and under different generic names, without any apparent recognition of the fact that they all belong to a large group, numerously represented in the warmer latitudes. It is probable that, upon closer comparison of the species scattered in different collections in Europe, the genus *Eriocera*, as defined here, will be subdivided in smaller groups, and that some of the genera, alluded to above as belonging to *Eriocera*, will be found to coincide with these groups.

These exotic species are distinguished for the most part by their brilliant coloring; that of their wings especially distinguish them from the North American and the European species; they are often dark, with bands and spots of a lighter color. The Asiatic species are often of a deep velvet black, with brown wings, banded and spotted with white.

It seems that *Eriocera* with *five* posterior cells are more
abundant in Asia, whereas those with *four* prevail in South
America. The three Asiatic species, described in Wiedemann:
basilaris, acrostacta, and *mesopyrrha,* and Macquart's *bicolor*
(if the two latter are *Eriocera*) have five posterior cells; *Physecrania* Bigot, from Africa, likewise. Nevertheless, *Limnobia
diana* Macq., from Bengal, *Caloptera nepalensis* Westw.,[1] from
Nepaul, and *Limnobia sumatrensis* Macq., from Sumatra, have
four posterior cells. The numerous *Eriocerae* from South America which I have seen in the Berlin Museum, as well as the
above-quoted South American species, described by Wiedemann,
Macquart, and Guérin, all have four posterior cells. That this
law should be general, I doubt very much, but it is remarkable
enough that it should be so prevalent, and that among a considerable number of South American species there should not be
a single one with five posterior cells, while in North America,
among four species which are known, one has that number of
cells.

Another, not less remarkable circumstance is, that among this
large number of specimens, described in works or seen by me in
collections, I did not find a single one provided with very long
antennæ in the male sex, such as distinguish three North American species of *Eriocera* and one *Penthoptera.* Many species,
it must be admitted, were represented by females only; the antennæ of several others were broken; but among the twenty-four
species of the Berlin Museum, eleven were represented by males
with well-preserved antennæ, and all these antennæ were short.

Among the Diptera included in amber, which I have had an
opportunity to examine in Mr. Loew's collection, there is the
genus *Allarithmia,* with a single species, *A. palpata.* (Loew,
Bernstein u. Bernsteinfauna, 1850, p. 38), which is a female
Eriocera with four posterior cells, ten-jointed antennæ, and an
elongated last joint of the palpi. There were, moreover, two
species of *Eriocera* represented by males with long antennæ.
One of them has been mentioned in the above-quoted paper of

[1] Westwood's *Caloptera nepalensis* has only four posterior cells, if this
author is right in quoting Guérin's figure of the South American *Erioptera. Pterocosmus* Walker, with several Asiatic species, has also four cells,
if I decipher right the description of the wing in *List,* etc. I, p. 76; but I
may easily have been mistaken in my interpretation.

Mr. Loew under the name of *Aniromera succini;* the other was at the time undescribed. Thus while on one side we have four North American species, three of which with long antennæ, and three amber species, two of which with long antennæ; on the other side we see dozens of exotic *Eriocera*, and, as far as known, not a single one with long antennæ among them. A new proof of the remarkable relationship of the North American and the amber fauna!

Table for determining the species.

1	Five posterior cells.	1 spinosa O. S.
	Four posterior cells.	2
2	Body light reddish.	3 wilsonii, n. sp.
	Body dark gray or brown.	3
3	Halteres pale.	2 longicornis Walk.
	Halteres brown.	4 fuliginosa O. S.

Description of the species.

A. Antennæ of the male very long and much longer than those of the female.

     1. Antennæ of the male glabrous on the upper side, and with a series of bristles inserted at regular intervals, on the under side (subgenus **ARRHENICA**).

1. E. spinosa O. S. ♂ and ♀.—Fuscescens, thoracis vittis fuscis; antennis maris corpore duplo longioribus, in pagina inferiori serie spinarum parvarum; halteres capitulo obscuro; cellulis posterioribus quinque; ovipositor feminæ valvis superioribus longis, acuminatis.

Brownish, thorax with brown stripes, antennæ of the male more than twice the length of the body, on the under side with a row of spines or bristles; knob of the halteres dark; five posterior cells; ovipositor of the female with elongated, pointed upper valves. Long. corp. ♂, 0.45—0.6; ♀, 0.9.

Syn. *Arrhenica spinosa* O. Sacken, Proc. Ac. Nat. Sc. Phil. 1859, p. 244.

Male. Head very downy, brownish-gray, tawny on the under side and on the front side of the tubercle; palpi dark brown, long; first, second, and fourth joints elongated; antennæ more than twice as long as the body, black, two basal joints tawny; if bent backwards, the tip of the third joint would reach a little beyond the root of the wings; the fourth joint is longer than the third, and each of the following joints is longer than the preceding one; the sixth is as long or longer than all the others together. Thorax brownish-gray, clothed with a soft grayish down; four brownish stripes above, the intermediate ones approximated; pleurae with a hoary reflection on their lower part; halteres pale at the basis, knob blackish; coxæ hoary, trochanters and basis of the femora yellowish-tawny; femora and tibiæ tawny, with brown tips; tarsi brown. Abdomen dark brownish, downy; lateral edges, especially beyond the third segment, yellowish, venter paler; forceps tawny; its structure like Tab. IV, fig. 20. Wings tinged with brownish; costal and subcostal cells of a more saturated tawny color; stigma oblong, brown, placed between the subcostal and stigmatical cross-veins; first submarginal and first posterior cells about equal in length; the second submarginal is longer; five posterior cells; petiole of the second cell about as long or a little longer than the cell itself.

Female. Like the male, but much larger; body of a reddish-brown, instead of a grayish-brown tinge, less downy; the antennæ are not longer than the head and thorax taken together; they have no spines, but only sparse hairs; ten indistinct joints can be counted; ovipositor ferruginous; upper valves elongated, almost imperceptibly arcuated, ending in a blunt point.

Hab. Trenton Falls, N. Y.; Massachusetts (Scudder). I possess two males and one female. The front femora of one of the males are much shorter than those of the other.

2. E. longicornis WALK. ♂ and ♀.—Obscure cinerea, thoracis vittis obscuris; antennis maris corpore duplo longioribus; in pagina inferiori serie spinarum parvarum; halteribus pallidis; cellulis posterioribus quatuor; ovipositor fœminæ brevis, valvis superioribus breviusculis, obtusis.

Dark gray, thorax with blackish stripes; antennæ of the male twice the length of the body, on the under side with a row of small spines; halteres pale; four posterior cells; ovipositor short; upper valves shorter than the lower ones, obtuse. Long. corp. 0.4—0.5.

Syn. *Anisomera longicornis* WALKER, List Dipt. Brit. Mus. I, p. 82.
Arrhenica longicornis O. SACKEN, Proc. Ac. Nat. Sc. Phil. 1859, p. 243.

Head gray, frontal bump very large, abrupt; palpi black, antennæ black; two basal joints grayish; antennæ of the male three or four times longer than the body; the third joint, if bent backwards, would reach beyond the root of the wing; every following joint is longer than the preceding; the sixth joint as long as the fourth and fifth together; the spines on the lower surface of the antennæ become short and indistinct towards its end; besides the spines there is a microscopic pubescence on the same side of the antennæ; antennæ of the female hardly reaching beyond the root of the wings; no spines, but hairs; two basal joints and base of the third yellowish; third joint as long as the two first taken together; the fourth less than half so long as the third; the fifth a little longer than the fourth; the following three joints are of about the same length; the ninth is a little longer and the tenth a little shorter than the preceding ones. Thorax gray; a long straight pubescence on the sides in the male, no such pubescence in the female; three blackish stripes on the mesonotum; intermediate stripe conciform; the lateral ones abbreviated before and extended beyond the sutura behind; the lower portion of the pleura hoary; scutellum and metathorax gray; halteres pale; coxæ gray, trochanters and femora tawny, except the tip of the latter, which is brown; tibiæ and tarsi dark brown. Abdomen grayish-black; forceps of the same color; ovipositor of the female very short; its structure like that of *Anisomera*; upper valves blunt, much smaller than the lower ones. Wings slightly tinged with brownish; veins, but especially the profurca, the central cross-veins, and the fifth longitudinal vein faintly clouded with brown; the second submarginal cell a little longer, the first distinctly shorter than the first posterior cell; four posterior cells; stigma brown.

Hab. Trenton Falls, N. Y.; Maine (Packard); Illinois (Kennicott); Massachusetts (Packard). Three males and two females. One of the males has the front and middle femora about half so long as the hind ones; another specimen, however (from Massachusetts), has the front femora at least two-thirds the length of the hind ones; the middle femora are a little shorter. The latter specimen, moreover, has a brownish abdomen, with distinct yellowish lateral margins, and a dark tawny forceps (it resembles the abdomen of *E. spinosa*); the thoracic stripe is not attenuated posteriorly; the frontal bump is smaller, etc. I am not sure whether it is a different species or not. The third male specimen, as well as the females, have their feet broken off, which prevents me from making any general statement about the relative length of the femora in this species.

2. Antennæ of the male much longer than those of the female, finely pubescent on both sides.

3. E. wilsonii, n. sp. ♂.—Ferruginea, maculis humeralibus atris; antennis maris corpore longioribus, pubescentibus; cellulis posterioribus quatuor; halteribus fuscis.

Ferruginous, with deep black humeral spots; antennæ of the male longer than the body, pubescent; four posterior cells; halteres brown. Long. corp. 0.4.

Male. Body yellowish-red; palpi rather short, brownish towards the tip; antennæ more than once and a half the length of the body; clothed on both sides with a delicate, short pubescence; on the under side with some scattered stronger bristles; the third joint, if bent backwards, would reach beyond the basis of the abdomen; the fourth is nearly of the same length with the third; the basal portion of the antennæ is red; the remainder, beginning with the tip of the third joint, brown. Thorax shining above, with two more or less distinct, often almost obsolete, brownish stripes; a deep black, elongated spot between the collare and the root of the wings; a brownish spot above it, near the suture, and another one on the other side of the suture, above the root of the wings; knob of the halteres more or less dark brown. Abdomen, including the forceps of the males, reddish-yellow. Feet yellowish tawny, tip of the femora, of the tibiæ, and the latter portion of the tarsi brownish. Wings with a pale brownish-yellow tinge; stigma pale brownish; often, but not always, a stump of a vein near the origin of the præfurca; four posterior cells.

Hab. Delaware (Dr. Wilson); three male specimens.

B. Antennæ short in both sexes.

4. E. fuliginosa O. S. ♂ and ♀.—Obscure fusca, alis fuscis; antennis maris et feminæ æque longis, brevibus; cellulis posterioribus quatuor; halteribus fuscis.

Dark brown, wings brown; antennæ in both sexes of the same length, short; four posterior cells; halteres brown. Long. corp. 0.4—0.5.

Obs. *Erioceca fuliginosa* O. Sacken, Proc. Ac. Nat. Sc., Phil. 1859, p. 243.

Lower part of the head and rostrum tawny; palpi black; antennæ black; short in both sexes; when bent backwards, they would not reach beyond the root of the wings; basal joints yellowish-ferruginous. Thorax dull dark brown, with a slight yellowish-gray reflection above; four more or less distinct dark brown

stripes on this grayish ground; halteres brown; feet ferruginous;
tips of the femora and of the tibiæ brown; tarsi brown. Abdomen
brown, shining; male forceps tawny; its structure like Tab. IV,
fig. 28; ovipositor ferruginous, tawny at the basis. Wings
brown, clouded along the veins; stigma still darker brown; four
posterior cells; first submarginal cell but little more than half the
length of the second; the marginal cross-vein close by the inner
end of the first submarginal cell.

Hab. Berkeley Springs, Virginia; Washington, D. C. I had
nine male and one female specimen when I first described this
species. I possess, moreover, two males from Virginia and a
female from Ohio, the coloring of which is very like that of *E.
longicornis*, gray with brownish stripes on the thorax; the wings
are only slightly tinged with brownish; the knob of the halteres
is dark brown; the first submarginal cell is short, with the cross-
vein close by its inner end. The difference in the coloring from
the typical specimens of *E. fuliginosa* is very considerable; but
I fail to discover any essential differences.

Gen. XXXIV. PENTHOPTERA.

Two submarginal cells; four or five posterior cells; a discal cell; the
subcostal cross-vein at the very tip of the auxiliary vein; the first submarginal cell shorter than the second; *stigma very small, occupying but a
small portion of the interval between the tip of the auxiliary vein and the
marginal cross-vein*; wing-veins distinctly pubescent. Globosity on the
front comparatively small; antennæ six-jointed in the male, sometimes
much longer than those of the female, sometimes of the same length;
antennæ of the female ten-jointed, comparatively short. Tibiæ with short
spurs at the tip; ungues small; empodia small, but distinct. Male forceps
like that of *Erioeera*.

This genus has been proposed by Dr. Schiner for the European
species *P. chirothecata* Scop. and *cimicoides* Scop., with the first
of which the North American *P. albitarsis* is most unmistakably
allied. Although these three species have all the characters of
Erioeera, it is easy to perceive peculiarities in their general
appearance and their coloring, which justify their separation.
The wings are more elongated, the wing-veins seem to be more
slender, less dark in coloring; the cells in the apical portion of
the wing are longer, the veins enclosing them less diverging, more
parallel, and much more distinctly pubescent; the fringe of hairs
along the posterior margin of the wings is longer; the stigmata

very much smaller, occupying but a small portion of the space between the tip of the auxiliary vein and the marginal cross-vein; the subcostal cross-vein is still nearer to the tip of the auxiliary vein; the marginal cross-vein, on the contrary, a little more distant from the tip of the first longitudinal vein. Both *P. chirothecata* and *P. albitarsis* have the tarsi white—a striking character not observed in the genus *Eriocera*; compared to the tibiæ, the tarsi are shorter here than in *Eriocera*, especially the hind ones.

As in *Eriocera*, the antennæ of the male are sometimes very long, and much longer than those of the female (*P. albitarsis*); sometimes they are short in both sexes (the two European species). The occurrence, in the different species, of either five or of four posterior cells also reminds of the former genus (*P. albitarsis* and *chirothecata* have five, *P. cimicoides* four of such cells).

The antennæ of the male are apparently six-jointed; on those of a fresh specimen of the female of *P. albitarsis* I have distinctly counted ten joints. Those of the two European species, in both sexes, when bent backwards, would hardly reach beyond the root of the wings; the third joint is the longest; the flagellum is sparsely clothed with hairs. The antennæ of the female of the North American species have exactly the same structure; those of the male are nearly as long as the body, filiform, covered with a short, soft pubescence. The structure of the palpi seems to be like that of *Eriocera*. The male forceps, likewise, resembles that of *Eriocera*; the ovipositor has the ordinary structure; the upper valves are slender, pointed, and very gently arcuated.

As I have observed in my remarks on the preceding genus, the subdivisions of *Eriocera* have been too little studied yet, as to decide upon the relative value and position of the allied genera; *Penthoptera* is among the number of the latter.

Dr. Schiner has described a new species (*P. fuliginosa*) from Columbia, South America (*Reise d. Novara, Diptera*. p. 42).

The name of the genus is probably derived from πένθος, sorrow, and πτερόν, wing, in allusion to the dark-colored wings of the European species.

Description of the species.

1. P. albitarsis, n. sp. ♂ and ♀.—Fuscana, capite superne pruinoso, tarsis albis; antennis maris longitudine corporis, femina multo brevioribus; cellulis posterioribus quinque.

17 October, 1868.

Brownish; head above with a thick bluish bloom; tarsi white; antennæ of the male as long as the body; those of the female much shorter; five posterior cells. Long. corp. 0.25—0.3.

Head brownish above, with a bluish bloom, which sometimes entirely conceals the brown; yellowish-tawny below; palpi brownish, except the basis, which is yellowish; antennæ brown, two basal joints yellowish-tawny; those of the male nearly as long as the body, clothed with a dense, delicate pubescence; those of the female, if bent backwards, would hardly reach beyond the root of the wings. Thorax yellowish-tawny, brownish above, shining, and with a slight gray or bluish bloom upon the brown; four darker stripes are sometimes indistinctly marked; halteres brownish; abdomen brown, venter yellowish, the male forceps and the basis of the ovipositor are likewise yellowish; coxæ yellowish, feet brown, tarsi white; last joint somewhat brownish. Wings slightly tinged with brownish; stigma almost imperceptible; first submarginal cell but little shorter than the first posterior; marginal cross-vein at a considerable distance beyond the inner end of the first submarginal cell; five posterior cells; the petiole of the second is rather long.

Hab. New London, Conn., on the sea-beach, a female; Pennsylvania (Cresson), a male. I have only these two specimens before me; the male is considerably smaller than the female, the petiole of the second posterior cell is comparatively much longer, the wings are more brown; but the agreement of the two specimens in other respects is perfect. Both specimens had only the hind tarsi left.

Section VI. AMALOPINA.

Two submarginal cells; four or five posterior cells; discal cell closed or
open; subcostal cross-vein far removed from the tip of the auxiliary
vein and anterior to the origin of the second longitudinal vein (Tab. II,
fig. 14–18). Tibiæ with spurs at the tip; empodia distinct. Eyes
pubescent; front usually with a more or less distinct gibbosity. Normal
number of antennal joints sixteen or thirteen.

The *Tipulidæ* of this section form two natural groups, based
upon the number of joints of their antennæ, and the peculiarities
of their venation.

Pedicia and *Amalopis* have 16-jointed antennæ; the second
submarginal cell is (in all cases which came under my observation) never longer, although generally but very little shorter, than
the first posterior cell; the prefurca is rather elongated (Tab. II,
fig. 14, 15); the palpi seem to be usually longer than in the following group.

Dicranota, *Rhaphidolabis*, and *Plectromyia* have 18-jointed
antennæ; the second submarginal cell is never shorter than the
first posterior, generally a little longer; the prefurca is very short
(Tab. II, fig. 16–18; for more details concerning the differences
between these two groups, compare the genus *Amalopis*).

The characters common to the two groups, and at the same
time distinctive of the *Amalopina* are: the position of the subcostal cross-vein; the pubescent eyes; the frequent occurrence
of the frontal gibbosity; the frequent absence of the discal cell,
especially in the second group; the peculiar shape of the penultimate posterior cell (compare Tab. II, fig. 14–18), the inner end
of which is always much more extended inwards than in the
majority of the brevipalpous *Tipulidæ*. This character, imparting a pentagonal shape to the discal cell whenever it is closed,
is also of general occurrence among the *Tipulidæ longipalpi*.
Among the latter the penultimate posterior cell, as a rule, has

its inner end in one line with the inner end of the last posterior
cell; a form of venation which is not altogether foreign to the
Amalopina also (compare *A. vernalis* O. S., *opaca* Meig., etc.).

This last character, the peculiar shape of the penultimate
posterior cell, is only wanting in the genus *Ula*, which, with its
17-jointed antennæ and its pubescent wings, seems to form a
group for itself, without any particular affinity to the other two;
its position among the *Amalopina*, however, is abundantly vindi-
cated by its other characters.

The separation of the *Amalopina* from the genus *Limnobia* in
the sense of Meigen is of too recent date yet, as that we should
know much about its relative position with regard to the other
sections of the *Tipulidæ*. The pubescence of the eyes seems to
be peculiar to the *Amalopina*, and has not been observed in any
other *Tipulidæ*, except in *Trichocera*. And it is singular enough
that in all the species hitherto observed this character should be
accompanied by another, equally peculiar to this group, the position of the subcostal cross-vein, anterior to the origin of the
second longitudinal vein and so far removed from the tip of the
auxiliary vein. The coincidence of such characters, together
with the structure of the male forceps (differing from the types
prevailing in the other sections) constitute a compact and well
characterized group.

About the occurrence of *Amalopina* in the other parts of the
world, besides Europe and North America, almost nothing is
known. The venation of *Polymera fusca*, from Brazil, figured
in Wiedemann's *Auss. Zw.* Vol. I. Tab. VI, fig. 6, 4, strongly
reminds of *Rhaphidolabis*; the tibiæ of this genus have spurs at
the tip; the antennæ are 28-jointed, pubescent (sometimes, however, 14-jointed? comp. Wied. l. c. p. 554). I have never seen this
genus; the descriptions of Wiedemann and Macquart (*Dipt. Exot.*
I, 1, p. 64, Tab. 8) are not sufficient to determine its position with
certainty (that of Wiedemann is translated in the Appendix II).

Gen. XXXV. AMALOPIS.

Two submarginal cells; five posterior cells; discal cell generally present,
sometimes wanting; the subcostal cross-vein is more or less anterior
to the origin of the second longitudinal vein; the second submarginal
cell is never longer (usually distinctly shorter) than the first posterior
cell; the tip of the wing is rounded in both sexes (not sinuate posteriorly

as in *Pediria*). Tibiæ with spurs at the tip; empodia distinct; ungues smooth. Eyes pubescent; front with a gibbosity behind the antennæ; the latter 16-jointed, short (not reaching much beyond the collare when bent backwards). Male forceps more or less club-shaped, with stout, branched horny appendages.

Rostrum short, with large, hairy lips; epistoma much broader than long; palpi comparatively long; the last joint is longer than the preceding, but usually shorter than the two preceding joints taken together.[1] The eyes are pubescent, separated above by a moderately broad front; on the under side of the head, the space separating them is narrow; the gibbosity on the front, behind the antennæ, is sometimes small, but always perceptible. Antennæ 16-jointed, very short; first and second joints of the usual shape; the flagellum of some species (as *A. vernalis* O. S., *auripennis* O. S., *immaculata* M.) is strongly incrassated at the basis, the joints being closely packed together; the tip is tapering and slender; in other species, however, this incrassation is not perceptible, and the joints are well separated from each other (*A. calcar* O. S.); the under side of the flagellum, especially in the males, is clothed with a short, dense pubescence; the opposite side has longer, verticillate hairs. Collare rather long, well developed; thoracic suture well marked. Feet long, moderately strong; the spurs at the tip of the tibiæ vary in length and distinctness; in *A. calcar* they are very long and divaricate, and therefore conspicuous; much less so in the other species; front tarsi (♂) rather long, about once and a half or once and a quarter the length of the tibia; hind tarsi as long or a little longer than the tibia; the four last tarsal joints taken together are equal to three-quarters or more of the first joint. The wings (compare Tab. II, fig. 14, wing of *A. calcar*; fig. 15, of *A. inconstans*) are of moderate breadth; generally slightly broader in the female. The tip of the auxiliary vein is nearly opposite the tip of the fifth longitudinal vein; the subcostal cross-vein is more or less anterior to the origin of the second longitudinal vein; the distance between them is equal to about one length of the great cross-vein in *A. auripennis* and *calcar*, two such lengths in *A. inconstans*, three lengths or more in *A. hyperborea*, *immaculata*, and *vernalis*. The tip of the first longitudinal vein is opposite the tip of the

[1] I have observed the palpi of living specimens of *A. calcar*, *inconstans*, and *vernalis*.

third branch of the fourth vein; the marginal cross-vein is at, or
very near this tip. The præfurca, the origin of which is about
the middle of the length of the wing, is rather long, arcuated or
angular near the basis (in the latter case generally with a stump
of a vein); its further course is generally straight, *in a line with
the third longitudinal vein.* The relations between the two
branches of the second vein, the third vein, and the small cross-
vein are very peculiar in this genus, and deserve a particular
attention (compare the figures 14 and 15 of Tab. 11): 1. The
small cross-vein always connects the fourth longitudinal vein with
the second vein or the posterior branch of this vein; never with
the third vein, as is almost universally the case among the
Diptera; in other words, the third vein in the genus *Amalopis*
(at least in all the instances observed by me) always issues from
the second beyond the small cross-vein. Hence, it is a peculiarity of *Amalopis* (and this applies also to *Pedicia*), that the
*second submarginal cell is never longer than the first posterior
cell,* generally a little shorter. From among all the other
Tipulidæ, I am aware of two genera only, where the position
of the small cross-vein, above alluded to, is to be met with:
Ptychoptera and *Bittacomorpha.* Even in *Erioptera* (subg.
Molophilus, compare Tab. I, fig. 19), the venation of which
otherwise reminds of *Amalopis,* the small cross-vein has the
usual position, between the third and the fourth veins. 2. The
first submarginal cell is either shorter than the second, which is
the normal venation among the *Tipulidæ;* or it is longer than
the second submarginal (Tab. 11, fig. 14), a form of venation
occurring also among the *Eriopterina* of the subgenus *Molophilus*
(see Tab. I, fig. 19), and the *Ptychopterina* (Tab. 11, fig. 19, 20).
We might express the difference between these two forms of venation by saying that, in the first case, the second vein is forked, in
the second case, the third; but this would be a deviation from
the terminology adopted by us and according to which it is
always the second and never the third vein which bears the fork.
The first submarginal cell is *longer* than the second in the
American species *A. hyperborea, vernalis, calcar,* and the
European species *A. unicolor* Schum. and *immaculata* Schum.);
the first submarginal cell is *shorter* than the second in *A.
auripennis* O. S., in the normal specimens of *A. inconstans*

O. S., and in the European species *A. littoralis* M., *schineri* Egg., *occulta* M. The structure of the posterior fork of the fourth vein undergoes some modifications which deserve likewise to be mentioned. In most of the species (*auripennis, hyperborea, calcar, inconstans,* and the European *littoralis* M., *tipulina* Egg., *schineri* Kolen., *unicolor* Schum., *immaculata* Schum.) this fork is petiolate, or in other words, the inner end of the *fourth* posterior cell (enclosed by this fork) is more remote from the basis of the wing than the inner end of the discal cell, or when it is open, of the third posterior cell. In *A. vernalis,* however, as well as in the European *A. occulta* M., *gmundensis* Egger, and *opaca* Egger, the posterior fork of the fourth vein is sessile, that is, the origin of the branch forming it is coincident with the first branching of the fourth vein; hence, the inner end of the fourth posterior cell is equidistant from the basis of the wing with the inner end of the discal cell, or, when it is open, of the third posterior cell. The discal cell is closed in the normal specimens of *A. calcar, vernalis,* and *inconstans;* it is likewise closed in the two remaining North American species, *A. auripennis* and *A. hyperborea,* of which, however, I have only single specimens before me; also in the European *A. tipulina* Egger. In the European *A. littoralis* M., *schineri* Kol., and *unicolor* Schum., the discal cell seems to be variable, sometimes closed, often open. In *A. occulta* M., *immaculata* Sch., *gmundensis* and *opaca* Egger, it is open (at least in normal specimens).[1] The shape of the discal cell is usually pentagonal; but in *A. vernalis,* owing to the above-mentioned structure of the posterior fork of the fourth vein, it is elongated and narrow. When the discal cell is closed, the second posterior cell is usually petiolate; in *A. vernalis* it is sessile; in most specimens of *A. inconstans* it is sessile or subsessile. The small cross-vein is generally in one line with the inner end of the discal cell (or of the third posterior cell, when the discal is open), and often with the great cross-vein; this relation is somewhat variable in *A. inconstans.* The fifth longitudinal vein is somewhat arcuated towards the end; the sixth and seventh are straight, or almost so. In *A. hyperborea* the second basal cell is divided in two by a supernumerary cross-vein; the same is the case with the Euro-

---

[1] The data about the European species are taken from Dr. Schiner's work.

penn *A. varinervis* Zett. The stigma is elongated and but little defined.

The abdomen of the male is elongated, often attenuated at the basis, and more or less club-shaped at the tip. The forceps of *A. inconstans* (Tab. IV, fig. 30) consists of a pair of coriaceous basal pieces, hollow inside (*c c*); each of them has a large horny appendage, with two branches directed upwards (*a a*), and a soft fleshy and putrescent lobe (*b*); moreover, there is a pair of smaller horny appendages (*h*) inside of the forceps (compare also the details given in explanation of the plate). The forceps of the other species seems to be formed pretty much on the same plan. The ovipositor of the female has moderately long and broad, somewhat arcuated and pointed upper valves.

The species of *Amalopis* are of medium size, some of them comparatively large; they occur in damp situations; nothing is known about the habits of their larvæ, which are probably aquatic, like those of *Pedicia*. *Amalopis* is very closely allied to the latter genus, and it is rather difficult to find a satisfactory character to distinguish them. From *Dicranota*, *Rhaphidolabis*, and *Plectromyia*, the present genus, as well as *Pedicia*, are distinguished by the number of antennal joints, by the circumstance that, on account of the peculiar position of the small cross-vein, already explained, the second submarginal cell is never longer than the first posterior, and by the frequent occurrence of the form of venation in which the first submarginal cell is longer than the second (compare also the general remarks on the *Amalopina*, p. 259).

I possess five North American species of *Amalopis*, and Dr. Schiner enumerates nine European ones, some of which, however, are probably synonymous. I have every reason to believe that *Limnobia varinervis* Zett., from Norway, which I know only from the description (Zett. *Dipt. Scand.* X, p. 8818), is an *Amalopis*. *Limnobia congrua* Walker, *List*, etc. I, p. 49, from Swan River, is an *Amalopis*; I have seen it in the British Museum.

The genus *Amalopis* (from ἁμαλός, soft, and ὄψ, face) was first proposed by Mr. Haliday for *Limnobia occulta* M., in Walker's *Ins. Brit. Diptera*, Vol. III, 1856. It was not incorporated into the work, however, but introduced in a note among the Addenda and Corrigenda (l. c. p. xv), after the work had been completed. Mr. Haliday points out the hairy eyes, the frontal tubercle, and the absence of a discal cell of this species, and says that it is the type of a new genus *Amalopis*. In the *Proc. Acad. Nat. Sci. Philad.* 1859, p. 245, I have further developed this suggestion, by adding to the characters of *Amalopis* the position of the subcostal cross-vein, and establishing upon that character the group of *Pediciæformia* (now *Amalopina*). At that time I described three North American species, to which I have since (*Proc.*, etc. 1861, p. 291) added two new ones. Dr. Schiner (*Fauna Austr. Diptera*, 1864, Vol. II, p. 527) referred to *Amalopis* the European species belonging to it, and which had been previously mixed up with the *Limnobiæ*.

Crunobia, a generic name proposed by Kolenati for *Amalopis schineri* Kol. (*Wien. Entom. Monatschr.* IV, p. 393; 1860), is a synonym of *Amalopis*.

The genus *Tricyphona*, established by Zetterstedt, in the *Ins. Lapponica*, 1840, and retained in all the later publications, even in Dr. Schiner's *Fauna Austriaca, Diptera*, is, according to my opinion, not sufficiently distinguished from *Amalopis*, to be retained as a separate genus. I suspected this already in 1859, but it has become evident to me recently, since I obtained specimens of *T. immaculata* M., the only species upon which this genus is based. If *T. immaculata* has been separated from *Limnobia* so early, it was principally on account of its discal cell being always open, a character of altogether secondary importance. Although the name *Tricyphona* is older than *Amalopis*, I believe that, as a matter both of right and of expediency, the latter name has to be maintained.[1] The genus *Bophræsia* Rondani, is a synonym of *Tricyphona*.

---

[1] The almost absolute rules of priority recognized for specific names are not equally applicable to the generic ones. In the present instance the genus *Amalopis* may be said to have been unknown until 1856, when Mr. Haliday pointed out one of its principal features, and 1859, when I showed its true extent and defined its character. Zetterstedt's definition of *Tricyphona* is not applicable to *Amalopis*, as it is principally based upon the absence of the discal cell, a character of mere casual occurrence. If the mere invention of a name gave a right to priority, we should call *Rhamphidia* by the name of *Helius* St. Fargeau, and adopt *Helobia* St. Fargeau, instead of *Symplecta*.

Table for determining the species.

1 { Anterior margin of the wings shaded with brownish.
            1 inconstans *O. S.*
  { Anterior margin of the wing not shaded with brownish. 2

2 { Wings spotted with brown. 3
  { Wings not spotted with brown. 4

3 { The inner end of the fourth posterior cell is in one line with the inner
    end of the fifth and of the discal cells. 5 vernalis *O. S.*
  { The inner end of the fourth posterior cell is beyond the inner end of
    the fifth and of the discal cells. 4 hyperborea *O. S.*

4 { First submarginal cell shorter than the second. 2 auripennis *O. S.*
  { First submarginal cell longer than the second. 3 calcar *O. S.*

Description of the species.

1. A. inconstans O. S. ♂ and ♀.—Ochracea, thorace rufescente,
abdomine obscuriori; alarum margine antica et venulis transversis infuscatis; praefurca initium appendiculatam; cellula submarginalis
prima secundâ brevior.

Ochraceous, thorax reddish, abdomen somewhat darker; anterior margin
of the wings and transverse veins infuscated; the praefurca has a stump
of a vein near its origin; the first submarginal cell (in normal specimens) is shorter than the second (Tab. II, fig. 15). Long. corp. 0.45—
0.55.

Syn. *Amalopis inconstans* O. Sacken, Proc. Ac. Nat. Sc. Phil. 1859, p. 247.

Coloring very inconstant; ochraceous, more or less mixed with
brown on the thorax and the abdomen; sometimes altogether
without brown. The following is the description of the specimens with a fully developed dark coloring:—

Rostrum and palpi brown; front grayish; under side of the
head yellowish; antennae pale, but little longer than the head;
basal joint generally brownish; flagellum with moderate verticils.
Collare ochraceous, a black ring near the head, a brown stripe
along the middle; mesonotum yellowish-orange, with a slight
brown tinge along the middle; stripes indistinct; back of the
suture, the thorax is brownish; scutellum and metathorax are
paler in the middle; pleura pale; halteres pale; feet yellow,
femora and tibiae faintly brownish at the tip; tips of the tarsal
joints, and their last joint brown. Abdomen brown, especially
towards the tip; male genitals brown; ovipositor reddish. Wings
tinged with light brownish; anterior margin, especially within

the costal and subcostal cells, infuscated; all the cross-veins have brown clouds, as well as the origin of the prefurca.

This is the normal coloring, but among eighteen specimens which I had before me, only four showed it in its full development. All the others were more or less paler about the collare, the scutum, the scutellum, the metathorax, and the abdomen; sometimes with slight indications of brown, sometimes without any. The coloring of the wings is also variable, the fuscous tinge of the anterior margin and the clouds on the cross-veins being sometimes very pale. Still, a trace of the brown tinge of the anterior margin of the wings and a brown ring on the anterior part of the collare, near the head, are always left, and help to recognize the species.

The venation of this species is also very variable. In the majority of specimens the first submarginal cell is shorter than the second (Tab. II, fig. 15); in other words, it is the second longitudinal vein which is forked. Sometimes (in two specimens among eighteen) the reverse is the case; it is the third vein which is forked, and hence the first submarginal cell is longer than the second.

In normal specimens the second posterior cell is sessile; in rather rare cases it is petiolate. The discal cell, in the majority of specimens, is closed; in three specimens among eighteen I find it open. The position of the great cross-vein is also somewhat variable; sometimes it is opposite the inner end of the discal cell, sometimes beyond it. The presence of a stump of a vein, usually long and distinct, near the basis of the prefurca, is a very constant character of this species. Adventitious cross-veins in the second submarginal cell are of frequent occurrence; sometimes two or three in succession. Occasionally they occur also in other cells, for instance in the second posterior cell. (Tab. II, fig. 16, represents a strongly colored wing of *A. inconstans* with two adventitious cross-veins in the second submarginal cell.)

Hab. Atlantic States, rather common in the spring; I have collected it in abundance at the Virginia Springs and in the White Mountains; also near Washington and New York.

I possess two specimens from Europe which are similar, in all respects, to the paler varieties of *A. inconstans*. The description of *A. tipulina* Egger (Schiner's *Fauna Austriaca, Diptera*, II, p. 528), agrees quite well with these specimens. The question arises whether *A. tipulina* is distinct from *A. littoralis* Meig.?

2. A. auripennis O. S.   ♂.—Fuscana, alis immaculatis, venolis transversis cvatralibus anguste fusco-marginatis; cellula submarginalis prima secundâ parum brevior.

Brownish, wings immaculate, central cross-veins slightly clouded with brown; the first submarginal cell is a little shorter than the second. Long. corp. 0.3.

Syn. *Amalopis auripennis* O. Sackén, Proc. Ac. Nat. Sc. Phil. 1859, p. 247.

Head grayish, vertex slightly brownish in the middle; palpi brown, somewhat pale at the basis; antennæ very short, three or four basal joints yellowish, the remainder brownish; joints from the fourth to the tenth short, crowded, gradually attenuated towards the tip, where they have very long verticils. Thorax grayish above, with three brown stripes; the intermediate one broad, bifid posteriorly; pleura, scutellum, and metathorax grayish; halteres pale; coxæ pale; feet pale tawny, tips of the femora infuscated; those of the tibiæ and tarsi likewise; spurs at the tip of the tibiæ distinct, of moderate length. Abdomen brown, with a sparse yellowish pubescence; margins of the segments and venter paler. Wings uniformly tinged with yellowish; otherwise hyaline, their surface shining; a narrow, inconspicuous brown cloud along the central cross-veins; similar clouds at the origin of the præfurca, the marginal cross-vein, and the tip of the auxiliary vein; stigma pale. Subcostal cross-vein anterior to the origin of the præfurca by not more than one length of the great cross-vein; origin of the præfurca with a stump of a vein; the first submarginal cell is very little shorter than the second, its petiole being very short, sometimes obsolete; the anterior branch of the second vein is arcuated at its basis, as usual; otherwise, the course of both branches of this vein and of the third vein is straight; the discal cell is closed, and the second posterior cell (in the only specimen in my possession) is petiolate.

Hab. Massachusetts (Scudder); a single male.

This species seems to be very like the European *A. occulta* Meig.; only the latter has an open discal cell, and its fourth posterior cell is sessile.

3. A. calcar O. S.   ♂ and ♀.—Ochracea, thorace rufescente; alis unicoloribus; cellula submarginalis prima secundâ longior; tibiarum calcaribus longiusculis.

Ochraceous, thorax reddish; wings unicolorous; first submarginal cell longer than the second (Tab. II, fig. 14); spurs of the tibiæ rather long. Long. corp. 0.45—0.55.

Syn. *Amalopis culcer* O. Sacken, Proc. Ac. Nat. Sc. Phil. 1859, p. 247.

Front and vertex grayish; epistoma brownish-gray; palpi yellow at the basis, two last joints infuscated; antennæ yellowish, infuscated at the tip; joints of the flagellum, except the first, short subcylindrical, with short verticils; finely pubescent on the under side. Thorax yellow; four reddish or brownish-red, often indistinct, stripes; halteres pale; coxæ and basis of the femora pale yellow; feet yellowish-brown or brownish-yellow, tip of the tarsi darker; the spurs at the tip of the tibiæ, and especially of the hind ones, are longer than usual in this species, divaricated. Abdomen yellowish at the basis, more brownish towards the tip, especially in the male. Wings hyaline, with a slight yellowish tinge; stigma pale; the distance between the subcostal cross-vein and the origin of the præfurca is about equal to the length of the great cross-vein; the second submarginal cell is shorter than the first; the second posterior cell is usually petiolate; discal cell generally closed (the venation is represented, Tab. II, fig. 14).

Hab. Massachusetts; Upper Wisconsin River; White Mountains, N. H., where I found it in abundance in June. It seems to be a rather northern species, as I never found it near Washington.

4. A. hyperborea O. S. ♂.—Fusca, alis fusco-maculatis; venula supernumeraria transversali in cellula basali secunda; cellula submarginali prima secundâ longior.

Brown, wings spotted with brown; a supernumerary cross-vein in the middle of the second basal cell; the first submarginal cell is longer than the second. Long. corp. 0.45.

Syn. *Amalopis hyperborea* O. Sacken, Proc. Ac. Nat. Sc. Phil. 1861, p. 292.

The only specimen in my possession being spoiled by mould, the following description is somewhat incomplete:—

Body brownish, antennæ brown; feet brownish, basis of the femora paler, tip of the femora and of the tibiæ infuscated; tarsi dark brown towards the end; halteres infuscated in the middle; their basis, and the greater part of the knob yellow. Second submarginal cell much shorter than the first, its petiole being comparatively long, but little shorter than the præfurca; the latter is comparatively short, strongly arcuated at the basis, and with

an oblique stump of a vein; subcostal cross-vein anterior to the
origin of the præfurca by about four lengths of the great cross-
vein; the fourth posterior cell has its inner end a little before the
middle of the discal cell; a supernumerary cross-vein in the
middle of the second basal cell. Wings rather broad, with a
slight brownish-yellow tinge and numerous brown spots; there
are seven larger spots along the anterior margin (one at the
humeral cross-vein, another a little beyond it, a third at the subcostal cross-vein, a large spot at the origin of the præfurca, the
following three at the tips of the auxiliary, first and second longitudinal veins); similar, but smaller spots at the tips of the veins
along the posterior margin, beginning with the posterior end of
the fork inclosing the second posterior cell; brown clouds in the
axillary and spurious cells, near the posterior margin; a spot at
the inner end of the second basal cell; cross-veins and inner ends
of the forks clouded with brown; the middle of the second submarginal cell clouded.

Hab. Labrador; a single male.

Observation. In reading over the descriptions of the *Limnobiæ*
in Prof. Zetterstedt's *Diptera Scandinavica*, Vol. X, with the view
of locating as much as possible all the anomalous species, I notice
the description of *Limnobia varinervis* Zett. (l. c. p. 3813), from
Norway, which agrees in many points with *A. hyperborea*. It is
certainly an *Amalopis*, and possibly the same species as *A. hyperborea*. *A. varinervis* has the discal cell quite often open.

5. **A. vernalis** O. S. ♂ and ♀. — Fusana, alis fusco-maculatis;
  cellula submarginali prima secundA longior; cellula posterior quarta
  longa, æqualis.

Brownish, wings with brown spots; the first submarginal cell is longer
  than the second; fourth posterior cell long, sessile. Long. corp. 0.3—0.4.

Syn. *Amalopis vernalis* O. Sacken, Proc. Ac. Nat. Sc. Phil. 1861, p. 291.

Head brownish-gray, front somewhat infuscated in the middle,
palpi brown; antennæ not much longer than the head, brown, two
basal joints paler; flagellum stout at the basis, joints very short,
their pubescence short. Thorax grayish-yellow above, with four
brown stripes; the intermediate ones separated by a delicate line;
pleuræ and metathorax brown, with a grayish bloom; halteres
pale, the middle of the stem, and the basis of the knob infuscated.

Abdomen brown, lateral and posterior margins of the segments pale ; male forceps and the basis of the ovipositor yellowish. Feet brownish, pale at the basis ; spurs at the tip of the tibiæ very small. Wings faintly tinged with brownish ; six or seven pale brown clouds along the anterior margin, and smaller clouds at the tips of the veins along the posterior margin; cross-veins and inner ends of the forks likewise clouded. The most striking feature of the venation is the length of the fourth posterior cell, the inner end of which is in one line with the inner ends of the fifth posterior and of the discal cell ; the second submarginal cell is shorter than the first ; the petiole of the former is not half so long as the præfurca; the origin of the præfurca has a stump of a vein ; the second posterior cell is usually sessile, sometimes petiolate ; the subcostal cross-vein is anterior to the origin of the præfurca by three or four lengths of the great cross-vein.

Hab. White Mountains, N. H., in June ; Washington, D. C., early in the spring.

Gen. XXXVI. PEDICIA.

Two submarginal cells ; five posterior cells ; discal cell closed ; the subcostal cross-vein is nearly opposite or a short distance before the origin of the second longitudinal vein, but a long distance before the tip of the auxiliary vein; the first submarginal cell is longer than the second ; the central cross-veins run in a very oblique direction, almost parallel to the posterior margin ; the latter is somewhat sinuated in the male, near the apex of the wing, which is thus drawn out in a point, instead of being rounded, as usual. Tibiæ with spurs at the tip ; empodia distinct ; ungues smooth. Eyes pubescent ;[1] front with a small gibbosity ; the antennæ 16-jointed, short. Male forceps somewhat club-shaped, with large horny appendages.

This genus is very closely allied to *Amalopis*, and besides the larger size and the striking coloring, which give it a peculiarly distinguished aspect, I can discover only the following differences : 1. The last joint of the palpi is flagelliform, and from once and a quarter to once and a half the length of the three preceding joints taken together (in the species of *Amalopis*, which I have observed when alive, the last joint was less in length than the two preceding taken together). 2. The central cross-veins (in this case the small and the great cross-vein, and, between them, the cross-vein forming the inner end of the discal cell) are in a straight

[1] The pubescence is often rubbed off in dry specimens.

line which runs more obliquely than in any species of *Amalopis*, and if prolonged, would form a very acute angle with the line of the anterior margin; in *Amalopis* the line of the central cross-veins is nearly at right angles with the anterior margin, or at least at a much less acute angle. 3. The posterior margin of the wing is somewhat excised towards the apex in such a manner that the wing is not rounded at the tip, but somewhat pointed, the point being directed backwards; this character belongs to the male sex only; in the female the apex of the wing is rounded, as usual. 4. The wings are kept divaricate, when in repose, whereas the species of *Amalopis* usually fold them.

These characters are barely sufficient to establish a claim to generic separation, and the genus *Pedicia*, defined in such a manner as to include all the species of *Amalopis*, would not have been an unnatural one.

The forceps of the male, built upon the same plan as that of *Amalopis*, has large, horny appendages, projecting in a curved point above; the ovipositor is comparatively short, moderately broad at the basis, pointed at the tip; the shorter lower valves bare, on the inside, a fringe of recumbent, strong bristles.

A single European and a single North American species of *Pedicia* are known, and both are so much alike that it requires a close comparison to distinguish them. *P. contermina* Walk., from Nova Scotia, is very probably only a variety of *P. albivitta; P. rivosa* shows occasionally the same abnormity. *P. gracilis* Walker (*List*, etc. I, p. 87), from an unknown locality, seems to be a distinct species.

Pedicia inhabits marshy woods; Dr. Schiner (*Fauna Austr. Dipt.* II, p. 537) observed it also in mountainous regions upon willow trees, so high that the net could not reach them. The larva has been observed by Scheffer, in well-water (Rossi, *System. Verz.* etc. p. 9).

This genus was first introduced by Latreille, in 1809 (*Genera Crust. et Insector.* Vol. IV, p. 255), who placed it among the *Tipulidæ longipalpi*. The relationship of *Pedicia* and *Amalopis* has been first pointed out by me in *Proc. Acad. Nat. Sci. Philad.* 1859, p. 246.

The name may perhaps be derived from πηδίον, a field.

Observation. In two male specimens of *P. albivitta* which I have before me, I perceive something very like a pair of ocelli on

the front, very near the basis of the antennæ. I do not see them,
however, on the front of a female *P. rivosa*, which I can likewise
compare. This may be owing to shrinkage. *Pedicia* and *Trichocera* would thus afford the only known instances of ocelli among
the *Tipulidæ*.

1. P. albivitta WALK. ♂ and ♀.—Alis hyalinis, costâ, venâ longitudinali quintâ et venulis transversis centralibus fusco-marginalis.

Wings hyaline; the costa, the fifth longitudinal vein, and the central cross-
veins margined with brown. Long. corp. 1.2—1.4.

SYN. *Pedicia albivitta* WALKER, List, etc. Vol. I, p. 37.—O. SACKEN, Proc.
Ac. Nat. Sc. Phil. 1859, p. 248.

Head and palpi brown, the former with a grayish bloom; antennæ not much longer than the head, yellowish-brown; flagellum
stout at the basis, gradually attenuated. Thorax pale brown,
with a silvery gray reflection; a brown double stripe in the
middle above, and less distinct stripes on the sides; another
brown stripe runs from the collare to the root of the wings, and
from there to the hind coxæ. Abdomen with a row of brown
spots on five segments; they are elongated and pointed behind,
with a yellowish-red spot at the basis of each; the remaining
portion of their intervals is silvery white; venter with a longitudinal brown band, interrupted by a reddish tinge at the incisures of the segments, and somewhat attenuated in the middle
of each segment; tip of the abdomen brownish. Feet stout,
hairy, femora tawny; their tips brown; tibiæ and tarsi brown.
Wings hyaline; a brown band along the costa, another along the
fifth longitudinal cell; they coalesce at the inner end of the basal
cells, and are connected by a cross-band along the central cross-
veins; the band along the costa is yellowish in the costal cell, and
somewhat expanded round the origin of the præfurca.

Hab. Trenton Falls, N. Y.; New London, Conn.; Massachusetts (Mr. Scudder). This species seems to be chiefly northern; I have seen a specimen, however, which was said to have
been caught in Maryland.

At first sight, this species looks very like the European *P.
rivosa* L.; still the longitudinal brown band along the abdomen,
in the latter, seems to be more continuous, and not composed of a
series of spots. A careful comparison of a larger number of

specimens would probably disclose some other differences. The picture of the wings is the same.

Gen. XXXVII. ULA.

Two submarginal cells; four posterior cells; a discal cell; the subcostal cross-vein is a considerable distance anterior to the origin of the second vein; the latter is near the middle of the length of the wing. Whole surface of the wing finely pubescent. Tibiae with distinct spurs; empodia distinct. Eyes pubescent; no striking gibbosity on the front; antennae 17-jointed; first joint not usually short.

The eyes are remote, being separated on the upper side of the head by a rather broad front; on the under side they are contiguous; the front, even in fresh specimens, does not show the gibbosity visible in the other genera of *Amalopina*. Rostrum somewhat prolonged, cylindrical, but shorter than the head; palpi elongated, slender; last joint elongated, but not strikingly prolonged. Antennae 17-jointed (I have counted the joints of a fresh specimen of *Ula elegans*, ♀); they are comparatively longer than those of *Amalopis* and *Pedicia*, and, if bent backwards, would reach the root of the wings, even in female specimens; the first joint is remarkably short (the fresh specimen of *U. elegans*, ♀, observed by me, had this joint shorter than the second, difficult to perceive on account of its smallness); the joints of the flagellum are elongated, subcylindrical, clothed on the under side with a distinct pubescence, more dense in the male, and provided with moderately long verticils. The collare is moderately developed; thoracic suture well marked; the depression between it and the scutellum shallow. Feet of moderate length, finely pubescent; fore tarsi a little longer, hind tarsi a little shorter than the corresponding tibiae; the spurs of the latter are small, but distinct; empodia rather large. The wings are finely and evenly pubescent on the whole surface; those of the female are broader than those of the male. The subcostal cross-vein is placed before the middle of the length of the wing, at more or less distance from the origin of the second longitudinal vein, and nearer to the root of the wing than the tip of the seventh longitudinal vein; the origin of the second vein is near the middle of the wing, a little more distant from the root of the wing than the tip of the seventh longitudinal vein; praefurca comparatively long (much longer than in *Dicranota* and the two genera allied to it), angular, and often with a sinum of a vein near the basis; the remainder of its course perfectly straight; the small cross-vein is opposite the tip of the sixth vein; the second submarginal cell is of the same length with the first posterior cell, or very nearly so; its basis is pointed; the first submarginal cell is a little shorter than the second, its petiole being as long as the great cross-vein, or a little shorter; the course of the veins, bordering these cells, is almost straight; the marginal cross-vein is very near the tip of the first longitudinal vein, which is nearly opposite the tip of the last branch of the fourth longitudinal vein; the tip of the auxiliary vein is nearly opposite the basis of the first submarginal cell. The discal cell is moderately elongated; narrower at the basis than towards the tip; the second and third posterior cells of nearly equal length; the great cross-vein somewhat beyond the basis of the discal cell; fifth longitudinal vein gently arcuated near the tip; sixth and seventh nearly straight. Abdomen of the male subclavate at the tip; the forceps has a pair of large horny appendages, very well perceptible even in dry specimens (I have not examined it in living specimens); female ovipositor rather short, arcuated, pointed, moderately broad.

Ula is easily distinguished from all the *Amalopina* by its pubescent wings. The presence of only four posterior cells, the abortiveness of the first submarginal cell in comparison to the second, and the length of the antennæ distinguish it from *Pedicia* and *Amalopis;* the constant presence of a discal cell, the length of the præfurca, and the number of joints of the antennæ separate it from *Dicranota* and the two genera related to it.

Besides the two North American species described below, there are two or three European ones; the European *Ula pilosa* Stan. is very like the North American *U. paupera;* and there exists an undescribed European species closely resembling *U. elegans.* The two species referred by Mr. Schiner to this genus: *sororcula* Zett. and *pilicornis* Zett. (*Dipt. Scand.* X, p. 3885 and 3888), I do not know; but as Mr. Zetterstedt distinctly mentions, in the description of his *Limnobia pilicornis,* that the subcostal cross-vein is at the tip of the auxiliary vein (the expression: "nervus longitudinalis primus apice bifidus," in that author's terminology, means nothing else), this species cannot well be *Ula.* It is more probably an *Ulomorpha.* *Ula* has also been discovered in amber; *Haploneura hirtipennis* Loew (*Bernstein u. Bernsteinfauna*),

of which I have seen the original specimen, is undoubtedly no
Ula.

The genus Ula (from ὀκλός, soft) was first introduced by Mr.
Halliday, in 1833 (Entom. Magaz. I, p. 153), for U. pilosa Stan.
(U. mollissima Hal.). Macquart took this species for a Cylindrotoma (C. macroptera Macq.; compare, however, about this
synonymy, the remark under the head of the Cylindrotomina
below). Mr. Lioy, overlooking the existence of the genus Ula,
established for this species the genus Macroptera (Lioy, Atti Inst.
Ven. 3d ser. 1863, Vol. IX, p. 224). The position of Ula among
the Amalopina (Pedicizformia ollm), based upon the pubescence
of its eyes, the position of the subcostal cross-vein, etc., has been
pointed out by me in 1859 (Proc. Acad. Nat. Sci. Philad. 1859,
p. 109).

The larvæ inhabit fungi, and have been observed by Stannius
(Reitr. z. Entom. Schl. p. 205) and Perris (Ann. Soc. Entom. de
France, 1849, p. 331, Tab. VII, fig. 4). Stannius, who found
the larva of Ula pilosa in an Agaricus, merely says that it is very
like that of Limnobia xanthoptera (compare above, p. 86).
Perris found the same larva in Hydnum erinaceum. According
to his account it has along the sides short, erect reddish hairs; in
other respects, its characters seem to agree exactly with those of
the other tipulideous larvæ. The pupa state was assumed underground.

1. U. elegans, n. sp. ♀.—Cinerea, abdomine fusco; alis fuscomaculatis.

Grayish; abdomen brownish; wings spotted with brown. Long. corp.
0.24.

Head gray, palpi brown; antennæ brown, paler at the base.
The black ground-color of the thorax above is entirely concealed
under a thick gray bloom; stripes hardly perceptible; pleuræ
slightly hoary. Halteres yellowish. Abdomen pale brown; last
segment paler; ovipositor short, broad, curved. Feet brownish,
darker towards the end. Wings with a brown spot on the origin
of the præfurca, a brown band between the costa and the fifth
vein, along the central cross-veins; brown clouds at the tip of the
first longitudinal vein and at the inner end of the second and
third posterior cells; fifth longitudinal cell margined with brown,
especially towards the tip.

Hab. White Mountains, N. H.; a single female; July, 1863.
I have seen an undescribed European species, which is very
like *U. elegans*, perhaps identical with it.

2. *U.* **pampera** O. S. ♀.—Pallide fuscana, fronte cinerea, alis immaculatis.

Pale brownish, front gray, wings immaculate. Long. corp. about 0.3.

Syn. *Ula pilosa* O. Sacken (non Schum.), Proc. Ac. Nat. Sc. Phil. 1859,
p. 231.

Front and vertex grayish; rostrum yellowish; palpi and antennae brown; the two basal joints of the latter yellowish; the
third joint is longer than the two first taken together, nearly
cylindrical; the following joints are not much shorter than the
third, but gradually diminish in length towards the tip of the antenna; the flagellum is clothed on the under side with a delicate
pubescence; the verticils are of moderate length. Thorax brownish-yellow, the mesonotum is brownish in the middle, somewhat
shining, although covered with a yellowish bloom; pleurae paler,
with a slight hoary bloom; halteres pale, knob infuscated at the
tip; feet tawny, infuscated at the tips of the femora, of the tibiae,
and of the tarsi; coxae and basis of the femora paler. Abdomen
brownish, venter paler; ovipositor falciform, short, ferruginous.
Wings with a faint brownish tinge, finely, densely, and uniformly
pilose over the whole surface; stigma elliptical, but little darker
in color than the wing itself; a very faint brownish cloud on the
small cross-vein.

Hab. Washington, D. C., a single female.
In my former publication, I had identified this specimen with
Ula pilosa Schum.; I prefer to give it another name now, as
experience has taught me since that such an identification, based
upon a description and not upon an actual comparison of specimens, is not always safe.

I possess a male specimen from the Trenton Falls, N. Y., the
antennae of which have a different structure: the joints of the
flagellum are much shorter, elongated-elliptical, rather than cylindrical; those of the latter part of the flagellum are longer and
more slender than those near its basis; the thorax is dark brown
above, covered with a grayish dust; the forceps of the male has
large horny appendages, yellow, brown at the tip; the stigma is

darker at both ends than in the middle. In other respects the resemblance between this specimen and *U. paupera* is very great.

Gen. XXXVIII. DICRANOTA.

Two submarginal cells; four or five posterior cells; discal cell open (adventitiously closed in abnormal specimens); *there are two marginal cross-veins between the first and the second longitudinal veins*; the subcostal cross-vein is a considerable distance before the origin of the second longitudinal vein (Tab. II, fig. 16). Tibiæ with small but distinct spurs at the tip; empodia distinct. Eyes pubescent; distinct gibbosity on the front, behind the antennæ; the latter 13-jointed.

The eyes are remote, being separated on the upper side of the head by a rather broad front; the latter shows in fresh specimens a distinct gibbosity behind the antennæ,[1] which seems to shrink in dry specimens. Rostrum and proboscis short; palpi short. Antennæ 13-jointed; the structure of those of the European species is thus characterized by Mr. Haliday (Walker, *Ins. Brit. Diptera*, Vol. III, p. 307): "*Male:* Antennæ a little longer than the thorax; third and following joints oval. *Fem:* Antennæ submoniliform, a little shorter than the thorax." In the North American *D. ricularis* the antennæ of both sexes are very similar in structure; if bent backwards, they would not reach much beyond the collare; first joint subcylindrical, the second short, cyathiform, the third obconical, attenuated at the basis; the following joints subglobular, gradually becoming narrower towards the tip; the flagellum is clothed with some short, scattered hairs, which can hardly be called verticils, and I do not perceive the delicate pubescence, often occurring in males of *Tipulidæ*.

The antennæ of the male of *D. eucera* are of an entirely different structure; they are twice the length of head and thorax taken together; the flagellum is clothed with a dense, delicate pubescence, without any verticils; the joints are cylindrical, elongated, of nearly equal length, except the last, which is shorter. The head is rather closely applied to the well-developed collare; the thoracic suture is well marked. The feet are long, moderately strong; the spurs at the tip of the tibiæ, although short, are very distinct. The wings have *four* posterior cells in two European

---

[1] This statement is repeated from *Proc. Acad. Nat. Sci. Philad.* 1859, p. 249, as I have not had any opportunity of seeing fresh specimens since.

species (*D. pavida* Hal. and *guerinii* Zett., which, however, may be synonyms; compare Walker, l. c. p. 896, No. 1), as well as in the two North American species described by me; they have *five* posterior cells in two European species (*D. ruficornis* Schum. and *D. bimaculata* Schum). The discal cell is open in normal specimens; it is, however, adventitiously closed in some rare specimens of the North American *D. rivularis*; the same seems occasionally to take place among the European species (compare Schiner, *Ins. Austr. Diptera*, II, p. 530, where the author, speaking of the discal cell, always takes care to say "usually" absent). In other respects, the venation is the following (compare Tab. II, f. 16, wing of *D. rivularis*, ♀): the subcostal cross-vein is about the middle of the length of the wing or a little before it, at a distance from the origin of the second longitudinal vein which is somewhat variable in different specimens, but always equal to several lengths of the great cross-vein; the origin of the second longitudinal vein is a little nearer to the root of the wing than is the tip of the sixth longitudinal vein; the præfurca is very short and arcuated. The small cross-vein is opposite the tip of the sixth vein; the second submarginal cell is almost of the same length with the first posterior cell; the first submarginal cell is but little shorter than the second, as its petiole is very short; the course of the veins, bordering these cells, is nearly straight; there are two marginal cross-veins; one very nearly at the tip of the first longitudinal vein; the other not far from the origin of the anterior branch of the second vein; the stigma is between them. The anterior fork of the fourth vein, when present (in the species with five posterior cells), is always very short; the fork of the posterior branch of the fourth vein is nearly twice its length; the great cross-vein is at the same distance from the root of the wing as the small cross-vein; the fifth longitudinal vein is gently arcuated towards the tip; the sixth and seventh are nearly straight. The European species, judging by the existing figures, in all respects agree in the venation with the American ones (compare the figures of the wing of *D. pavida*, in Walker, l. c. Tab. XXX, fig. 7 a, *D. bimaculata*, ibid. fig. 7 b); *D. ruficornis* Schum., if the figure is correct (Schum. *Beitr.* etc. Tab. IV, fig. 2), has both the præfurca and the anterior fork of the fourth vein much longer than the other species. The wings of the females are distinctly broader than those of the males.

Abdomen of the male depressed, subelavate at the tip; the male forceps is analogous to that of *Amalopis* and *Pedicia* in structure ;[1] abdomen of the female more cylindrical; upper valves somewhat arcuated, moderately long and broad.

Dicranota is closely allied to *Rhaphidolabis* and *Plectromyia* by its 13-jointed antennæ and its venation; but it is sufficiently distinguished by the presence of two marginal cross-veins. While the only known species of *Plectromyia* has four posterior cells and the two species of *Rhaphidolabis* five, *Dicranota* has some species with four and others with five posterior cells. In all other respects, the similitude of the venation of these three genera, which extends to all the relative proportions of cells and veins, is very striking and indicates the closest relationship.

Two North American species are described by me. The four European species have been sufficiently adverted to above, and I am not aware of any other species of this genus ever having been published, unless it is *Limnobia stignatella* Zett. (compare the foot-note below), which may be a *Dicranota*.

The genus *Dicranota* was first proposed by Mr. Zetterstedt for his *D. guerini*, in 1840 (*Insecta Lapponica*, p. 851); but that this author did not recognize the true character of the genus appears from the fact that even in his later work *D. bimaculata* Schum. is left by him in the genus *Limnobia* (Zett. *Dipt. Scand.* X, p. 3897, 72).[1] Mr. Haliday, in Walker's often quoted work, puts three species under the head of *Dicranota: pavida* Hal. (*syn. guerini?*), *bimaculata* Schum., and *senilis* Hal. The latter, as I have already shown, in 1859, can hardly be a *Dicranota*, nor can it belong to the *Amalopina*, if Mr. Westwood's figure (Walker, l. c. Tab. XXVII, fig. 3) is correct: the subcostal cross-vein is posterior to the origin of the second longitudinal vein; there is only one marginal cross-vein, and the discal cell is present. The wings are those of *Limnophila*, but if the antennæ are really 13-jointed, it is difficult to decide where this species belongs to. In 1859 (*Proc. Acad. Nat. Sci. Philad.* p. 249) I described the first North American species of *Dicranota*, and completed the definition of the genus by noticing its pubescent

<hr/>

[1] This is repeated from *Proc. Acad. Nat. Sci. Philad.*, 1859, p. 249; I have not had any fresh specimens for examination since.

[1] In the same work, Vol. X, p. 3643, there is a *Limnobia stignatella* Z-tt., from Lapland, which seems to be a *Dicranota* with five posterior cells.

eyes, the position of the subcostal cross-vein, etc., and assigning it its true place among the Amalopina (*Pediciformia*, olim). The name of the genus is derived from δικρανος, fork.

Description of the species.

1. D. rivularis O. S. ♂ and ♀.—Obscure cinerea, thorace vittis fuscis: halteribus pallidis; antennis maris brevibus; cellulis posterioribus quatuor.

Dark gray, thorax with brown stripes, halteres pale; antennæ of the male short; four posterior cells. Long. corp. 0.28—0.3.

8yn, *Dicranota rivularis* O. Sacken, Proc. Ac. Nat. Sc. Phil. 1859, p. 249.

Head dark yellowish-gray, front and vertex slightly brownish; rostrum, palpi, and antennæ blackish; the latter short in both sexes, not reaching the base of the wings; joints of the flagellum subglobular. Thorax dark gray, with three distinct blackish-brown stripes; the intermediate one broad, and, in some specimens, distinctly divided by a longitudinal paler line; scutellum and metathorax dark gray, the posterior half of the latter blackish; halteres pale; coxæ gray, feet blackish, trochanters and basis of the femora paler. Abdomen blackish cinereous, indistinctly whitish along the lateral margins; male genitals gray. Wings (Tab. II, fig. 18, wing of the female) slightly tinged with gray; stigma indistinct, situated between the two marginal cross-veins; præfurca very short, and hence the distance between its origin and the nearest marginal cross-vein is not longer (usually shorter) than the interval between the two cross-veins.

Hab. Washington, D. C.; five males and two females were caught, early in April, in the act of flying close to the surface of a little stream in the woods; the females were in copulation.

One of the males has the discal cell closed on both wings; some of the specimens have a stump of a vein on the præfurca.

2. D. eucera, n. sp. ♂.—Obscure cinerea, thorace vittis fuscis; halteribus infuscatis; antennis maris thorace multo longiore; cellulis posterioribus quatuor.

Dark gray, thorax with brown stripes; halteres with an infuscated knob; antennæ of the male much longer than the thorax; four posterior cells. Long. corp. 0.26.

Very like the preceding species, and distinguished principally by the structure of the antennæ of the male, which are twice as

long as the head and thorax taken together, the flagellum with
nearly cylindrical, elongated, densely pubescent joints, of nearly
equal length, except the last, which is shorter. The knob of the
halteres is distinctly infuscated; the stigma, likewise, is slightly
brownish; the vertex seems to be darker than in *D. rivularis*;
the wings of the male are somewhat narrower, and the præfurca
a little longer; the interval between its origin and the nearest
marginal cross-vein, in both specimens which I have before me,
is longer than the interval between the two cross-veins.

I have two males in my possession, taken together with the
specimens of *D. rivularis*. At that time (compare *Proc. Acad.
Nat. Sci. Philad.* 1859, p. 250) I was uncertain whether they did
not belong to the latter species. I venture now to describe them
as distinct; the antennæ are of a length which is otherwise unusual in the genus.

Gen. XXXIX. PLECTROMYIA.

Two submarginal cells; four posterior cells; discal cell open; the subcostal cross-vein is a considerable distance before the origin of the second
longitudinal vein; the marginal cross-vein is very near the tip of the first
longitudinal vein (Tab. II, fig. 18). Tibiæ with exceedingly minute spurs
at the tip; empodia small, but distinct. Eyes pubescent; antennæ 13-
jointed. The upper horny appendage of the forceps of the male is flat,
rounded, with a serrate edge.

A rather broad front separates the eyes above; in well preserved dry specimens, it rises abruptly above the antennæ and is
rather convex, without showing any trace of a bump (having
neglected to describe it from a fresh specimen, I have abstained
from any statement about it in the generic character). Rostrum
short; palpi short; the first joint is the longest, the others stout,
short; the last is not much longer than it is broad. Antennæ
13-jointed (I have counted the joints on fresh specimens); first
joint elongated, subcylindrical; the joints of the flagellum, except
the first, which is subconical, are rounded, slightly elongated,
with short verticils; they are clothed with a short pubescence,
which is more dense in the male; if bent backwards, the antennæ
would not reach the root of the wings. Collare well developed,
with a short, neck-like prolongation towards the head; the mela-
notum moderately gibbose above it; thoracic suture well marked.
The feet are long (although much shorter than in *Rhaphidolabis*);

the spurs are so minute as to be perceptible only with great difficulty; the angues are very minute; the empodia distinct; the
first joint of the tarsi is about equal in length to the tibia, or
even longer (on the foremost pair of the feet); the four following
joints, taken together, are a little longer than half the length of
the first joint. The wings (Tab. II, fig. 18) are moderately
broad; the subcostal cross-vein is a little before the middle of
length of the wing, at a distance before the origin of the second
longitudinal vein equal to about two lengths of the great cross-
vein; the origin of the second longitudinal vein is a little nearer
to the root of the wing than is the tip of the sixth longitudinal
vein; the præfurca is comparatively short and arcuated. The
small cross-vein is opposite the tip of the sixth vein; the second
submarginal cell is of the same length with the first posterior
cell; the first submarginal cell is only a trifle shorter than the
second, as its petiole is short and in some specimens almost imperceptible; the course of the veins, bordering these cells, is
straight, only the anterior branch of the second longitudinal vein
is somewhat arcuated; the marginal cross-vein is at the very tip
of the first longitudinal vein, which tip is nearly opposite the tip
of the second branch of the fourth longitudinal vein; the posterior
branch of the latter vein alone is forked, and hence there are only
four posterior cells; the second of these (confluent with the discal
cell, which is open) has its basis on the same line with the small
cross-vein; the third posterior cell is much shorter; the great
cross-vein is about the middle of the distance between the bases
of the second and third posterior cells, or a little before this
middle; the fifth longitudinal vein is gently arcuated towards its
end; the sixth and seventh are straight. The abdomen is short
and comparatively stout; the male genitals are conspicuously
club-shaped; the forceps consists of a pair of subcylindrical basal
pieces, with two horny appendages upon each; the upper or outer
ones among these are rounded at the end, densely and sharply
serrated along the edge of the rounded part, thus looking like the
end of a spur; the lower or inner appendage is more slender.
The ovipositor of the female is comparatively long, moderately
broad, arcuated.

This genus, described here for the first time,[1] is very closely

---

[1] It was merely mentioned, without any description, in the synoptical
table of the genera which I gave in the *Proc. Entom. Soc. Philad.* 1863, p.

allied to *Rhaphidolabis*, but the body is less slender, the male genitals not club-shaped and of a different structure; the feet comparatively much shorter. The venation is pretty much the same in both genera, as the comparison of the descriptions will show, except that *Plectromyia* has only four posterior cells, and that the subcostal cross-vein is less near the root of the wing. The discal cell is absent in all my specimens.

The name of the genus is derived from κλῆστρον, spur, and μυῖα, fly, in allusion to the shape of the appendage of the forceps.

Description of the species.

1. **F. modesta**, n. sp. ♂ and ♀.—Fuscano-ochracea, thorace vittis subobsoletis, capite cano pollinoso, abdomine fusco; alis hyalinis immaculatis.

Brownish-ochraceous, thorax with indistinct stripes, head with a hoary bloom; abdomen brown, wings hyaline, immaculate. Long. corp. 0.17—0.18.

Ground color of the head brown, entirely concealed above by a thick hoary bloom; rostrum somewhat paler; palpi and antennæ brown. Thorax brownish-ochraceous, hardly shining above, in consequence of a dull grayish dust; three pale brown, rather indistinct stripes; the intermediate one double; stem of the halteres pale, the knob brownish; feet tawny, coxæ and basis of the femora paler, tip of the tibiæ and the tarsi brown. Abdomen brown; genitals paler. Wings hyaline, immaculate; veins brown.

Hab. White Mountains, N. H., June, 1864; five specimens.

GEN. XL. RHAPHIDOLABIS.

Two submarginal cells; *five posterior cells;* discal cell closed or open; the subcostal cross-vein is a considerable distance before the origin of the second longitudinal vein; the marginal cross-vein is very near the tip of the first longitudinal vein (Tab. II, fig. 17, wing of *R. tenuipes*). Feet long, slender; tibiæ with minute spurs at the tip; empodia small, but distinct. Eyes pubescent; the front with a bump; antennæ 13-jointed. The forceps of the male of *R. tenuipes* has long, needle-like, horny appendages.

As I have taken some notes from a living specimen of *R. tenuipes*, I consider it as the type of the genus. In the following

225. The name *Asteolabis*, which I gave it at that time, I give up as objectionable, and replace it by *Plectromyia*, a name I originally intended to give to the genus now called *Atarba*.

description, whenever I was not sure whether a character would be likewise applicable to *R. flaveola*, of which I could compare only dry specimens, I have taken care to mention that this character belongs to the typical species.

The eyes are distinctly pubescent, with a rather broad front between them above, and more closely approximated on the under side of the head; seen from the side, the front of *R. tenuipes* shows a distinct hump behind the antennæ, which is much less visible in dry specimens. The rostrum is short; the palpi (*R. tenuipes*) short, joints stout, except the basal one, which is attenuated. Antennæ 13-jointed (I have counted the joints of a fresh specimen of *R. tenuipes*), short; if bent backwards, they would not reach much beyond the collare; joints of the flagellum oblong, clothed in the male (*R. tenuipes*) with a dense, delicate pubescence, and the alternate ones with short verticils. Collare well developed, rather broad, and with a neck-like prolongation towards the head; the mesonotum rather gibbose above it; thoracic suture well marked. The feet are very long and slender (especially in *R. tenuipes*); the spurs are exceedingly short, and may be easily overlooked; the ungues are very minute; the empodia distinct (for the proportions in length of the tibiæ and tarsi, compare the description of the species). The wings (Tab. II, fig. 17, wing of *R. tenuipes*) are a little longer than the body; comparatively narrow in *R. tenuipes*; broader in *R. flaveola*; the tip of the auxiliary vein is almost opposite the tip of the fifth longitudinal vein; the subcostal cross-vein is at one-third of the length of the wing, a considerable distance before the origin of the second vein, and but a little more distant from the root of the wing than the anal angle; the præfurca is comparatively short, and very much arcuated; it is much shorter in *R. tenuipes*, where its origin is nearly opposite the tip of the sixth vein (a little anterior to it); in *R. flaveola* the origin of the second vein is opposite the tip of the seventh vein, and the præfurca is therefore a little longer. The small cross-vein is opposite the tip of the sixth longitudinal vein (*R. tenuipes*), or a little anterior to it (*R. flaveola*); the second submarginal cell is of the same length with the first posterior cell (or only a trifle longer in *R. tenuipes*); the first submarginal cell is a little shorter than the second, its petiole being shorter than the great cross-vein; the course of the veins, bordering these cells, is

straight, only the anterior branch of the second longitudinal vein
is somewhat arcuated (especially in *R. tenuipes*, where the
posterior branch is also, but very slightly, arcuated); the marginal cross-vein is very near the tip of the first longitudinal vein
(at this very tip in *R. tenuipes*); the tip of the first longitudinal
vein is opposite the tip of the third branch of the fourth longitudinal vein. Both branches of the fourth longitudinal vein are
forked; the anterior fork is very short, the second posterior cell,
which it incloses being about one-third the length of the first
posterior cell; the basis of the third posterior cell in *R. tenuipes*
(which has no discal cell), is in one line with the small cross-vein,
and rather pointed; in *R. flaveola* the third posterior cell is
divided in two by the cross-vein, which forms the subtriangular
discal cell; the fourth posterior cell is about half the length of
the first; the fifth is somewhat longer than the fourth; the great
cross-vein is a little beyond the first forking of the fourth longitudinal vein; the fifth, sixth, and seventh longitudinal veins are
nearly straight, somewhat, but not conspicuously, arcuated.

The abdomen is elongated and slender; the male genitals
rather club-shaped, consisting of the usual basal pieces, with
horny appendages; one of the latter, in *R. tenuipes*, is elongated,
needle-shaped, and conspicuous in living specimens, although not
visible in dry ones;[1] the ovipositor (*R. flaveola*) has rather long,
broad, arcuated upper valves, and blunt, without being actually
rounded at the tip; the lower valves are shorter, but also rather
broad; the ovipositor of *R. tenuipes* is likewise comparatively
long, and arcuated, but narrower and more pointed.

This genus, described here for the first time, although it was
mentioned by name in the *Proc. Entom. Soc. Philad.* 1865, p.
225, is closely allied to *Plectromyia*, but easily distinguished
from it by the greater slenderness of the body and especially of
the abdomen, which has the male genitals distinctly club-shaped;
by the structure of the male genitals, and by the venation of the
wings, which have five, instead of four posterior cells.

Although *R. flaveola* differs from *R. tenuipes* by the presence

---

[1] I add this detail from memory, as the description of the forceps, taken
down from a living specimen, has been lost with my original manuscript.
Although I have caught a specimen since, I have omitted to describe its
forceps.

of a discal cell and by its coloring, their relationship in other
respects is so great that I have no hesitation in placing them in
the same genus. Should a more detailed study of the organization of *R. flaveola* necessitate its separation, *R. tenuipes* should
be retained as the type of the genus.

I am not aware of the existence of this genus in any other
country.

The name *Rhaphidolabis* is derived from ραφις, needle, and
λαβις, forceps.

Description of the species.

1. R. tenuipes, n. sp.   ♂ and ♀.—Fusca, thoracis vittis fuscis; alis
immaculatis, cellula discoidali nulla.

Fuscous, thorax with fuscous stripes, wings immaculate; no discal cell.
Long. corp. 0.2.

Head blackish-fuscous; front gibbose, somewhat cinereous
along the eyes, darker in the middle; antennæ and palpi black.
Thorax fuscous, very little shining, and with a slight hoary
bloom; stripes dark brown, almost black; the intermediate one
cuneiform, the lateral ones prolonged beyond the suture behind;
in the darker specimens, the stripes are divided only by a grayish
bloom, visible at the humeri, and extending backwards in the
shape of a line between the intermediate and the lateral stripes;
in paler-colored specimens the stripes are well marked upon a
pale brownish yellow ground. Pleuræ, scutellum, and metathorax
brownish, more or less mixed with yellow. Halteres infuscated,
pale at the base. Abdomen fuscous, with scattered pale hairs;
forceps fuscous. Coxæ yellowish, sometimes more or less tinged
with brown; feet dark tawny; femora pale at the base. On the
foremost pair of feet of the male the first joint of the tarsi is
considerably longer than the tibia; the four following joints,
taken together, are much less than half the length of the first
joint; nearly the same proportions prevail on the two other pairs
of feet, only the first tarsal joint is not much longer than the
tibia. Wings (Tab. 11, fig. 17) with a slight grayish tinge, immaculate, veins brown; stigma long, very slightly tinged with
brownish; the præfurca is short, arcuated; its origin is a little
before the tip of the sixth longitudinal vein (for the details of the
venation compare the generic characters).

Hab. Maryland; Saratoga Springs, N. Y.

2. R. flaveola, n. sp. ♂ and ♀.—Flava tota; alis immaculatis collis discoidali instructis.

Entirely yellow; wings immaculata, with a discal cell. Long. corp. 0.2.

The whole body, including the feet, is of a pale yellow color; the thorax above, as well as the pleura, have a slight hoary bloom; the wings are hyaline, with pale brown veins, except the costa, which is yellowish; the stigma is elongated, colorless; the details of the venation have been given above, in the generic character. The first tarsal joint (in the female specimen) is about equal in length to the tibia; the four following joints, taken together, are rather more than half the length of the first (the feet of the male specimen are broken).

I possess a male, taken by me in Maryland; a female, taken by Mr. Scudder, on Mt. Greylock, Mass., is much paler in coloring, almost whitish, but agrees in all the other characters.

Section VII. CYLINDROTOMINA.

One submarginal cell; the first longitudinal vein is incurred at the tip towards the second, instead of ending in the costa (exception: *Phalacrocera replicata* Lin., where the first vein takes the usual course); four or five posterior cells; a discal cell. The auxiliary vein is abruptly interrupted, just before the stigma, without ending either in the costa or in the first longitudinal vein. Eyes glabrous. Normal number of the antennal joints sixteen.[1] Tibiæ with spurs at the tip. Empodia distinct. Forceps and ovipositor of a peculiar structure (compare below).

1. Definition and Affinities.

We have here a small, but very remarkable group of species, occupying an isolated and intermediate position between the *Tipulidæ brevipalpi* and *longipalpi*. Their affinity to the former is justified by the following characters: 1. The structure of their palpi, the last joint of which, although somewhat elongated, never has the whiplash shaped appearance peculiar to the *Tip. longipalpi*; 2. The absence of the peculiar fold which, in most of the *Tipulina*, runs across the wing, beginning in the region of the stigma; 3. The length of the inner marginal cell, which, in the majority of *Tipulina*, is much shorter; 4. The shape and position of the penultimate posterior cell, which is situated behind the discal cell, instead of being alongside of it, which is the case among the *Tipulina*; 5. The number of posterior cells which, as a rule, is *four* among the *Cylindrotomina*, five being the exception; whereas *five* is the rule among the *Tipulina*: 6. The number of antennal joints, *sixteen*, is also the prevailing number among the *Tipulidæ brevipalpi*, whereas *thirteen* is the usual number among the *Tipulidæ longipalpi*.

[1] The European authors (Walker, Zetterstedt, etc.) call the antennæ 17-jointed, which may be due to the fact that in dry specimens the prolongation of the last joint looks like an additional one.

19 November, 1868.

The *Cylindrotomina* possess other characters, however, which are foreign to the *Tip. brevipalpi*.

1. The *Cylindrotomina* have a single submarginal cell and spurs at the tip of the tibiae. The *Tip. brevipalpa* with a single submarginal cell, as far as known, never have any spurs on the tibiae.[1] The presence of these spurs is a point of affinity to the *Tipulina*. The divaricated spurs of *Phalacrocera* remind very much of *Tipula*.

2. The course of the veins immediately surrounding the stigma is very peculiar here. The first longitudinal vein, instead of ending in the costa, is incurved towards the second vein, and ends in it (fig. 4). The marginal cross-vein (usually connecting the first and second longitudinal veins and thus dividing the marginal cell in two sections) is absent; instead of it, there is a short, generally oblique and often indistinct cross-vein between the first vein and the costa (fig. 4 a); this cross-vein is inserted a short distance anterior to the tip of the first vein. A glance at the venation of a genuine *Tipula* (fig. 6) at once shows its homologies

Fig. 4.

Fig. 5.

Fig. 6.

with that of the *Cylindrotomina*. In *Tipula* the second longitudinal vein has a short fork (fig. 6, b, c), which is wanting in the *Cylindrotomina*; the first vein ends in the anterior branch of this fork; the prolongation of this anterior branch, together with a short cross-vein (a) between the first vein and the costa (which cross-vein is homologous to the above-mentioned cross-vein of the *Cylindrotomina*) inclose a small trapezoidal cell, very characteristic of the *Tipulina* (fig. 6, between a and b). To complete the resemblance, it would be necessary for the second vein of the *Cylindrotomina* to emit a short branch; and this is actually the case with the European species *Phalacrocera replicata* (fig. 5), where

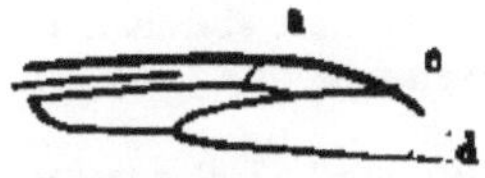

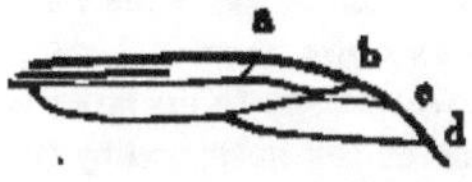

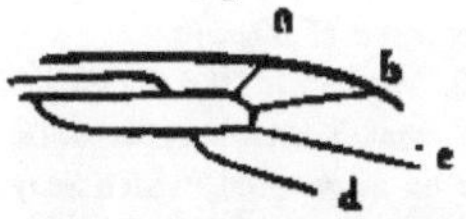

[1] Compare the genus *Atarba*, which may be an exception.

the vein *b* may bo considered as homologous to *b*, in fig. C, although it appears to be merely the prolongation of the first vein. Thus *Phalacrocera*, the general appearance, antennæ, etc. of which are so much like *Tipula*, seems also to indicate a translation towards this genus in its venation. And that this interpretation of the course of the first vein in *Phalacrocera* is not altogether arbitrary, is proved by the North American *Ph. tipulina*, closely allied to the European species, but in which, nevertheless, the first vein ends in the second, as it does in the other *Cylindrotomina*, and the branch *b* is wanting. But there are a few *Tipul. longipalpi* (for instance *Dolichopeza*) where the second vein has no fork, and then the resemblance to the *Cylindrotomina* in that portion of the venation is complete.

3. In all the specimens which I have had an opportunity to examine, the auxiliary vein does neither join the costa (as in the majority of the *Tip. brevipalpi*), nor the first longitudinal vein (as in the *Tip. longipalpi*), but it stops short abruptly, just before the stigma (compare above, the figures 4 and 5); some distance before its abrupt termination, sometimes close by it, the auxiliary vein is connected with the first longitudinal vein by a short, often indistinct cross-vein. Thus, in this important character, the *Cylindrotomina* hold the middle between the *Tip. longipalpi* and *brevipalpi*.

We may sum up the preceding examination by saying that the *Cylindrotomina*, with all the prevailing characters of the *Tip. brevipalpi*, show important aberrations in the course of the veins in the vicinity of the stigma, aberrations which prove a leaning towards the *Tip. longipalpi*. The latent affinity to the latter is further proved by the presence of spurs on the tibiæ, and by the general appearance; the coloring of the *Cylindrotomina* reminds very much of the two principal genera of the *Tipulina—Cylindrotoma* of *Pachyrrhina*, and *Phalacrocera* of *Tipula*.

If I have gone into some detail with regard to the above indicated structural homologies, it is not that I attach an absolute importance to them. New forms may be discovered, which may perhaps overthrow the supposed homologies between the venation of *Cylindrotoma* and *Tipula*; but the perusal of my statements will, I hope, in one way prove useful to those who may have to describe these new forms; it will indicate to them the characters deserving to be mentioned in their descriptions, characters which otherwise would probably be overlooked by entomologists who have not made the *Tipulidæ* their especial study.

The structure of both male and female genitals of the *Cylindrotomina* shows some peculiarities which deserve to be noticed.

In the forceps of the male *Cylindrotomina* which I have had an opportunity to examine, the claw-shaped horny appendages inserted at the tip of the movable basal pieces do not meet or overlap each other, as usual. In the state of repose they are folded backwards, like the blade of a penknife, towards the upper side of their basal pieces. A very characteristic, long, horny, linear organ, which I have called *aculeus*, usually protrudes when the forceps is opened, and sometimes remains hanging on the outside even in dry specimens. This organ consists of three slender horny styles, connate at their basis, which is especially the case with *Phalacrocera tipulina*; each of the styles has a knob at the tip in *Cyl. nodicornis* O. S. and in *Triogma*; in *Cylindrotoma americana* these styles are so far connate that the aculeus assumes the shape of a lamella with three sharp points at its tip,[1] separated by deep indentations.

The ovipositor of the female is distinguished by its short, broad, foliaceous valves, rounded at the tip. Nothing similar is to be found among the *Tipulidæ*. The ovipositor of *Cyl. distinctissima* has a still more complicated structure, which will be described in its place.

2. HISTORICAL ACCOUNT.

The history of this group is short, as the recognition of its true characters is only of recent date. The principal European *Cylindrotomina* were known for a long time before any connection was discovered between them, and on the other hand the genus *Cylindrotoma* was first established and long maintained, upon a purely artificial character, which caused many foreign elements to be introduced in it.

The genus *Cylindrotoma* has been adopted by Macquart in 1834 (*Hist. Natur. des Dipt.* Vol. I, p. 107); he formed it out of two European (*distinctissima* and *macroptera*) and a North American

<hr>

[1] The forceps of the European *Cyl. glabrata* Meig. seems to be built upon a different plan; but I cannot well judge of it from a single dry specimen. The structure of its aculeus, as far as I could perceive, is the same as in *Cyl. nodicornis* O. S.

species (*macrocera* Say). The first of these three species has remained as the type of the genus ; the second, according to the interpretation of Stæger, Loew, and others, is synonymous with *Ula pilosa* Scham. ; the third is a *Limnophila*. The only character which has induced Macquart (compare Macq. *Dipt. Exot.* I, p. 67) to separate these species from *Limnobia*, and to place them under a common generic appellation, is the structure of their antennæ, which have elongated, cylindrical joints.[1] In the *Diptères Exotiques* the same author added three more species to the genus, all of which are *Eriocera*, and have antennæ of an entirely different structure (*arrostarta* Wied., from Java, *ruficornis* Macq, and *erythrocephala* Wied., both from Brazil)! This shows the vagueness of Macquart's conception of the genus he was introducing.

Stæger (*Kröyer's Tidskr.* III, p. 36) based his definition of *Cylindrotoma* likewise on the structure of the antennæ.

In 1849 Mr. Loew described *Cylindr. nigriventris* from Siberia. He observes correctly that *C. distinctissima* has to be considered as the type of the genus, and that the two other species, added by Macquart, do not belong to it. Nevertheless, the four species found by the same author in amber and mentioned by him as *Cylindrotomæ* (*Cb. d. Bernstein und die Bernstein-fauna*, 1850), belong all to the genus *Limnophila*.

Mr. Zetterstedt (*Dipt. Scand.* X, p. 3900; 1851) placed *Ula pilosa* in the genus *Cylindrotoma*, together with *C. distinc-tissima*; at the same time *Trioyma exsculpta* and *Phal. repli-cata* are left among the *Limnobiæ*, although their relationship to *Cylindrotoma* is noticed (l. c. page 3879).

Mr. Haliday (in Walker's *Insecta Britannica, Diptera*, III, p. 312; 1856) gave a detailed account of the generic characters of *Cylindrotoma*, in which the peculiarities of the venation are correctly stated.

This recognition of the true characteristics of *Cylindrotoma* could not be considered as completed as long as this genus was not placed in the same group with *Limnobia trisulcata* and

[1] It is singular that Macquart in characterising the genus calls the antennæ 12-jointed, whereas the figure he gives of *C. distinctissima* shows 17 joints. His figure of *C. macroptera* shows 13 joints, in conformity to the description, and if this statement is correct, the species cannot be *Ula pilosa*.

Limnobia replicata Lin. This step was taken by Dr. Schiner
(*Wiener Ent. Monatschr.* 1863, and *Fauna Austriaca*, 1864).
He pointed out this relationship, proposed for these species the
new genera *Triogma* and *Phalacrocera*, and gave to the whole
group the name of *Limnobina cylindrotomiformia*.

In 1865 (*Proc. Entom. Soc. Philad.* Vol. IV, p. 224) I described for the first time North American insects of this group;
four species, belonging to the three above-named genera. The
position assigned to the *Cylindrotomina* in the present publication differs from that which they occupy in Dr. Schiner's work,
next to the *Limnobina anomala*. This change of place is intended
to indicate the affinities between the *Cylindrotomina* and the
Tipulina; it has the further advantage of removing the *Cylindrotomina* from among the spurless *Tipulidæ*, and placing them
in the midst of those which are provided with spurs.

3. DISTRIBUTION IN GENERA.

Dr. Schiner has distributed the European *Cylindrotomina*
among three genera: *Triogma*, with one species (*T. trisulcata*
Schum.); *Phalacrocera*, with *P. replicata* L., and *Cylindrotoma*
with *C. distinctissima* M., glabrata M., nigriventris Loew, and
diversa Walk. *C. glabrata*, however, by the structure of its
antennæ, of its male forceps, and by its venation, is sufficiently
distinct from *C. distinctissima* to be set up as a separate genus.
The two remaining species of *Cylindrotoma* I have not seen, but
judging from the description of one of them, *C. nigriventris*, it
is closely allied to *C. distinctissima.*

Among the North American species we have in *Triogma exsculpta* O. S. a form closely analogous with *T. trisulcata;* in
Cylindrotoma americana O. S. a form almost identical with
C. distinctissima. The coloring of *C. nodicornis* O. S. is so
much like that of the European *C. glabrata*, that, at first glance,
they might be taken for the same species; and one is surprised
to find, upon examination, that they show not unimportant differences in the structure of the antennæ, of the male genitals,[1] and
in the venation of the wings. The forceps of *C. nodicornis* O. S.,

---

[1] I have seen but one dry specimen of *C. glabrata*, ♂, and can but imperfectly judge of its forceps. It would be interesting to investigate
whether it is really so different from the typical form of the *Cylindrotomina*
as it appears to me.

the absence of the small cross-vein on the wings, and the sculpture of the thorax remind of *Triogma* so much, that before I
had seen *C. glabrata*,, I preferred to place *C. nodicornis* in the
genus *Triogma*, rather than to connect it with *C. americana*
(compare my description of this species in *Proc. Entom. Soc.
Philad.* 1865). The fact is that these species represent a grada-
tion which baffles every attempt at a generic arrangement.
The North American *Phalacrocera tipulina* O. S. shows an
important difference in the venation from the typical *Phalacrocera*, the European *P. replicata;* but the resemblance in their
coloring and general appearance is very great.

In order to avoid the establishment of a new genus for almost
every species known, which would probably necessitate a similar
process for every species to be discovered hereafter, I have preferred to retain Dr. Schiner's three genera, although since the
discovery of the North American species those genera rest more
upon the general appearance of the insects than upon characters
which admit of a strict definition. Acting upon this principle,
I have placed in the genus *Cylindrotoma*, the insect which I had
described in 1865 under the name of *Triogma nodicornis*.

4. Larva.

The early stages of the *Cylindrotomina* seem to be as anomalous as the structure of the perfect insect. The larva of *C. distinctissima*, instead of being found underground, or in decayed
wood or in fungi, like most tipulideous larvæ, assumes the habits
and more or less the exterior of a lepidopterous larva, and lives
upon the leaves of certain plants. The larva of *Phalacrocera
replicata*, still more singular in structure, lives under water, upon
water plants (more details about both larvæ will be given below).

5. Geographical Distribution.

Besides the six species from the old world and the four from
North America, which have been mentioned on the preceding
pages, no other described *Cylindrotomina* can be named here
with any degree of certainty. *Cylindrotoma albitarsis*, from
Java, described by Doleschall, *Natuurk. Tijdschr. Nederl. Indie*,
Vol. XIV, p. 15, Tab. IV, fig. 1, can hardly be a *Cylindrotoma*,
and its venation seems to show some analogy to that of *Limnobia
trentepohlii* Wied. (*Auss. Zw.* I, p. 551, Tab. VI, 6, fig. 12), from

Sumatra. About *Cylindr. ornatissima* Doleschall, from Amboina
(l. c. Vol. XVII, p. 60), I have no opinion, and I may say the
same about *Cylindr. hyaloptera* Philippi, from Chile (*Verh.
Zool. Bot. Ges. in Wien*, 1865, p. 614). The descriptions of both
species are too short to enable me to judge whether these species
are really *Cylindrotoma* or not.

Gen. XLI. CYLINDROTOMA.

First longitudinal vein incurved at the tip towards the second and ending in it (and not in the costa) ; a marginal, a submarginal, a discal, and
five posterior cells.[1] Antennæ 16-jointed, *joints subcylindrical, elongated ;
first joint short, not longer than the second*. Eyes bare, separated by a
rather broad interval above and below the head. Tibiæ with distinct spurs
at the tip. Empodia distinct. Forceps of the male with claw-shaped
horny appendages, which, in the state of repose, are folded backwards,
like the blade of a penknife, towards the upper side of their basal pieces :
a long, narrow, linear lamella, deeply tridentate at the tip, protrudes when
the forceps is opened. Coloring yellow, with black stripes and spots.

Head rather broad posteriorly. Proboscis very short ; palpi
somewhat elongated, last joint elongated ; in *C. americana* it is
about equal in length to the two preceding joints taken together.
The antennæ of the male with elongated, almost cylindrical joints ;
finely pubescent, with short, thin, rather scattered verticils ; those
of the female shorter, less pubescent. In both sexes, the first
joint is remarkable for its shortness. Collare moderately developed. Thorax short, stout. Feet slender ; spurs at the tip
of the tibiæ of moderate length ; fore coxæ short ; empodia distinct ; excision at the basis of the last tarsal joint of the male, on
the under side, rather small, and this joint not particularly
modified. Abdomen long, slender, conspicuously club-shaped at
the tip, in the male ; the long, narrow, linear, horny lamella, which
usually protrudes when the living insect opens its forceps, ends
in three sharp points. The ovipositor of the female of *C. distinctissima* has a very peculiar structure. It is rather large ; the
upper valves are lamelliform towards the tip, and the lower ones
are curved in such a manner as to leave a considerable empty
space between them and the upper ones. Although I have not
seen the female of *C. americana*, I have no doubt, from its close

[1] *Four in Cyl. nodicornis* O. S. ; it will be explained below, that this
generic character applies only to the typical species, *C. distinctissima* and
americana.

resemblance to the European species, that the ovipositor has a similar structure. The peculiarities of the venation, compared to that of the other *Tipulidæ*, have been explained in the general remarks on the *Cylindrotomina* (p. 290); the auxiliary vein stops short abruptly, and is somewhat indistinctly connected near its tip with the first longitudinal vein; the latter, instead of ending in the costa, is incurved towards the second longitudinal vein, and ends in it; a more or less indistinct cross-vein connects it with the costa; the second longitudinal vein forms with the third a fork, neither of the branches of which is in a straight line with the præfurca (a different structure of this fork characterizes *Phalacrocera*); the small cross-vein is always present and not rendered obsolete, as in *Triogma*, by the contact of the sub-marginal with the discal cell; the discal cell is elongated, and its inner end is nearer to the root of the wing than the inner end of the submarginal cell; of the three veins emitted by the discal cell towards the margin of the wing, the anterior one in the European *C. distinctissima* and in *C. americana* has a branch-vein, including one more posterior cell, of which these species have thus *five* instead of *four*. (Judging by Dr. Schiner's expressions about this character, it seems as if it was not altogether constant, and that occasionally specimens of *C. distinctissima* with *four* posterior cells occur; but this must be a very rare exception.)

The generic character, as defined above, applies to the European *C. distinctissima* and the American *C. americana*. *Cylindrotoma glabrata* M. and *nodicornis* O. S. have been included in the genus, in order to avoid the necessity of introducing a new one (compare above, p. 295). They differ from the typical species in the following characters: the first joint of their antennæ has the usual elongated shape, and is distinctly longer than the second; the antennæ of the male are of an entirely different structure; the head is more narrowed posteriorly, the thorax less short and differently sculptured; the tip of the abdomen of *C. nodicornis* O. S. is narrower and less conspicuously club-shaped; the lamella of the forceps consists of three linear, horny styles, connate at their bases, and each with a small knob at the tip; the ovipositor of the female consists of four broad valves, rounded at the tip, and joined to each other without leaving an open interval between them; the discal cell is much shorter, and

Its inner end is farther from the root of the wings than the inner end of the submarginal cell; the small cross-vein, although present in *C. glabrata*, is wanting in the majority of the specimens of *C. nodicornis*; and lastly, there are *four*, instead of *five* posterior cells.

However much *C. glabrata* and *nodicornis* may differ from *Triogma* in their general appearance and in their coloring, they have more affinity to this genus than to the typical *Cylindrotoma*. This affinity appears: in the structure of the antennæ, the sculpture of the thorax, the shape of the discal cell, the number of posterior cells, the structure of the lamella of the male forceps. The American *C. nodicornis* O. S. differs from *C. glabrata* in having, in normal specimens, the submarginal cell in close contact, at the basis, with the discal cell (Tab. I, fig. 7, wing of *C. nodicornis*), in consequence of which the small cross-vein is wanting. The same is the case with both species of *Triogma*. In the *Proc. Entom. Soc. Philad.* 1865, p. 239, I did not hesitate to locate *C. nodicornis* in the genus *Triogma*; but at that time I had not seen the European *C. glabrata.* It will be necessary ultimately to establish a new genus for these two species (it may be called *Liogma*, from the character of the furrows which are more smooth than those of *Triogma*). But I abstain from characterizing this genus, as I am not quite certain about the position of *C. nigriventris* Loew, and *diversa* Walk., which I have not seen.

The word *Cylindrotoma* is derived from κύλινδρος, cylinder, and τέμνω, I cut, in allusion to the shape of the antennal joints of the typical species.

The larva of *Cylindrotoma distinctissima* lives on the under side of the leaves of different plants, as *Viola, Anemone, Stellaria*, and eats elongated holes in them; it is green, elongated, flattened, linear, but little attenuated at both ends, with a longitudinal crest along its back, consisting of a row of fleshy processes, pointing backwards; the lateral margin is broad, with many excisions, formed by fleshy points. The larva, before transforming, leaves the plant upon which it fed, and fastens itself to some grass-stalk, upon which it undergoes the pupa state. The pupa is not unlike that of some Lepidoptera; the thorax bears several horny processes. The first description and the only figure of this larva have been given by Schellenberg (*Genres de*

Monches Dipteres, 1803, Tab. XXVII), a circumstance which has been entirely overlooked since, probably because this author took the insect for a *Pachyrrhina*). Bole (*Krijer's Tidskr.* 11, p. 234; 1834) made a short mention, and Zeller (*Isis*, 1813, p. 808) gave the best description of the larva.

Description of the species.

1. C. americana O. S. ♂.—Flava, capite flavo, thorace nigrofasciato, antennarum articulis subcylindricis, elongatis; cellulis posterioribus quinque.

Yellow, head yellow, thorax striped with black, antenna with subcylindrical, elongated joints; five posterior cells. Long. corp. 0.45.

SYN. *Cylindrotoma americana* O. SACKEN, Proc. Entom. Soc. Phil. 1865, p. 236.

Head pale yellow, rounded and but little attenuated posteriorly; a pale brown spot on the vertex; palpi brown; the antennæ, if extended backwards, would reach the end of the second abdominal segment; two basal joints pale yellow, the first not much longer than the second; third joint yellow at the extreme basis only, elongated, cylindrical; the following joints brown, a little shorter than the third, elongated, subcylindrical, slightly attenuated at the basis; they are nearly of the same length to the end of the antenna; the flagellum is clothed on both sides with a delicate and dense pubescence, among which some longer, but also very delicate verticills are scattered. Thorax pale yellow, opaque above, with a black, opaque stripe in the middle, reaching from the scutellum to the collare, and divided longitudinally by a very narrow yellow line; the lateral stripes are dark brown, sometimes pale brown, abbreviated anteriorly and reaching beyond the suture posteriorly; a brown spot on the pleuræ, between the root of the wings and the collare and another brown spot on each side of the sternum, between the first and second pair of coxæ; halteres pale, dusky at tip; feet yellow, tarsi brown towards the tip. Abdomen brownish-yellow, darker along the lateral margins; its tip (in the male) is rather stout, club-shaped. Wings hyaline, very slightly tinged with yellowish-cinereous; stigma short, pale; the præfurca and the remaining portion of the second vein are almost of equal length; the first vein ends in the second at about the middle of the outer section of the latter; submarginal cell a little longer than the first pos-

terior; small cross-vein short; discal cell rather large, elongated;
its inner end pointed and nearer to the basis of the wing than
the inner end of the submarginal cell; the posterior end of the
discal cell emits four veins towards the margin; the anterior
among these veins is very arcuated at its basis, so that the cell it
forms seems to be curved out of the first posterior cell; great
cross-vein somewhat beyond the basis, but before the middle of
the discal cell; fifth longitudinal vein incurred at the tip (more
structural details about this species have been given among the
generic characters).

Hab. White Mountains, N. H., end of June, 1864; two male
specimens.

Observation I. I have not seen the female of this species, but
I suppose that its antennæ are a little shorter and its wings somewhat smaller; at least these characters distinguish the female of
C. distinctissima. I suppose also that in the American species,
as in the European, the venation may be somewhat variable, and
that in some cases the second posterior cell may be petiolate,
instead of sessile.

Observation II. I will mention here some peculiarities of the
suture of the thorax of this species, which I have omitted in
its description, as unimportant for its recognition. The thoracic
transverse suture is marked by a very delicate groove in the
shape of a Y or of a fork, the two ends of which run parallel
towards the collare, and the handle reaches the scutellum; a
transverse impression on each side connects this fork with the
sides of the thorax, near the root of the wings, and thus com-
pletes the transverse suture. These slender grooves on the
thoracic dorsum foreshadow the more distinct sculpture of *Triogma.* The scutellum in both genera has two distinct pits near
its basis.

Observation III. The European *C. distinctissima* is almost
identical with *C. americana.* The three specimens of the former,
which I can compare, show the following differences: the dark
spot on the head and the stripes of the thorax are not brown, but
of an opaque black; there is a black spot, divided in two parts by
a fine longitudinal yellow line, on the posterior part of the metathorax (there is no vestige of such a spot in *C. americana*); the
feet are also of a darker coloring, and the tips of the femora and of
the tibiæ are distinctly infuscated; the wings have a more distinct

grayish tinge, and the stigma is likewise more distinctly colored.
The paleness of my two American specimens may be accidental;
still, they would show at least a vestige of the spot on the metathorax, if it occurred in better-colored specimens.

2. C. medicornis O. S. ♂ and ♀.—Obscure flava, capite nigro,
thorace nigro-vittato, antennis moniliformibus, articulis earum brevibus, subcordiformibus; cellulis posterioribus quatuor.

Dark yellow, head black, thorax with black stripes, antennæ moniliform,
their joints short, almost heart-shaped; four posterior cells. Long. corp.
0.4—0.42.

Syn. *Triogma medicornis* O. Sacken, Proc. Entom. Soc. Phil. 1865, p. 239.

Head black, shining; palpi brownish; antennæ dark brown,
reaching a little beyond the basis of the abdomen in the male and
somewhat shorter in the female; two basal joints and the basis
of the third brownish-yellow; first joint cylindrical, of moderate
length; the second short; the joints of the flagellum, especially
the middle ones, are not much longer than broad, expanded on
the under side so as to appear almost heart-shaped, and connected by short pedicels, so as to make the antenna appear
moniliform; the last joint is abruptly narrower than the preceding and about twice its length, subcylindrical; it shows a
coarctation in the middle, which is more apparent in some (fresh)
specimens than in others, and then the antennæ may be taken for
17-jointed; in the female the joints of the flagellum are much
less expanded, and only seven or eight intermediate joints have a
strikingly heart-shaped appearance; towards the tip, they become
gradually narrower; in both sexes, the antennæ are clothed with
a soft, dense, pubescence, much denser on the under side, and
much more striking in the male than in the female; besides, each
joint has several verticils about the middle. Thorax honey-
yellow, with three black, shining, often confluent stripes; sternum
between the first and second pairs of coxæ, black, shining; this
black coloring is extended upwards, across the pleuræ, in the
shape of a black, but not shining stripe; a black opaque spot
near the base of the halteres, aciculate on its surface; metathorax,
or at least its posterior part, black, its surface rugose (very dark
specimens, with confluent thoracic stripes, have all these spots
and stripes darker and more extended; those specimens, on the
contrary, which have the thoracic stripe separated by yellow,

especially towards the scutellum, have also the other black marks
smaller in extent and paler in coloring, often pale brown, and the
sternum is black on the sides only, yellow in the middle). A well-
marked groove extends from the scutellum along the middle of
the intermediate stripe, and is interrupted long before reaching
the collare; the intervals between the intermediate and the lateral
stripes are rugose-punctate. Halteres pale, knob dusky. Feet
brownish-yellow; tip of the femora, of the tibiæ, and of the two
first tarsal joints, infuscated; two or three last tarsal joints
brown. Abdomen brownish, last segments darker, venter paler;
genitals brownish-yellow. Wings (Tab. I, fig. 7) tinged with
brownish-cinereous; stigma elliptical, brownish; submarginal cell
longer than the first posterior; discal cell of variable, generally
of moderate size, nearly quadrangular; four posterior cells;
position of the great cross-vein variable, sometimes a little before,
sometimes a little beyond the inner end of the discal cell; the
small cross-vein is usually wanting, that is, the inner end of the
submarginal cell is more or less contiguous to the inner end of
the discal cell; the extent of this contiguity is variable in different specimens; sometimes the small cross-vein is present, but
then it is short (among twenty-one specimens which I have compared, only four had the cross-vein); the fifth longitudinal vein is
incurved at its tip.

Hab. Washington, D. C.; New York; White Mountains, N. H.;
Illinois (LeBaron); New Jersey (Cresson). Not rare in May
and June.

The aculeus of the male forceps is very often projecting in the
dry specimens of this species. It consists, as observed on p.
299, of three horny, slender styles, connate at the basis, separated
and somewhat club-shaped at the tip.

The resemblance between this species and the European *C.
glabrata* M. is complete, as far as their coloring is concerned;
and it is therefore the more remarkable that they should differ so
much in some structural details. The antennæ of the male *C.
glabrata* are much shorter; if extended backwards, they would
not extend much beyond the roots of the wings; the joints are
short subcylindrical, attenuated at the basis. The wings are
distinctly longer, and the submarginal cell is not in contact with
the discal cell, so that the small cross-vein is present. The

forceps, as I have already alluded to above (p. 294), seems to
have a different structure.

Gen. XLII. TRIOGMA.

First longitudinal vein incurved at the tip towards the second and ending in it (and not in the costa); a marginal, a submarginal, a discal, and
four posterior cells; *the small cross-vein is wanting*, the submarginal cell,
at its inner end, being in immediate contact with the discal cell. Antennæ
16-jointed; first joint elongated; joints of the flagellum short subcylindrical or subglobular, attenuated at the basis; broader in the male than
in the female. Eyes glabrous, separated by a rather broad interval above
and below. Tibiæ with distinct spurs at the tip. Empodia distinct.
Forceps of the male analogous to that of *Cylindrotoma*; the aculeus is
three-branched, the single branches with a knob at the tip. The ovipositor
of the female has short, broad valves, obtuse at the tip. Coloring dull
brownish or grayish; head and thorax conspicuously sculptured with deep
punctures.

Head rather broad posteriorly; proboscis and palpi rather
short. The antennæ of the male have more rounded joints of
the flagellum than those of the female; they are clothed on the
under side with a delicate pubescence; in the female these joints
are rather subcylindrical; in both sexes each joint is attenuated
at the basis, and there are short verticils about the middle of
each (I possess only the male of *T. trisulcata*, and the female
of *T. exsculpta*). The collare is moderately developed, in the
shape of a transverse fold. The thorax of the two species at
present known is sculptured in a manner quite unusual among
the *Tipulidæ*, and even among the Diptera in general; there is
a more or less distinct groove running from the collare backwards,
along the middle of the mesonotum; on each side of it, there is
a densely rugoso-punctate stripe; the upper part of the metathorax is also densely rugoso-punctate. Feet rather strong, fore
coxæ short, spurs at the tip of the tibiæ of moderate length;
empodia large, distinct; last joint of the tarsi in the male only
slightly excised at the basis on the under side, and its shape not
modified. The forceps of the male is very much like that of
Cylindrotoma. Although I have not had the opportunity to
examine the forceps of living specimens, I could perceive in the
dry specimen of a male *T. trisulcata* the presence of a three-
branched aculeus, with knobs at the end of the branches, similar

to that of *Cyl. nodicornis* O. S. The ovipositor of the female has short, broad, obtuse valves.

The principal feature of the venation, the course of the first longitudinal vein, which does not end in the costa, but is incurred at the tip towards the second vein, is the same here as in *Cylindrotoma*. The auxiliary vein ends abruptly at the inner end of the stigma, and has but an indistinct connection with the first longitudinal vein (I perceive this in *T. exsculpta* only). A slight vestige of an oblique cross-vein connects the latter part of the first vein with the costa. The absence of the small cross-vein seems to be a peculiarity of this genus; the inner end of the submarginal cell thus comes in immediate contact with the discal cell.

The relationship of *Triogma* and *Cylindrotoma* is very great, and the principal differences consist in the structure of the antennæ, the number of posterior cells, and the absence of the small cross-vein in the former genus; in the shape and sculpture of head and thorax, and in the general coloring.

This genus was proposed by Dr. Schiner, in 1863, for the European *Limnobia trisulcata* Schnm.; the North American species is an exactly analogous form. These two species are the only ones of the genus at present known.

The name of the genus is derived from τρεις, three, and τυπος, furrow, in allusion to the thoracic furrows.

Description of the species.

1. T. exsculpta O. S. ♀.—Fusca, alis infuscatis; thorace apice medio impresso; vittis ejus lateralibus, capite metanotique parte anteriori rugoso-punctatis.

Brown, wings tinged with brownish; thorax with an impressed groove in the middle; its lateral stripes, the anterior part of the metathorax, and the head are rugoso-punctate. Long. corp. 0.37.

Syn. *Triogma exsculpta* O. Sacken, Proc. Entom. Soc. Phil. 1865, p. 239.

Whole body dull brown; front and vertex rugoso-punctate, with a longitudinal furrow in the middle; palpi brown; antennæ, basal joints brown, flagellum paler, joints of the latter subovate. Thorax with a deep longitudinal furrow in the middle; the lateral stripes are marked by a deep, irregular punctation; from the anterior part of these rugoso-punctate stripes a similar punctation extends backwards, along the sides of the mesonotom; the anterior part of the metathorax is deeply rugoso-punctate, and some parts of the pleura are also punctate. Halteres dingy brownish-tawny; coxæ brown, feet tawny, clothed with black hairs. Abdomen brown. An indistinct cross-vein connects the latter part of the first longitudinal vein with the costa; discal cell elongated, quadrangular; stigma indistinct, colorless.

Hab. Pennsylvania (Cresson); a single female specimen.

This species is very like the European *T. trisulcata* in its sculpture, but is manifestly different from it. The coloring of the European species is more blackish than brownish; the hind port of the pleuræ, the anterior part of the metathorax, and the basis of the coxæ are yellow, the antennæ and feet are darker, the stigma is brownish, etc.

Gen. XLIII. PHALACROCERA.

First longitudinal vein incurved at the tip towards the second and ending in it (*P. tipulina*), or ending in the costa and connected with the second by a cross-vein (*P. replicata*); a marginal, a submarginal, a discal, and four posterior cells; the anterior one of the three short veins connecting the discal cell with the margin is arcuated, in consequence of which the first posterior cell is attenuated at the basis (and not square, as usual); a distinct small cross-vein is present. Antennæ 16-jointed; first joint elongated, joints of the flagellum elongated, almost cylindrical, with short verticils. Eyes glabrous, separated by a rather broad interval above and below. Tibiæ with distinct spurs at the tip. Empodia distinct. Forceps of the male analogous to that of *Cylindrotoma*; the scabrous is three-branched, the branches connate at the basis, pointed at the tip; valves of the ovipositor broad. Body brownish, head and thorax grayish, without any conspicuous punctures.

Dr. Schiner established this genus, in 1863, for the European *P. replicata*, which is easily distinguished from all the known *Cylindrotomina* by the course of the first longitudinal vein ending in the costa and being connected with the second vein by a short cross-vein. But it became much more difficult to define this genus since the discovery of the North American *P. tipulina*, which does not possess this character. In this species the first vein is incurved towards the second and ends in it, just as it does in all the other *Cylindrotomina*. The affinity of the two species is otherwise evident, and in their sculpture, coloring, and general appearance, they are sufficiently distinguished from the other

20   November, 1868.

Cylindrotomina, to form a separate genus. (Compare the general remarks on the genera of this section, p. 295.)

The head is somewhat attenuated posteriorly; the palpi of *P. tipulina* have the last joint elongated, longer than the two, but shorter than the three preceding taken together. The first joint of the antennæ is cylindrical, elongated; the second cyathiform; the joints of the flagellum (in *P. tipulina*) are elongated, cylindrical, slightly incrassated near the basis; the verticils are upon this incrassation, and therefore before the middle of the joint. These antennæ have exactly the same structure as the antennæ of many *Tipula*. In *P. replicata*, the joints of the flagellum are not incrassated at the basis, and the exceedingly short verticillate hairs are inserted in the middle of the joint; thus the likeness to *Tipula* is not so striking. Besides the verticils, the antennæ of the male of *P. tipulina* have a dense, delicate pubescence. The collare is somewhat more developed and broader in *P. tipulina* than in *P. replicata*. The thorax has the stout, compact shape, common to the *Cylindrotomina*; the thoracic suture is well marked, grooved in the middle, more shallow on the sides; the intervals between the thoracic stripes are somewhat depressed, but shallow and not marked with a groove or with conspicuous punctures; two distinct impressions at the basis of the scutellum. Feet long and rather strong; spurs long, divaricate; empodia distinct; last joint of the tarsi in the male distinctly excised at the basis on the under side.

The forceps of the male is very much like that of *Cylindrotoma;* the claw-shaped horny appendages are turned, in the state of repose, towards the upper anterior margin of the abdominal segment; the aculeus consists of three horny styles, connate at the basis, sharp and pointed at the tip (I have seen only the aculeus of *P. tipulina*). The ovipositor of *P. replicata*, according to Dr. Schiner, is short, with broad foliaceous valves.

The venation is somewhat different in the two only known species. The difference in the course of the first longitudinal vein has been alluded to above; I have also shown before, when speaking of the general characters of the *Cylindrotomina* (p. 290), that it would be perhaps a more correct interpretation of the course of the first vein of *P. replicata*, if we considered this vein as ending in the second vein, and the latter emitting a branch towards the anterior margin. The venation of *P. replicata* viewed

In this way, would be analogous to that of most *Tipulæ*. The præfurca (in *P. tipulina*) forms a perfectly straight line with the third vein; the remaining portion of the second vein looks therefore as if it was emitted from this continuous vein; it is almost angular at the basis, and emits from this angle a short stump of a vein, projecting inside of the marginal cell; owing to this peculiar course of the second vein, the submarginal cell is square at its inner end, which is in a straight line with the inner end of the first posterior cell.

In *P. replicata* the third vein is much less conspicuously in a straight line with the præfurca; the remaining portion of the second vein is gently arcuated, and not angular at its inner end; there is no stump of a vein upon it; the submarginal cell is distinctly longer than the first posterior, and hence, their inner ends are not in one line. In both species the second posterior cell is attenuated at the inner end, its line of contact with the discal cell being very short; in some specimens (according to Dr. Schiner's statement) this cell is actually. petiolated; the discal cell is elongated; the fifth longitudinal vein is abruptly incurved towards the margin at its tip; the sixth is straight; the seventh nearly so; the posterior margin of the wing has the propensity to fold (hence the name of the European species *P. replicata*).

Heretofore, only the two above-named species of *Phalacrocera* have been described. The name of the genus is derived from φαλακρος, bald, in allusion probably to the almost glabrous antennæ of the European species.

The larva of *P. replicata* has been described by Degeer, Vol. VI, p. 351, Tab. XX. It lives in the water, among aquatic plants and mosses, is greenish-brown, bearing a number of long, soft and flexible filaments, looking like spines. It remained all winter in the larva state, although a crust of ice formed on the vessel which contained it. In May, the larva transformed into pupa and floated in this state on the surface of the water. The posterior end of the pupa has several pairs of hooks, by means of which it can seize the stems of the plants and descend below the surface of the water.

Description of the species.

1. **P. tipulina** O. S. ♀.—Fuscescens, capite et thorace supra obscure cinereis, hoc obsolete vittato, pleuris canis; vena longitudinalis prima in secundam, non in costam, excurrit.

Brownish; head and thorax dark cinereous above, the latter with obsolete stripes; the first longitudinal vein ends in the second, not in the costa. Long. corp. 0.55.

Syn. *Pholacrocera tipulina* O. Sacken, Proc. Entom. Soc. Phil. 1863, p. 241.

Head considerably narrowed posteriorly, blackish above, with a yellowish-cinereous bloom and a small reddish spot in the middle of the vertex, posteriorly; the under side of the head is brownish; proboscis brownish-yellow; palpi brown; the antennæ, if extended backwards, would reach the end of the second abdominal segment; they are dark brown or black; the first half of the first joint and the basis of the third are reddish; the first joint cylindrical, elongated; the second short; the third and the following joints are elongated, cylindrical, somewhat incrassated on their anterior half, and with the verticils inserted on that incrassation; the flagellum is clothed on both sides with a very short and soft pubescence (the structure of the antennæ is remarkably like that of some *Tipula*). Thorax above with a yellowish-cinereous bloom, concealing the blackish ground color; the latter is more apparent in the place of the usual stripes, whereas the cinereous bloom is more dense in the somewhat impressed intervals between the stripes; sternum black between the first and second pairs of coxæ and this black color extends upwards, in the shape of a stripe over the pleuræ; a black spot near the basis of the halteres; the remaining portion of the pleuræ brownish-yellow; the whole of the pleuræ is covered with a dense hoary bloom, so that their black portions are visible in a certain light only; collare rather broad, brownish; scutellum and metanotum brownish-yellow, the latter with a yellowish, shining reflection; halteres dusky; coxæ yellowish, with a hoary bloom; femora tawny, yellowish at the basis, and infuscated at the tip; tibiæ brownish, darker at the tip; tarsi brown. Wings with a brownish-cinereous tinge, stigma pale brownish, small, oblong (the venation has been described among the generic characters). The first longitudinal vein in this species, as in all the *Cylindrotomina*, is incurved towards the second, and has, at some distance before the tip, a rather indistinct, slender, oblique cross-vein connecting it with the costa.

Hab. White Mountains, N. H.; two male specimens.

Section VIII. PTYCHOPTERINA.

Only a single longitudinal vein posterior to the fifth vein ; two submarginal cells. Labium largely developed ; palpi long. Tibia with spurs at the tip. Thoracic suture deeply sinuate.

The five known genera of this section form two distinct groups, distinguished by the following characters :—

1. No subcostal cross-vein ; first submarginal cell much longer than the second ; three or four posterior cells ; collare obsolete ; a peculiar, small spatulate, membranaceous, ciliated organ at the foot of the halteres : *Ptychoptera, Bittacomorpha.*

2. A subcostal cross-vein is present ; the second submarginal cell is much longer than the first ; the number of posterior cells is raised to six, in consequence of the presence of a supernumerary longitudinal vein in the first posterior cell ; collare large : *Protoplasa, Tanyderus, Macrochile.*[1]

Ptychoptera alone occurs in Europe : it is common to that continent and to America ; *Bittacomorpha* and *Protoplasa* have been found in North America only ; *Tanyderus* in South America ; *Macrochile* is included in the Prussian amber.

This section is the most aberrant of all the *Tipulidæ.* The venation shows peculiarities not found elsewhere ; the large development of the labium, the prolonged epistoma, the deeply sinuate thoracic suture, etc., separate the *Ptychopterina* entirely from the rest of the family, and the latter character may be indicative of a relationship to the *Blepharoceridæ.*

Gen. XLIV. PTYCHOPTERA.

Two submarginal cells, the first much longer than the second : no subcostal cross-vein ; no discal cell ; four posterior cells, the second very short ; only a single longitudinal vein after the fifth vein (Tab. II, fig. 19,

---

[1] I do not know about the collare of *Macrochile.*

wing of *P. rufocincta*). Antennæ 15-jointed; last joint very small. Tibiæ with strong, divaricate spurs at the tip; empodia large. Thoracic suture deeply sinuate. Abdomen of the male club-shaped at the tip, with a coriaceous, often apparently double, forceps.

Head transverse, sessile; epistoma projecting, subtriangular, rounded at the tip; proboscis with very large suctorial flaps; palpi very long; last joint whiplash-shaped, once and a half the length of the three preceding joints taken together, or longer; among the three first joints the second is the longest.[1] Eyes large, separated by a broad space on the upper and on the under side of the head. The antennæ of the male are comparatively long; bent backwards, they reach somewhat beyond the basis of the abdomen; those of the female are shorter; they are sixteen-jointed; scapus short, the first joint being but little longer than the second; the first joint of the flagellum is cylindrical, twice the length of the second; the following joints are almost cylindrical, slightly decreasing in length towards the tip, clothed with a microscopic down, and with scattered, verticillate hairs; the last joint is very small in the European species; in the American *P. rufocincta* it is hardly perceptible even in fresh specimens. The collare is small, almost obsolete, concealed under the somewhat projecting mesonotum; the latter is gibbose; the thoracic suture forms a deep sinus in the middle, the bottom of which nearly reaches the scutellum; the sides of this sinus are prolonged anteriorly in the shape of furrows, as far as the anterior margin of the mesonotum; the metathorax is large, convex. The abdomen of the male is narrow and rather abruptly club-shaped at the tip; the forceps of *P. rufocincta*, which I have examined upon a fresh specimen, has the following structure: the last dorsal segment of the abdomen has a strong excision in the middle; under it is the forceps, which consists of an elongated, curved, coriaceous outside lobe, and an inner piece, apparently horny, fastened to the lobe; between the two halves of the forceps, the horny aculeus is visible. In the European species the tip of the abdomen shows four rather long, projecting appendages, having

---

[1] In describing the generic character, I had, besides *P. rufocincta*, specimens of the European *P. albimana* and *contaminata* before me. Some data, for instance those on the forceps and on the palpi, are taken from a fresh specimen of *P. rufocincta*; its palpi, when extended backwards, could almost reach the second abdominal segment.

the appearance of a double forceps; but the upper pair seems to
represent the last dorsal segment of the abdomen, only very much
excised, and with the sides developed into elongated, forceps-like
appendages. Interpreted in such a manner, the structure of the
forceps in the American and in the European species is perfectly
homologous. The abdomen of the female is also narrowed at
the basis, broader in the middle; the upper valves of the ovipositor of *P. rufocincta* are broad, convex above. Feet rather
strong, especially the hind tibia and tarsi; coxæ moderately developed; tibiæ with strong, divaricate spurs at the tip; the
tarsal joints in the male are attenuated at the extreme basis,
which is not the case in the females; the fourth tarsal joint of the
male has the basis incrassated, and with a tuft of hair; the ungues
are very small, the empodia rather large and not linear, as usual
among the *Tip. brevipalpi*, but short and transverse. Wings
of moderate breadth, in some species comparatively broad; the
surface is clothed with a microscopic pubescence, visible under a
lens of moderate power, and especially dense in the apical portion.
The peculiarities of the venation are numerous; the principal
ones are: the absence of the subcostal cross-vein; the length of
the first submarginal cell, which is usually twice the length of the
second; in other words, it is not the second longitudinal vein
which is forked, as in most *Tipulidæ brevipalpi*, but the third; the
central cross-veins are nearly in the middle of the wing; there is
no discal cell; the anterior branch of the fourth vein alone is
forked, and this fork is very short; the latter portion of the fifth
vein is bisinuated; a striking fold, almost like a spurious vein,
runs along the last longitudinal vein, crosses the anal cell, and
ends at the tip of the fifth vein; beyond the fifth longitudinal
vein, there is only a single vein, and not two, as in all the *Tipulidæ brevipalpi*; this vein apparently represents the seventh
longitudinal vein, the sixth being obsolete; it is strongly arcuated
at the tip (compare the wing of *P. rufocincta*, Tab. II, fig. 19).
In the first posterior cell there is a longitudinal fold, which has
not attracted any attention before, but deserves to be noticed, as
it seems to foreshadow the supernumerary longitudinal vein,
which, in *Protoplasa* and its congeners, divides the first posterior
cell in two parts. This fold is especially distinct in the European
P. albimana, where it assumes the appearance of a spurious vein,
abruptly terminating somewhat beyond the inner end of the

second submarginal cell; it is much weaker in *P. contaminata* and in the North American *P. rufocincta.*

The venation of the three species which I have seen (*P. albimana, contaminata, rufocincta*) is pretty much the same; only in *P. albimana* the præfurca is shorter and the first submarginal cell is not sessile, but has a short petiole. The American *P. rufocincta* has also a very short præfurca.

Mr. Westwood (*Introd.* II, p. 526) was the first to call attention to a singular organ in the shape of a membranaceous, spatulate, small appendage, ciliated on the margin (Westw., l. c., fig. 126, 7), and inserted at the foot of the halteres of *Ptychoptera.* I notice the same appendage in *Bittacomorpha,* but none in *Protoplasa.* Its use or homology is unknown; it has nothing in common with the tegulæ, which are usually inserted more in front of the halteres.

Five European species are known; a sixth, *P. pectinata* Macq. (*Hist. Nat. Dipt.* I, 75), from the North of France, is distinguished by the antennæ being pectinated, as in *Ctenophora.* It seems to be very rare; Mr. Roudani introduced for it the new genus *Ctenocerria.* The American species, *P. rufocincta,* is quite common. I have never found *P. 4-fasciata* Say (*Long's Exped.* etc. p. 359), also described by Wiedemann; nor *P. metallica* Walker (*List,* etc. I, p. 80), from Hudson's Bay. No *Ptychopteræ* from any other part of the world seem to have been published.

The insects of this genus are found in the vicinity of stagnant waters, where their larvæ live. The larvæ and pupæ have very early attracted the attention of naturalists, and have been often figured (Réaumur. *Mém.* Vol. V; Lyonnet, *Œuvres posthumes,* Tab. XVIII, fig. 1–7; Van der Wulp, *Handel. Nederl. Entom. Ver.* I, 1, p. 31; Lacordaire, *Introd. à l'Entom.* Tab. II, fig. 5; Tab. V, fig. 20, gives a copy of Lyonnet's figure). The larvæ have a long tube at the end of the body, which they raise to the surface of the water for breathing. In the pupæ, one of the horny processes, which distinguish the thorax of all the pupæ of *Tipulidæ,* is enormously prolonged, likewise for the purpose of breathing under water (compare p. 10).

The genus *Ptychoptera* (from πτυχή, fold, and πτερόν, wing) has been introduced by Meigen, in 1803 (*Illiger's Magazin,* II, p. 262).

Description of the species.

1. P. rufocincta O. S. ♂ and ♀.—Nigra, antennæ, basi ex. epid, nigra; epistoma fulvum; pedes fulvi; abdomen nigrum, fasciis ferraginosis; alis maculis basali et famelis tribus fuscis.

Black, antennæ, except the basis, black; epistoma fulvous, feet fulvous; abdomen black, with ferruginous bands; wings with a brown basal spot and three brown bands. Long. corp. 0.28—0.32.

Syn. *Ptychoptera rufocincta* O. Sacken, Proc. Ac. Nat. Sc. Phil. 1859, p. 232.

Head black, shining, proboscis and epistoma reddish-yellow; basal joints of the antennæ brownish; flagellum black. Thorax black, less shining than the head; pleuræ reddish-yellow; a silvery reflection is sometimes perceptible upon them; halteres pale, somewhat dingy; feet reddish-yellow; tips of the femora, of the tibiæ, and the larger part of the tarsi brown; the first joint of the posterior tarsi yellowish. Abdomen black, with ferruginous bands, which occupy the anterior portion of the segments; the last segments, including the forceps and the ovipositor, are reddish-yellow; the venter is yellowish. Wings with a brown spot at the basis, an abbreviated pale brown band across the middle of the two basal cells; another band along the central cross-veins, reaching the fifth longitudinal vein; a third band, consisting sometimes of two unconnected spots at the inner end of the two forks, in the apical portion of the wing; the interval between the costa and the first vein is more or less brownish. These bands, especially the last, are sometimes very weakly marked. Præfurca very short, arcuated; first submarginal cell sessile or nearly so.

Hab. United States, not rare. Pennsylvania; Washington, D. C.; Dobb's Ferry, N. Y.; Virginia (Dr. Wilson); Quebec (Couper); Illinois (LeBaron); White Mountains, N. H., etc.

Gen. XLV. BITTACOMORPHA.

Two submarginal cells, the first much longer than the second; no submental cross-vein; no dimal cell; three posterior cells, the inner cells of which are nearly in one line; only a single longitudinal vein after the fifth vein (Tab. II, fig. 20). Antennæ 20-jointed. Tibiæ with small spurs at the tip; first joint of the tarsi very much incrassated; empodia distinct. Thoracic suture deeply sinuate. Abdomen slender, very elongated, with a forceps consisting of four coriaceous, digitiform, somewhat curved appendages (Tab. IV, fig. 31, 31 a).

Head rather large, transverse, applied to the thorax with a

rather broad surface; epistoma narrow, very much prolonged, pointed at the end; proboscis with large suctorial flabs; palpi very long, all the joints being elongated. Eyes large, separated by a moderately broad interval on the upper side of the head, and a broader one on the under side. The antennæ of the male are twice the length of the head and the thorax, or more; first joint very small; the second but very slightly larger; the flagellum is filiform, and consists of (apparently 19) subcylindrical joints of nearly equal length; only the first is a little longer; it is clothed with a microscopic down, without any longer hairs. The thorax is very small in comparison to the size of the body; the collare is not visible, the head being in contact with the mesonotum; the thoracic suture is deeply sinuate in the middle; the metathorax is large and convex. The abdomen of the male is long and narrow, attenuated at the basis; the forceps (Tab. IV, fig. 31, from below, 31 a from above) consists of two pairs of digitiform, somewhat curved coriaceous appendages.

The ovipositor of the female, which I have not observed on living specimens, does not show the usual horny, pointed valves. I perceive only a pair of small, very little projecting valvules, apparently of a thin, coriaceous consistency, sickle-shaped, rounded at the tip. Feet long, femora remarkably slender, especially on their basal half; tibiæ somewhat stouter than the femora, with small spurs at the tip; the first joint of the tarsi is somewhat longer than the four following taken together, incrassated, spindle-shaped; the second joint is once and a half the length of the third; the fourth and fifth are very small, and their length, taken together, is hardly equal to the third joint; the empodia are broad, transverse. Wings shorter than the abdomen, small and narrow for the size of the insect; glabrous, hyaline; the stigma is hardly indicated by a narrow streak along the first longitudinal vein; the tip of the auxillary vein is opposite the tip of the fifth vein; no subcostal cross-vein; marginal cross-vein at the tip of the first longitudinal; præfurca very short; first submarginal cell nearly three times the length of the second; three posterior cells, none of the branches of the fourth vein being forked; the inner ends of the first submarginal and of the three posterior cells are nearly in one line; the section of the fifth posterior vein beyond the great cross-vein is bisinuated (as in *Ptychoptera*); only one longitudinal vein beyond the fifth; the two basal cells do not reach much beyond the middle of the wing (Tab. 11, fig. 20).

The peculiar membranaceous, spatulate, ciliated appendage, inserted at the foot of the halteres, and observable in *Ptychoptera*, exists also in *Bittacomorpha*.

The relationship of *Bittacomorpha* and *Ptychoptera* is very great and evident, all the difference of the outward appearance notwithstanding. A rather large, transverse head, closely applied to the thorax, a pointed epistoma, long palpi, large lips, a small antennal scapus, a sinuate thoracic suture, an almost obsolete collare, a large metathorax, the spatulate appendage, are characters common to both genera. The male forceps of both have a similar structure; the venation is almost the same; if we suppress the fork, inclosing the second posterior cell of *Ptychoptera*, we obtain the venation of *Bittacomorpha*.

The only known species of the genus, *B. clavipes*, was first described by Fabricius, as *Ptychoptera clavipes*, in 1781. Mr. Westwood erected the genus *Bittacomorpha* for it (*Lond. and Edinb. Philos. Mag.* 1835, p. 281). It has been found in North America only.

The name is derived from *Bittacus*, a neuropterous insect, and μορφή, shape, on account of a slight resemblance between the two genera.

Description of the species.

1. B. clavipes Fab.   ♂ and ♀.—Nigra, mesonoti villa, metathorax, pleurisque albis; pedibus albofasciatis.

Black, a stripe on the mesonotum, the metathorax and the pleura white; feet banded with white.   Long. corp. 0.55.

Syn. *Tipula clavipes* Fabricius, Spec. Insect. II, 404, 19; Mantissa Ins. II, 323, 21; Ent. Syst. IV, 239, 25.
   Ptychoptera clavipes Fabricius, Syst. Antl. 22, 4.—Wiedemann, Auss. Zweifl. I, p. 69.
   Bittacomorpha clavipes Westwood, Lond. and Edinb. Philos. Mag. 1835, p. 281.

Head silvery white in front, vertex black on both sides; proboscis, palpi, and antennæ brownish-black; thorax velvet black above, with a white longitudinal line in the middle of the mesonotum; pleura silvery white, sericeous; metathorax likewise; scutellum yellowish; halteres with a brownish knob; femora

pale at the basis, their latter half blackish; tibiæ black, with a
brown ring near the basis; first joint of the tarsi black, white at
the basis; the second and the third white; the two last joints
black; abdomen brownish-black, the posterior margins of the
segments, beginning with the second, paler. Wings hyaline.
Hab. North America, not rare. Newfoundland, common
(Westw.); Nova Scotia (Brit. Mus.); Washington, D. C., not
rare; Upper Wisconsin River (Kennicott); Florida, where I
caught it in March. This insect occurs early in the spring and
also, but more seldom, in autumn; usually in the vicinity of
water, especially in woody localities. A number of *Billaco-
morphæ*, flying slowly, as they do, and keeping their feet, variegated with snow-white, extended like the radii of a circle, present
a very striking appearance.

Gen. XLVI. PROTOPLASA.[1]

Two submarginal cells, the second much longer than the first; a subcostal cross-vein at the tip of the auxiliary vein; a discal cell; *six posterior cells, in consequence of the first being divided in two by a supernumerary
longitudinal vein; the penultimate posterior cell contains a supernumerary
cross-vein; only a single longitudinal vein after the fifth vein; anal angle
projecting, square.* Antennæ 15-jointed. Tibiæ with spurs at the tip.

Head elongated; eyes separated by a moderately broad front
above, almost contiguous on the under side of the head; epistoma
longer than broad; the proboscis, together with its large, fleshy
flabs, is not much shorter than the head; palpi longer than the
head, joints elongated.[4] Antennæ (♀?) apparently 15-jointed,

---

[1] I possess two, somewhat injured specimens of *P. fitchii*. Only a single
antenna seems to be entire, and I count 15 joints upon it. One of the
specimens has no head; the neck of the other is so twisted that I did not
perceive its length, until my attention was called upon it by the description of *Tanyderus Philippi*; this is the reason why the length of the neck
is not mentioned in *Proc. Acad. Nat. Sci. Philad.*, 1859.

[4] In *Macrochile Loew* (comp. below) the length of the palpi is dependent
on the elongation of all the joints, not of the last chiefly, as in *Ptychoptera*.
The second and the last joints are represented by Mr. Loew as being of
equal length, and somewhat longer than the first and the third. In *Tanyderus Philippi*, likewise, all the joints are elongated, the last not being
much longer than the preceding ones. As far as I can perceive, the palpi
of *Protoplasa* have a similar structure, although I cannot describe them
accurately from a dry specimen.

not longer than the head and proboscis taken together; first joint
very short; second stout, subglobular; flagellum gradually
attenuated; its first joint is attenuated at the basis, a little
longer than broad; the following two or three joints are short,
square; the next ones are somewhat more oval, elongated; the
flagellum is clothed with moderately long hairs. Collare extended
into a long neck; thoracic suture (as far as I can perceive on my
specimens) deeply sinuate; scutellum large, very much projecting;
metathorax usually small. Abdomen rather short, stout. Feet
moderately long and stout; tibiæ armed at the tip with moderately long, strong, divaricate spurs; empodia indistinct; ungues
smooth.[1] Wings (Fig. 7) broad, with a very projecting, square
anal angle; the venation
is very peculiar; auxiliary
vein comparatively short,
reaching but little beyond
the middle of the wing; subcostal cross-vein at its tip;
the first longitudinal vein

Fig. 7.

reaches far beyond the auxiliary vein; there is no marginal cross-
vein, and hardly any vestige of a stigma; the origin of the præfurca
is unusually near the basis of the wing; it has a conspicuous stump
of a vein on its curvature; the first submarginal cell is less than
half so long as the second; the first posterior cell is a little
shorter than the second submarginal; it is divided longitudinally
in two halves by a supernumerary vein, which starts from the
middle of the small cross-vein and runs parallel to the two ad-
joining longitudinal veins; discal cell very long, in the shape of
a narrow triangle, truncate at the tip; its inner end, as well as
the inner ends of the two last posterior cells are somewhat anterior
to the inner end of the first posterior cell; the penultimate posterior cell is formed by the last branch of the fourth vein (or the
posterior intercalary vein, comp. p. 34), which, in this case, issues
alone by the inner end of the discal cell; this penultimate posterior
cell has a supernumerary cross-vein in its middle; the fifth vein
is somewhat angular, the sixth nearly straight; the spurious cell
is very large, triangular; in consequence of the great length of

[1] The two last statements are repeated from *Proc. Acad. Nat. Sci. Philad.*
1859; I cannot well verify them now, as there is only a single foot left.

the cells in the apical portion of the wing, the basal cells are short; the first is longer than the second.

I am uncertain about the sex of my specimens, as the tip of the abdomen shows no trace either of a forceps or of an ovipositor; I am inclined to think that they are females, and that the ovipositor of this genus has very short, almost indistinct horny appendages, or none at all.

The next relatives of *Protoplasa* are, the amber genus *Macrochile* Loew, and the Chilian genus *Tanyderus* Philippi.

Tanyderus Philippi (*Verh. Zool. Bot. Gesellsch.* in *Wien*, 1865, p. 780, Tab. XXIX, fig. 57) shows, in almost all respects, the greatest resemblance to *Protoplasa;* the same large suctorial flabs and long palpi; long neck; projecting scutellum; venation almost identical; anal angle likewise square, only more pointed; the wings pictured in a similar manner. The only differences which I can discover are: the antennae are longer and consist of at least twenty-five joints, the last ones being difficult to count; the first vein and both branches of the second vein are very much arcuated, whereas they are nearly straight in *Protoplasa;* there is no supernumerary cross-vein in the penultimate posterior cell, but there is one in the first posterior cell (which does not exist in *Protoplasa*). "The abdomen of the male," says Dr. Philippi, "ends in two filaments." As this author had only one of the sexes before him, did he not mistake the female for a male? *Tanyderus* is represented by a single species, *T. pictus*, from Chile.

Macrochile Loew (*Linnaea Entomologica*, Vol. V, p. 402, 1851, Tab. II, fig. 24) is also remarkably like *Protoplasa;* nearly the same venation, the same square anal angle,[1] long proboscis, large lips, and long palpi. The only striking difference in the venation is, that the supernumerary cross-vein in the penultimate posterior cell, which distinguishes *Protoplasa*, is wanting here, as in *Tanyderus*, and that the præfurca is rounded near its origin, and has no stump of a vein. The eyes of *Macrochile*

---

[1] From *teino*, to extend, and *dips*, neck.

[2] From *makros*, large, and *xeilos*, lip.

[3] This is not mentioned in Mr. Loew's description, nor represented on his figure, but I have ascertained it on the original specimens, which I have seen. The statement about the structure of the antennæ, which I make further below, I owe to a written communication of Mr. Loew.

are contiguous above the antennæ, which are likewise longer
than those of *Protoplasa*, and nineteen-jointed; their structure
is nearly the same; the collare is short, and in this respect
Macrochile differs from the two other genera. *Macrochile* is
represented by a single species, *M. spectrum*, found in the Prussian amber.

Macrochile, *Protoplasa*, and *Tanyderus* thus form a group of
closely allied genera, distinguished by the presence of a discal
cell, of a supernumerary longitudinal vein in the first posterior
cell, the great length of the second submarginal cell in comparison
to the first, the shortness of the basal cells, and some other very
striking characters.   That they are more closely allied to the
Ptychopterina than to any other known group of *Tipulidæ* is
proved by the presence of only six longitudinal veins, by the
large development of the auctorial flabs, the great length and
structure of the palpi, and the sinuosity of the thoracic suture
of *Protoplasa*.   *Ptychoptera* and *Bittacomorpha* have no discal
cell, the second submarginal cell is only half so long as the first,
and the first posterior cell is not divided in two by a superna-
merary longitudinal vein, although this vein is foreshadowed by
a fold which appears in its place in *Ptychoptera*.

The genus *Protoplasa* (from κρῶτος, the first, and πλάσω, to
form, in allusion to its relationship to a species belonging to a
previous geological period) has been introduced by me in the
Proc. Acad. Nat. Sci. Philad. 1859, p. 252.

Description of the species.

1. P. Gichii O. S.—Fuscano-cinerascens; alis maculis ocellaribus
brunneis in fascias confluentibus ornatis.

Brownish-gray; wings banded with brown, the bands consisting of confluent brown spots. Long. corp. 0.3—0.36.

Syn. *Protoplasa fitchii* O. Sachsu, Proc. Ac. Nat. Sc. Phil. 1859, p. 252.

Head grayish, epistoma, proboscis, and palpi brownish; antennæ paler.   Thorax brownish-gray, opaque, stripes hardly
visible; halteres with brown knobs; feet yellowish; knees, the
tips of the tibiæ, of the first tarsal joint, and of the tarsi brown.
Abdomen brownish; posterior margins of the segments paler.
Wings whitish, with a brown picture occupying nearly the
whole surface; on all the cross-veins and at the origins and the

tips of the principal veins the brown of this picture is paler, forming ring-like spots or ocelli; the principal ones of these ocelli are: one, at the origin of the præfurca, connected with a brown spot, occupying the greater part of the base of the wing; another at the inner end of the first posterior cell, a third on the great cross-vein, and a fourth on the supernumerary cross-vein in the penultimate posterior cell; these three ocelli form a part of a broad brown band, running from the anterior to the posterior margin; the two next ocelli (one at the inner end of the first submarginal vein, the other at the posterior end of the discal cell) form, with two small ocelli on the hind margin of the wing, a second band, running across the wing; this band emits a branch which runs towards the tip of the wing and fills the whole apical portion of the double first posterior cell; there are some small ocelli along the apical margin of the wing.

I possess two specimens of this insect, for which I am indebted to Dr. Fitch; I am not aware of the precise locality, where they were taken; but it was probably either in the State of New York, or in the Green Mountains of Vermont. As stated above, I am in doubt as to the sex of these specimens.

APPENDIX I.

SPECIES DESCRIBED BY PREVIOUS AUTHORS AND NOT CONTAINED IN THE PRESENT MONOGRAPH.

Say, Journal of the Academy of Natural Sciences in Phila-
delphia, III, p. 28.

Limnobia humeralis.

Dusky, beneath pale; wings hyaline, immaculate.
Inhabits Pennsylvania.

Antennæ fuscous, first joint and rostrum dull yellowish; front
and vertex dull cinereous; thorax dark livid; humerus, two
obsolete lines, and lateral margin as far as the wings yellowish;
pleura and pectus pale yellow; scutel and metathorax color of
the thorax; nervures dark brown, corresponding in arrangement
with Meigen's fig. 2, pl. 6; feet dark brown; tergum dull yellowish, with a black line; venter white.

Length, two-fifths of an inch (fem.).

Say, Long's Expedition, Appendix.

Page 339. Ptychoptera 4-fasciata.

Wings hyaline, with four brown bands.
Inhabits Pennsylvania.

Head and thorax blackish-brown; antennæ, palpi, mouth and
hypostoma, except near the base of the antennæ, whitish; wings
with four brown, subequidistant bands, of which the third reaches
the inner margin and the others are abbreviated; pleura, pectus,
and feet yellowish-white, the incisures of the latter dusky.

Length to the tip of the wings nearly half an inch.

This species is infested by a parasite of the genus *Ocypete.*
It occurred in June.

21 November, 1868.   (321)

Page 360. **Trichocera scutellata.**

Dark fuscous, scutel whitish.

Inhabits Northwest Territory.

Palpi blackish; thorax slightly tinged with livid; anterior angles and neck segments dull yellowish-piceous; scutel dull whitish; wings immaculate, whitish at base; polsers white, with a fuscous capitulum; coxæ and thighs at base, dull yellowish. ♂ and ♀. Length of the body three-twentieths of an inch. Taken, in September, at the falls of Kakabikka, beyond Lake Superior. The posterior margin only of the scutel is dull yellowish-white in the male. This species seems to be closely allied to *T. parva* Melg.

Wiedemann, Aussereuropaische Zweiflügelige Insecten, Vol. I, p. 29.

Limnobia gracilis.

Brunnea, glabra; thoracis lateribus, pleuris abdominisque segmentis mediis apice flavidis.

Saftbraun, glatt; Seiten des Rückenschildes, der Brust und Spitze der mittleren Hintereibsabschnitte gelblich. ♀ Linien lang; ♂.

Pennsylvania.

Fühlerwurzel gelblich, Geissel braun. Untergesicht lichtgelblich. Stirne und Hinterhaupt braun. Rückenschild saftbraun, glatt; Schultern und Selten lichtgelblich, Brustseiten und Brust gleichfalls; Schildchen und Hinterrücken saftbraun. Hintereib viel länger als die Flügel, saftbraun, an der Wurzel mit weisslichen Flecken; erster Abschnitt am längsten, an der Spitze, wie auch der zweite und dritte, gelblich; folgende an den Einschnitten sehr schmal und wenig merklich weisslich; After gelblich; Bauch saftbraun mit gelblichen Einschnitten. Flügel wenig gelblich, mit braunem Randmale; Adern wie Meigen's Tab. VI. fig. 2. Schwinger gelblich, mit braunem Knopfe. Beine saftbraun.

(*Translation.*)—Brown, glabrous; sides of the mesonotum, pleura, and the posterior margins of the intermediate abdominal segments yellowish. Male seven lines long.

Basis of the antenna yellowish, flagellum brown; under side of the face pale yellowish. Front and vertex brown. Thorax brown above, smooth; humeri and margins of the mesonotum pale yellowish, pleura and

sterunm likewise; scutellum and metathorax brown. Abdomen much
longer than the wings, brown, with whitish spots near its basis; the first
joint is the longest; its posterior margin, as well as that of the second
and third joints, yellowish; the following joints have narrow and but little
perceptible whitish margins; tip of the abdomen yellowish; venter brown,
with yellowish margins of the segments. Wings but slightly yellowish,
with a brown stigma; veins like Meigen, Tab. VI, f. 2. Halteres yellowish, with a brown knob; feet brown.

A. Fitch, *Winter Insects of Eastern New York.*

Trichocera brumalis.

Brownish-black; wings and legs pallid at their bases; poisers
blackish; their pedicels whitish.

Length of the male 0.18; of the female 0.25, the wings ex-
panding twice these measurements.

Thorax with an obscure grayish reflection. Abdomen in the
male cylindrical, slightly narrower towards the tip; in the female
elongated oval and pointed at the tip; each segment with a
strongly impressed transverse line in its middle, and the posterior
margin elevated into a slight ridge. Ovipositor fulvous, sometimes tinged with blackish. Wings hyaline, faintly tinged with
dusky; inner margins ciliated with quite short hairs; nervures
blackish. Legs very long, slender and fragile, blackish; femora
brown, gradually paler towards their bases.

Common in forests in the winter season, coming out in warm
days, flying in the sunshine and alighting upon the snow, its
wings reposing horizontally upon its back, when at rest. Even
when the temperature is below the freezing point and the cold so
severe as to confine every other insect within its coverts, it may
be met with abroad, upon the wing. It is a plain, unadorned
species, closely allied in its characters to the European *T. hie-
malis*, but in a number of impaled specimens before me I can
detect no stripes or bands upon the thorax, whilst the very obvious character of the legs and wings, being pallid at their bases,
I do not find mentioned as pertaining to that species.

Macquart, Diptères Exotiques, Vol. I, 1, p. 66.

Limnophila carbonaria Bon.

Thorace nigro; alis fuscis, maculis fasciisque hyalinis.
Tête testacée; parties postérieure du front brune. Museau

court. Trompe et palpes bruns. Antennes : les premiers articles
d'un fauve brunâtre; les autres brunâtres; premier assez court;
troisième et suivants oblongs, ovales; les derniers manquent.
Thorax d'un noir luisant; côtés d'un brun luisant. Abdomen
manque. Pieds : hanches fauves, ainsi que les cuisses antérieures:
le reste manque. Balanciers bruns. Ailes brunes: une point
blanc à la base des cellules basilaires; une tâche hyaline avant la
base de la marginale; une bande hyaline avant la base de la
sous-marginale; l'intérieur de la discoïdale et des postérieures
hyalin; deux marginales, deux sous-marginales; deuxième postérieure assez petite, à long pétiole.   (De la Caroline.)

(*Translation.*)—Thorax black; wings brown, with hyaline spots and
bands.

Head tentaceous; back part of the front brown. Rostrum short; proboscis and palpi brown. Antennæ: first joints brownish-fulvous; the
others brownish; the first rather short, the third and following oblong,
oval; the last joints are wanting. Thorax black, shining; pleuræ brown,
shining. The abdomen is wanting. Feet: coxæ fulvous, as well as the
fore femora; the remainder is wanting. Halteres brown. Wings brown;
a white dot at the inner end of the basal cells; a hyaline spot before the
inner end of the marginal cell; a hyaline band before the inner end of the
submarginal cell; the inside of the discal and of the posterior cells is
hyaline: two marginal and two submarginal cells; the second posterior
cell is short, with a long petiole.   (From Carolina.)

*Walker, List of the Specimens of the Dipterous Insects in the
    Collection of the British Museum, Vol. I.*

Page 60. Ptychoptera metallica.

Nigro-ænea, abdomine apice fulvo, pedibus fuscis, femoribus
fulvis, alis cinereis.

Body black; head and chest bronze; abdomen bronze black,
tawny at the tip; legs brown, pubescent; thighs tawny, with
brown tips; wings gray, tawny along the fore border; veins
brown; poisers dull tawny. Length of the body 3 lines, of the
wings 8 lines.

St. Martin's Falls, Albany River, Hudson's Bay.

Some of the characters of this species differ from those of the
other *Ptychopteræ*: the fifth longitudinal vein extends beyond
two-thirds of the length of the wing, and there joins the fore
border, the fourth is adjacent to the fifth till near the tip, and
after emitting a branch, which runs parallel to it, is forked beyond

three-fourths of the length of the wing; the forks are very short
and one joins the fore border, the other joins the branch before
mentioned; the latter, soon after its origin is divided, and its
lower branch is again divided; at the source of its first division
a short cross-vein joins it to the third, which is forked near the
tip of the wing; the second is simple, but is joined to the third
by a cross-vein, which has an outward angle, whence a vein proceeds to the hind border, near the tip of the wing; the first is
forked.

Page 52. Chlonea aspera, n. sp.

Obscure fulva, hirsutissima, antennis nigris, pedibus fulvis.

"Body dark tawny, very hairy; eyes black; feelers black, beset
with long hairs, tawny at the base, a little longer than the head;
legs tawny, long, stout, and very hairy. Length of the body 9 lines.
"St. Martin's Falls, Albany River, Hudson's Bay."

Chlonea scita, n. sp. Fem.

Pallide fulva, hirsuta, antennis nigris.

Body pale tawny, longer and more slender than that of the
preceding species, and much less hairy; eyes black; feelers black,
less hairy than those of C. aspera, longer than the head; legs
tawny, paler, more slender, less hairy, and a little longer than
those of C. aspera.

Page 54. Trichocera bimacula, n. sp.

Cano fulva, thorace cano trivittato, abdomine fusco fasciato,
antennis tarsisque fuscis, pedibus fulvis, alis limpidis, fusco bi-
maculatis.

Head and chest overspread with a slight hoary bloom; head
tawny, palpi and eyes black, feelers brown, slender, pubescent,
more than half the length of the body; chest brown, three indistinct hoary stripes on the disk of the shield; breast tawny, abdomen with alternate tawny and brown rings; legs tawny, slender,
pubescent; knees and feet brown; wings colorless, with two
small pale brown spots on the disk; veins brown; poisers tawny.
Length of the body 9 lines; of the wings 5 lines.

Nova Scotia. From Lieut. Redman's collection.

Trichocera gracilis, n. sp. Fem.

Nigra, gracilis, pedibus fuscis, alis subcinereis, immaculatis.

Body black, slender, dull; scutcheon and breast piceous; feelers black, nearly half the length of the body; legs brown; wings slightly gray, not spotted; veins black; poisers tawny, with piceous knobs. Length of the body 2 lines; of the wings 5 lines.

New York Factory. Presented by Dr. Rae.

Walker, Diptera Saundersiana.

Page 434.   Div. L   Meig. Dipt. I, p. 131, Tab. V, fig. 6.

Limnobia turpis, Fœm.

Nigro-fusca; antennæ setaceæ, moniliformes, thorace breviores; caput et thorax cinereo tomentosa; abdomen piceum, apice fulvum; pedes fulvi, femoribus tibiisque apice, tarsisque nigris; alæ subcinereæ, venulis transversis infuscatis.

Blackish-brown. Antennæ black, setaceous, moniliform, rather shorter than the thorax. Head and thorax with cinereous tomentum. Abdomen piceous, tawny at the tip. Oviduct cylindrical, rather long. Legs tawny; tarsi and tips of the femora and of the tibiæ black. Wings grayish; veins brown, testaceous towards the base; transverse veinlets clouded; stigma brown. Halteres testaceous. Length of the body 5 lines; of the wings 10 lines.

Canada.

Page 434. Div. a.

Mediastinal vein at a little before two-thirds of the length of the wing; subcostal ending at about three-fourths of the length, connected with the radial by a transverse veinlet at its tip; radial and cubital springing from a common petiole, which is less than half their length, and which forms a right angle near its base; radial forked near its base; cubital forming near its base a very obtuse angle, whence proceeds the first externo-medial; the latter is rectangular near its base and is forked towards its tip, and is connected with the third externo-medial by two transverse veinlets; the outer one of these forms a slight angle, whence proceeds the second externo-medial vein; third externo-medial connected with the subanal by a transverse veinlet, which joins the middle of the hind side of the discal areolet.

Limnobia biterminata, Förm.

Fulva; antenum fuscæ, setaceæ, pilosæ, submoniliformes, basi fulvæ; abdomen fuscum, basi fulvom; pedes testarel, longi, graciles; alæ subcinereæ, venis fuscis, venulis transversis opud costam nebulosis; halteres testacei.

Tawny. Antennæ brown, setaceous, pilose, submoniliform, tawny at the base, not half the length of the thorax. Abdomen brown, tawny at the tip. Legs testaceous, long, slender. Wings very slightly grayish; veins brown, testaceous at the base; transverse velulots towards the costa clouded with brown. Halteres testaceom. Length of the body 6 lines; of the wings 10 lines. United States.

Page 457. Div. s.

Structure of the wing-veins much like that of Div. N. Melg. Dipt. I, p. 188, Tab. VI, fig. 5, but the petiole whence spring the radial and cubital veins forms a right angle and emits the stump of a vein near its base, and the veinlet between the third externo-medial vein and the subanal is nearer the middle of the hind side of the discal areolct, which is as long as the second externo-medial vein.

Limnobia ignobilis, Förm.

Cinerea; caput antice fulvum; palpi and antennæ nigræ basi fulva; antennæ setaceæ, non moniliformes, thorace multo breviores; thorax fusco trivittatus; latera pectusque cana; abdomen subtus fulvum, apice rufescens; pedes fulvi; alæ subcinereæ, venulis transversis fusco subnebulosis.

Cinercous. Head tawny in front. Palpi and antennæ black, tawny at the base. Antennæ setaceous, not moniliform, much shorter than the thorax. Thorax with three brown stripes; sides and pectus hoary. Abdomen tawny beneath, reddish at the tip; oviduct rather long. Legs tawny; tarsi blackish (?). Wings grayish; veins black, tawny at the base; transverse velulets slightly clouded with brown. Halteres tawny. Length of the body 5½ lines; of the wings 12 lines.

North America.

Zetterstedt, Diptera Scandinaviæ, Vol. X, p. 3777.

Erioptera fascipennis.

Grisea; antennis obscuris; alis cincreo-hyalinis, undique villo-
sulis, fasciâ nubeculari abbreviatâ, brunneâ; halteribus albidis.
♂ ♀. Long. ♂ 2½, ♀ saltem 3 lin.
Zett. Ins. Lapp. 881, 9, etc.
Tota griseo-fusca, opaca, pubescens. Antennæ obscuræ. Oculi
nigri. Palpi fusci, articulo 2do incrassato. Thoracis limbus
humeralis pallidus. Scutellum testaceum. Abdomen distincte
pallido pubescens, in ♂ Uncâ utrâque laterali et unicâ mediâ
dorsali obscurioribus, in ♀ stylis caudalibus ferrugineo-flavis.
Alæ sordide albidæ, irisantes, undique pube brevissimâ tenu-
issimâ vestitæ, nervis brunneis. Nubecula distincta, saturate
brunnea; ex hac descendit fera ad medium alæ fascia augusta
indeterminata valde obsoleta fusca, nervos tracesversos transiens;
hæc vero pictura in ♀ paulo perspicalior quam in ♂. Areola
obovata nervos tres simplices emittit. Nervus longitudinalis 8vus
longiusculus, leniter flexuosus, apice ad marginem interiorem alæ
non longe ab octavo remotus. Nervulus connectens¹ adest.
Halteres albidi. Pedes pubescentes, fusci, femoribus basi paullo
dilutioribus.

[*Translation.*—Gray, antennæ dark, wings grayish-hyaline, pubescent
on the whole surface, and with an abbreviated clouded brown band;
halteres whitish; ♂, ♀.
Altogether grayish-brown, opaque, pubescent; antennæ dark; eyes
black; palpi brown, second joint incrassated. Humeral border of the
thorax pale; scutellum testaceous; abdomen with a distinct pubescence
of pale hairs, in the male on each side with a darker lateral line and a
similar one in the middle; in the female, the ovipositor is ferruginous-
yellow. Wings of a sordid whitish, iridescent, clothed on the whole
surface with a very short and delicate pubescence; the veins brown.
Stigma distinct, saturate brown; a narrow, indefinite, very obsolete brown
band runs from it along the central cross-veins; this picture is more
distinct in the female than in the male. Discal cell obovate; it emits
three simple veins; the last longitudinal vein is elongated, gently sinuated; its tip is rather approximated to the tip of the preceding longitudinal
vein. The connecting nervule is present.¹ Halteres pale. Feet pubescent,
brown; femora paler at the basis.]

---

¹ Marginal cross-vein.

Westwood, London and Edinb. Philos. Magazine, 1835.

Gymoplietia annulata, ♀.

Nigra, thorace coxisque luto fulvis; alis fuscis; abdomino sericic subaurea obtecto; tibiis annulo centrali albo, tarsisque basi fulvescentibus; antennis ♀ 17-articulatis, articulis 3-9 ramum brevem obtusum emittentibus, 10mo interne acuto producto, reliquis simplicibus. Long. corp. 5 lin.; exp. alar. 9½ lin. *Hab.* Amcr. Sept. Mus. D. Hope.

[*Translation.*—Black, thorax and coxa of a bright fulvous; wings brown; abdomen with a somewhat golden, sericeous reflection; tibiæ with a white band in the middle; tarsi yellowish at the basis; antennæ of the female 17-jointed; the joints 3-9 emit a short, obtuse branch; the tenth has a sharp projection on the inside; the following joints simple. Length of the body 5 lines; expanse of the wings 9½ lines. *Hab.* North America; collection of Mr. Hope.]

APPENDIX II.

ON THE GENERA OF TIPULIDÆ BREVIPALPI NOT INDIGENOUS IN EUROPE OR
IN THE UNITED STATES.

PERIPHEROPTERA[1] Schiner.

(Section LIMNOBINA; compare above, p. 53.)

The following is translated from Dr. Schiner's article in the
Verhandl. Zool. Bot. Gesellsch. in Wien, 1866, p. 933 :—

"Head attached rather low, short-necked, seen from above almost triangular; oculpal strongly developed; eyes round, large, separated by the
broad front; ocelli wanting; palpi four-jointed, the last joint shorter than
the preceding; antennæ short, 14-jointed; first joint cylindrical, the
second short and stout, the joints of the flagellum rounded, rather closely
applied to each other, gradually diminishing in size; the last joint bud-
shaped; all joints with delicate bristles near the basis. Thorax very
convex; transverse suture deep; scutellum narrow, metathorax well developed; halteres large, with a big knob. Abdomen comparatively short,
seven-jointed; genitals of the male in the shape of a forceps; the strong
appendages are excised on the inside, pointed at the tip; ovipositor of the
female horny, almost as long as the three last joints taken together. Feet
very long and slender, tibia without spurs, the ungues dentate on the
under side, empodia rudimentary. Wings elavate in their outline, the
alulæ almost wanting; auxiliary vein long, connected about the middle
of the wing by a cross vein with the first longitudinal vein; the latter
vein is incurved at the tip in the second vein, and connected by a cross-
vein with the costa; the origin of the second vein is much beyond the
middle of the wing; this vein is not forked; third longitudinal vein
simple, strongly arcuated at the basis; the fourth vein is emitted by the
fifth normally far from the root of the wing; the discal cell emits three
simple veins; the fourth vein is in a line with its posterior branch; fifth,
sixth, and seventh veins nearly straight.

Type of the genus: *P. nitens*, n. sp.; Columbia, South America."

---

[1] From στρογγύλος, rounded, and πτερόν, wing.

Dr. Schiner's work, *Reise, etc. der Novara, Diptera*, does not contain any further details, except the description of the species *P. nitens* and a figure. *Peripheroptera* is evidently related to *Dicranomyia*; like some species of the latter genus, it has a very short præfurca, and the tip of the first longitudinal vein is incurved towards the second.

GYNOPLISTIA[1] Westw.

(Section LIMNOPHILINA; compare p. 192.)

Gynoplistia Westw., *Lond. and Edinb. Phil. Mag.* VI, p. 280 (syn. *Anoplistes* Westw., *Zool. Journ.* No. 20), is characterized thus :—

"Related to *Ctenophora*. Antennæ unipectinate in both sexes, ♂ 18-, ♀ 17-jointed; venation like that of *Ctenoph. flaveolata*."

Three species from New Holland and a fourth from North America are described. The author divides the genus in two sections : one, with the male antennæ having the joints 8–17 unipectinate ; the other, the joints 3–17.

Macquart (*Dipt. Exot.* I, 1, p. 43) adds some new characters to the generic description, and in a subsequent volume (l. c. *Suppl.* I, p. 10) observes that *Gynoplistia* belongs to the *Tipulidæ* with short palpi, and not to those with long palpi, as might be inferred from Mr. Westwood's statement on its relationship to *Ctenophora*.

Those *Gynoplistiæ* which I have seen in the European collections undoubtedly belong to the section *Limnophilina*; their venation is like that of a *Limnophila* with five posterior cells ; the structure of the male genitals of an Australian species which I have seen shows the operculo mentioned by Macquart (l. c. p. 43). I had no opportunity for studying these species in detail ; nor do I know whether a *Gynoplistia*, from South America, which I have seen in the Berlin Museum, really belongs to the same genus with the Australian species ; the degree of relationship of *Gynoplistia* to *Ctedonia* Phil. is likewise unknown to me.

---

[1] From γυνή, female, and λιστζω, I arm.

CEROZODIA[t] Westw.

(Section LIMNOPHILINA ? compare p. 192.)

Cerozodia Westw., *Lond. and Edinb. Phil. Magaz.* VI. p. 281 (syn. *Ozocera* Westw., *Zool. Journ.* No. 20; nec *Ozodicera* Macq.), from Australia, is described thus:—

Limnobia affinis; antennæ thorace paulo longiores, articulis 32; 3-31 ramnium longum emittenti; palpi perbreves; alarum nervi ut in *Gynoplistia* cili dispositi.

This last mention seems to indicate that this genus belongs to the *Limnophilina*. I do not know anything about this genus, nor do I find it mentioned in subsequent publications, except Macquart's naked quotation (*Dipt. Exot.* I, 1, p. 65).

CLONIOPHORA[t] Schiner.

(Section LIMNOPHILINA; compare p. 192.)

The following has been translated from Dr. Schiner's article in the *Verh. Zool. Bot. Gesellsch. in Wien*, 1866, p. 932:—

Head rounded; eyes somewhat projecting, rostrum moderately prolonged, truncate in front, and beset with bristly hairs. Palpi four-jointed, the second joint short spade-shaped, third and fourth slender, nearly of the same length. Antennæ 16-jointed, first joint cylindrical, the second short cyathiform, 3-13 on the inside with a single lateral projection, which is very short on the joints 9 and 13; the last joints narrow and elongated, finely bristly. Thorax stout; abdomen more than three times the length of the thorax, somewhat flattened, the horny ovipositor very much projecting, almost as long as half the abdomen, stout at the basis, gradually attenuated, ending beyond the middle, in two slender, somewhat arcuated valves; the lower valves do not reach beyond the middle of the upper ones. Feet rather strong, tibiæ with spurs, empodia strongly developed. Wings long and comparatively more narrow than in the genus *Gynoplistia*; the auxiliary vein is long, connected with the first longitudinal by a crossvein near its tip; the venation is otherwise like that of *Gynoplistia*, only the terminal portions of the veins are all longer and more straight; halteres long with a large knob.

Type of the genus: *C. subfasciata* Walker; Australia.

---

[t] From αἴρω, horn, and ζώδιον, branched.

[t] Apparently from κλών, the hip, and φέρω, I bear.

PARATROPESA[1] Schin.

(Section LIMNOBINA ANOMALA; see p. 132.)

The following is translated from Dr. Schiner's article in the
Verh. Zool. Bot. Gesellsch. in Wien, 1866, p. 932:—

"Head, seen from above, almost triangular, the occiput strongly developed; the rostrum, somewhat projecting eyes situated quite anteriorly; front broad and flat; ocelli wanting; rostrum very short; palpi four-jointed, the two last joints nearly of the same length; antennæ 15-jointed; first joint elongated, cylindrical, the second short, truncate in front, the joints of the flagellum oblong, diminishing in size towards the tip, finely pubescent; the last joint attenuated at the basis, not shorter than the preceding joint. Thorax very convex, rather abrupt in front, the collare being almost at a right angle to the mesothorax; it is strongly narrowed in front. Abdomen seven-jointed, about twice the length of the thorax, narrow and slender; forceps of the male rather strong; appendages folded backwards; a short, blunt intermediate piece near the basis. Feet slender; hind femora longer than the abdomen; the first joints of the tarsi long and rather strikingly incrassated, spindle-shaped, with a dense, short pubescence; ungues distinct; the empodium strongly developed, the pulvilli rudimentary. Wings broad, the anal angle much developed; auxiliary vein close by the first longitudinal; the latter gradually approaching the costa and merging into it without being incurved towards it; the second longitudinal vein originates about the middle of the wing, strongly arcuated in its whole course, almost at a right angle at its origin; forked not far from its tip; the anterior branch of the fork is short, the posterior one is in a line with the remainder of the vein; the marginal cross-vein is long and perpendicular, connecting the first and second veins in the region of the stigma; the inner end of the submarginal cell is in a line with the marginal cross-vein, and in immediate contact with the discal cell; the small cross-vein is therefore wanting; the discal cell emits three simple veins, running toward the margin; fifth vein quite straight; the sixth and seventh have nothing peculiar.

Type of the genus: *P. singularis*, n. sp.; Columbia, South America."

Although Dr. Schiner is in doubt about the relationship of this
genus, I have shown above (p. 132) that, according to my opinion,
it is related to *Trucholabis*.

[1] Probably from παράτροπος, deflected, averted.

CTEDONIA[1] Philippi.

(Section LIMNOPHILINA.)

The following has been translated from Dr. Philippi's article
in the *Verh. Zool. Bot. Ges. in Wien*, 1865, p. 602 (Tab. XXIII,
fig. 2):—

Head small, globose, attenuated behind, produced anteriorly in a stout,
horizontal rostrum. Eyes globose, rather remote. No ocelli. The antennae in length are equal to about three-quarters of the head and the
thorax taken together; from 15- to 24-jointed; first joint cylindrical, stout,
the second equal to one-third of the first, subglobular; the following eight
(or twelve) cylindrical, subequal, emitting a filament and thus forming a
comb; the projection of the third joint is on the external side, and short;
the fourth joint has one on the inside and another on the outside; the
joints 5, 6, 7, 8, 9, 10 and beyond, have on the inside a long projection;
joint 11 has a short one on the inside; the nine following joints are cylindrical, and difficult to distinguish. Palpi four-jointed, joints cylindrical,
the fourth stout, rather short, although a little longer than the third. The
tibiae have two spurs at the tip.

Four species from Chile are described. The wings, as I
judge by the plate, have two submarginal, five posterior, and a
discal cell; the second submarginal and first posterior have their
inner ends almost in a line; the second marginal is but little
shorter than the submarginal. The venation is altogether like
that of an ordinary *Limnophila*.

POLYMERIA[2] Philippi.

(Section LIMNOPHILINA?)

The following is translated from Dr. Philippi's article on the
Diptera of Chile in the *Verh. Zool. Bot. Ges. in Wien*, 1865, p.
608 (Tab. XXIII, fig. 3):—

"Head produced in a rostrum, as in *Tipula*; third joint of the palpi
stout, the fourth slender. Antennae short, 16-jointed; first joint elongated,
cylindrical, stout; the second stout, subglobular; the following gradually
decrease in size, short, with long hairs. Wings with six[3] posterior cells,

---

[1] From εκτενής, comb.

[2] From πολύς, much, and μέρος, part.

[3] Philippi says: six posterior cells; but both figures given by him show
only five.

the third petiolate; the veins, especially the apical ones, pubescent. Otherwise like *Tipula*."

Five species, all from Chile, are described. The generic character does not mention whether there are any spurs at the tip of the tibiæ or not; but in the description of one of the species, *P. ludca*, I find the statement "that the tibiæ have no spurs." If this is correct, the genus would have to be placed among the *Eriopterina*. The comparison to *Tipula* renders the question of the location of this genus somewhat doubtful. The venation is not unlike that of *Dactylolabis* (Tab. II, fig. 7).

LACHNOCERA[1] Philippi.

(Section LIMNOPHILINA? or ERIOPTERINA?)

The following is translated from Dr. Philippi's article in the *Verh. Zool. Bot. Gesellsch.* in *Wien*, 1865, p. 615, Tab. XXIII, fig. 5:—

"Antennæ, at least those of the male, are as long as the body, 13-jointed (?); first joint cylindrical, stout, elongated; the second of the same length with the first, gradually attenuated; the following ones slender, stouter in the middle, on both sides with long, hirsute hairs; the last joints are rather indistinct. Proboscis short; fourth joint of the palpi equal to the third in length (?). Wings with two marginal cells: the first large; the second short, separated from the first by an oblique vein; a single submarginal cell; four posterior cells; discal cell pentagonal; basal cells elongated, the second longer. Feet slender."

The genus is represented by a single species, *L. delicatula* Phil., from Valdivia, 2½ lines long. The figure represents a venation not unlike that of *Goniomyia*. *Lachnocera* may therefore be related to this genus, or to the *Limnophilæ* with four posterior cells.

POLYMERA[2] Wied.

(Section unknown; perhaps AMALOPINA?)

The following is extracted from Wiedemann's *Aussereurop. Zweifluegelige Insecten*, Vol. I, p. 57:—

Antennæ 28 articulate: articulus primus globosus; secundus cylindri-

---

[1] From λάχνη, woolly hair, and κέρας, horn.
[2] From πολύς, much, and μέρος, part, in allusion to the numerous joints of the antennæ.

cus, elongatus; basis articulorum sequentium multo breviorum, pilis
verticillalis.

Pedes longissimi.

Habitus *Limnobiæ.* Nomen a *culis*, multum, et *μέρος,* part.

[*Translation.*—Antennæ 22-jointed; first joint globose, the second cylindrical, elongated; the following joints much shorter, with verticillate hairs
at their basis. Feet very long. Appearance of a *Limnobia*; the name, etc.]

Two species from South America are described; they are 3
and 3½ lines long; one is black, with brown wings, banded with
white, the other brown, with hyaline wings. Wiedemann's figure
(l. c. Tab. VI, b, fig. 4) represents a venation not unlike that
of *Rhaphidolabis,* only all the cells in the apical portion of the
wing are exceedingly long, the small and the great cross-veins,
as well as the inner end of the discal cell, being before the middle
of the length of the wing.

Macquart (*Dipt. Exot.* I, p. 64) gives a description and a figure
of *Polymera fusca* Wied. To the generic characters he adds
that the rostrum is very short; the palpi of equal length, the last
joint slender, pointed; collare indistinct; feet slender; tibiæ
with spurs at the tip; tarsi longer than the tibiæ. Wings with
pubescent veins. Abdomen of the male flattened, with an elongated forceps.

Macquart's figure (l. c. Tab. VIII, fig. 1) shows a distinct thoracic suture and a venation similar to that figured by Wiedemann.
As this insect has five posterior cells and spurs at the tip of the
tibiæ, if it fits in any of our sections at all, it must belong either
to the *Limnophilina* or to the *Amalopina.* The venation, especially the absence of a discal cell, reminds us of the *Amalopina.* But
the male forceps, consisting, if Macquart represents it correctly,
of two elongated slender halves, leaving an empty space between
them, is very different from the forceps of the *Amalopina.* The
presence of spurs on the tibiæ of *Polymera* excludes the probability of its relationship to the *Eriopterina.*

EXPLANATION OF THE PLATES.

Remark. The wings figured on Plates I and II are all magnified about 4½ times, except the wings fig. 2 and 11 of Plate II, which are magnified 9½ times.

PLATE I.

1. **Dicranomyia** loxoiphenia *Schm.*
2. **Dicranomyia** pcmpensis *O. S.*
3. **Dicranomyia** haertica *O. S.*
4. **Trochobola** aroca *Say.*
5. **Elephantomyia** westwoodi *O. S.*
6. **Toxorrhina** maora *O. S.*
7. **Cylindrotoma** somcosxia *O. S.*
8. **Dicranoptycha** boenira *O. S.*
9. **Orimarga** alpina *Zetterst.*
10. **Elliptera** omena *Schiner.*
11. **Antocha** opalizafa *O. S.*
12. **Teucholabis** complexa *O. S.*
13. **Atarba** picticornis *O. S.*
14. **Rhypholophus** rubiled *O. S.*
15. **Rhypholophus** rebelica *O. S.*
16. **Erioptera** chloropuylla *O. S.*
17. **Erioptera** venusta *O. S.*
18. **Erioptera** armata *O. S.*
19. **Erioptera** sp. nov. (The wing was taken from a Californian specimen, closely allied to *E. hirtipennis* O. S.)
20. **Symplecta** punctipennis *M.*

PLATE II.

1. **Trimicra** filipes *Fab.*
2. **Goniomyia** sculptrella *O. S.*

23 December, 1868.

(337)

3. Limnophila (Prionolabis) RUFIBASIS *O. S.*
4. Goniomyia SUBCINEREA *O. S*
5. Gnophomyia TRISTISSIMA *O. S.*
6. Limnophila ARMILATA *O. S.*
7. Limnophila (Dactylolabis) MONTANA *O. S.* (The spots on this wing are omitted in the figure.)
8. Epiphragma SOLATRIX *O. S.*
9. Limnophila QUADRATA *O. S.*
10. Limnophila LUTEIPENNIS *O. S.*
11. Cryptolabis PARADOXA *O. S.*
12. Anthomera HUMERALIS *O. S.* ♀.
13. Trichocera BIMACULA *Walk.*(?). The spots of this wing are omitted in the figure.
14. Amalopis CALCAR *O. S.*
15. Amalopis INCONSTANS *O. S.* The wing represented on this figure has two supernumerary cross-veins in the second submarginal cell, which do not exist in normal specimens.
16. Dicranota BIVITTATA *O. S.* ♀.
17. Rhaphidolabis TENUIPES *O. S.*
18. Plectromyia MODESTA *O. S.*
19. Psychoptera SCROGSICTA *O. S.*
20. Bittacomorpha CLAVIPES *Fab.*

PLATE III.

1. Dicranomyia DEFECTA *O. S.*; forceps from below.
　Fig. 1a. the same from above; aa. soft, fleshy lobes; bb. horny, falciform appendages, movable with the lobes, and closely applied to them, although fastened by the basis only; cc. horny, projecting points of the internal apparatus.
2. Dicranomyia BADIA *Walk.*; forceps from above; aa and bb are the same as in fig. 1; dd. horny, square appendages, each bearing a pair of bristles; e. point of the anal style, visible between the two lobes.
3. Dicranomyia LIBERTA *O. S.*; forceps from above; aa. and bb. as in fig. 1; dd. horny, rostriform appendage, with a bristle.—Fig. 3a. point of the anal style, seen from below.
4. Dicranomyia CLAVATUS *O. S.*; one-half of the forceps from above; a, b. as in fig. 1; e. anal style.
5. Rhiphidia DOMESTICA *O. S.*; forceps from above and open; the lettering is the same as in the preceding figures.—Fig. 5a represents the same forceps from below and closed.

[6. **Limnobia** SOLITARIA *O. S.*; forceps from above, half closed; *aa* are coriaceous, movable; *bb.* hooked appendages, consisting of two, closely applied lamina; the outer one horny; the inner one apparently coriaceous; *e.* the anal style; *cc.* projecting internal organs; *bb.* soft eminences (perhaps rudiments of the large soft lobes of *Dicranomyia*).

7. **Limnobia** INDICINA *O. S.*; forceps from above; the lamina *bb* are double.

8. **Elephantomyia** WESTWOODI *O. S.*; one-half of the forceps; *aa.* horny appendages.

9. **Teucholabis** COMPLEXA *O. S.*; forceps from above; 9a. one-half of the same, from below; *aa, bb.* horny appendages.

10. **Antocha** SAXICOLA *O. S.*; forceps from above; *aa.* double appendages, consisting of a horny and of a soft part, closely joined.

11. **Dicranoptycha** KIONIPES *O. S.*; forceps from above; *y.* short, black bristles; *xx.* indistinct horny appendages. When this species opened its forceps, a delicate, horny apparatus (figured separately, fig. 11a) was spread outside of it; *bb* is a slender forceps, moving independently of *aa*, and closing at the point *c*.

12. **Dicranoptycha** SOBRIA *O. S.*; one-half of the forceps.

13. **Cryptolabis** PARADOXA *O. S.*; forceps from above.
  13a. the same from below; *aa.* horny appendages, small and indistinct, being closely applied to the fleshy part of the forceps; *b* seems to be the rudiment of an anal style.
  13b. the tip of the abdomen of the female, from the side.
  13c. the same from above; both show that there are no visible horny lamina; the prominences *aa* are beset with microscopic bristles.

PLATE IV.

14. **Erioptera** ARMATA *O. S.*; forceps from above.
  14a. the same, from the side; its structure is somewhat complicated; besides the coriaceous parts, *dd*, there are two pairs of horny appendages; one of them is seen at *b*, in fig. 14a; when detached, it looks like fig. 14b, in which the portion *bb* is closely applied to the coriaceous part *d* and *c* branches off. The other pair of appendages, *w*, of fig. 14a, is slender and curved.

15. **Erioptera** CALOPTERA *Say*; forceps from below.

16. **Erioptera** VENUSTA *O. S.*; forceps from above.
  16a. the same, from below; the horny appendages, *aa*, seen from below, appear double, consisting of the horny part, *bb*, and the membranaceous appendage, *cc*; fig. 16b represents it detached; its margin *d* is horny, the rest is membranaceous; these two appendages have an interval between them, although they move simultaneously.

17. Goniomyia SLANDA *O. S.;* forceps from above and open.

18. Goniomyia COGNATELLA *O. S.;* half the forceps, from above.

19. Gnophomyia TRISTISSIMA *O. S.;* forceps from above, half open.
19a. ovipositor of the same species.

20. Drioptera VENTRALIS *O. S;* half the forceps.

21. Symplecta PUNCTIPENNIS *M.;* forceps from above; *a* and *b* are horny.

22. Cladura FLAVOFERRUGINEA *O. S.;* forceps from the side; *a* is convex, and seems to be horny inside; *c* is the forceps.

23. Limnophila APRILINA *O. S.;* forceps from above; the outer horny appendages have a longitudinal notch, represented on fig. 23a.

24. Limnophila ULTIMA *O. S;* forceps from below.

25. Limnophila LUTEIPENNIS *O. S.;* forceps from above; so, movable appendages; the outer ones horny.

26. Limnophila (Dactylolabis) MONTANA *O. S.;* forceps from above, closed (it is distinguished at once by the position of the appendages).
26a. the same, from the side; *c.* inner horny points, protruding when the forceps is opened.

27. Limnophila (Prionolabis) RUFIBASIS *O. S.;* forceps from above, open; *os,* large, strong appendages, serrated on the inside; *bb,* also horny, figured separately, 27a.
27b is a slender, horny organ, which protrudes, when the forceps is opened; otherwise it is concealed.

28. Eriocera FULIGINOSA *O. S.;* forceps from above; *aa* are horny; *bb* soft; *c* is curved downwards, like fig. 27b.

29. Eriocera (Arrhenica) SPINOSA *O. S.;* forceps from above; *a.* horny, *b.* soft appendages; *cc.* internal clutching apparatus; the latter is figured separately, fig. 29a; at *d* is a joint, by means of which it is moved.

30. Amalopia INCONSTANS *O. S.;* forceps from above, and half open; it is difficult to convey a correct idea of it in a drawing; the horny points, *f, g, h,* are all curved upwards; the point *f* is bifid (fig. 30a); *bb* are soft; *cc* hollow inside; *h* is figured separately at 30b.

31. Bittacomorpha CLAVIPES *F.;* forceps from below.
31a. the same, from above.

INDEX.

ADDITIONS AND CORRECTIONS.

Page 18, line 4 from the top: "1. In the *T. longipalpi*, the auxiliary vein ends in the first longitudinal, etc." In the genus *Pachyrrhina* the auxiliary vein, immediately before its termination in the first longitudinal, often has a stump of a vein, which, in some species, almost looks like a cross-vein, connecting it with the costa.

Page 19, line 14 from the top: "The *Tip. longipalpi* usually keep the wings divaricate in repose," etc. *Pachyrrhina* and even some *Tipula*, keep the wings folded in repose. The rule is less general than has been stated by former authors.

Pages 88, 89, 90: In the three Latin diagnoses on these pages, read "venula transversa" instead of "transversalis."

While this volume was in press, two new species, *Goniomyia maraca* and *Erioptera forcipula*, have been added to it. The numerical data on pages 35 and the following were printed before this addition was made, and have to be modified accordingly. The abnormal character of one of these species, *Goniomyia maraca*, requires that it should be quoted along with the genus *Cladolipes* (on page 24 and in the third foot-note on page 44), as an instance of an exceptional disappearance of one of the branches of the second longitudinal vein. For the same reason, on page 25, line 5 from the top, instead of "in *Goniomyia*," read "in *Goniomyia maraca*."

On the same page, 25, the genus *Paratropeza* Schiner (compare page 132) may be quoted as forming an apparent transition between the *Tipulidæ* with one and those with two submarginal cells. It has a cross-vein in the marginal cell, which might be taken for a branch of the second vein, if every other character did not point to a relationship with *Tricholabis*. Hence I look upon it as having only a single submarginal cell, while Dr. Schiner placed it among those with two such cells. Dr. Schiner's work was received by me while this volume was in press.

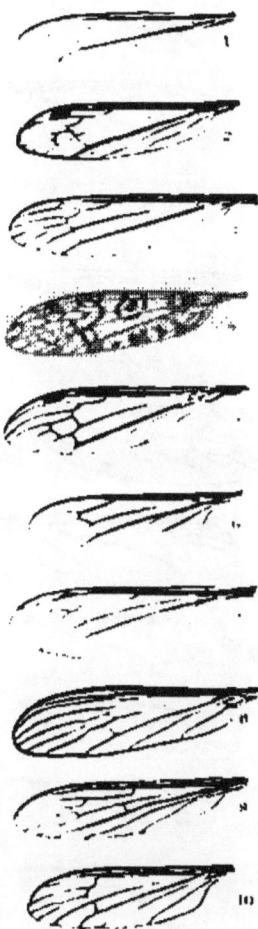
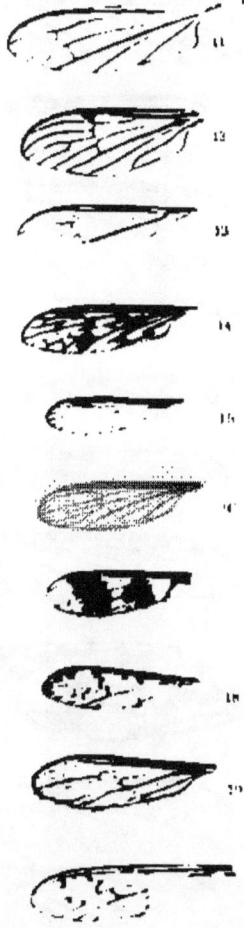

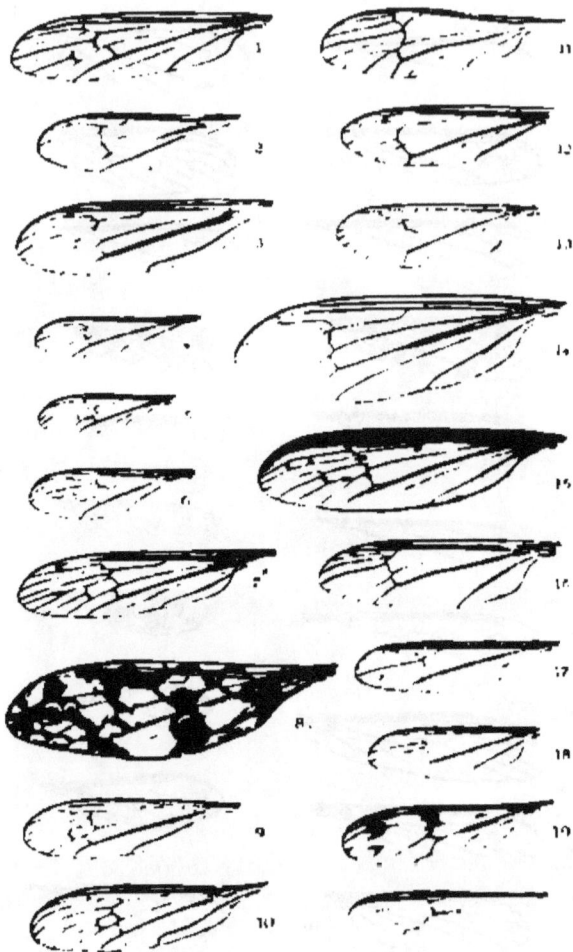

Pl II

www.ingramcontent.com/pod-product-compliance
Lightning Source LLC
Chambersburg PA
CBHW021105270326
41929CB00009B/739